THE THEORY AND PRACTICE OF FUTURES MARKETS

THE THEORY AND PRACTICE OF FUTURES MARKETS

Raymond M. Leuthold, *University of Illionis, Urbana-Champaign*

Joan C. Junkus, *DePaul University*

Jean E. Cordier, *Institut de Gestion Internationale Agro-Alimentaire*

Lexington Books
D.C. Heath and Company/Lexington, Massachusetts/Toronto

Library of Congress Cataloging-in-Publication Data

Leuthold, Raymond M.
The theory and practice of futures markets/Raymond M. Leuthold, Joan C. Junkus, and Jean E. Cordier.
p. cm.
Includes notes and index.
ISBN 0-669-16260-4 (alk. paper)
1. Commodity exchanges. 2. Financial futures. 3. Stock index futures. I. Junkus, Joan C. II. Cordier, Jean E. III. Title.
HG6024.A3L48 1989
332.64'4—dc19 87-45248

Published simultaneously in Canada
Printed in the United States of America
International Standard Book Number: 0-669-16260-4
Library of Congress Catalog Card Number 87-45248

The paper used in this publication meets the minimum requirements of American National Standard for Information Sciences—Permanence of Paper for Printed Library Materials, ANSI Z39.48-1984. ∞™

88 89 90 91 92 8 7 6 5 4 3 2 1

TO OUR SPOUSES

CONTENTS

PREFACE

The Theory and Practice of Futures Markets is an introductory text about commodity and financial futures and options markets. It is written for advanced undergraduate students and Master's- or MBA-level graduate students. The text can be used in classes in agricultural economics, economics, and finance. It is designed both to provide a general introduction to the theory of pricing and risk management in futures and to discuss the problems and issues involved in the application of this theory to particular types of futures contracts. It integrates theory and practical application. Since the primary function of futures markets is risk management, the book focuses on how individuals and firms can manage risks through hedging programs and through the use of options markets. Many examples are presented on how to use the market for hedging and arbitraging.

The book is unique in that it covers commodity, interest rate, stock index, and currency futures contracts along with options on these contracts. It integrates research knowledge and backgrounds from agricultural economics, economics, and finance.

The information presented can be used to apply the general concepts of futures markets to a broad array of futures contracts. Adequate institutional and theoretical background are provided to instruct students in conducting proper trades and for understanding why and how the markets can be used to manage risks. The book demonstrates the concept of optimal hedging and shows how one can assess market performance and forward pricing efficiency of futures markets. The book ends with a discussion of the regulatory environment for futures markets. The chapters are arranged so that instructors can select without loss of continuity among those chapters dealing with commodities, interest rate, stock index, currency, or option contracts (chapters 7–13) as dictated by the needs of their class.

The book will also be of interest to professionals in a number of industries (food processors, metals, energy, agricultural products) and financial institutions (banks, savings and loans, pension funds, insurance companies, and other firms subject to interest rate risk). The book will prove valuable for private investors with financial or economic backgrounds and for staff members of large firms or institutions dealing with futures and options markets.

The book begins (chapters 1–6) with an introduction to the organization and functioning of futures markets. Included is a comprehensive analysis of the economic function performed by all types of futures markets. This material will be of interest to all readers. The second part (chapters 7–12) is oriented to specific groups or types of contracts. How to use these markets for risk management is demonstrated through specific hedging, pricing, and arbitrage examples for many contracts. Readers may wish to select among these chapters according to their commodity or instrument specialty and interests. Chapter 13 is about futures options and chapter 14 discussed regulation.

The book begins with a presentation of the institutional background necessary for understanding the organization and operation of futures markets. Chapter 1 describes the functions and characteristics of futures markets. Chapter 2 provides a broad overview of exchanges and contracts, their history, terms and definitions, trading of contracts, traders, contract specifications, the operation of the clearing house, and the function of margins.

The theory of price relationships and basis are presented in chapter 3 for both storables and nonstorables. The theoretical concepts are shown to apply to both commodity contracts and financial instrument (interest rate) contracts. Chapter 4 presents alternative trading activities on futures markets and their motivations. Different types of procedures for speculation are outlined. Chapter 5 introduces concepts of individual trading behavior. Standard techniques of choices under uncertainty and the foundations of portfolio analysis are used to derive optimal hedging rules in both simple and generalized cases. Finally, chapter 6 outlines the concept of market equilibrium and how to assess the market performance and forward pricing efficiency of futures markets and whether these markets contain a risk premium. This chapter ends with a discussion of the influence of futures markets on the price variability of the underlying cash commodity or instrument.

The next six chapters describe specific pricing patterns and relationships for agricultural, interest rate, stock index, and currency contracts and give several hedging and arbitraging examples for managing risks. Chapter 7 describes the pricing and basis patterns for grains and livestock and chapter 8 presents hedging examples for these commodities. The latter chapter also discussed the steps in making marketing decisions in a risky environment and the use of futures markets in international trade. Chapters 9 and 10 provide pricing relationships and hedging and arbitraging examples for interest rate contracts, concentrating principally on Treasury Bills and Treasury Bonds. Emphasis is given to the relationship between the yield curve and the prices of these instruments and their futures contracts. The last section of chapter 9 outlines spread relationships and trades. Chapter 11 discusses stock index futures pricing and the procedures for hedging stocks, utilizing concepts of portfolio management. Mention is also made of the stock market crash of October 19–20, 1987. Chapter 12 provides a background on the pricing relationships and risk management (hedging) opportunities in foreign currency futures markets.

Chapter 13 concentrates on options of futures contracts. Basic terminology and definitions provide a background before uses and opportunities of options in risk management and pricing formulas are presented. The last chapter, chapter 14, presents a history of the development of the regulatory process in futures and options markets, and discusses many regulatory issues of current concern. Included is an evaluation and historical background of the concerns toward market manipulation. The chapter concludes with a discussion of the performance of futures markets relative to its functions, which were introduced in chapter 1.

For some parts of the book, students will find knowledge of introductory calculus and finance theory helpful for full understanding. However, much of this material is placed in appendixes and should not be a detraction for most readers.

No book can be written without the assistance of others. Much of the information in this book comes from various lecture materials used by the authors in many individual classroom experiences. Principal acknowledgment is to the students who over the years have provided us the benefit of their comments and suggestions, often by asking questions and requesting clarifications. The authors are also grateful to those many researchers who keep pushing the frontier of knowledge in providing fuller understanding of futures and options markets. We have tried to pass much of that new knowledge on to the reader in this text.

Special thanks go to those on two continents who have typed large parts of the original manuscript and the numerous revisions. We note especially the able assistance of Dianne Lafenhagen and Eleanor Kisinger in this regard. Part of this work was supported by a DePaul Univesity Research Grant, support which is greatly appreciated.

INTRODUCTION

1

Futures markets have captured the public's attention. Since the early 1970s world activities and expanding markets have attracted a wide variety of new traders to the futures markets. Public interest in commodity, currency, stock and financial instrument price fluctuations has moved news about futures markets from the financial page to the front page. More and more raw material producers, processors and users, financial intermediaries, and international trading firms use these markets to manage their price, interest rate, and exchange rate risks. Speculators around the world interpret this information and enter these markets as investors, either individually or as members of commodity funds and trading clubs. In addition, politicians and regulators observing rapidly fluctuating prices and large trading volume have become interested in learning about futures markets. The linkages between futures, stock, options, and other financial markets have become a focal point of interest and concern.

The explosion of futures market trading relates to world economic events that created higher and more volatile prices and interest rates. This environment results in greater uncertainty in decision making. Many markets are now much more international in nature than just a decade ago. Large capital flows seem to know no boundaries, responding to alternative investment opportunities around the world. Furthermore, there has been a proliferation of new contracts on the futures market over the last twenty years. Futures trading has expanded beyond the traditional storable agricultural commodities and metals to contracts in livestock, wood products, petroleum products, foreign currencies, financial instruments, and stock and other price indexes. There is a constant stream of proposals for new contracts every year.

Agricultural contracts helped lead futures trading to larger volumes beginning in the 1970s due to rising commodity and energy prices. Adverse weather around the world, changing government policies in agriculture, growing international trade, and the formation of OPEC dramatically altered traditional markets. Further growth in futures trading volume came from the introduction of new contracts, especially financial instruments. Foreign currency futures were introduced after exchange rates were allowed to fluctuate in 1971 and the U.S. dollar was removed from the gold standard. These events, coupled with changing fiscal and monetary policies, led to freely fluctuating interest rates in the late 1970s and beyond. This brought the introduction of several interest rate futures contracts, followed by a host of stock index contracts. History has now recorded the high volatility of the stock market with the rapid rise of stock prices during the first half of 1987 following by the crash of October 19, 1987. Finally, this growth in futures trading has been supported by the introduction in the 1980s of options on many futures contracts.

These changes in futures trading in the last few years have been so dramatic that the traditional agricultural commodity contracts dropped below 50 percent of the total volume of futures trading in the United States in 1982. By 1985 agricultural commodity contracts were less than one-fourth of the total volume. In fact, the Treasury bond contract itself exceeded the total of all agricultural commodity contracts in futures trading volume beginning in 1985.

The total number of contracts traded annually and their monetary value have increased many fold over the last few years. Futures markets are one of the fastest growing industries in the world business community. Figure 1–1 shows this rapid growth in the volume of trading in the United States for selected years. From 1970 through 1980 futures trading volume grew almost 580 percent. Add to the 228.9 million contracts for 1987 another 46.2 million option contracts on futures. This latter extension of futures markets just began in late 1982. The total face value of all futures contracts now traded amounts to several trillion dollars annually.

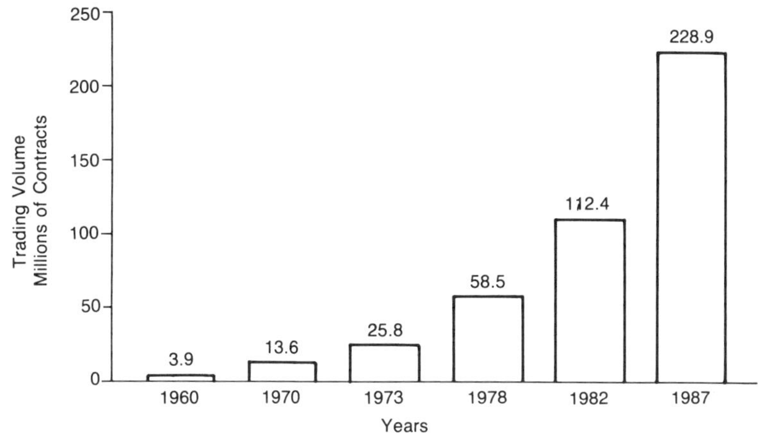

Figure 1-1. Trading Volume in U.S. Futures Markets for Selected Years

Thus, futures markets attracted new contracts as perceptions of futures trading changed. Trading volume increased because of these new contracts and because of increased price and asset risks faced by business firms. Futures markets aid firms in managing these risks and in reducing related costs. This additional hedging use of the markets requires more speculators for the necessary liquidity. Speculators are attracted to the markets to participate in the information gathering process and to manage investment portfolios. Other means exist for firms and investors to manage risks, but futures markets are popular, useful, and can be very effective.

FUNCTIONS AND CHARACTERISTICS OF FUTURES MARKETS

Futures markets perform several functions. Primarily, they (1) facilitate the management of risk; (2) aid firms in discovering forward prices; (3) provide a means for firms to request and secure additional operating capital; and (4) provide a source of information for decision making. These functions are emphasized in the following discussion of the characteristics of futures markets.

Futures markets are effective, in part, because of their close approximation to the classical concepts of pure competition. Authorities did not plan this structure; it evolved out of the existing market forces. Regulation has attempted to preserve the market structure. Many buyers and sellers participate in most futures contract markets, which means that no one trader noticeably influences prices. Contracts are perfectly homogeneous except for price and maturity date, and the cost of entry is small.

The existence of futures markets has created a flow of information far exceeding what would otherwise be the case. This allows for much more intelligent decision making. Futures markets are a place where information is interpreted and exchanged, and the information they provide for decision making may well be their most significant economic role for both participants and nonparticipants. Futures markets can make cash markets more efficient through this information role. The efficiency of futures markets themselves is an often investigated topic as it closely relates to information availability.

Futures markets are extensions of cash markets. They evolved out of existing market forces, and their purpose is to make cash markets work better. They are about the forward pricing of commodities and instruments—a speculative, unavoidable process. To understand a futures market well, a trader must understand the underlying cash market.

Due to this relationship with cash markets, futures markets are primary price discovery markets for many commodities, instruments, and indexes. Futures prices are base reference values for producers, processors, and consumers of many goods and services both nationally and worldwide. Futures markets facilitate the marketing and transference of ownership of goods and services, and increase the information content of spot market prices. Futures markets attract speculators who search for information and whose trading should improve rational price formation. Speculation is not costless because information is costly, but these activities can reduce total marketing costs for everyone.

Information systems about futures markets have become very sophisticated and technologically advanced. For example, highly complex computer systems track the value of stock portfolios to signal instant arbitrage opportunities with an appropriate stock index futures contract. Complex computer models also track price data for trading signals from a multitude of technical trading indicators. Finally, computers create international linkages for exchanges and firms to transfer information immediately and to trade around the world twenty-four hours a day.

Firms and businesses face risks as they buy inputs, perform a service on them, and then sell products. During this process price relationships may change so much that the firm cannot cover all its costs. These risks are themselves a cost. To be successful, such firms need skills in managing risks. The futures market is one possible means for managing this risk.

Effective risk management has financial consequences. Firms that can reduce risks should have a higher probability of making a profit. Such firms should, theoretically, be able to command additional operating capital. Lenders should be more willing to lend money to those enterprises that can show lower probabilities of financial loss and bankruptcy. Lenders themselves can manage these interest rate risks directly on the futures market. In all cases firms are managing portfolios of assets, and success depends on their ability to manage portfolios optimally.

Speculators are important for effective futures markets. Speculation is an essential element in the formation of any market price. As others do, speculators manage portfolios of risky investments and interprete information. They must assess the expected returns from an investment and weigh that against the potential risk. Their characteristics range from one-time traders to those earning a living by trading on the market. The effectiveness of futures markets in providing risk management opportunities to hedgers depends on the abilities and numbers of speculators. They provide the necessary market liquidity. As they trade, speculators must judge that the market is in error, or that prices are too high or too low. In addition, they must manage their risk capital and understand risk-return tradeoffs.

Futures markets are a zero-sum game, meaning for every dollar won on the market, someone else loses a dollar. The markets are very competitive. They pit the price forecasting and capital management skills of one person against those of another person. Through the process of trading, speculators and hedgers can potentially reach their price, income, and financial goals. The interaction of all traders together interpreting information makes the market effective.

Futures markets have the image of being fast-moving markets. It is not that their prices necessarily fluctuate more than other prices, but that futures trading is done on the margin. Small amounts of money command large contracts; this risk capital can balloon in size or evaporate quickly. Trading in futures contracts requires constant attention; this is not a place where one can invest money and then forget about it.

The benefits of a futures market come from improving the scope and flexibility of decision making for a firm. Futures trading is a highly standardized way to enter into fixed-price forward contracts; it is economical in execution and secure in performance. Ownership responsibilities are shifted to someone else, and firms can thereby organize production operations more efficiently.

Futures markets have unique and complex rules, regulations, and practices. Because most futures contracts are liquidated through offsetting transactions before they mature, futures trading does not appear to deal with real commodities or financial instruments. There is little direct exchange of ownership or title through futures markets. Thus, they are essentially "paper" markets.[1]

Anyone who posts a small margin deposit as a performance guarantee can trade in the futures market without possessing the underlying physical commodity or instrument. A trader can sell commodities or instruments for deferred delivery without having them or knowing where to acquire them. Hence, the number of outstanding contracts and volume of trading can exceed the physical supply of the commodity or instrument available to satisfy the contracts. Yet, that feature need not cause any marketing or pricing problems.

This is not to deny that futures markets, as with many other markets, overreact to certain situations and cause short-run price distortions. Because of their central nature, distortions and volatility in futures markets can dramatically affect prices in related markets. Comprehensive rules and regulations are important in reducing and preventing such occurrences.

Nevertheless, futures trading has survived and expanded because the markets serve a useful economic purpose. Futures contracts are useful in production, financing, storage, pricing, distribution, and consumption of goods and services. Their direct role is in facilitating risk transfer and forward pricing. These functions in turn play an important role in the allocation of resources by guiding production, inventories, and rational decision making. The markets exist because of support from commercial firms that need to manage risks and make decisions. Futures trading activity is closely tied to the commercial patterns of hedging, not speculative activities. Firms do not need to participate in the market to benefit from the information which flows from it. Futures markets also facilitate the use or existence of other market coordinating mechanisms, such as cash forward contracts. They are often a cheap source for information and risk transfer. The continued existence of futures markets affects how commercial agents in cash markets organize themselves for decision making, price discovery, risk management, and the collection and interpretation of information.

PURPOSE AND ORGANIZATION

The purpose of this book is to describe the basic features and theories of futures markets, and to relate them to traditional concepts and theories of finance. Futures markets are financial markets with traders exchanging commodity or product obligations for monetary obligations. This book incorporates business and financial tools of analysis along with descriptions of futures markets and how to trade them. Underlying concepts and theoretical relationships are emphasized. Traditional agricultural and nonagricultural commodities are discussed along with the financial instrument, currency, stock index, and option contracts. Standard theories of finance, such as optimal portfolios and capital asset pricing models, are also presented to put futures markets into a proper financial framework.

The literature in futures markets and finance has developed down two somewhat separate, but yet parallel, paths. Interest in bridging these study areas comes in part from the trading of futures contracts in financial instruments and exchange rates, but also from the overlapping research topics in the two areas. For instance, theoretical developments and empirical tests concerning efficient markets and portfolio management are found in both the agriculture and finance literature. This book is an attempt to improve trading and analytical skills of all students of futures markets by presenting the underlying theories of futures and financial markets in a coordinated conceptual context designed for practical use.

The first six chapters of this book present a basic discussion of primary concepts of futures markets applying to all futures contracts. Chapters 7 through 13 cover different groups of contracts and specific issues related to using them for hedging and speculation purposes. The last chapter discusses the regulation of U.S. futures markets and the impact of the markets on social welfare.

NOTE

1. A.B. Paul, K.H. Kahl, and W.G. Tomek, *Performance of Futures Markets: The Case of Potatoes.* United States Department of Agriculture Technical Bulletin No. 1636 (Washington, D.C.: 1981), p. 18.

FUTURES CONTRACTS, EXCHANGES, AND TRADING

2

This chapter discusses the institutional features, operating procedures, and jargon of the futures market. Understanding these elements is necessary before one can move to the underlying theories, uses of the market, and research implications. Trading in this market is exciting, but one must first know the rules and its unique features.

This chapter begins with instructions on how to read futures quotations in the newspaper and a description of futures market exchanges and contracts traded. Next is a short history of futures trading. Futures contracts are defined and the procedure for trading contracts is discussed along with the characteristics of the various traders. The chapter ends with a description of how the clearinghouse operates and the cash flow implications of trading at the margin.

READING FUTURES PRICES

Table 2-1 presents the futures prices for Wednesday, February 10, 1988, published in the *Wall Street Journal.* The *Journal* is one of the most complete and widely available sources for futures prices. Along with prices and the price range for the day, the paper also indicates the contract size, lifetime price range for each contract, open interest, and volume of trading. Other contract specifications such as quality and delivery conditions are not shown, but can be obtained from the exchanges.

Starting with corn, table 2–1 shows that the nearby corn contract, March, opened on this Wednesday at $2.03 3/4 per bushel, traded in a range during the day from $2.04 per bushel to $2.00 3/4 per bushel, and settled or closed at $2.02 3/4 per bushel, down 3/4 cents from the settlement (close) on Tuesday, February 9. This means that 5,000 bushel corn contracts for March delivery declined in value on that day by $37.50. Likewise, the settlement price for the March feeder cattle contract can be read as 83.15 cents per pound as listed, or as it is more commonly referred to, $83.15 per hundredweight (cwt). The reading of prices for most other food commodities, metals, and currencies is straightforward from the contract definitions.

Interest rate contracts fall into two different categories: One is Treasury bonds where the March settlement price is 95–01. This means bonds are being priced for March at 95 and 1/32d percent of par value. The second category is Treasury bills. The settlement price of 94.52 is an index of 100 minus the discount of 5.48. Notice the discount is listed as is the yield for Treasury bonds. Stock index numbers reflect the value (price) of the underlying index. Pricing procedures for all contracts correspond to cash market practices, and more detail on interpreting the prices for different contracts is provided later in the text.

The newspaper also shows the open interest for each contract, that is the number of contracts in existence after the close of trading for that day. Note that open interest is usually greatest for nearby contracts and becomes smaller for each succeeding distant maturity. Commercial users place most of their trades in the nearby maturities as more information exists about those months. Finally, listed for each commodity or instrument is the estimated total volume of trading for that day, actual volume for the previous day, and total open interest with its one-day change.

EXCHANGES AND CONTRACTS

EXCHANGES

Futures contracts trade on organized exchanges licensed by the government. It is illegal in the United States to trade futures contracts other than at these appointed markets. There are several exchanges in the United States and a large number

Table 2-1. Futures Prices

FUTURES PRICES

Wednesday, February 10, 1988

Open Interest Reflects Previous Trading Day.

–GRAINS AND OILSEEDS–

CORN (CBT) 5,000 bu.; cents per bu.

	Open	High	Low	Settle	Change	Lifetime High	Lifetime Low	Open Interest
Mar	203¾	204	200¾	202¾	– ¾	222¾	171	53,975
May	209	209½	207	208¾	– ¼	225½	174	40,423
July	212½	213	210½	212½	+ ¼	226½	180	31,418
Sept	214¼	215¼	213	214½	+ ½	223	180¾	5,471
Dec	218¼	218½	216	218	– ¼	218½	184	17,923
Mr89	225	225	223	224¾	– ¼	225	193½	981
May	229	229	227¼	228¾	– ½	229½	207½	108

Est vol 27,500; vol Tues 29,214; open int 150,299, +1,370.

OATS (CBT) 5,000 bu.; cents per bu.

	Open	High	Low	Settle	Change	Lifetime High	Lifetime Low	Open Interest
Mar	190¾	191	189	190	– 1	205½	129½	3,677
May	178½	179¼	177	178	– 1¾	194½	150¾	2,337
July	172½	172½	170½	170½	– 2¼	177	144	1,064
Sept	169	170	169	169½	– ½	173	143	963
Dec	176	177	176	176½	– ½	180	162	260

Est vol 1,000; vol Tues 1,022; open int 8,301, –189.

SOYBEANS (CBT) 5,000 bu.; cents per bu.

	Open	High	Low	Settle	Change	Lifetime High	Lifetime Low	Open Interest
Mar	609¾	614	607	612¾	+ 3	642½	474	38,393
May	619	621	616	620¾	+ 2	651	476	28,220
July	628	630	624½	629¾	+ 2½	657	488½	25,889
Aug	629	631½	627	631½	+ 3	656	512	3,713
Sept	629½	630½	627	630½	+ 1½	653	503	2,657
Nov	637½	638¼	633½	637½	+ ¾	656	499¼	21,623
Ja89	644	645	642	645	+ 1½	662	553	658
Mar	649½	652½	649½	652½	+ 1½	667	579	101

Est vol 23,000; vol Tues 28,816; open int 121,260, +1,906.

SOYBEAN MEAL (CBT) 100 tons; $ per ton.

	Open	High	Low	Settle	Change	Lifetime High	Lifetime Low	Open Interest
Mar	177.50	178.40	176.60	178.00	+ .60	205.00	135.00	13,279
May	177.60	178.00	176.30	177.90	+ .40	199.00	148.00	17,810
July	179.10	179.80	178.20	179.50	+ .40	198.00	148.10	12,424
Aug	180.30	181.00	179.50	180.80	+ .30	198.00	148.00	5,162
Sept	181.20	182.00	181.00	181.50	+ .30	189.00	153.00	3,623
Oct	182.00	182.50	182.00	182.50	....	186.00	159.00	2,220
Dec	183.50	184.50	183.50	183.50	– .20	187.00	159.00	4,695

Est vol 13,000; vol Tues 12,300; open int 64,301, +1,198.

SOYBEAN OIL (CBT) 60,000 lbs.; cents per lb.

	Open	High	Low	Settle	Change	Lifetime High	Lifetime Low	Open Interest
Mar	21.35	21.42	21.11	21.23	– .10	23.55	16.29	31,983
May	21.70	21.70	21.40	21.48	– .16	23.70	16.50	21,541
July	21.91	21.97	21.66	21.72	– .19	23.90	16.65	19,357
Aug	22.05	22.10	21.80	21.82	– .19	23.90	16.71	4,247
Sept	22.10	22.10	21.85	21.85	– .20	23.77	16.55	3,457
Oct	22.20	22.22	21.85	21.85	– .27	23.65	17.25	2,223
Dec	22.20	22.25	21.95	21.95	– .25	23.75	18.30	4,307
Ja89	22.35	22.35	21.95	21.95	– .20	23.30	21.45	160

Est vol 25,000; vol Tues 15,745; open int 87,275, +1,079.

WHEAT (CBT) 5,000 bu.; cents per bu.

	Open	High	Low	Settle	Change	Lifetime High	Lifetime Low	Open Interest
[illegible]	[illegible]	[illegible]	[illegible]	[illegible]	¼	[illegible]	253	20,928

	Open	High	Low	Settle	Change	Lifetime High	Lifetime Low	Open Interest
July	1,769	1,775	1,755	1,765	+ 10	2,160	1,741	4,790
Sept	1,807	1,807	1,788	1,792	+ 9	2,204	1,770	3,574
Dec	1,839	1,839	1,820	1,827	+ 7	2,197	1,809	4,129
Mr89	1,850	1,856	1,850	1,860	+ 6	2,088	1,844	1,912
May	1,880	1,885	1,880	1,881	+ 7	2,088	1,880	866

Est vol 3,181; vol Tues4,300; open int 28,697, –775.

COFFEE (CSCE)–37,500 lbs.; cents per lb.

	Open	High	Low	Settle	Change	Lifetime High	Lifetime Low	Open Interest
Mar	136.20	137.16	136.20	136.90	+ .33	178.00	105.00	9,476
May	139.20	139.75	139.10	139.69	+ .32	150.00	108.00	9,969
July	141.00	141.70	141.00	141.70	+ .30	145.30	110.00	4,257
Sept	142.75	143.35	142.75	143.29	– .11	145.00	111.01	1,884
Dec	145.24	145.50	145.24	145.50	– .24	146.50	114.00	854

Est vol 2,600; vol Tues3,767; open int 26,547, +377.

COTTON (CTN)–50,000 lbs.; cents per lb.

	Open	High	Low	Settle	Change	Lifetime High	Lifetime Low	Open Interest
Mar	61.50	62.10	61.10	61.40	– .12	81.25	47.50	11,570
May	62.20	62.70	61.80	61.97	– .28	81.70	53.40	12,601
July	62.50	63.10	62.10	62.47	– .18	81.40	53.90	5,271
Oct	60.12	61.10	59.80	60.75	+ .15	73.00	59.80	1,344
Dec	59.11	59.90	58.70	59.50	+ .05	70.20	58.70	6,073
Mr89	60.02	60.40	60.02	60.60	+ .10	67.90	60.02	450
May	....	....	....	61.05	+ .40	65.15	61.10	107

Est vol 5,500; vol Tues 3,928; open int 37,431, –509.

ORANGE JUICE (CTN)–15,000 lbs.; cents per lb.

	Open	High	Low	Settle	Change	Lifetime High	Lifetime Low	Open Interest
Mar	166.45	168.90	166.30	168.30	+ 1.40	177.00	119.00	3,041
May	162.40	164.00	162.25	163.80	+ .90	176.75	119.40	4,688
July	162.25	162.50	161.70	162.00	– .05	178.25	124.00	2,947
Sept	161.50	162.00	159.55	159.75	– 1.75	177.00	125.00	1,194
Nov	161.00	161.00	160.50	160.25	– 1.00	172.75	132.00	820
Jan89	157.50	157.50	157.50	157.60	– 1.65	171.25	132.00	251

Est vol 2,000; vol Tues 2,024; open int 12,975, +282.

SUGAR–WORLD (CSCE)–112,000 lbs.; cents per lb.

	Open	High	Low	Settle	Change	Lifetime High	Lifetime Low	Open Interest
Mar	8.38	8.70	8.38	8.44	+ .25	10.83	6.39	40,579
May	8.40	8.62	8.36	8.40	+ .09	10.60	6.60	39,606
July	8.35	8.48	8.23	8.26	+ .04	10.38	6.79	15,002
Oct	8.30	8.43	8.20	8.26	+ .09	10.35	7.00	36,437
Mr89	8.36	8.50	8.29	8.30	+ .03	10.32	7.99	14,597
May	8.54	8.55	8.54	8.37	– .04	10.20	8.15	421

Est vol 24,397; vol Tues32,386; open int 146,643, –3,148.

SUGAR–DOMESTIC (CSCE)–112,000 lbs.; cents per lb.

	Open	High	Low	Settle	Change	Lifetime High	Lifetime Low	Open Interest
May	22.10	22.12	22.10	22.10	– .03	22.14	21.35	1,671
July	22.12	22.15	22.12	22.15	+ .01	22.20	21.55	2,254
Sept	22.08	22.10	22.08	22.10	+ .01	22.10	21.52	1,987
N[illegible]	[illegible]	[illegible]	21.89	21.90	[illegible]	[illegible]	[illegible]	[illegible]

–WOOD–

LUMBER (CME)–130,000 bd. ft.; $ per 1,000 bd. ft.

	Open	High	Low	Settle	Change	Lifetime High	Lifetime Low	Open Interest
Mar	197.10	199.00	195.30	197.00	+ .20	199.40	156.00	3,009
May	193.50	195.50	192.80	193.60	+ .40	195.60	164.50	2,251
July	191.00	192.10	190.00	190.60	+ 1.00	192.00	165.20	1,062
Sept	188.10	189.40	187.70	188.40	+ .30	188.70	164.80	535

Est vol 1,177; vol Tues 1,662; open int 6,972, –12.

–FINANCIAL–

BRITISH POUND (IMM)–25,000 pounds; $ per pound

	Open	High	Low	Settle	Change	Lifetime High	Lifetime Low	Open Interest
Mar	1.7560	1.7615	1.7535	1.7560	+ .0115	1.8845	1.5870	36,923
June	1.7450	1.7500	1.7430	1.7440	+ .0115	1.8780	1.5280	2,828

Est vol 6,890; vol Tues 20,284; open int 39,784, –89.

CANADIAN DOLLAR (IMM)–100,000 dlrs.; $ per Can $

	Open	High	Low	Settle	Change	Lifetime High	Lifetime Low	Open Interest
Mar	.7871	.7875	.7848	.7864	–.0015	.7898	.7052	20,922
June	.7841	.7847	.7820	.7834	–.0017	.7870	.7325	4,002
Sept	.7800	.7807	.7787	.7804	–.0019	.7847	.7307	736
Dec	.7776	.7784	.7765	.7774	–.0021	.7825	.7390	234

Est vol 3,964; vol Tues 2,672; open int 25,950, –226.

JAPANESE YEN (IMM) 12.5 million yen; $ per yen (.00)

	Open	High	Low	Settle	Change	Lifetime High	Lifetime Low	Open Interest
Mar	.7775	.7791	.7761	.7769	–.0005	.8320	.6672	49,463
June	.7824	.7841	.7812	.7819	–.0005	.8390	.6735	3,167
Sept	.7874	.7885	.7874	.7875	–.0005	.8485	.7075	212

Est vol 20,130; vol Tues 17,517; open int 52,946, –602.

SWISS FRANC (IMM)–125,000 francs-$ per franc

	Open	High	Low	Settle	Change	Lifetime High	Lifetime Low	Open Interest
Mar	.7254	.7275	.7243	.7252	+.0021	.7955	.6450	32,183
June	.7337	.7359	.7325	.7334	+.0021	.8040	.6580	2,183
Sept	.7420	.7435	.7408	.7415	+.0019	.8120	.6950	97

Est vol 21,844; vol Tues 29,630; open int 34,500, –90.

W. GERMAN MARK (IMM)–125,000 marks; $ per mark

	Open	High	Low	Settle	Change	Lifetime High	Lifetime Low	Open Interest
Mar	.5928	.5946	.5923	.5933	+.0027	.6426	.5359	43,811
June	.5975	.5995	.5972	.5981	+.0027	.6494	.5410	6,431
Sept	.6028	.6040	.6028	.6033	+.0027	.6555	.5609	218

Est vol 16,077; vol Tues 20,787; open int 50,564, –256.

EURODOLLAR (LIFFE)–$1 million; pts of 100%

	Open	High	Low	Settle	Change	Lifetime High	Lifetime Low	Open Interest
Mar	93.14	93.23	93.14	93.21	+ .06	93.67	90.00	17,412
June	92.98	93.08	92.98	93.08	+ .10	93.39	89.89	9,101
Sept	92.68	92.76	92.68	92.77	+ .09	93.13	89.74	4,418
Dec	92.39	92.44	92.39	92.46	+ .08	92.93	89.80	1,221
Mr89	92.14	92.14	92.14	92.20	+ .07	92.14	90.86	406

Est vol 6,125; vol Tues 5,441; open int 32,640, +563.

STERLING (LIFFE)–£500,000; pts of 100%

	Open	High	Low	Settle	Change	Lifetime High	Lifetime Low	Open Interest
Mar	90.42	90.54	90.40	90.48	+ .04	91.70	88.60	15,140
June	90.31	90.42	90.30	90.38	+ .06	91.54	89.28	11,068
Sept	90.21	90.32	90.21	90.30	+ .06	91.27	89.26	2,611
Dec	90.14	90.21	90.12	90.20	+ .07	91.12	89.22	1,776
[illegible]	[illegible]	[illegible]	[illegible]	90.06	+ .06	90.83	89.25	1,454
[illegible]	[illegible]	[illegible]	[illegible]	[illegible]	[illegible]	[illegible]	89.65	660

Table 2–1 continued

Sept	328½	329¼	327	332	+ 4	330½	272	919
Dec	337¾	339	337	342½	+ 5	340½	289	775

Est vol 9,000; vol Tues 12,380; open Int 43,389, –158.

WHEAT (KC) 5,000 bu.; cents per bu.

Mar	324	324½	320	322	– 2	326¾	262½	16,456
May	321	321¼	318¾	321	....	325	262¼	7,012
July	320	322½	318	321½	+ 2	322½	272	488
Sept	322	327	322	325	+ 2	327	313	198

Est vol 5,191; vol Tues 6,130; open Int 28,590, +843.

WHEAT (MPLS) 5,000 bu.; cents per bu.

Mar	308	309	304	308½	+ ½	324	266	5,757
May	308½	310	307	310	+ 1¾	315	286½	3,095
July	307½	310	307	309¼	+ ¾	311½	304	357
Sept	310	310	309½	310	....	312½	309½	126

Est vol 1,306; vol Tues 1,913; open Int 9,338, +70.

BARLEY (WPG) 20 metric tons; Can. $ per ton

Mar	74.00	74.00	73.60	73.70	– .70	87.00	67.10	6,469
May	76.30	76.30	75.90	75.90	– .40	83.80	69.00	6,625
July	78.00	78.20	78.00	78.00	– .50	80.30	71.00	4,073
Oct	82.30	82.40	82.00	82.30	– .40	82.90	75.00	1,764
Dec	83.10	83.10	82.80	.82.80	– .30	83.10	79.80	362

Est vol 1,440; vol Tues 1,764; open Int 19,327, +201.

FLAXSEED (WPG) 20 metric tons; Can. $ per ton

Mar	236.00	236.50	235.00	236.20	– .20	252.50	208.10	2,767
May	242.50	242.50	241.00	242.00	– .50	260.00	214.00	2,635
July	247.00	247.70	246.80	247.50	– 2.00	264.10	232.50	712
Oct	....	....	....	256.50	– 1.50	272.50	243.00	138

Est vol 335; vol Tues 372; open Int 6,301, -54.

RAPESEED (WPG) 20 metric tons; Can. $ per ton

Mar	305.20	305.20	303.40	303.80	– .90	315.80	231.50	8,214
June	307.20	307.20	305.40	306.20	– .40	321.30	252.90	13,676
Sept	307.20	307.20	305.50	306.00	– 1.00	318.50	259.80	4,113
Nov	305.00	305.00	303.60	304.40	– .20	316.50	261.80	5,802
Jan89	307.30	308.80	307.30	308.60	– .10	310.20	304.50	233

Est vol 1,600; vol Tues 6,473; open Int 32,038, –1,051.

RYE (WPG) 20 metric tons; Can. $ per ton

Mar	110.00	110.70	109.70	110.70	+ .70	112.80	91.10	810
May	106.00	106.00	105.70	106.00	+ .10	107.50	99.50	1,298
July	....	....	....	106.50	....	107.00	101.00	374

Est vol 275; vol Tues 160; open Int 2,501, –5.

–LIVESTOCK & MEAT–

CATTLE–FEEDER (CME) 44,000 lbs.; cents per lb.

Mar	83.25	83.67	82.95	83.15	– .07	83.67	66.20	7,413
Apr	81.90	82.25	81.42	81.62	– .12	82.25	67.20	5,153
May	80.75	80.75	80.00	80.12	– .50	80.82	68.20	5,110
Aug	79.75	79.95	79.10	79.25	– .52	79.95	68.30	1,966
Sept	78.80	79.00	78.45	78.50	– .50	79.10	69.40	743
Oct	78.50	78.60	78.00	78.00	– .50	78.70	69.70	840
Nov	....	....	....	78.80	– .30	79.10	70.25	153

Est vol 2,875; vol Tues 3,844; open Int 21,391, +173.

COPPER (CMX)–25,000 lbs.; cents per lb.

Feb	102.00	106.50	102.00	106.25	+ 4.25	127.00	99.50	68
Mar	97.50	101.90	97.50	101.70	+ 4.60	127.80	60.70	18,490
May	89.10	93.80	89.10	93.50	+ 5.20	109.00	60.90	11,908
July	82.00	85.30	82.00	85.70	+ 4.80	99.70	62.30	6,738
Sept	79.60	82.20	79.60	82.70	+ 4.50	96.00	59.45	2,075
Dec	78.00	79.50	77.40	80.70	+ 4.50	96.50	64.70	2,920
Mr89	77.40	78.50	77.40	80.20	+ 4.50	93.00	66.50	607

Est vol 7,500; vol Tues 7,180; open Int 42,944, –382.

GOLD (CMX)–100 troy oz.; $ per troy oz.

Feb	442.90	444.00	440.20	440.60	– 1.00	510.00	371.00	1,546
Apr	446.80	448.20	443.20	443.90	– 1.00	514.00	378.00	82,758
June	451.00	452.30	448.00	448.30	– 1.10	523.00	399.00	17,616
Aug	456.50	456.50	452.50	452.80	– 1.20	527.00	425.00	7,829
Oct	458.50	461.50	458.50	457.50	– 1.30	533.50	429.00	9,294
Dec	465.20	466.80	462.20	462.30	– 1.40	546.00	430.00	11,769
Fb89	470.00	470.00	469.00	467.40	– 1.50	549.50	465.00	5,358
Apr	476.50	476.50	476.50	472.70	– 1.60	550.00	470.00	4,646
June	482.30	483.20	482.30	478.10	– 1.70	570.00	476.00	6,380
Aug	488.50	488.50	488.50	484.90	– .80	575.00	482.20	2,421
Oct	494.00	495.00	494.00	489.90	– 1.90	575.50	488.00	2,697
Dec	499.50	499.50	499.50	496.10	– 2.00	504.00	495.00	922

Est vol 27,000; vol Tues 41,939; open Int 153,239, –2,630.

GOLD (IMM)–100 fine troy oz.; U.S. $ per fine oz.

Mar	....	....	....	441.80	– .80	509.50	472.50	102
July	....	....	....	451.40	– .40	513.40	487.40	2

Est vol 0; vol Tues 0; open Int 104, .

PLATINUM (NYM)–50 troy oz.; $ per troy oz.

Feb	....	....	....	454.10	+ 1.50	482.00	451.00	21
Apr	463.50	466.00	455.50	456.10	+ 1.50	670.80	439.50	12,565
July	468.00	470.50	461.00	461.10	+ 1.50	667.50	443.00	4,007
Oct	473.50	475.00	468.50	466.60	+ 1.50	667.50	452.00	2,043
Ja89	476.00	476.00	476.00	472.10	+ 1.00	646.00	459.00	111

Est vol 4,790; vol Tues 4,830; open Int 18,748, +104.

PALLADIUM (NYM) 100 troy oz.; $ per troy oz.

Mar	122.75	123.00	121.75	122.20	+ .40	160.50	103.65	3,107
June	120.25	121.00	120.00	120.70	+ .90	160.00	103.65	2,245
Sept	....	....	....	119.70	+ .90	142.25	103.65	740
Dec	120.00	121.00	120.00	118.95	+ .90	139.50	104.50	390

Est vol 354; vol Tues 599; open Int 6,483, +77.

SILVER (CMX)–5,000 troy oz.; cents per troy oz.

Feb	....	....	....	628.2	+ 1.7	700.0	649.0	3
Mar	634.5	637.0	628.5	630.5	+ 1.5	1030.0	552.0	37,235
May	644.0	645.0	637.0	638.6	+ 1.5	1041.4	557.0	17,189
July	652.0	652.0	645.0	646.5	+ 1.5	1053.0	580.0	12,548
Sept	655.0	657.0	655.0	654.0	+ 1.5	1064.0	588.0	6,757
Dec	672.0	672.0	664.0	666.4	+ 1.5	1082.0	606.0	5,644
Mr89	683.0	683.0	683.0	679.3	+ 1.5	1073.0	684.0	1,318
May	....	....	....	688.3	+ 1.5	948.0	714.0	479
July	702.0	703.0	699.0	698.0	+ 1.5	985.0	692.0	367

Est vol 10,600; vol Tues 12,476; open Int 81,611, +238.

Est vol 15,486; vol Tues 19,231; open Int 32,998, +1,567.

LONG GILT (LIFFE)–£50,000; 32nds of 100%

Mar	118-06	118-28	118-01	118-27	+ 0-30	125-00	110-26	24,167
June	118-04	118-24	118-02	118-27	+ 0-30	121-17	117-05	3,465

Est vol 33,386; vol Tues 41,125; open Int 27,632, –1,512.

EURODOLLAR (IMM)–$1 million; pts of 100%

	Open	High	Low	Settle	Chg	Yield Settle	Yield Chg	Open Interest
Mar	93.23	93.24	93.19	93.23	+ .05	6.77	– .05	130,455
June	93.08	93.14	93.07	93.12	+ .08	6.88	– .08	86,466
Sept	92.77	92.83	92.76	92.82	+ .09	7.18	– .09	42,050
Dec	92.47	92.53	92.45	92.51	+ .09	7.49	– .09	21,628
Mr89	92.20	92.25	92.18	92.24	+ .09	7.76	– .09	15,089
June	91.96	92.02	91.95	92.01	+ .08	7.99	– .08	11,686
Sept	91.80	91.82	91.76	91.82	+ .07	8.18	– .07	9,732
Dec	91.63	91.66	91.61	91.66	+ .07	8.34	– .07	7,073
Mr90	91.49	91.52	91.48	91.52	+ .07	8.48	– .07	9,108
June	91.37	91.40	91.36	91.40	+ .07	8.60	– .07	10,033
Sept	91.27	91.30	91.26	91.30	+ .07	8.70	– .07	6,079
Dec	91.18	91.21	91.18	91.21	+ .07	8.79	– .07	4,913

Est vol 63,410; vol Tues 55,027; open Int 354,312, +3,009.

U.S. DOLLAR INDEX (CTN) 500 times USDX

Mar	90.92	91.07	90.72	90.88	– .34	102.05	86.07	4,275
June	91.35	91.45	91.20	91.33	– .37	101.20	86.60	2,473

Est vol 1,000; vol Tues 1,849; open Int 6,758, +339.
The Index: High 90.88; Low 90.62; Close 90.78 –.29

5 YR TREAS NOTES (CTN) $100,000; pts. 32nds of 100%

Mar	101-02	101-09	01-015	01-085	+ .075	7.69	– .06	7,478
June	00-165	100-23	100-16	100-23	+ .075	7.82	– .06	2,579

Est vol 2,000; vol Tues 1,899; open Int 10,057, +704.

CRB INDEX (NYFE) 500 times Index

Mar	229.90	230.65	229.55	230.30	+ .70	242.25	210.00	1,384
May	228.60	229.25	228.60	229.10	+ .80	237.50	217.10	345
July	228.80	229.00	228.50	229.00	+ .60	235.90	218.50	424
Sept	228.70	228.70	228.70	228.90	+ .60	236.70	226.50	253

Est vol 350; vol Tues586; open Int 2,406, –83.
The Index: High 232.01; Low 231.21 ; Close n.a.

TREASURY BONDS (CBT)–$100,000; pts. 32nds of 100%

Mar	94-20	95-05	94-16	95-01	+ 15	8.522	– .051	249,748
June	93-19	94-04	93-14	94-00	+ 16	8.635	– .056	56,143
Sept	92-19	93-05	92-16	93-02	+ 16	8.740	– .057	9,197
Dec	91-24	92-11	91-24	92-07	+ 16	8.836	– .057	3,055
Mr89	91-08	91-17	91-08	91-14	+ 16	8.926	– .058	3,197
June	....	....	....	90-23	+ 16	9.009	– .059	2,455
Sept	....	....	....	90-01	+ 16	9.090	– .060	373
Dec	....	....	....	89-12	+ 16	9.169	– .060	134
Mr90	....	....	....	88-24	+ 16	9.244	– .061	47

Est vol 205,000; vol Tues 196,466; op Int 324,380, +597.

TREASURY NOTES (CBT)–$100,000; pts. 32nds of 100%

Mar	98-13	98-28	98-13	98-25	+ 11	8.181	– .051	58,578
June	97-22	98-02	97-22	97-31	+ 10	8.303	– .047	16,441

Feb	72.20	72.57	71.82	72.07	– .12	72.57	55.10	7,765
Apr	72.55	72.65	71.80	72.10	– .47	72.90	57.70	39,371
June	70.80	70.85	70.15	70.27	– .65	71.25	60.60	21,076
Aug	68.27	68.27	67.60	67.65	– .62	68.47	59.17	12,471
Oct	67.30	67.30	66.55	66.62	– .57	67.60	58.65	7,081
Dec	67.50	67.60	66.97	67.05	– .47	67.90	60.25	1,924

Est vol 25,404; vol Tues 25,128; open Int 89,701, +933.

HOGS (CME) 30,000 lbs.; cents per lb.

Feb	49.10	49.20	48.30	48.57	– .50	49.20	37.55	1,938
Apr	46.80	47.35	46.50	46.62	– .57	47.35	35.90	13,568
June	49.90	50.35	49.45	49.60	– .40	50.35	37.50	5,680
July	49.65	49.85	49.30	49.45	– .25	49.85	41.15	2,051
Aug	48.80	49.15	48.30	48.35	– .52	49.15	39.95	6,487
Oct	43.95	44.00	43.30	43.40	– .45	44.00	37.52	856
Dec	44.00	44.10	43.80	43.90	– .30	44.20	38.30	411

Est vol 8,410; vol Tues 10,347; open Int 31,005, +489.

PORK BELLIES (CME) 40,000 lbs.; cents per lb.

Feb	56.50	57.80	56.35	57.75	+ 1.42	69.00	49.00	454
Mar	57.00	58.50	56.77	58.22	+ 1.30	68.62	49.60	2,972
May	58.80	59.90	58.50	59.57	+ 1.07	67.75	51.00	3,714
July	58.90	60.25	58.75	59.70	+ 1.10	66.47	51.00	1,780
Aug	57.50	58.60	57.35	57.92	+ .65	60.00	50.10	1,178

Est vol 5,061; vol Tues 4,436; open Int 10,139, –49.

–FOOD & FIBER–

COCOA (CSCE)–10 metric tons; $ per ton.

Mar	1,706	1,725	1,693	1,704	+ 9	2,160	1,681	4,694
May	1,740	1,755	1,727	1,735	+ 8	2,152	1,715	8,732

ACC–Amex Commodities Corp.; CBT–Chicago Board of Trade; CME–Chicago Mercantile Exchange; CMX–Commodity Exchange, New York; CRCE–Chicago Rice & Cotton Exchange; CSCE–Coffee, Sugar & Cocoa Exchange, New York; CTN–New York Cotton Exchange; IPEL–International Petroleum Exchange of London; IMM–International Monetary Market at CME, Chicago; KC–Kansas City Board of Trade; LIFFE–London International Financial Futures Exchange; MCE–MidAmerica Commodity Exchange; MPLS–Minneapolis Grain Exchange; NYFE–New York Futures Exchange, unit of New York Stock Exchange. NYM–New York Mercantile Exchange; PBOT–Philadelphia Board of Trade; WPG–Winnipeg Commodity Exchange.

Feb	633.0	633.0	625.0	626.0	+ 1.0	1003.0	569.0	47
Apr	637.0	641.0	633.0	634.0	+ 1.0	1015.0	576.0	6,130
June	648.0	650.0	642.0	642.5	....	1030.0	600.0	3,531
Aug	657.0	659.0	650.0	651.0	+ 1.0	1004.0	643.0	220
Dec	675.0	675.0	667.0	668.0	+ 2.0	946.0	660.0	1,102

Est vol 500; vol Tues 637; open Int 11,213, –146.

CRUDE OIL, Light Sweet (NYM) 1,000 bbls.; $ per bbl.

Mar	17.17	17.29	17.11	17.13	– .29	21.15	14.70	55,447
Apr	17.11	17.26	17.06	17.09	– .27	21.15	14.70	75,817
May	17.10	17.18	17.02	17.04	– .24	21.20	14.70	30,713
June	16.98	17.07	16.91	16.94	– .23	21.20	14.78	18,631
July	16.86	16.96	16.81	16.84	– .23	20.17	14.85	8,962
Aug	16.86	16.87	16.70	16.74	– .23	20.10	14.85	4,699
Sept	16.66	16.79	16.66	16.64	– .23	19.70	14.95	2,646
Oct	16.70	16.70	16.70	16.54	– .23	19.70	14.90	1,454
Nov	16.60	16.60	16.60	16.44	– .23	16.85	14.90	251
Dec	16.50	16.50	16.50	16.34	– .23	18.15	14.99	310
Ja89	16.47	15.48	16.47	16.24	– .23	16.48	16.00	102

Est vol 84,369; vol Tues 59,963; open Int 199,032, –181.

HEATING OIL NO. 2 (NYM) 42,000 gal.; $ per gal.

Mar	.4780	.4790	.4720	.4728	– .0132	.5840	.4324	25,057
Apr	.4670	.4695	.4620	.4627	– .0121	.5790	.4119	13,170
May	.4575	.4595	.4540	.4545	– .0103	.5650	.4025	6,756
June	.4505	.4540	.4490	.4490	– .0103	.5540	.3995	3,126
July	.4530	.4530	.4490	.4490	– .0098	.5490	.3975	2,506
Aug	....	....	....	.4540	– .0098	.5445	.4110	510
Sept	.4630	.4630	.4630	.4610	– .0098	.5230	.4175	198
Oct	....	....	....	.4680	– .0098	.5090	.4410	116
Nov	....	....	....	.4750	– .0098	.4950	.4340	121
Dec	....	....	....	.4820	– .0098	.4925	.4620	153

Est vol 20,410; vol Tues 17,502; open Int 51,713, +57.

GAS OIL (IPEL) 100 metric tons; $ per ton

Feb	136.50	139.00	136.00	137.00	– 2.00	184.00	134.00	6,659
Mar	139.00	139.75	137.50	138.00	– 2.50	185.00	130.00	15,589
Apr	138.00	138.75	137.25	137.75	– 1.75	167.00	129.00	7,003
May	137.50	138.75	137.50	137.50	– 1.50	166.00	128.00	8,614
June	141.00	140.50	138.50	139.50	– 1.75	151.75	129.50	3,754
July	140.25	140.25	139.50	139.50	– 2.00	148.50	131.00	1,344

Actual Wednesday; vol 6,807; open Int 42,969, n.a..

GASOLINE, Unleaded (NYM) 42,000 gal.; $ per gal.

Mar	.4675	.4700	.4640	.4648	– .0109	.5700	.4073	12,566
Apr	.4770	.4780	.4725	.4728	– .0107	.5800	.4180	15,440
May	.4835	.4845	.4790	.4797	– .0103	.5610	.4245	10,329
June	.4853	.4860	.4810	.4818	– .0107	.5400	.4310	2,461
July	.4835	.4842	.4805	.4805	– .0105	.5150	.4510	2,052
Aug	.4780	.4795	.4780	.4770	– .0115	.4865	.4540	152

Est vol 9,261; vol Tues 8,343; open Int 43,000, +628.

Sept	....	....	....	97-06	+ 10	8.422	– .047	309

Est vol 20,000; vol Tues 16,098; open Int 75,328, –598.

TREASURY BONDS (MCE)–$50,000; pts. 32nds of 100%

Mar	94-22	95-05	94-00	95-02	+ 13	8.518	–.0045	5,398
June	93-20	94-03	93-20	94-02	+ 15	8.628	–.0052	137

Est vol 3,000; vol Tues 3,726; open Int 5,558, +168.

TREASURY BILLS (IMM)–$1 mil.; pts. of 100%

						Discount		Open
	Open	High	Low	Settle	Chg	Settle	Chg	Interest
Mar	94.52	94.53	94.48	94.52	+ .03	5.48	– .03	16,193
June	94.36	94.39	94.35	94.39	+ .05	5.61	– .05	6,114
Sept	94.07	94.12	94.07	94.12	+ .05	5.88	– .05	961
Dec	93.75	93.82	93.75	93.81	+ .06	6.19	– .06	168
Mr89	93.56	93.56	93.50	93.56	+ .05	6.44	– .05	121

Est vol 2,962; vol Tues 3,392; open Int 23,597, +76.

–INDEXES–

MUNI BOND INDEX(CBT)$1,000; times Bond Buyer MBI

								Open
	Open	High	Low	Settle	Chg	High	Low	Interest
Mar	90-22	91-17	90-22	91-15	+ 26	91-15	71-12	14,627
June	89-02	89-26	89-02	89-24	+ 24	89-25	70-03	2,347
Sept	87-19	88-11	87-19	88-10	+ 24	88-08	81-02	415
Dec	86-30	86-30	86-28	86-30	+ 24	86-29	83-08	145

Est vol 5,000; vol Tues 3,974; open Int 17,539, +191.
The Index: Close 92-01; Yield 7.92.

S&P 500 INDEX (CME) 500 times index

Mar	254.50	258.20	253.60	257.95	+ 3.05	344.90	181.00	114,128
June	255.50	259.40	255.00	259.25	+ 3.10	347.90	190.00	6,995
Sept	259.30	260.55	256.60	260.30	+ 2.75	343.50	193.00	137

Est vol 43,617; vol Tues 43,421; open Int 121,261, +2.
Indx prelim High 256.92; Low 251.72; Close 256.66 +4.94

NYSE COMPOSITE INDEX (NYFE) 500 times index

Mar	143.20	145.15	142.70	145.00	+ 1.55	193.00	112.00	4,149
June	144.15	145.70	143.55	145.85	+ 1.55	194.60	113.00	1,113
Sept	145.15	146.00	145.00	146.65	+ 1.55	149.15	128.50	532

Est vol 8,650; vol Tues 9,848; open Int 5,824, +48.
The Index: High n.a.; Low n.a.; Close 144.24 +2.61

KC VALUE LINE INDEX (KC) 500 times index

Mar	212.25	215.75	211.60	215.45	+ 2.60	287.20	170.00	1,609

Est vol 280; vol Tues 221; open Int 1,646, .
The Index: High 213.74; Low 210.61; Close 213.61 +3.04

MAJOR MKT INDEX (CBT) $250 times index

Feb	384.75	393.25	384.40	392.85	+ 7.75	414.75	368.50	2,326
Mar	385.50	393.75	385.00	393.25	+ 7.50	509.00	330.00	410

Est vol 7,000; vol Tues 3,868; open Int 2,848, –27.
The Index: High 391.69; Low 382.47; Close 391.65 +9.18

scattered around the world in England, Canada, Japan, Australia, India, France, Brazil, Hong Kong, the Netherlands, and elsewhere. The two largest exchanges are in Chicago: the Chicago Board of Trade and the Chicago Mercantile Exchange. They serve as a focal point for futures trading around the world. Among active markets, the Chicago Board of Trade is the largest and oldest for it began trading futures contracts in 1865. Outside the United States the most active futures trading occurs in London where there are several small exchanges.

Originally organizations for trading cash (also called spot or physical) commodities, older exchanges gradually undertook the trading of futures contracts. Newer exchanges organize under corporate laws strictly to trade futures contracts. The Chicago Board of Trade specializes in futures contracts for grains, oilseeds, metals, and financial instruments, while the Chicago Mercantile Exchange handles livestock, foreign currency, and financial instrument contracts. Smaller exchanges in the United States typically have less than five or six active contracts and most foreign exchanges offer only one or two. Products such as wheat, silver, and gold trade on more than one exchange and in more than one country. Table 2–2 lists ten active exchanges in the United States and the volume of trading for their most active contracts from 1982 to 1987. Also indicated is the year each contract began trading.

Exchanges are voluntary associations of people who have a common interest in trading futures contracts. Exchanges exist to provide the facilities and rules for trading. The exchanges themselves do not trade contracts, nor do they become involved in setting prices. Their objectives are (1) to provide a place for trading, (2) to establish trading rules and standards of business conduct, (3) to supervise and enforce those rules and standards, (4) to write contracts, (5) to settle disputes and guarantee contract settlements, and (6) to collect and disseminate market information to the public. The exchanges are responsible for the financial and business integrity of their own members and contracts.

Exchanges organize similar to corporations. They hire personnel to oversee administration, operations, and support services such as research, education, and data distribution. They also often have a board of directors from the outside. Officers, directors, and committees elected from the membership are responsible for the policies of the exchange and enforcement of the rules. Typical committees include business conduct, education, membership, arbitration, and new contracts. Particularly important and powerful is the arbitration committee that must settle trading disputes. Trading mistakes, often unintentional, cause disputes and involve money. Members are bound by commercial law, so when individuals cannot reconcile a dispute, the arbitration committee acts as a review board and makes the final decision. Only constitutional matters, issues of exchange bylaws, and rule violations such as price manipulation are taken to a court of law.

Table 2-2. U.S. Exchanges and Selected Futures Contracts[a]

Exchanges and Contracts	Volume Traded (in millions) 1987	1986	1985	1984	1983	1982
Chicago Board of Trade						
Wheat (1865)[b]	1.9	2.1	2.1	3.0	3.9	4.0
Corn (1865)	7.3	6.2	6.4	9.1	11.9	7.9
Oats (1865)	0.3	0.1	0.1	0.2	0.4	0.4
Soybeans (1936)	7.4	6.1	7.4	11.4	13.7	9.2
Soybean oil (1950)	3.9	3.2	3.6	4.0	3.9	3.0
Soybean meal (1951)	3.8	3.0	3.3	3.8	3.9	2.8
Silver (1,000 oz) (1969)	0.5	0.5	1.0	1.9	2.6	0.8
Gold (kilo) (1974)	0.2	0.1	0.2	0.3	0.3	—
GNMA mortgages (1975)	0.0	0.0	0.1	0.9	1.7	2.1
T-notes (1982)	5.3	4.4	2.9	1.7	0.8	0.9
T-bonds (1977)	66.8	52.6	40.4	30.0	19.6	16.7
Major Mkt. Index (1984)	—	0.0	2.1	1.5	—	—
MMI Maxi (1985)	2.6	1.7	0.4	—	—	—
Municipal bonds (1985)	1.6	0.9	0.3	—	—	—
Total	101.6[c]	81.1	70.6	67.7	62.8	48.2
Chicago Mercantile Exchange						
Live hogs (1966)	2.0	1.9	1.7	2.2	2.8	3.6
Pork bellies (1961)	1.1	1.1	1.5	1.9	2.4	2.8
Live cattle (1964)	5.2	4.7	4.4	3.6	4.3	4.4
Feeder cattle (1971)	0.6	0.4	0.5	0.3	0.5	0.6
Lumber (1969)	0.4	0.5	0.6	0.8	0.7	0.5
British pound (1972)	2.6	2.7	2.8	1.4	1.6	1.3
Canadian dollar (1972)	0.9	0.7	0.5	0.3	0.6	1.1
Deutsche mark (1972)	6.0	6.6	6.4	5.5	2.4	1.8
Japanese yen (1972)	5.4	4.0	2.4	2.3	3.4	1.8
Swiss franc (1972)	5.3	5.0	4.8	4.1	3.8	2.7
Gold (1974)	0.3	—	—	0.0	1.0	1.5
T-bills (1976)	1.9	1.8	2.4	3.3	3.8	6.6
Domestic CD (1981)	0.0	0.0	0.1	0.9	1.1	1.6
Eurodollar (1981)	20.4	10.8	8.9	4.2	0.9	0.3
S&P 500 Index (1982)	19.0	19.5	15.1	12.4	8.1	2.9
S&P 100 Index (1983)	—	0.0	0.0	0.2	0.4	—
Total	71.3	59.8	52.1	43.5	37.8	33.6
Kansas City Board of Trade						
Wheat (1877)	1.0	0.7	0.7	1.0	0.9	1.0
Value Line Index (1982)	0.5	1.0	1.2	0.9	0.7	0.5
Total	1.5	1.7	2.0	1.9	1.7	1.5
Minneapolis Grain Exchange						
Wheat (1885)	0.3	0.3	0.3	0.3	0.4	0.3

Table 2-2 continued

Exchanges and Contracts	Volume Traded (in millions) 1987	1986	1985	1984	1983	1982
MidAmerica Commodity Exchange[d]						
Wheat (1880)	0.2	0.3	0.3	0.4	0.3	0.2
Corn (1880)	0.3	0.4	0.5	0.6	0.6	0.3
Soybeans (1936)	0.4	0.7	0.8	1.3	1.2	0.5
Silver (1968)	0.0	0.0	0.1	0.0	0.1	0.1
Gold (1974)	0.0	0.0	0.0	0.0	0.3	0.4
Live cattle (1978)	0.0	0.1	0.1	0.1	0.1	0.1
Live hogs (1974)	0.0	0.1	0.1	0.1	0.1	0.2
T-bonds (1981)	1.0	0.5	0.3	0.3	0.3	0.4
Swiss franc (1983)	0.1	0.1	0.1	0.1	0.0	—
Deutsche mark (1983)	0.1	0.1	0.1	0.1	0.0	—
Total	2.4	2.4	2.5	3.1	3.2	2.4
Coffee, Sugar, and Cocoa						
Coffee "C" (1955)	1.0	1.1	0.6	0.5	0.4	0.6
Sugar No. 11 (1941)	3.9	3.6	3.0	2.5	3.2	2.0
Cocoa (1925)	0.9	0.8	0.8	1.1	1.2	0.6
Total	5.8	5.5	4.6	4.2	4.9	3.3
Commodity Exchange						
Copper (1953)	2.6	1.9	2.4	2.5	3.2	2.4
Silver (1933)	5.1	3.8	4.8	6.7	6.4	2.9
Gold (1974)	10.2	8.4	7.8	9.1	10.4	12.2
Total	17.9	14.2	15.1	18.4	20.0	17.5
NY Cotton and Citrus						
Cotton No. 2 (1870)	1.4	1.0	0.6	1.1	1.6	1.3
Orange juice (1966)	0.3	0.2	0.2	0.3	0.1	0.2
Dollar Index (1985)	0.4	0.2	0.1	—	—	—
5-Year T-note (1987)	0.4	—	—	—	—	—
Total	2.5	1.5	0.9	1.5	1.7	1.5
NY Futures Exchange						
NYSE Comp Index (1982)	2.9	3.1	2.8	3.5	3.5	1.4
CRB Index (1986)	0.1	0.1	—	—	—	—
Total	3.1	3.2	2.8	3.5	3.5	1.5
NY Mercantile Exchange						
Palladium (1968)	0.2	0.1	0.1	0.2	0.2	0.0
Platinum (1956)	1.4	1.6	0.7	0.6	1.1	0.7
Potatoes (1941)	0.0	0.0	0.0	0.0	0.0	0.1
No. 2 heating oil (1981)	4.3	3.3	2.2	2.1	1.9	1.7

Leaded reg. gas (1981)	—	0.8	0.7	0.7	0.4	0.1
Unleaded reg. gas (1984)	2.1	0.4	0.1	0.0	—	—
Crude oil (1983)	14.6	8.3	4.0	1.8	0.3	—
Total	22.5	14.6	7.8	5.3	3.9	2.6
Total All Contracts[e]	228.9	184.4	158.7	149.4	139.9	112.4

[a]*Source:* Futures Industry Association

[b]Year contract began trading (Commodity Futures Trading Commission Yearbooks).

[c]Totals do not necessarily equal the sum of the columns due to rounding errors and omitting minor contracts.

[d]Contract sizes on the MidAmerica Commodity Exchange are smaller than similar contracts on other exchanges, usually one-half or one-fifth in size.

[e]The total omits the Amex Commodity Exchange and the Chicago Rice and Cotton Exchange (formerly the New Orleans Commodity Exchange).

MEMBERSHIPS AND SEATS. U.S. exchanges limit membership to individuals, and only members of the exchange can trade contracts on the trading floor. Leasing or renting of memberships to nonmembers and joint ownership are often allowed. Corporations cannot hold memberships, although many companies underwrite the purchase of memberships for their own employees. Members come from all areas of commercial and financial trade. They include producers, merchants, processors, distributors, exporters, importers, brokerage houses, financial institutions, and professional speculators.

Most exchanges have a specific number of memberships, or seats, which can be bought or sold. Some, like the Winnipeg Grain Exchange, have no limit on memberships. The Chicago Board of Trade had over three thousand members at one time, but the base number has remained at 1,402 since the 1950s. The Chicago Mercantile Exchange has a base membership of 500, plus an additional 650 original seats with the associated International Monetary Market. However, both major Chicago exchanges are expanding memberships. They have developed associated memberships that allow individuals to trade only specific minor or new contracts, but not the principal or original contracts of the exchange. In some cases these partial seats will become full-fledged memberships after a number of years. Other exchanges have smaller membership rolls than the two major Chicago exchanges. The increased volume of business during the last decade has put considerable pressure on exchanges to expand memberships.

The value of seats on exchanges has changed dramatically in recent years. In the early 1960s, memberships in Chicago traded for less than $5,000, but in 1987 some sold for over $400,000. Their value varies considerably as trading business increases and decreases, and seat prices fall rapidly during periods of economic stagnation. Seats in other exchanges are usually less valuable than those in Chicago.

To become a member of an exchange is relatively easy. An applicant must attest to good character, financial responsibility, and reasonable net worth. The latter varies among exchanges and whether applicants are acting on their own behalf or to represent a company. After an application is approved, memberships trade through a bid and ask negotiation. The purpose for owning a membership is either (1) to gain access to the exchange for trading or; (2) to obtain reduced commission rates offered to members, whether they trade through agents or directly themselves. Members pay smaller commissions than nonmembers, especially floor traders who get in and out of the market within the day.

Nonmembers can easily trade in the futures market by becoming the customer of either an account executive (also known as a registered representative or associated person) or a futures commission merchant. These agents solicit orders, collect customer funds, and execute trade orders requested by their public clients. Most account executives associate with major brokerage houses who sponsor exchange memberships. The house asks clients to sign a customer agreement stating financial responsibilities and rules for trading orders. Alternatively, customers can join a commodity fund where a general partner controls a pool of money and obtains assistance for trading decisions.

Finally, most exchanges are nonprofit organizations. They finance themselves through a combination of investments, dues, and/or fees. Some exchanges own buildings or other securities from which they obtain rent or returns. However, the principal source of operating money for most exchanges comes from assessing a fee for each trade. Thus, their amount of operating capital is a function of trading volume and contract popularity. Exchanges cannot require people to trade, so their financial health and existence depend on contracts and services offered. As a result, exchanges grow or die. New exchanges develop where there is an interest, such as the New York Futures Exchange established in 1980. Inactive exchanges that once offered contracts include Duluth, Milwaukee, Portland, Seattle, and St. Louis. The New Orleans exchange reactivated trading in 1980, but closed its doors again in 1983 due to insufficient volume. Small size and high operating costs were instrumental in four New York exchanges agreeing to share a common trading floor.[1]

CONTRACTS

Table 2–2 showed that the list of actively traded futures contracts is large. In 1986 trading occurred on about 85 different contracts, although around 130 different contracts had approval for trading in the United States. The list of contracts is always changing as exchanges constantly compete with each other in offering new ones.

Historically, the standard commodities traded were grains, oilseeds and their products, cotton, and metals—all storable commodities traded internationally. The biggest break from these traditional commodities came in the mid-1960s with the successful trading of nonstorable livestock contracts—live cattle and live hogs. Foreign currencies followed in the early 1970s, then interest bearing instruments in the mid-to-late 1970s, and stock indexes and options on futures contracts in the 1980s. This is not to overlook the introduction of more food products, forest and petroleum products, and metals during this same twenty-year time span. Nevertheless, the recent explosion and proliferation of contracts involved financial instruments and stock indexes. Table 2–2 shows this trend, and notes that the most actively traded contract since 1982 has been Treasury bonds, the first time in history this honor did not go to an agricultural commodity. Stock index contracts and crude oil have also quickly surpassed many traditional agricultural commodities in trading volume. In 1987 the Treasury bond contract itself comprised 29 percent of all futures trading.

Outside the United States there are futures contracts for most major grains, various oils, cocoa, coffee, copper, copra, cotton, financial instruments, gold, ground nuts, jute, lead, ocean shipping rates, pepper, rubber, shellac, silk, silver, sugar, tin, wool, zinc, and futures options.

Equally impressive is the list of commodities once actively traded, but no longer in existence. The Chicago Mercantile Exchange was originally a butter and egg exchange. Butter is no longer traded and eggs vanished for a while, but reappeared in a different form only to vanish again. Lard and cottonseed oil were active commodities before expiring in the 1960s. Turkeys and broilers have been tried off and on with mixed success. Onions were legislated out of existence in 1958. Unsuccessful trading attempts have been made for wine, scrap iron, boneless beef, diamonds, and apples, to name a few. Many recently introduced currencies, interest rate instruments, petroleum products, lumber products, metals, and price indexes have failed after only a year or two of trading.[2] Exchanges continually search for those contracts that will trade actively.

CHARACTERISTICS. Common characteristics of commodities traded are difficult to list. Curiously, some products are successful, but closely related substitutes are not. Frozen pork bellies, or unsliced bacon, trade actively while there is no futures contract for hams, even though every hog has two of each. There is a contract for frozen concentrated orange juice, but not for any other citrus juice. Some metals succeed, but not others. Swiss francs are popular, but not French francs. Major market stock indexes trade actively, but over-the-counter indexes failed.

In 1948 Julius B. Baer and Olin G. Saxon developed a list of common characteristics of commodities traded on futures markets.[3] These are: (1) homogeneity of product; (2) capability of standardization and grading; (3) large demand and supply; (4) centralized market; (5) uncertain demand and supply and fluctuating prices; and (6) storability. The success of recent contracts reduces this list. Commodities no longer need to be storable, nor flow through a centralized market. A list of common characteristics of futures contracts today would be: (1) homogeneity of item, or at least not identified with a producer or manufacturer (i.e., fungible); (2) capable of description, including standardization and grading; (3) variable or uncertain prices; (4) active and large commercial market; and (5) availability of public information.[4] In addition, contracts must fulfill an economic need, contract terms must be evenly balanced between buyers and sellers, and trading must be liquid.

HISTORY

Closely associated with the development of civilization, the trading of commodities traces back to the Roman and Greek empires.[5] More modern practices of trade evolved in Europe from the eleventh to fourteenth centuries. The number of commodities traded multiplied rapidly and trade centers were established in northern Italy, Flanders, and Champagne. Markets were characterized by fairs that rotated from city to city throughout the year. In association with the fairs came trading institutions and standardized practices. Although most trading was spot, one document that emerged was the *lettre de faire,* a forward contract specifying delivery and payment of products in the future. Initially between first buyer and seller, these *lettres de faire* eventually evolved into documents traded in forward markets among third parties before delivery occurred. They appeared to differ from modern futures contracts in the lack of standardization, homogeneity, and formalized trading rules.

The fairs gradually moved northwards and began year-round activities at specific locations, known as exchanges. One such exchange was the Royal Exchange in London, which opened in 1570. At the exchanges, dealers acting as agents absorbed price risks that merchants sought to avoid through the use of forward transactions. The dealers assured both sellers and buyers of a market, and attempted to profit from price differences. Grading and standardization became important parts of the marketing process.

Apparently, organized futures trading in rice took place in Japan in the seventeenth century. The government banned this highly developed system in 1869. In Europe the 1600s saw forward trading on Dutch tulips, which collapsed in speculative frenzy. Warrant trading of pig iron existed in England in the eighteenth century. Other forward markets developed in the nineteenth century, especially in England and the United States. Of special note was the forward market for flour in Buffalo and New York City in the 1840s.[6]

DEVELOPMENT IN THE UNITED STATES

The development of modern futures trading in the United States closely corresponds with the growth of Chicago as a commercial center. A village in 1833, Chicago's location between the Great Lakes and the fertile land of Illinois favored it as a center for internal trade. New railroads emerged from the city in several directions, moving primary commodities into the city and goods manufactured there and in the east out of the city. Of local importance was the opening in 1848 of the Illinois-Michigan Canal, connecting the Illinois River and Lake Michigan and providing water transportation between productive farmlands and market outlets. This canal reduced transportation costs and active grain trading developed immediately along the river and canal. Chicago became a major grain terminus and in 1848 the Chicago Board of Trade opened with 82 members to trade cash commodities.

Along the Illinois River, merchants purchased corn and wheat from local farmers after harvest. They stored the grain until the following spring and shipped it to Chicago after the ice melted. Because farmers usually demanded immediate cash payments, the merchants either had to pay them directly from their own funds or borrow the money. Lenders, however, hesitated to make loans when the price of stored grain was uncertain. Merchants then made contracts in Chicago for delivery of grain at a firm price in the spring. As a result, they shifted the risk of price changes away from themselves to Chicago businessmen prepared to take the risk. As soon as the merchants no longer carried all the price risk associated with grain inventories, lenders became more willing to loan them money. At the same time the Board of Trade developed a system of standards beginning with an inspection and weighing system for wheat. This system and associated quality standards increased the physical efficiency of handling grain and issuing warehouse receipts in Chicago.

These initial grain contracts were forward commitments calling for deferred delivery of a standard quality commodity at an agreed price to be paid on delivery. They reduced the pricing and financing risks of river merchants holding stored grain. Gradually, country and Chicago merchants found third parties willing to buy the contracts and assume the price risks. As other traders joined, the contracts began changing hands several times before delivery occurred.

This system continued to develop and evolve until futures contracts traded at the Chicago Board of Trade in 1865. Making them distinguishable from forward contracts, these contracts were standardized, traded on an exchange with a specific set of rules, openly reported, and available with only margin funds deposited to gurarantee performance.[7] Standardization here included contract size, grading definitions, and delivery procedures. The concept of offsetting a contract before maturity did not begin until 1882, and establishing the clearinghouse as third party to all transactions was formalized in 1891 at the Minneapolis Grain Exchange.[8] These features completed the evolution of forward contracts to futures trading with the latter being traded on an impersonal basis for some purpose other than the exchange of title. This entire evolutionary process took about fifty years to develop the futures contracts and trading procedures we now know.

Paralleling market development in Chicago was the growth of New York as an international trade center. Major shipping routes linked it to other major ports around the world. Regarding futures markets, a cotton exchange developed in New York not only because of its location between southern plantations and northern processing mills, but also because of its long-standing trade relation with England.

Cotton futures trading began in New York in 1872, to be followed by Liverpool, England, and New Orleans about a decade later. In the 1880s coffee and sugar began trading in New York. Between 1900 and 1920, futures contracts for butter and eggs were established in Chicago, and the Chicago Mercantile Exchange officially opened in 1919. The first metals traded were copper and tin in 1929 and silver in 1931. Soybeans began trading at the Chicago Board of Trade in 1936, but were temporarily suspended during World War II. Each of these early contracts developed in response to similar commercial needs and followed similar evolutionary patterns. Producers, processors, and users of cash commodities faced risks associated with pricing, inventory management, and financing. Systems of exchanging cash contracts for future delivery gradually developed in each case into formalized futures trading. Futures markets were not developed by sinister people simply to provide a separate market for speculators and gamblers. Futures markets are firmly rooted in commerce and serve as an extension of the cash market. They would not exist otherwise.

Because the overall market structure was in place, contracts for foreign currencies and financial instruments did not require long incubation periods. Still, these new contracts require strong commercial ties. The Bretton Woods agreement which fixed exchange rates collapsed in 1971 and the International Monetary Market began trading foreign currency futures in May 1972. Also, a ban on U.S. citizens owning gold was lifted, paving the way for gold futures. Interest rate futures contracts began in 1975 because the risk exposure by borrowers and lenders in home mortgages is analogous to that for grain dealers. The pricing of credit instruments and stock indexes is much like that of grains, livestock, and metals.

This quick review of market development in the United States cannot ignore parallel developments elsewhere around the world. The nineteenth century saw markets develop in England and Germany much as they did in New York and Chicago. Other markets followed in India, Japan, and various countries in Europe and Southeast Asia.

Futures trading has not always been active. Trading in the United States was very low during the Great Depression because of extremely low farm prices. Price fixing during World War II took away risks and the need for much futures trading. Government agricultural price support programs, especially during the 1950s and early 1960s, reduced downside price risks and the need for futures trading. However, recent economic events, adverse weather shocks, and changing government programs have resulted in more volatile prices and interest rates. These increased price risks have led many managers to utilize the futures market.

TRADING OF FUTURES CONTRACTS

THE FUTURES CONTRACT

SPECIFICATION. A futures contract is a legally binding agreement between a buyer and seller to exchange a commodity or instrument (or its cash value) later at a particular price, quantity, quality, location, and time. It is a promise to consummate something in the future. The contract does not necessarily involve the exchange of an actual cash commodity or instrument. A contract is created when the buyer and seller enter the futures market and make the agreement. Exchanges place no limit on the number of contracts in existence, in contrast to corporations that offer a specific number of shares of stocks. When the contract is created, no title changes hands and only a small amount of money is posted by both sides to guarantee performance.

Unlike many other legally binding agreements, futures contracts can easily be liquidated. In fact, only about 2 percent of the contracts ever mature. Traders seldom enter the futures market for the purpose of delivering or acquiring the underlying cash instrument. Most traders use contracts either to protect themselves from price fluctuations or to profit from them. These purposes are best served when traders liquidate their futures contracts prior to delivery date, that is, sell their contracts if they were buyers, and vice versa. Traders view the holding of contracts as a temporary matter. They use the futures market for reasons other than exchange of title.

Almost every aspect of the futures contract—its size, place of delivery, quality, and maturity month—is highly standardized. Standard contract sizes are shown in table 2-1; however, there are some exceptions. For example, the Mid-American Commodity Exchange in Chicago offers futures contracts for many grains in 1,000-bushel units and contracts for livestock, currencies, and financial instruments typically one-half the size shown in table 2-1. Most contract sizes correspond with standard units of trade in the cash market. For example, 5,000 bushel grain contracts would fill a railroad car.

Agricultural contracts specify which quality and grade of the commodity is acceptable. However, some substitution and variation are allowed at either a price premium or discount. Traders who make and accept delivery must check these provisions carefully. Quality and grade are not a problem for most financial instrument contracts. An exception is long-term instruments, like Treasury bonds, where many bonds are eligible for delivery and traders must determine which ones meet contract specifications and are also cheapest to deliver.

DELIVERY. Most commodity and instrument contracts specify four to seven delivery months per year. The specified delivery months remain the same every year. The delivery months for most foreign currency, financial instrument, and stock index futures contracts are March, June, September, and December—the last month of each calendar quarter. Some of the metals have contracts for most months of the year.

The months selected for agricultural commodities correspond with existing trade practices. For example, the delivery months for corn are December, March, May, July, and September. December, the first delivery month after the fall harvest, is when the Great Lakes freeze, stopping all exporting by ship until March. Planting begins in May when traders can make initial approximations of the size of the new crop. July is mid-growing season and allows further reflection on growing conditions and potential crop size. This assists traders in deciding how much of the old crop to save or sell. September is the last month of the old crop year and just prior to the harvesting of the new crop. Wheat has the same contract delivery months as corn, but harvest begins in southern United States in June. Hence, the July contract is the first contract of the new crop year. November serves as the first contract of the new crop year for soybeans, which has seven delivery months. The contract months for cattle and hogs are every alternate month except the seventh month, July, for hogs. For most commodities and instruments there is insufficient trading volume to support a delivery contract for every month.

Each contract states explicitly the delivery location. For most agricultural commodities, metals, and forest products, this involves either licensed warehouses or approved livestock yards. Some products have multiple delivery points for the seller to select among, although some locations may be at a price discount. Beginning in December 1983, a shipping certificate replaced delivering the actual commodity for cattle. Financial contracts name financial institutions within large cities or rely on wire transfers for delivery. Sometimes due bills substitute for the instrument itself. Delivery is easy for those financial instruments which exist as computer entries at large financial institutions. In any event, when the cash commodity or instrument is delivered and inspected or checked, the buyer receives a warehouse receipt, inspection certificate, or similar document indicating ownership and commodity location. It is a myth that agricultural products are delivered to your doorstep.

SETTLEMENT. Cash settlement of contracts instead of physical delivery was instituted in 1982 for Eurodollar and stock index contracts. Since then, this method of settlement has been adapted to several more contracts, including physical commodities and financial instruments. For example, the feeder cattle contract changed to cash settlement in 1986. The success of cash settlement may lead to the introduction of new contracts, specifically price indexes where physical delivery is impossible, and physical contracts where the commodity is not easily defined or the contract size does not match standard commercial trading units. When delivery occurs under cash settlement, the seller gives the buyer a sum of money equal to the current value of the contract less the amount the buyer originally agreed to pay. Because the contract is marked-to-market (defined later in this chapter) daily, the final adjustment is the difference between the previous day's closing futures price and the last day's cash price or value. Critical for the acceptance of cash settlement is the availability on a regular basis of a reliable cash price or index for determining the final contract value.

Futures contracts are valid and enforceable, but few ever mature. Traders usually offset them prior to maturity. If delivery occurs, title then changes hands and the buyer must pay the seller. Written into the contract are the terms of payment once the receipt confirming delivery is accepted. Because the receipts, or certificates, are negotiable, one can post them as colateral for a loan.

Also stated in the contract are the procedures for default by either the buyer or seller. Usually the party being defaulted can enter the cash market to buy or sell the desired commodity or instrument, if it exists. The account of the defaulting party is then debited or credited accordingly. Alternatively, the exchange can exercise emergency powers and determine an appropriate settlement price between the parties as the New York Mercantile Exchange did in the celebrated potato default in 1976. In any event, defaults are extremely rare and none has ever occurred on the Chicago Board of Trade or Chicago Mercantile Exchange.

FUTURES CONTRACTS VERSUS FORWARD CONTRACTS

Futures contracts are very similar to forward cash contracts. Almost everyone signs one of the latter at least once during their lifetimes, especially if they buy houses or new automobiles. Futures and forward cash contracts are agreements between two parties to make or take delivery of a particular good or service at a certain future date for a given price. That is, both call for deferred performance in product exchange and specify the basic terms. However, there are some important differences. Futures contracts trade openly or publicly on organized exchanges, while forward cash contracts, especially in agriculture, usually trade one-on-one or privately between the buyer and seller. Futures contracts trade in a more liquid environment and the market is often easier to enter and exit. Forward contracts are typically not fungible. Futures contracts are standardized and homogeneous in quantity, quality, location, and delivery time, while forward contracts are usually individualized or tailored to specific needs. The latter have virtually no trading rules outside that specified in existing contract law. Futures contracts trade in very formalized environments with performance guaranteed by the exchange's clearinghouse. Most futures contracts are offset before maturity, while most forward cash contracts end in spot delivery. Forward contracts seldom involve third parties. Finally, futures contracts require margin deposits and have brokerage fees, while forward contracts usually have neither, but may have legal fees.

The major distinctions between the two contracts are their payment schedules and revenue flows. A purchaser of either contract agrees to buy the specified item in the future at some forward price that exists at the time of contract initiation. In both cases no money changes hands initially. As prices change for futures contracts, however, one party must immediately pay the other party the change in the value of the contract. Thus, when the maturity date arrives, the payment required by the buyer becomes the current spot price because installments have been paid or received throughout the life of the contract as prices change. In contrast, for cash forward contracts money only changes hands at the time of maturity in a lump sum cash transfer. The payment is the original contract price. These two procedures result in quite different revenue flows between contracting parties. Under constant interest rates, forward prices and futures prices can be essentially equivalent, but as John Cox, Jonathan Ingersoll, and Stephen Ross point out, that is usually not the case.[9] The flow of funds in futures markets results from the marked-to-market concept.

Forward contracts and futures contracts are complements with each other, but not perfect substitutes. They cannot be perfect substitutes due to the lumpiness of futures contracts, differences in payment and settlement patterns generating different revenue flows, and differences in basis risks.[10] Forward contracts with fixed prices may have no basis risk. Nevertheless, forward and futures contracts often exist side-by-side for many goods and services. Futures contracts provide flexibility to undo forward commitments and liquidity which may reduce transaction costs, price premiums, and search costs. Futures markets may provide more accurate prices than alternative marketing devices for efficient production, processing, and trading decisions. They are a source of information used in many alternative contracting procedures. However, forward contracts exist for the purpose of spot delivery at a fixed price, given variety, and specific location—all of which may differ from the futures contract specifications.

TRADING CONTRACTS

Futures contracts trade in pits. Pits are often hexagonal structures with four or five steps descending into the center. They are shaped so that all traders can see one another. Contracts for each of the delivery months trade in different areas of the pit, often with the nearby contract trading in the center. However, traders can trade in any delivery month with anyone else in the pit without changing location.

An active trading pit may contain several hundred traders at any one time. Less active pits may be in the form of a ring with a rail outside of which traders stand or a table they trade across. Very inactive trading pits consist of a blackboard on which traders write bids, offers, and/or trade confirmations.

Trading begins with the ringing of a loud bell. Similarly, a bell terminates trading. Often warning bells ring seconds before the close and opening; rules strictly prohibit trading before the opening or after the close. Sometimes the close for an expiring delivery month is at a separate, earlier time than normal closing time to ensure less confusion and an orderly liquidation of a large number of orders at the last moment. For example, at the Chicago Board of Trade expiring commodity contracts stop trading at noon, seventy-five minutes before normal closing time. Trading time between the opening and close ranges from four to six hours.[11]

Prices are established in the trading pit through a multiple auction procedure in which both bids and offers are made. Traders negotiate to find the final trading price. Rules require that traders call out all bids and offers in a loud voice for all other traders to hear and to have equal opportunity of access. However, when many traders are in the pit, the high noise level may prevent any single trader from being heard. So, much of the communication is through hand signals. A palm held in is a bid to buy and palm held out is an offer to sell. Fingers held vertically show the quantity to trade, and fingers turned horizontally show the price of the bid or offer.

Traders record their transactions—the price, quantity, contract commodity, delivery month, and identification of the opposing trader—on a card. Staff personnel record this information in individual computerized accounts. After the close of trading the clearinghouse reconciles these records. Also, exchange reporters in each pit record the prices, feeding this information into a vast communication system. Using computers, telephones, and ticker tapes, this system, instantaneously distributes prices to electric display boards, desktop units, and printing machines around the world.

Trading floors are a hubbub of activity. At the ends of the floor are several desks where phone clerks, employed primarily by large brokerage houses, take public customer orders transmitted by account executives. These orders are time-stamped and carried by runners to the appropriate broker in the trading pit. After the order is transacted and the information recorded by the floor broker, the order returns via the runner to the desk for time stamping. It is then sent to the clearinghouse. The movement of the runners along certain paths resembles a well-organized ant hill when viewed from the visitors gallery overhead.

The futures market is one of open competition. Large trades transact in a manner of seconds. All traders have equal access to the bids and offers. Trading is public, and prices are communicated to the public instantly. These characteristics are important attributes of the futures market and differentiate it from other markets.

ORIGINATION AND SETTLEMENT OF CONTRACTS

Every contract has a buyer and seller. The buyer of the contract is "long" and the seller of the contract is "short." The number of longs in the market must equal the number of shorts. The long has made a contract to accept and purchase a good or service on a certain date in the future, and the short has promised to deliver the same good or service and accept payment for it in the future. For each person taking a position in the market, someone else must be willing to assume an opposite position. It is not necessary that either party to the contract have a position in the cash market when the futures contract is initiated. Traders can contract to forward sell a good or service even if they do not yet own it. The contract is merely a promise to meet certain conditions in the future, and traders seldom allow it to mature. If delivery is to occur, the seller can enter the cash market, acquire the commodity or instrument and satisfy the delivery conditions.

Futures contracts are settled by delivery or by making the opposite, or offsetting, transaction in the futures market. For most contracts, if a trader originally makes a contract to buy or sell some item in the future, at any date before delivery is to occur the trader can make a contract to sell or buy that same item. Because one cannot hold both contracts to buy and sell the identical good or service on the same exchange, the second action offsets or cancels the first. Both contracts cease to exist. If prices have risen in the interim, the buyer makes a profit and the seller loses money. If prices have fallen, the seller profits and the buyer loses.

The futures market is, before commissions, a zero sum game. That is, for every dollar gained by someone, there is a dollar lost by someone else. Since there are an equal number of longs and shorts, gains by one side equal losses by the other side as prices change. There is an equal transfer of money among the traders.

The alternative method of settling contracts is through delivery when the contract matures. The long, or buyer, receives delivery of the cash commodity or instrument, and the short, or seller, makes delivery. When delivery occurs, title and money change hands; the contract terms are satisfied and it ceases to exist.

The relationship between open interest and trading volume was defined earlier. The following schematic illustrates this relationship:

Sequence of Events	Long Trader		Short Trader	Contracts	Open Interest	Trading Volume
1	A	← →	B	1	1	1
2	D	← →	C	2	3	2
3	E	← →	D	2	3	2
4	B	← →	A	1	2	1
5	C	← →	E	2	0	2
Total						8

Trader A first buys a contract and trader B sells. The open interest is one and the volume is one. Later C sells two contracts to D. The volume on this trade is two and total open interest in this market is now three. If D sells two contracts to E, volume is again two and open interest remains at three. D is now even and out of the market. Finally, if A sells a contract back to B, and E sells two contracts to C, then A, B, C, and E are all even and out of the market. Open interest is now zero, and total trading volume was eight. Note that every contract gets counted once in volume when created, again every time one side changes ownership, and once again when offset. Clearly, open interest (at any one time) represents a stock variable and volume represents a flow variable.

On a typical trading day, volume may show that as many as one-third of the contracts trade. However, the change in open interest from one day to the next is usually very low. That is, despite a large amount of day trading, there may be very little change in market commitment at the end of the day. Volume typically exceeds, but is never less than, the change in open interest. Only at the extremes of creating new contracts or liquidating existing contracts are volume and the change in open interest equal. Sometimes in stock index contracts the volume of trading for one day exceeds the open interest.

Finally, trading on a contract usually begins about twelve to fifteen months prior to its maturity date. However, some metal and financial instrument contracts begin trading almost two years ahead of maturity. Exchanges permit trading when they feel traders are interested and create a liquid market.

THE TRADERS

A variety of people take part in pit trading. Some are brokers acting on instructions from public customers transmitted by futures commission merchants. Other traders in the pit carry out instructions from firms involved in the daily cash market. Professional speculators in the pit trade to profit from price fluctuations resulting from the flow of orders. This participation of a variety of traders with different objectives makes the futures market competitive and gives it liquidity.

BROKERS. The largest group of traders in the pit are floor brokers who fill orders for outside speculators and hedgers. They are responsible for filling orders rapidly and with little or no price concession. Some brokers take orders from several firms, others become very specialized. For example, some trade only nearby contracts of one commodity for a single firm. Some brokers associate with commission firms; others operate independently.

Brokers earn a living by receiving a fee for filling outside orders and/or by trading for their own accounts. These two sources of income can create conflicts of interest. Rules govern the brokers in an attempt to prevent them from abusing this dual trading situation. For example, they should not trade for their own account in front of any customer market order that might affect the price. Also, they must offer all customer orders publicly and not match them against their own accounts. The exchanges enforce these rules through surveillance. Time stamping of trades is a part of this procedure.

Still, brokers need their own accounts to absorb mistakes. If a broker fills an order differently from the customer's request, the balance goes into the broker's personal account. Mistakes are made both to the advantage and disadvantage of the broker. Brokers are very skilled; they must manage many trades, each of various sizes and specific instructions. They have to anticipate orders as well as remember the resting orders in their hands. During active trading, their skill in accurately and rapidly filling orders is critical.

PROFESSIONAL SPECULATORS. Another large group of traders on the floor are speculators who mainly trade for their own accounts. Previous writers divide these speculators into three groups, but with different names. Thomas Hieronymus classifies them as scalpers, pit traders, and floor traders.[12] Holbrook Working calls them unit-change scalpers, day-trading scalpers, and day-to-day scalpers.[13] The basic differences between these three groups is length of time and number of contracts they hold. Nevertheless, their roles are all the same: to provide liquidity to the market, interpret information, and bridge the gaps between outside orders that vary in time and size.

The first group of scalpers buys contracts one tick (the smallest amount prices can move) below the last market price or sells one tick above the last price. That is, they attempt to buy at the bid price or sell at the offer price.[14] Their activity allows rapid filling of orders with only minimum price concession. They usually hold contracts for only a few minutes, trying to take advantage of price moves. Their skill lies in anticipating short-run price fluctuations during the day and avoiding being caught on the wrong side of a price move. They are continually in the market as both buyer and seller. Scalpers such as these provide liquidity and are called market makers.

Pit traders (day-trading scalpers) usually take larger positions and hold them for longer time periods than the group just described. However, it is unlikely that traders in either group will hold positions overnight. This second group is more likely to take the opposite position of large hedging orders, bridging the time gap until the speculating public enters the market later in the day. Obviously, they become very skilled interpreting the trends and forces within the market and anticipating actions by others. For example, they try to position themselves to profit from price moves which result from a rush of orders that must be executed after a particular market situation occurs. Their success depends on buying contracts before prices rise and selling before prices fall; they must anticipate price moves.

The third group, floor traders or day-to-day scalpers, are professional speculators who can take large positions and hold them for several days. They are called position traders. They try to remain flexible and often deal in multiple markets. They are typically well financed and capable of standing for delivery or making delivery if needed. Thereby, they remain aware of the factors affecting cash market activities. Of course, the distinctions between the preceding three groups are not absolute; any one trader could perform the roles mentioned in each group.

Professional speculators, or floor traders, are important for providing the necessary liquidity which makes markets function smoothly, and bridges the time gaps between outside orders. The success of a futures market is critically dependent on the number of orders flowing to the market. A large share of daily liquidity results from "locals" or floor traders. Working estimated that floor traders accounted for 50 percent of the transactions in wheat futures during one specific day at Chicago.[15] However, these traders held only 14 percent of the open contracts. Floor traders hold small or no overnight positions and their variation in trading "was in rough proportion to that of total trading in the market."[16]

SPREAD TRADING. Important for all professional speculators is the understanding and taking of spread positions, sometimes called arbitrage. Spreading is the purchasing of one futures contract while simultaneously selling another futures contract to profit from changes in price relationships. Spread trades can be interdelivery (between different delivery months), intermarket (between different exchanges), intercommodity (between different commodities or instruments), or some combination of these. Examples of each of these are given in chapter 4. As we outline in chapter 3, the economic relationships between contract delivery months and between products are important and explainable. Spread trading is a means of keeping prices properly aligned with each other according to economic expectations. Because futures prices tend to fluctuate together, spread trading is usually less risky than position trading. All the traders described earlier are active in spread trading.[17]

Leo Melamed, in describing spreaders' activities, calls them "artists."[18] "His [the spreader] aptitude, agility, and ability to detect the slightest market shift is extraordinary. He is constantly active, moving as a buyer of one month to a seller of another, and immediately back again." Spreaders are constantly looking for the smallest increment of profit. Also, spreaders are an important source of liquidity, especially in distant contract months, enabling the market to absorb the pressures of large hedging transactions.

HEDGERS. The final group in the trading pits are those traders representing commercial firms who use the market for hedging. Depending on the firm, they may have one or several representatives or traders on the floor at any one time. They place orders in direct response to commercial cash market activities, and their trading strategies vary considerably among firms. Some firms hedge net cash positions, while others hedge each cash position. Because large hedging orders can cause considerable price concessions, firms often attempt to disguise their activities through multiple floor trading activities and/or through multiple traders.

Nevertheless, large hedging orders often affect prices; buy orders cause price increases and sell orders cause price dips. Working terms this the "execution cost of hedging." For some traders it is a large proportion of their hedging costs, which can serve as a major source of income to speculators, or scalpers.[19] Working noted that the level of income for speculators directly relates to total hedging activities as scalpers absorb the hedging orders and take market or spread positions on price dips and bulges. The market is unable to instantly absorb large orders.

THE PUBLIC. The largest single group of traders involved with futures markets is the customer public who place orders with account executives or associated persons at their local brokerage houses. Public traders provide liquidity, interpret information, and facilitate the management of risks for hedgers. They are a necessary ingredient for the market to work smoothly and actively. Some public customers make decisions and act on their own, others follow their account executives' advice, while others join a trading club or limited partnership where an organizer makes decisions and takes market positions. Public customers come from all walks of life and geographic areas. Their motives are usually to earn a positive return on risk capital. They view the market as an investment medium.

The public traders comprise varying portions of the number of contracts (open interest). They typically hold one-quarter to one-third of the long-term financial instruments contracts and one-third to one-half of the wheat and soybean contracts.

Alternatively, small traders often comprise two-thirds of the frozen pork bellies and oats markets.

ASSOCIATED PARTIES. There are many additional people associated with futures trading. The public places trades with a futures commission merchant (FCM), a firm or person soliciting outside orders. FCMs and their associated persons (APs), or account executives (AEs), must register with the Commodity Futures Trading Commission (CFTC) and/or the National Futures Association. These registered persons are certified, attesting to their integrity and ability to handle customer accounts. Also, FCMs are responsible for assuring that the public customer has sufficient net worth, a credible employment history, an appropriate personality and understands the nature of futures market risk before trading. All customers must sign risk disclosure statements.

A commodity trading advisor (CTA) is an individual or corporation who advises others regarding commodity trades. They provide information services about contracts for pay. They can advise or manage individual discretionary accounts, commodity pools, or FCMs. They cannot pool individual clients into a common account.

A commodity pool operator (CPO) solicits and pools together funds for the trading of contracts. Pools are usually established for small investors so that risks and returns are shared. Many commodity pools organize as limited partnerships with the CPO as general manager. This limits the risks for individuals and avoids double taxation of winnings. Most pools hire a CTA for trading advice. A CPO can manage more than one pool.

Both the CTA and CPO must formally register with the CFTC, and the latter with the Securities and Exchange Commission. The CFTC reviews these registrations annually and has the right to reject or suspend CTA or CPO status. Protecting public clients and customer funds and maintaining public confidence in futures trading is the responsibility of the CFTC.

TYPES OF ORDERS

Traders establish or alter market positions by placing a variety of orders. The simplest is the *market order.* It instructs the broker either to buy or sell a certain number of contracts promptly for the most advantageous price. To complete the order, the broker may have to bid up the price to buy contracts or lower the price to sell them. When the market is active and the order is not too large, market orders can be filled with little or no price concession. The customer must rely on the skill of the broker to fill the order quickly and without price concession.

If traders wish to obtain the best possible price rather than buy or sell contracts quickly, they can place a *limit order.* This order specifies the time or price for executing a contract. The order may transact under reasonable conditions, but the trader runs the risk of not getting it filled at all. Limit orders execute only at the designated price or better, never at a price concession.

Traders guard against a disastrous loss or protect an existing profit by placing a *stop-loss order.* This order protects a customer in the market from a drastic increase or decrease in price. The trader requests with this order that the market position be liquidated if the price of the contract reaches a certain level. If the specified price is touched or passed, the stop-loss order becomes a market order and the broker executes it as quickly as possible. Some price concession may occur, depending how fast the broker can fill the order and how fast prices are moving. Sell stops instruct the broker to sell out a long position if prices fall to a specific level. Buy stops indicate the customer desires to buy back a short position when prices rise to a specified level.

The *spread order,* defined earlier, involves buying and selling interdelivery, intermarket, or intercommodity contracts simultaneously. Examples are given in chapter 4. Spread trades require very little margin money (discussed later), and usually smaller commissions than the trading of two separate contracts.

Several other orders exist but are less frequently used by the customer public than those described here. Most important is that the broker understand the customer's desires.[20]

RULES AND REGULATIONS

REGULATIONS. Both the federal government and exchanges regulate trading of futures contracts in the United States. Together they attempt to keep futures trading open and competitive, and relatively free of price fixing, distortion, and collusion.

The legislative basis for federal regulation in the United States is the Commodity Futures Trading Act of 1974, an extension of the Commodities Exchange Act of 1936. A five-person administrative body appointed by the president, the Commodity Futures Trading Commission (CFTC), oversees federal regulation. Its purposes are to ensure proper execution of customer orders and to prevent unlawful manipulation, price distortion, fraud, cheating, fictitious trades, and misuse of customer funds. It accomplishes these by (1) licensing futures exchanges; (2) registering brokers and futures commission merchants; (3) auditing records and bank accounts; (4) surveillance of trading; (5) regulating trader positions; (6) publicizing market reports; and (7) investigating complaints and prosecuting violators. The commission oversees exchanges by approving exchange rule alterations, contract modifications, and new contracts.

Exchanges work both independently of and in cooperation with the federal government to prevent many of the abuses mentioned previously. Exchanges are responsible for seeing that traders follow general business practices. They also set rules to ensure orderly trading. Both the exchange and CFTC have the authority to suspend trading, or call for liquidation trading only, if emergency or potential disorderly situations arise.

PRICE RESTRICTIONS. Each exchange sets daily price limits and minimum movements for price quotations for most contracts. For example, livestock prices must move at least $0.025 per hundredweight if they move at all. However, prices cannot vary more than $1.50 per hundredweight above or below the closing market price of the previous day. As a result, on any given day the price of livestock can fluctuate only within $3-per-hundredweight range. There is no restriction to its fluctuation within that range. In grain markets the minimum movement for price quotations is $0.0025 per bushel. The daily price limits are $0.10 for corn, $0.20 for wheat, and $0.30 for soybeans above or below the previous day's close. For Treasury bonds the minimum move is 1/32 of 100 percent, while the maximum price limit from day to day is 64/32. After the stock market crash of October 19, 1987, exchanges imposed daily price limits on stock index futures contracts ranging from 25 to 30 points. However, there have been no price limits on currency contracts since 1985.

For some contracts the daily limit rules modify during delivery months, and sometimes limits expand if prices move the limit in one direction for three consecutive days. Limits are sometimes eliminated for the last day of trading for a contract. Daily price limits are subject to change when economic conditions vary. Price limits allow the market to digest new information in an orderly fashion without overreacting, and thereby protect traders and their accounts. They give traders an opportunity to think about new market situations overnight before trading resumes.

When prices are at their daily limit, little or no trading takes place because there are no sellers at a limit up move or buyers at a limit down move. Traders try to avoid these market situations because of the lack of liquidity and flexibility. Thus, daily limits should be wide enough so that prices reach them infrequently and only after major news events. Price limits delay price adjustments and, under certain conditions, restrict market liquidity. During volatile situations cash and future price relationships may become distorted.

DELIVERY PROCEDURE. The delivery process for each futures contract is predetermined and unique. A fixed sequence of events involves the short who initiates the process and is making delivery, the long who is taking delivery, and the clearing association who matches these two traders and guarantees the process. For most traditional agricultural and metal contracts, Treasury bonds, and a few other financial contracts, the rules specify that delivery can occur any business day during the maturing month. The first business day of the month or the last business day of the preceding month is usually the first day of delivery, although there are exceptions.[21]

Once delivery begins, a specific procedure is followed. For example, Treasury bonds follow a three-day sequence: position day when the short gives notice of intent to deliver, notice of intention day when the oldest long receives notice of delivery, and delivery day when the bonds transfer from short's bank to long's bank.[22] A trader must be fully aware of similar dates and rules of any contract traded near its maturity. For many contracts trading terminates about eight days before the last day of delivery, or about the 20th of the month.[23] This rule, especially for agricultural commodities, ensures that parties who must deliver have enough days before the end of the month to move their cash commodity into position and avoid default. Any contracts outstanding after the close of trading must be settled by delivery before the end of the calendar month. Failure to do this means the traders are in default of the contract. Finally, traders must know contract specifications concerning location and quality.

For many financial instruments, delivery takes place in a very narrow span of time. For Treasury bills, currencies, and other similar contracts, the only day the seller can give notice of intent to deliver is the last day of trading; delivery usually occurs within one or two days following. Delivery of contracts which have cash settlement provisions, like stock indexes, occurs only on the last day of trading.

SPECULATOR TRADING LIMITS. There is a limit to the number of contracts speculators can hold at any given point in time. For corn and soybeans, no speculator may hold over 12 million bushels of futures contracts (net) of either commodity (2,400 contracts). The speculative position limit on Standard & Poor's 500 Stock Index contract is 5,000 contracts net. Other position limits can be as low as 300 contracts. These limits vary by contract and exchange as the government establishes some limits and the exchange others. Some limits apply to a single delivery contract while others apply to the sum of all delivery contracts held of a commodity. Some are gross positions, others net positions. They are all subject to change. This rule does not apply to hedgers, nor does it involve cash markets.

REPORTING REQUIREMENTS. All traders must file reports daily with the CFTC if they hold more than some given number of futures contracts in U.S. markets. For actively traded contracts this reporting limit is usually 100 contracts, while for others it is 25 or 50 contracts. Filing traders must report both their total cash and futures positions. They are then classified as either reporting speculator, reporting hedger, or reporting spreader. The remaining traders in the market become classified as nonreporting traders, but their motives in the market—that is hedging or speculating—are unknown.

COMMISSIONS. Finally, commissions are charged for trading on the futures market. The commission relates to the round turn, that is, both the originating and the offsetting of the contract. The trader pays when the market position is liquidated. The commission for a small, nonmember trader ranges from $60 to $90 per contract. However, large traders can negotiate lower commissions. Exchange members always pay less than nonmembers. There are also lower rates for day trades. Nonmember commissions are divided between the account executive who solicits the order, the brokerage house (futures commission merchant), and the exchange.

THE CLEARINGHOUSE AND MARGIN

The task of balancing all futures market transactions and money flows is the responsibility of the clearinghouse, a department within or separate corporation associated with each exchange. The clearinghouse: (1) matches and reconciles all futures transactions; (2) assures the financial integrity of the transactions; and (3) provides the mechanism for delivery. The clearinghouse is unique to futures markets, and critical to the markets' success. This system assures that traders who realize market gains are paid at the end of the day. The clearinghouse itself becomes the obligor to every futures contract, assuring financial integrity. It also becomes a party to and guarantees delivery.

Only members of the exchange, or the corporations who sponsor them, can become clearing members. Just a small number of them do become members because the financial requirements and responsibilities are substantial. Clearing members deposit a large sum of money into a guarantee fund; members of some clearing organizations must purchase shares of stock in the corporation. The guarantee fund is a reserve in case a trader defaults or has difficulties in paying debts incurred on the futures market. Exchange members who are not clearing members must clear their transactions through a clearing member and pay a fee for the service. Thus, clearing members are usually large corporations, financial institutions, brokerage houses, and partnerships of exchange members. The rigid financial requirements for clearing members keeps futures market exchanges free from financial emergencies and helps maintain a secure public image.

TRADING POSITIONS

As traders and brokers complete transactions in the trading pit, they note the necessary information on a card and send it to the clearinghouse. The clearinghouse assumes the opposite side of all transactions, the long side to all the shorts and the short side to all the longs. It becomes a party or obligor to all trades. However, because the number of longs always equals the number of shorts, the clearinghouse has no net position. This system allows traders to originate and offset contracts at any time without having to locate specific parties with whom they trade. The activities of the clearinghouse makes futures contracts impersonal and easy to negotiate. Traders can hold their positions for several months while the other side of the positions may trade over and over many times.

A few trade records at the end of each day do not match, because of errors written on the cards or clerical errors. The two parties involved must reconcile their differences through an "out trade." Usually differences are small and quickly resolved, but trading cannot open in the morning until the previous day's trades balance. On occasion, openings are delayed. Parties unable to solve their dispute go to the arbitration committee for resolution.

MARGINS

In addition to facilitating the trading and settlement of contracts, the clearinghouse performs a banking function by settling monetary differences. To trade futures contracts, every public hedger and speculator must have an account with a futures commission merchant. Exchange members must also maintain separate futures trading accounts. With every new trade, traders deposit money, called the *initial margin,* with their account executives. This customer margin serves as a security deposit or performance bond. Traders must make this deposit whether they enter the market from the long or short side. The initial margin for a public trader is about 10 percent of the value of the contract, although this percentage varies among speculators, hedgers, and spreaders. Ultimately, the minimum deposit required from traders depends on what the exchange considers an adequate guarantee. A brokerage house can require any public trader to post more than the minimum margin if it judges that the customer may have difficulty in fulfilling the contract.

After depositing the initial margin, traders must always keep a minimum amount of money, called a *maintenance margin level,* in their accounts. The maintenance margin level is roughly three-fourths of initial margin, and varies among the contracts. We discuss the procedure for maintaining the margin momentarily.

Actually, this system of initial or original and maintenance or variation margins applies to members of the clearing association; they in turn apply it to the FCMs for whom they clear, and FCMs duplicate the system to public customers. There are some exceptions to the rules, however. For example, although all customers must post margin with their FCMs, the FCMs are responsible to post margins only for the net positions of their customers. In other words, if a FCM's customers are equally long and short for a contract, the FCM need not post any margin with the clearing member or association. The FCM can deposit excess margin money in interest bearing securities; this is a major source of income for the FCM.

Margin deposits have several functions. First, they guarantee performance on futures contracts as both parties place funds on deposit. Second, they provide the futures market system with money so the clearinghouse can collect from traders who lose and pay those who gain. This provides the financial integrity of the system. And third, because the initial and maintenance margins are only a small fraction of the futures contract's full value, customers can participate in trading with a relatively small financial investment. Margin trading allows traders to attain considerable financial leverage. Nevertheless, commodity margins are quite different from margins on securities. Securities traders may deposit a margin or downpayment, but must borrow the balance. These shares themselves are collateral for the loan. In contrast, futures contracts require a much smaller initial investment, and there is no financial obligation to the balance of the contract value unless delivery occurs. A margined stock purchase gives the trader ownership to the stock and the right to receive dividends, but futures contracts only set conditions for exchange of physical commodity ownership in the future.

MARKING-TO-MARKET. The settlement of accounts through the clearinghouse is very straightforward. The official basis for transferring money among traders is the settlement price. Each delivery month of each commodity has a settlement price every day based on the closing price or the range of prices in the last few seconds of trading. Each exchange has its own method of calculating settlement prices. If the contracts held by a trader lost value during the day, the clearinghouse debits that trader's account. If the contracts gained in value, the account is credited. That is, the clearinghouse "marks-to-market" all open positions at the end of every day by transferring money from losers to winners, settling all accounts. Hence, in a sense the value of each futures position for the next day is zero. This unique feature of futures markets helps maintain financial integrity. It also distinguishes the market from all other stock, bond, and forward contract markets in cash flow requirements and implications for investment returns.

Suppose, for example, that two traders enter the corn futures market, one long and the other short a 5,000 bushel contract at $2.75 per bushel, and that the initial margin is $2,000. If the price rises, as shown for days 2 and 3 in table 2-3, money is added to the long trader's account and taken from the short's account. When prices rise, money flows from the short to the long. On day 4, however, the price suddenly drops $0.07, and the clearinghouse transfers $350 from the account of the long trader to the short's account. The clearinghouse acts only as a medium for the transfer of money. Because the amount gained always equals the amount lost, the clearinghouse breaks even. Payments are immediate. That is, after day 4 the traders are not long

Table 2-3. The Flow of Money between Traders' Accounts

		Trader A (long)		Trader B (short)	
Day	Settlement price per bushel	Cumulative profits	Equity in account	Cumulative profits	Equity in account
1	$2.75	$ 0	$2,000	$ 0	$2,000
2	2.77	+100	2,100	−100	1,900
3	2.78	+150	2,150	−150	1,850
4	2.71	−200	1,800	+200	2,200

or short corn at their initial price of $2.75, but at $2.71. The loser has already paid the winner and accounts balance. Futures positions are technically reset to zero, the consequence of daily marking-to-market.

MARGIN CALLS. When the equity in a trader's account falls below the maintenance margin level, the trader receives a *margin call* from the account executive. The trader must deposit additional funds to bring the equity position back up to the initial margin level. If the customer fails to deposit the funds, the account executive has authorization to close the trade. This system displays considerable flexibility, ranging from "mail a check tomorrow" to "have a certified check here within an hour," depending on customer-broker relations. Alternatively, as equity positions surpass initial margin levels, customers can withdraw all or part of the surplus if desired.

The examples in table 2-4 illustrate how an equity position can grow or diminish as prices fluctuate. A trader buys a 5,000-bushel contract of May corn at $2.75 per bushel. The initial margin is $2,000, and the maintenance margin level is $1,750. In example 1, at the end of the second day the price is $2.76. The trader makes $50, bringing the equity position up to $2,050. By the end of the third day, the price has fallen $0.03 to $2.73; the equity position is now $1,900. On the next day a $0.05 drop in the price brings the equity position down to $1,650, below the maintenance margin level of $1,750. The account executive makes a margin call. The customer desiring to maintain the market position must deposit $350 to restore the account to the initial margin level. However, the trader always has the option of getting out of the market rather than posting the additional funds.

In example 2 the price jumps from $2.75 to $2.85, increasing the value of the customer's position to $2,500. The customer may withdraw the $500 surplus. However, because futures prices fluctuate daily, it is not advisable to make small withdrawals perfunctorily.

Table 2-4. A Margin Call and Capital Withdrawal

	Settlement price per bushel	Cumulative profits	Capital	Equity in account
	Example 1			
Day 1	$2.75	$ 0	$2,000	$2,000
Day 2	2.76	+ 50	2,000	2,050
Day 3	2.73	−100	2,000	1,900
Day 4	2.68	−350	2,000	1,650
Margin call of $350		−350	2,350	2,000
	Example 2			
Day 1	2.75	0	2,000	2,000
Day 2	2.85	+500	2,000	2,500
Capital withdrawal of $500		+500	1,500	2,000

RULES AND PROCEDURES

Regulators and exchanges are very concerned about the financial integrity of futures markets, so they audit customer accounts carefully and frequently. Brokerage houses must maintain customer funds in a segregated account, and the house cannot use these funds for investment in securities or other futures contracts. They can, however, take this accumulated cash, called the float, and earn interest on it overnight with their bank at the repo rate. This produces a sizeable income for a house. If an individual customer's account is large enough, the customer can request the house purchase a Treasury bill and post it as initial margin. However, Treasury bills cannot meet margin calls.

Finally, the clearinghouse becomes involved as the intermediary if delivery occurs. Delivery is at the option of the seller, who must notify the clearinghouse of delivery intentions. The clearinghouse then passes the notice to the oldest long. For many contracts, there are provisions for retendering. That is, the long may go to the trading pit, sell a new contract and retender the notice. This may happen rapidly, so one notice retendered several times may satisfy many open contracts. Eventually, the contract lodges with someone who desires delivery. For some contracts, demand notices exist so that buyers and sellers interested in delivery at a specific location can match more rapidly. For those financial instruments where termination of trading and delivery coincide, retendering is not an issue.

The clearinghouse, as a party to all trades, is a part of the delivery process. It receives and makes payments, passes delivery notices, transfers title, insures the commodity meets specifications, and that it is in the proper location. The financial resources of the clearinghouse assure the integrity of the contract.

NOTES

1. Information about United Kingdom futures markets, contracts, and trading procedures is in M. Riess, "Comparing the U.S. and U.K. Futures Markets," in *Handbook of Futures Markets,* ed. Perry J. Kaufman (New York: John Wiley & Sons, 1984), 4.1–28; and C. Prior-Willeard, *Farming Futures: A Guide to the Agricultural Commodity Futures Markets* (Cambridge: Woodhead-Faulkner, 1984).
2. Further elaboration of successes, failures, survival rates, and longevity of contracts and competition among exchanges is in D.W. Carlton. "Futures Markets: Their Purpose, Their History, Their Growth, Their Successes, and Failures," *Journal of Futures Markets* 4 (1984): 237–71.
3. J.B. Baer and A.G. Saxon, *Commodity Exchanges and Futures Trading* (New York: Harper & Row, 1948).
4. See Carlton, "Futures Markets," for a comparable list.
5. This section relies on T.A. Hieronymus, *Economics of Futures Trading* (New York: Commodity Research Bureau, 1977); R.J. Teweles, C.V. Harlow, and H.L. Stone, *The Commodity Futures Game Who Wins? Who Loses? Why?* (New York: McGraw-Hill, 1974); W.C. Labys and C.W.J. Granger, *Speculation, Hedging, and Commodity Price Forecasting* (Lexington, Mass.: Lexington Books, 1970).
6. J.C. Williams, "The Origin of Futures Markets," *Agricultural History* 56 (1982): 306–16.
7. Margin, defined later in this chapter, is the practice of both parties posting money that is only a fraction of the value of the contract. It not only guarantees contract performance, but also increases financial leverage for traders.
8. A.E. Peck, "The Economic Role of Commodity Futures Markets," in *Futures Markets: Their Economic Role.* ed. A.E. Peck (Washington, D.C.: American Enterprise Institute, 1985), 6.
9. J.C. Cox; J.E. Ingersoll, Jr.; and S.A. Ross, "The Relation between Forward Prices and Futures Prices," *Journal of Financial Economics* 9 (1981): 321–46.
10. R.D. Nelson. "Forward and Futures Contracts as Preharvest Commodity Marketing Instruments," *American Journal of Agricultural Economics* 7 (1985): 15–23.
11. Proposals exist for twenty-four-hour trading, but so far no exchange has adopted those rules. Gold, silver, and many foreign currencies trade on several exchanges around the world, so individually each trades almost all day and night. The Chicago Mercantile Exchange has a satellite exchange in Singapore, allowing traders access to the same contract over extended hours. The Chicogo Board of Trade began evening trading of certain financial instruments in 1987. Technological advances in computers and electronic communication linkages make globalization of market and on-floor automation systems distinct realities.
12. Hieronymus, *Economics of Futures Trading,* 44–49.

13. H. Working, "Tests of a Theory Concerning Floor Trading on Commodity Exchanges," *Food Research Institute Studies,* supplement to 7 (1967): 5–48.
14. Scalpers are not subject to the full brokerage commissions that apply to outside traders, so they can profit from the smallest price moves.
15. Working, "Tests of a Theory."
16. Ibid., 11.
17. Hedging, defined thoroughly in chapter 4, is also a form of spread trading, or arbitrage. It is the taking of opposite positions usually of comparable size in the futures market, as opposed to the cash market.
18. L. Melamed. "The Futures Market: Liquidity and the Technique of Spreading," *The Journal of Futures Markets* 1 (1981): 405–11.
19. Working, "Tests of a Theory."
20. For a more complete list of orders, see Hieronymus, *Economics of Futures Trading,* 62–64.
21. See Teweles, Harlow, and Stone, *The Commodity Futures Game,* 62.
22. This specific procedure for Treasury bonds is more fully described in chapter 9.
23. For specifics, see Teweles, Harlow, and Stone, *The Commodity Futures Game,* 63.

BASIS AND THEORETICAL PRICE RELATIONSHIPS

3

Fundamental to understanding the futures market is understanding the basis and theoretical price relationships. The term *basis* describes price relationships. Basis is the difference between the quoted futures price for a particular delivery month and the cash price at the local market. It can have three dimensions: time, space, and quality. For many futures contracts the basis follows a predictable pattern, and traders must recognize deviations from that pattern. Basis takes on different meanings for different contracts.

Relative to price relationships, most futures contracts fall into one of two groups, storables or nonstorables, for contract delivery. The combined cash and futures markets for storable commodities and instruments, such as grains, metals, petroleum products, and Treasury bonds, are carrying charge markets. Not only is there a cost of carrying or holding the physical instrument, but traders can also carry the physical instrument from one delivery month to a more distant delivery month. Relative prices between the physical instrument in the cash market and the various futures contracts depends on the cost of carrying or storing the physical instrument over time.

Nonstorable, or perishable, commodities and instruments refer to such contracts as cattle, hogs, and Treasury bills. Nonstorable means that they can meet the contract specifications for delivery in only one particular month. A trader cannot buy the commodity or instrument in one maturity month and deliver the same item on the next contract. Treasury bills literally perish, while cattle and hogs change composition sufficiently so that they fail to meet contract specifications in a subsequent delivery month.

Discussed in this chapter are basis relationships for storable commodities and instruments, followed by the cash-futures price relationships for nonstorables. Also mentioned here are spread price relationships among futures contracts, a topic covered in more detail in later chapters.

STORABLES

The discussion of price relationships for storables begins with the grain commodities, products trading for over one hundred years. The same model applies to many other contracts also, such as metals, petroleum products, and frozen pork bellies. Emphasized here is the extension of the theoretical model to financial instruments.

COMMODITIES

Cash and futures markets for storable commodities combined to form carrying charge markets. In these markets there is a charge for holding the physical commodity, but not for holding futures contracts. The charge includes the costs for storing the physical commodity until delivery month. This is the time dimension of the basis. Prices in most local agricultural markets also reflect the spatial dimension, the cost of transporting the commodity to the par delivery point. Thus, the basis, or difference between futures and cash prices, reflects for most storable commodities both the carrying charge and transportation costs. Finally, for many agricultural products, differences in product quality between the cash commodity and specifications of the futures contract may also affect the size of the basis.

In this chapter, however, the discussion concentrates on the time dimension, or carrying charge. This is the price for the storage service of carrying inventory forward based on the demand for and supply of storage.[1] Presented first is the traditional theory of storage developed by Holbrook Working,[2] and then modeled by Michael Brennan.[3] This is only a partial equilibrium framework and ignores market and individual optimization and equilibrium among asset prices. We discuss these latter topics in chapters 5 and 6.

In a competitive industry in an uncertain world, a trading firm maximizing storage returns supplies storage or holds stocks to the amount that the marginal net carrying costs equals the expected change in their price during the time held.[4] The net marginal carrying costs in holding a specific level of stocks is equal to the marginal outlay on physical storage plus a possible marginal risk premium minus the marginal convenience yield on stocks. The marginal net cost of storage may be positive or negative.

The outlays on physical storage refer to out-of-pocket expenses such as rent for storage facilities, loading and unloading charges, interest, and insurance. These outlays increase as the quantity of stocks held by the firm increases. Typically, marginal outlays are fairly constant, or per unit storage costs do not change as inventory increases, until reaching warehouse capacity at which time marginal outlays increase.

Most suppliers of storage engage in production, processing, or merchandising, so storage may be adjunct to their main business. Thus, they gain a convenience yield from holding stocks because of the uncertainties in receiving the raw materials and uncertainties in consumer demand for products. If fixed costs are high, the loss from the interruption in production to such firms as flour millers and soybean processors may be substantial. Wholesalers gain convenience from holding inventory as it increases the chances of a customer sale or repeat business. Hence, the convenience yield explains why firms hold stocks when the apparent remuneration is less than storage costs.

The smaller the level of stocks, the greater is the convenience yield for holding an additional unit. The total convenience yield of stocks increases with quantities held until marginal convenience becomes zero at some large level of stocks. Consequently, marginal convenience yield is positive, having a large value at low levels of inventory, and negatively sloped as it approaches zero at some large level of stocks.

The carrying of stocks has some risk in an uncertain world, especially the risk of financial loss. The firm has the risk of an unexpected fall in prices, so the larger the quantity of stocks held, the larger can be the loss to the firm. This could seriously harm the firm's credit position and rating. Intuitively, the risk premium, if it exists, would be an increasing function of stocks, of the risk aversion factor of the trading firm, and of price volatility—all parameters defined in chapter 5. Thus, the marginal risk premium is either constant or an increasing function of stocks held. Normally, risk premium is a very small or nonexistent component of basis.

Letting X_t denote stocks held at the end of the period, $m_t(X_t)$ as the total cost of storage, $o_t(X_t)$ as the total outlay for physical storage, $r_t(X_t)$ as the total risk premium, and $c_t(X_t)$ as the total convenience yield, the total cost function can be expressed as:[5]

$$m_t(X_t) = o_t(X_t) + r_t(X_t) - c_t(X_t).$$

The net marginal cost function of storage has similar algebraic format and signs as this total cost function, indicating that the marginal cost function can be positive or negative.[6] That is, normally when stocks are adequate, the marginal convenience yield is small and the net marginal cost of storage positive. However, when stocks are small, the marginal convenience yield may be very large and outweigh the other two cost components so that net marginal costs of storage are negative.

Figure 3–1 shows the typical supply of storage curve (labeled *SS*) where $F_{t,T}$ is the futures price at time t for delivery of a commodity at time T, and S_t is the cash (spot) price at t.[7] It is analogous to a usual supply function derived from a marginal cost relationship. However, it becomes highly price inelastic as inventories approach the limit of available warehouse space, and is negative at very low inventory levels when the convenience yield dominates the cost components. The horizontal axis reflects inventory level while the vertical axis shows the marginal cost of storage, or basis, defined as futures ($F_{t,T}$) minus spot (S_t) price.

The demand for storage is derived from the demand for the consumption of a commodity. Because production is often seasonal and consumers want a stable flow of the commodity, a demand for storage results. Consumption in any period is equal to production during that period, plus stocks carried into the period, minus stocks at the end of the period. If, for convenience, current and subsequent levels of production and stocks are known, a rise in the price in period t leads to lower consumption in period t. This results in more commodity being carried out of period t into period $t + 1$, lowering prices in period $t + 1$. Conversely, lower stocks at the end of period t associate with lower consumption and higher prices in period $t + 1$. This results in a demand curve with a negative relation between the price difference of the two periods and storage level (*DD* in figure 3–1). The demand curve shifts from period to period, tracing out the more stable supply curve and showing how commodities move into or out of storage in response to favorable or unfavorable prices of storage.

The quantity of stocks which maximizes expected revenue is the familiar condition that expected marginal revenue equals net marginal costs. Using the preceding notation, this can be written as:

$$F_{t,T} - S_t = m_t'(X_t).$$

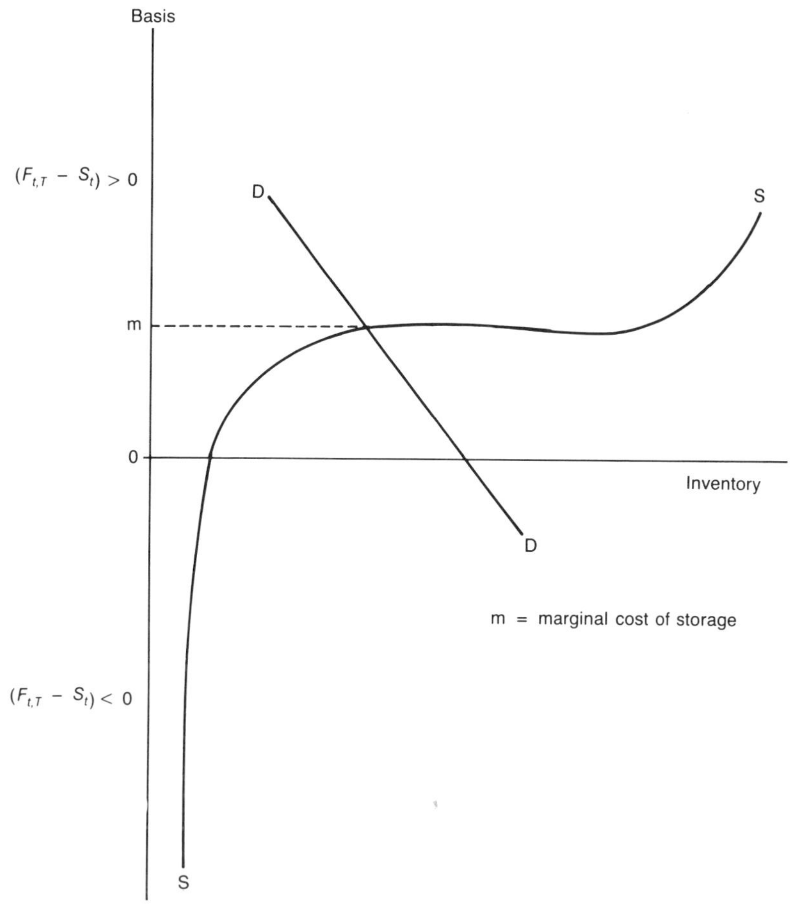

Figure 3-1. The Supply of Storage Curve

Hence, the basis for storable commodities, $F_{t,T} - S_t$, is the market price of storage, based on the supply of and demand for storage. The basis, in equilibrium, represents the net cost of storage. Figure 3-1 shows that this price of storage or basis and inventories are positively related; large inventories occur with a large basis, and small inventories associate with a small or negative basis.

Working noted that this price of storage may be negative, or that the market can show an inverse carrying charge.[8] The convenience yield described earlier explains this inverse carrying charge. Several authors, besides Working, have provided empirical evidence supporting the shape of the supply of storage curve as depicted in figure 3-1, including the inverse portion.[9]

Because of the existence of inventory, all futures prices for a commodity relate to each other. The difference in price between two futures contracts reflects the expected storage costs between the two associated delivery periods. Because the costs of storage are fairly constant within a storage season, cash and futures prices of storables are functionally related by these costs and the set of prices often move together as a constellation. They are highly interrelated. However, any one basis gradually gets smaller as the futures contract approaches the maturity date, meaning that cash and futures prices do not move exactly parallel with each other. On the first day of delivery at the par delivery point, cash and futures prices theoretically should be equal, or the basis equal to zero, as the commodity in the two markets becomes interchangeable and storage is no longer a factor. If these price relationships do not hold, arbitrage transactions are possible which can be profitable to the trader. In chapter 7 we provide further elaboration on such arbitrage transactions, seasonal basis patterns, procedure for computing costs of carry, maximum and minimum sizes of the basis for storables, and spread relationships among futures prices for agricultural commodities.

Working's theory of storage states that the price of storage is a function of current inventories. This even extends into the next crop year. Changing expectations about next year's crop influences current prices as well as next year's prices, and the price relationships remain at least in the same proportion to each other. F.H. Weymar expanded this theory of storage by arguing that the price of storage is not only a function of current inventories or stocks, but also of expected inventories if the time interval is over a long enough period.[10] For grains in the United States current stocks are a good proxy or forecast of expected stocks as users deplete only current stocks. However, for products like cocoa and coffee where harvests occur over an extended period, and where the countries who have the futures markets are major importers and stockholders of these commodities, expected stocks depend heavily on shipments anticipated before the future date. This is especially true if the future date is very distant. Hence, the price of storage in this case is:

$$F_{t,T} - S_t = f(X^*)$$

where X^* is the level of inventory expected at a future time. This concept provides a refinement, but does not detract from the basic theory nor from the importance of understanding the basis and its relationship to stocks.

More recently, Hans Stoll introduced finance theory to these concepts by explaining futures-spot price determination in the context of capital market equilibrium.[11] The problems addressed are how to allocate risks among stock, futures, and bond markets, and the allocation of storage stocks. Stoll determines equilibrium cash and futures positions for all traders and derives the optimal futures position and output for the individual storer. He shows the spot price to be the discounted value of the expected spot price adjusted to reflect expected marginal storage costs and storer attitudes toward and assessment of risk. Empirical measurement and testing of this model still remains to be done.

The seasonal basis pattern for storable agricultural commodities is presented in chapter 7. Also, we contrast futures contracts for metals with those for agricultural commodities.

FINANCIAL INSTRUMENTS

As with the storable commodity contracts discussed earlier, many financial futures involve underlying assets that are storable. That is, the assets are deliverable into several different maturity contracts. For example, for a number of financial futures contracts the underlying commodity is a long-term maturity bond with periodic interest payments and payment of principal at maturity. The most actively traded include the U.S. Treasury bond (T-bond), the ten-year U.S. Treasury note (T-note), and the five-year U.S. treasury note (FYTR). For the bond futures, any U.S. Treasury bond with at least fifteen years to maturity or call is eligible for delivery. Thus, some long-term maturity bonds can meet delivery specifications on the bond futures contract for several delivery months. Alternatively, a trader could accept delivery of a bond during one delivery month and redeliver that same bond during a later delivery month. Thus, prices on the deferred contracts should reflect the cost of carry on the long-term asset.

Stock index futures can also be considered storable and have as their underlying commodity a specific portfolio of common stocks. Examples of these futures include the Standard & Poor's 500 Stock Index (S&P 500) futures, the Major Market Index (MMI), and the New York Stock Exchange Index (NYSE). We discuss the pricing and specific details of these contracts in chapter 11.

BOND PRICING. There is a key relationship between interest rates or yields on financial assets and asset prices. Interest rates and prices are inversely related. As rates rise, the price or value of a financial asset declines. This is because the price of the asset is determined by discounting the value of the cash flow to be received from holding the asset (periodic interest payments and/or repayment of principal) back to the present by a market rate of return (R):

$$S = \sum_{t=1}^{m} C_t/(1 + R)^t.$$

Here, S is the spot price of the bond, C represents coupon payments, and M is the maturity of the bond. C_M would include both the last coupon payment and the

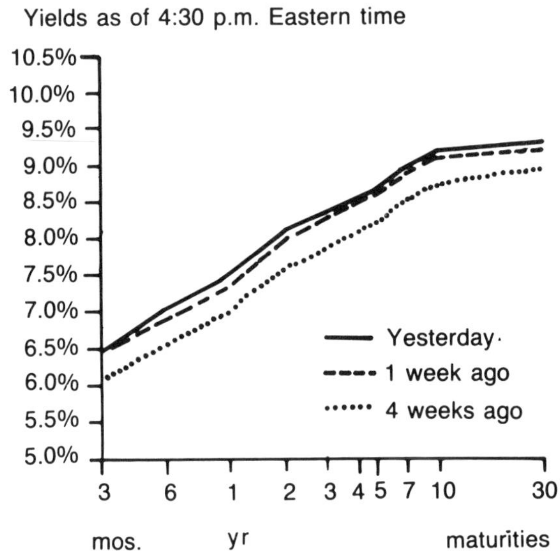

Figure 3–2. Yield Curve for Treasury Securities (May 25, 1988)

repayment of principal. Alternatively, given a market price for the bond, S, and its fixed coupon payments, C, a market yield to maturity, R, can be calculated.

THE YIELD CURVE. Before discussing carrying charges for such financial assets, it is first necessary to discuss the theories proposed to explain the relation of bond yield to maturity.

The difference in market yield for two different bonds depends on such bond characteristics as credit risk, coupon, and term-to-maturity. For bonds alike in risk, coupon, and call characteristics, but not maturity, have a relatively regular relationship between yield on the bond and maturity. This is the term structure of interest rates or the yield curve. For a yield curve based on Treasury securities, see figure 3–2.[12]

Three basic theories have been proposed to explain the shape of the yield curve: (1) the pure expectations hypothesis (PEH) that maintains the shape is a direct reflection of expectations on future interest rates; (2) the liquidity premium hypothesis that is similar to (1) but adds to all rates a risk premium that varies directly with time to maturity; and (3) the market segmentation hypothesis that maintains neither expectations nor risk premiums determine rates but rather the interaction of investor and debtor preference for maturity.

PURE EXPECTATIONS HYPOTHESIS. Under the PEH, the yield curve shape is determined by expectations on future rates. If rates are expected to rise in the future, the yield curve slopes upward. Thus, the current yield curve shows the market consensus on future interest rate movement.

The reasoning behind the theory is relatively simple. Assume that currently the yield curve is flat. However, if the general market consensus suddenly shifted to an expectation of higher rates in the future, two things would happen: Investors with excess funds would preferentially and almost exclusively choose short-term investments to have their money available for rollover when rates do, indeed, rise. Given the limited supply of short-term securities, such preferential investing causes prices of short-term securities to be bid up in the market, or short-term yields can fall because so many investors are willing to invest short term. At the same time, debtors such as the government and corporations would desire to borrow or sell securities almost exclusively at the long-term end of the maturity spectrum to lock in the currently low rate for as long as possible. Long-term rates must rise to attract investors, and the large supply of bonds relative to investors can cause bond prices to fall. The end result in equilibrium, then, would be a rising yield curve with low short-term rates and high long-term rates. If the market expects rates to rise, differential buying and selling results in an upward sloping yield curve. A similar explanation can be applied to expectations of declining rates. Although this explanation is a simplified reflection of the successive buying and selling decisions of market participants and the corresponding minute fluctuations in interest rates for various maturities, the basic decision making process seems a reasonable reflection of market reaction.

LIQUIDITY PREMIUM HYPOTHESIS. A second explanation of the shape of the yield curve derives from the existence of risk-averse investors in the market. If long-term investments are considered riskier than short-term, and if the preponderance of investors are risk averse, then a risk premium, called a liquidity premium, is required on long-term investments to induce the risk-averse investor to buy them. Under this second hypothesis, then, the yield curve contains a liquidity premium component that tends to bias all long-term rates upward to compensate for risk, with the size of the liquidity premium increasing with maturity. As figure 3–3 shows, the observable yield curve is determined partly by expectations, as in the first theory, but also partly by risk.

MARKET SEGMENTATION HYPOTHESIS. The third theory of the yield curve maintains that the key determinant of the yield curve shape is not expectations or risk per se but the institutional nature of borrowers and investors. Under this theory, market participants have strong preferences for a certain maturity due to the nature of their

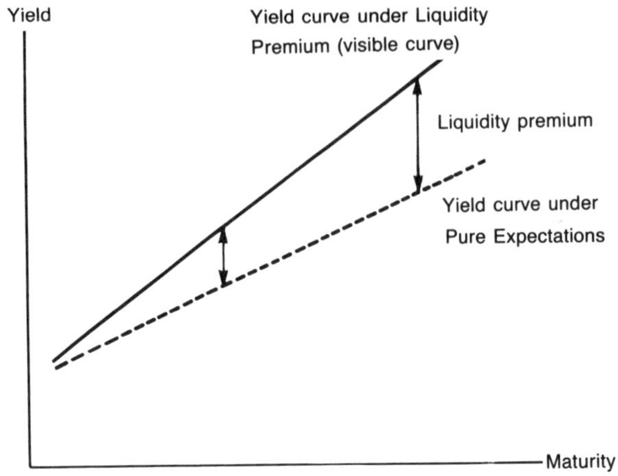

Figure 3-3. Yield Curves under Pure Expectations Hypothesis and Liquidity Premium Hypothesis

operations. Because most institutions strongly prefer to match asset and liability maturity, operating outside of this maturity poses significant risks. For instance, banks generally attempt to hedge the interest rate risk of their assets—commercial loans primarily—by concentrating on liabilities of equal interest rate sensitivity or maturity such as CDs or deposits. Similarly, pension funds or insurance companies concentrate on acquiring long-term investment assets to fund their essentially long-term liabilities. Because of this strong preference for one maturity segment over another, institutions in the capital market rarely can be induced to buy or borrow outside of the preferred segment. This obviously precludes borrowers and investors from preferentially buying and selling securities on the basis of current and expected rates, as we maintained in discussing the PEH. Thus, each maturity "habitat" has a relatively fixed supply and demand, and rates in any segment or maturity respond to changes in this supply and demand. The fact that the long-term segment of the yield curve generally exhibits higher rates is, under this theory, the consequence of prevailing supply and demand conditions in the long-term segment: Long-term rates may be high because of an abundance of long-term securities offered by corporations and the Treasury relative to the investors willing to acquire them.

THE BASIS. For storable financial asset futures, the shape of the yield curve determines the basis. For interest-bearing assets, the cost of carry consists of two components: first, the cost of acquiring and holding the asset until delivery of the futures; and second, the positive cash flow from the interest earned during this carry period. The cost of holding the asset relates to the short-term interest rate, *r*, since the time during which the trader borrows the purchase price (possesses a loan outstanding), or during which the money is invested, would be the time between contract delivery dates, or quarterly. Because the held asset generates coupon interest and capital gains or losses, assuming no change in the yield curve during the holding period, the second component—the yield earned on holding the interest-bearing asset—would reflect the long-term rate on the bond (y). Thus, the total cost of carry can be a positive or negative cash flow for the holder depending on whether short-term rates are less than long-term rates causing the yield curve to slope upward, or short-term rates are greater than long-term rates causing the yield curve to slope downward.

In equation form, the futures contract price ($F_{t,T}$) of a storable financial asset should be a function of the current price of the cash bond (S_t), the short-term interest rate paid to borrow the purchase price (r), and the long-term yield earned during the carry period (y):

$$F_{t,T} = S_t + rS_t - yS_t$$

$$F_{t,T} = S_t + (r - y)S_t.$$

Thus, the basis can be positive or negative depending on $(r - y)$, or the difference between short-term and long-term rates embodied in the yield curve.

If the yield curve slopes positively indicating that short-term rates are less than long-term rates, then the holder of the bond earns a higher rate from holding the bond as an asset than would be paid on the borrowed purchase price. Futures prices on the deferred contracts are thus lower than on nearby contracts to reflect this positive cash flow. The buyer of a contract for deferred delivery requires a lower price as an inducement to take the deferred delivery rather than hold the bond now. A positive yield curve results in a positive carry market.

Similarly, if short-term rates are greater than long-term rates, the holder of the bond must pay more in interest expense to borrow the purchase price than the income earned from holding the asset. In this case, the deferred futures price is higher than nearby prices to reflect the negative cost of carry, or negative cash flow. The bond holder agrees to sell in the futures market only if the futures price is high enough to compensate the trader for the expected cost of carrying the instrument through to the delivery date. Thus, for long-term financial asset futures, the spread in prices between delivery months reflects the shape of the yield curve, or the relative magnitude of short- and long-term rates.

The preceding argument demonstrates the relationship between cash short-term rates, long-term yields on the deliverable asset, and the cash-futures basis. If this relationship does not hold, certain arbitrage transactions are possible which result in a certain (riskless) profit with no investment by the arbitrageur. We discuss examples of these arbitrage trades in chapter 9.

NONSTORABLES

Nonstorable contracts are characterized by the inability of a trader to take delivery of the commodity or instrument during one delivery period and redeliver that same item on a later maturing contract. A particular financial instrument or cash agricultural commodity can satisfy the delivery requirements for only one specific maturity month. Consequently, the relationship between cash and futures prices for nonstorable commodities and instruments can be quite different from that for storable items. Next we discuss the characteristics of agricultural commodities and financial instruments.

COMMODITIES

The principal nonstorable agricultural commodities are live cattle and hogs. Although there is an inventory of livestock related to the animals on feed, no fixed storable supply exists as in the case for grains. The inventory is very fluid, composed of animals in many weight groups, with their weight and composition changing daily. Only a small number of animals are ready or available for consumption at any one time.

Hence, this continual production and distribution of livestock results in a basis that does not closely follow a theoretically expected pattern as in the case of storable commodities. No net cost of storage guides price relationships and inventory. Instead, varying production decisions are the primary influence on price relationships for nonstorables. The futures markets for nonstorable commodities are mainly for forward pricing because they do not assist in inventory rationing as in the case of grains.

The supply and demand for livestock and how traders expect these functions to change over time govern the basis for livestock. The current supply and demand determine the cash price of livestock today. The futures price reflects what traders expect supply and demand to be on some date in the future. Hence, the difference in these prices reflects what traders expect will happen to relative cash prices between now and that date. The size of the basis, or difference between the futures and cash prices, varies depending on how much traders believe the relative cash price will increase or decrease by the delivery month. Suppose, for example, that in April the cash price for cattle at a delivery point is $67 per hundredweight. If the June futures contract is trading at $69.50, the basis is $2.50. This shows that traders expect the cash price to increase relatively by about $2.50 by June as a result of changing supply and demand conditions (assuming a zero basis at maturity). A larger basis would reflect a greater relative cash price increase. Of course, cash and futures prices in June may be higher or lower than $69.50 depending on any new information, so the concept of relative changes in cash price is important.

If, on the other hand, traders expect the price to decrease by June, the present cash price will exceed the June futures price. In some years cash prices are below futures prices and in others above them, depending on whether traders believe cash prices will move up or down relative to futures before the contract matures. Thus, the basis for nonstorable commodities can be positive or negative.

Empirical analysis supports the theoretical model that the basis for nonstorables reflects the difference between current demand and supply and expected demand and supply.[13] In the short run demand is fairly constant and the primary factors determining basis are those representing shifts in supply.

An interesting question for nonstorables is the degree of interdependence, or independence, among cash and futures prices and among the futures prices themselves. Because storage does not exist to hold prices together, the set of cash and futures prices are not functionally related as in grain markets. Hence, one might argue that all the prices are independent of each other. However, for prices to be completely independent of each other the commodity would need to be perfectly nonstorable and that is usually not the case.

There are several reasons why cash and futures prices for livestock show some interdependence:[14] One, prices relate to each other because major inputs in animal feeding such as corn and soybean meal are storable and have highly interrelated price structures. Any change in their price levels or structure can affect all the livestock prices, current and forward. Two, cash and futures prices for nonstorables are subject to the same exogeneous shocks in the general economy that might influence such factors as consumer demand and interest rates. Three, livestock are not totally nonstorable as feeding programs can be lengthened or shortened by changing rations or rates of feed, thereby causing correlation among prices. There exist a host of contractual feeding arrangements and rates of gain programs in the spot market. Fourth, production lags are not fixed. Producers responding to current and expected prices can alter breeding schedules by keeping more or fewer female animals, affecting prices now and in the future.

The degree of interdependence varies by commodity and the length of time between the two prices being correlated. Empirical evidence shows that cash and futures prices are interdependent for nearby contract months, but do often move independently of each other for more distant contracts.[15]

There is another price relationship of interest for livestock and that is the one between distant fed animal futures contracts and the current cash price of feeder animals. This difference, weighted appropriately with other costs, reflects the cost of feeding animals and is called the price of feedlot services. It is somewhat analogous to the price of storage. Allen Paul and William Wesson showed that cattle feedlot placements are positively related to this feeding margin.[16] We describe in chapter 8 how producers use futures markets in these situations.

Although the basis in nonstorage markets reflects a different set of conditions than in storage markets, the basis pattern of the former does resemble that of the latter in one important way. Spot and futures prices for nonstorables, like those for storable commodities, must gradually come together as the delivery month approaches, regardless of whether the basis is positive or negative. During the delivery month at any local market, spot and futures prices should differ by the transportation costs to the delivery point. During the delivery month at the delivery point, the basis must be nearly zero no matter how large it may have been earlier. If the basis is not near zero at contract maturity, speculators may arbitrage between the spot and futures markets, forcing the prices together. In later chapters we discuss how certain market features, costs, and imperfections prevent the basis from being exactly zero.

When referring to the basis for any commodity, traders compare products of similar quality. Agricultural commodities vary considerably in quality, and the futures contract calls for a specific grade. The basis follows the expected patterns and closes near zero for only the cash prices representing the same quality or grade as the futures contract. Cash prices of premium products are higher than the futures price during the delivery month, and cash prices of inferior products are at a discount. For most part, these products of different grades are not deliverable on futures markets. Nevertheless, cash premiums and discounts due to quality remain fairly constant, meaning the futures market can still be quite useful. The user must adjust the basis according to these differences.

INTEREST RATE CONTRACTS

Several financial futures have as their underlying commodity a nonstorable financial asset. Examples of these contracts include the U.S. Treasury bill (T-bill) and the Eurodollar contract. Eurodollars are dollars deposited outside the United States. For these, the deliverable asset is one that has ninety days to maturity as of the futures delivery date. For instance, the June Eurodollar futures contract calls for delivery of $1 million of a Eurodollar deposit with a maturity of ninety days as of approximately June 15. Clearly, this timed deposit cannot be delivered into more than one contract. By the maturity of the September contract, the June ninety-day deposit will have matured.

The primary pricing relationship on such a nonstorable commodity as a T-bill is very similar to that of an agricultural nonstorable. The price set in the futures market for delivery in some later time period is equal to the spot price expected to prevail for the commodity at delivery time.

Treasury bills are priced at a discount from their face value, and the difference between the price paid for the T-bill and the maturity face value, called the discount, represents the interest earned on the bill until maturity. For instance, a $1 million face value Treasury bill with ninety days to maturity, yielding 8 percent on an annual basis would be priced as follows:

$$\text{Price} = \text{Face value} - \text{Discount}$$

$$\text{Price} = \text{Face value} - \frac{(\text{days to maturity} \times \text{annual yield} \times \text{face value})}{360}$$

$$= \$1{,}000{,}000 - \left(\frac{90}{360} \times .08 \times \$1{,}000{,}000\right)$$

$$= \$980{,}000.$$

The futures price of a Treasury bill contract would be equal to the face value of the cash instrument to be delivered, or $1 million, discounted by the rate expected to prevail on a ninety-day Treasury bill at delivery time:

$$\text{Futures price} = \text{Face value} - \frac{(\text{days to maturity} \times \text{expected yield} \times \text{face value})}{360}.$$

For instance, if an investor expected that three-month T-bills will yield 10 percent by September, then the September futures price would be equal to:

$$\text{Futures price} = \$1{,}000{,}000 - ((90/360) \times .10 \times \$1{,}000{,}000)$$

$$= \$975{,}000.$$

Thus, the pricing of a T-bill futures contract, or any nonstorable financial futures, is quite similar in principle to the pricing of any nonstorable agricultural futures contract. What is different in financial futures is that expectations of prices of short-term assets for future dates can be estimated from current cash market prices for these assets. As discussed earlier, the shape of the yield curve, constructed from current cash market yields, reflects expectations concerning interest rates. In chapter 9 we discuss a method of extracting an estimate of expected rates, the Implied Forward Rate, from current market rates. If these two expected rates, one from the futures price and one from the yield curve, are not equal, then we show that arbitrage transactions are possible between the cash and futures market; these can result in a riskless profit to the arbitrageur with no initial investment.

In sum, then, the basis for a nonstorable financial asset futures contract is, like livestock commodity contracts, a function of the expected price at maturity of the contract relative to the current price. Thus, if the yield curve is upward sloping, indicating an expectation of rising rates, the futures price of a deferred T-bill contract is less than the current price for the ninety-day T-bill, indicating a larger discount has been subtracted from the face value in the futures price. If the yield curve is downward sloping, futures prices on deferred contracts are greater than the current price for the T-bill, because a smaller discount has been subtracted in the futures price. Of course, the basis still must theoretically close to zero at delivery time.

NOTES

1. Storage refers to the commodity as inventory, not to storage space.
2. H. Working, "The Theory of Price of Storage," *American Economic Review* 39 (1949): 1254–62.
3. M.J. Brennan, "The Supply of Storage," *American Economic Review* 48 (1958): 50–72. See also L.S. Venkataramanan, *The Theory of Futures Trading* (New York: Asia Publishing House, 1965), chapter V.
4. As used in this chapter, stocks refer to an inventory of a physical commodity like grain, and not to shares of IBM.
5. This notation is from Brennan, "The Supply of Storage."
6. The net marginal costs function can be written as

   $$m_t'(X_t) = o_t'(X_t) + r_t'(X_t) - c_t'(X_t)$$

   based on the expected first and second derivatives of each of the cost components being

   $$o_t' > 0,\ o_t'' \geq 0,\ r_t' > 0,\ r_t'' \geq 0,\ c_t' \geq 0 \text{ and } c_t'' \leq 0.$$

   That is, o_t and r_t are increasing functions of X_t so at the margin they are either constant or increasing functions of X_t. c_t is also an increasing function of X_t, but c_t declines toward zero.
7. The letter S represents *spot price*, a term used in this text interchangeably with cash price.
8. H. Working, "Theory of the Inverse Carrying Charge in Futures Markets," *Journal of Farm Economics* 30 (1948): 1–28.
9. Brennan, "The Supply of Storage"; R.W. Gray and A.E. Peck, "The Chicago Wheat Futures Market: Recent Problems in Historical Perspective," *Food Research Institute Studies* 18 (1981): 89–116; L.G. Telser, "Futures Trading and the Storage of Cotton and Wheat," *Journal of Political Economy* 66 (1958): 233–55; S. Thompson, "Returns to Storage in Coffee and Cocoa Futures Markets," *Journal of Futures Markets* 6 (1986): 541–64. Also see A. Kamara, "Issues in Futures Markets: A Survey," *Journal of Futures Markets* 2 (1982): 261–94 for a much larger literature review.
10. F.H. Weymar, "The Supply of Storage Revisited," *American Economic Review* 56 (1966): 1226–34.
11. H.R. Stoll. "Commodity Futures and Spot Price Determination and Hedging in Capital Market Equilibrium," *Journal of Financial and Quantitative Analysis* 14 (1979): 873–94.
12. For a more complete discussion of the term structure of interest rates, see J.C. Van Horne, *Financial Market Rates and Flows* (Englewood Cliffs, N.J.: Prentice-Hall, 1978).

13. R.M. Leuthold, "An Analysis of the Futures-Cash Price Basis for Live Beef Cattle," *North Central Journal of Agricultural Economics* 1 (1979): 47–52; R.M. Leuthold and P.E. Peterson, "The Cash-Futures Price Spread for Live Hogs," *North Central Journal of Agricultural Economics* 5 (1983): 25–29.
14. D.L. Kendall and G.M. Scobie, "Intertemporal Price Relationships in Noninventory Futures Markets," *International Futures Trading Seminar*, vol. VII. (Chicago Board of Trade, 1981), 106–61.
15. W.G. Tomek, "An Analysis of the Futures-Cash Price Basis for Live Beef Cattle: Comment," *North Central Journal of Agricultural Economics* 2 (1980): 81–2; and Kendall and Scobie, "Intertemporal Price Relationships."
16. A.B. Paul and W.T. Wesson, "Pricing Feedlot Services Through Cattle Futures," *Agricultural Economics Research* 19 (1967): 33–45.

TRADING ACTIVITIES ON FUTURES MARKETS

4

Participants use markets to facilitate the exchange of products and services. The degree of organization of markets relates to various quality attributes of the product exchange. From a trader's standpoint, the main quality attributes are liquidity, low transaction costs, and integrity of the market through enforced safety rules. From society's point of view, these attributes expand to the absence of dominant positions and the quality of the price discovery system. The former may require many participants and a high level of public information.

Futures and option markets are useful because they provide the opportunity for traders to develop risk management programs. Exchanges develop the organizational structure of the markets to meet the quality requirements of individual traders as well as those of the whole economic society.

Futures and options markets exist because traders use them for economic purposes. We presume that most market participants have rational motivations. Thus, their methods of utilizing these markets are various, multiple, and complex. Depending on their business or private objectives, each trader has a unique procedure for using the instruments of these markets. Procedures vary according to each trader's constraints, education, market expertise, and financial well-being.

For practical reasons, however, we classify traders into broadly defined groups. We usually do this by defining different trading activities on the futures markets.

TRADERS

We traditionally divide traders in a futures market into two groups: The first are hedgers. They are producers, buyers, and users of the goods and instruments specified on the futures contract, or of goods and instruments whose prices are linked with prices on the futures market. That is, hedgers have or expect to have spot market positions. Most hedgers use the futures and options markets to diversify their business and financial risk associated with spot market activities. They are called hedgers because of the combined trading activities they practice in spot and futures markets. Hedging is a concept with various meanings for various traders; we explain hedging momentarily.

Speculators, the second type, have no spot market position and only futures market positions. These traders enter the futures market with some expected financial return. Speculators are not homogeneous in objectives, skills, and experience. Some enter the market in an attempt to make quick money, with little investment in information gathering and processing. Those who succeed in making money usually stay around and trade more. Those who lose find an alternative investment outlet.

Other speculators are more cautious, investing in market information and looking for a less variable return from their investment. They take diversified positions in the futures market, buying and selling different futures, looking for prices to increase or decrease. A subgroup of speculators, spreaders, buy and sell different futures contracts at the same time looking for price differentials among contracts to change.

Grouping traders into hedgers or speculators is traditional and official in the United States and in those countries where major futures markets exist. Hedgers and speculators face different rules in administrative and regulatory control, such as the size of futures positions, position reporting, margins, and commissions.

Unfortunately, these classifications become less distinct when hedgers start to speculate or when speculators diversify their portfolio risk into futures contracts and options (see chapter 5). Still, it is useful to describe their trading activities and to use the level of risk as the criteria for classification.

TRADING ACTIVITIES

Traditionally, speculation is a trading activity involving high risks, while hedging typically has low or medium risks. However, spreading and arbitrage activities have very low or no risks. In addition, hedging is really an arbitrage activity. In discussing each of these activities, we start with arbitrage, continue with spreading and hedging, and conclude with speculation.

ARBITRAGE

Arbitrage transactions are possible when theoretical or logical price relationships do not exist within the broadly defined market. These transactions exist on agricultural markets relating either to the time, quality, or spatial dimension. When market premiums or discounts are different from product values, differential arbitrage potential exists. For instance, traders look for price differentials which exceed the costs of transportation between two market locations. If corn is priced at $2.55 per bushel in one market and $3.22 in another, with a $0.59 transportation cost, a simple arbitrage transaction consists of buying in the lowest priced market and selling in the highest. Due to the arbitrage activity, prices should increase in the low-priced market and decrease in the other until the price differential reaches the cost of transportation. Such arbitrage opportunities are often short-lived and unstable.

Financial instruments traded on spot and futures markets allow for arbitrage transactions because of the redundant information created by the futures market over the spot market. As explained in chapter 3, implied forward rates, which are not quoted, can be computed from spot rates for instruments of different maturities. Any differential between these implied rates and quoted futures prices above transaction costs induces an arbitrage activity. We cover these transactions more thoroughly in chapter 9.

The essence of arbitrage in the financial markets involves using the discrepancy between borrowing money at a cheaper rate while acquiring an asset that pays a higher rate or has a lower price. The difference between these rates results in arbitrage profit.

Arbitrage opportunities also exist between futures markets dealing with the same or similar products. However, these trading opportunities become classified as spread trades which we discuss next.

SPREADING

Spread trading is the simultaneous buying of one futures contract while selling a related futures contract. Typically, these contracts are for different delivery months of the same commodity (instrument), but sometimes involve different commodities (instruments) or the same commodity (instrument) on different exchanges. These are, respectively, interdelivery, intercommodity, and intermarket spreads. Spread trades are usually less risky than position trades, requiring less margin money and having smaller potential for large gains.

The interdelivery spread is most common where a trader purchases contracts of one delivery month while simultaneously selling those of another delivery month; all contracts are of the same commodity or instrument on the same exchange. The success of this strategy depends on a thorough understanding of the basis and price relationships. For storables, the spread can depend on the expected change in the cost of carry between delivery months. Likewise, for nonstorables spread traders also believe that price relationships change due to changing economic conditions.

As an example, if the futures price for May corn exceeds that of March corn and a trader believes that the difference between the two prices will decrease due to, say, falling interest rates, then the trader should sell May corn and buy March corn. The opposite trade is made if the trader believes that the difference between the two prices will increase.

Table 4-1 shows an example of the first situation. On January 10 the price of May corn is \$2.56 and the price of March corn is \$2.35. The trader buys March corn and sells May corn, believing the difference will decrease. This is a bull spread. On February 19 the trader liquidates the spread trade and makes a profit of \$0.07 per bushel, before commission. The trader was not concerned about the change in price level, only the change in the spread.

A bear spread is when the trader sells the nearby contract and buys the deferred contract. In the case of March-May corn, a bear spread trader may believe the difference

Table 4-1. A Spread Trade in Corn

	Dollars per Bushel				
Date	March Corn		May Corn		Spread
January 10	Long @	$2.35	Short @	$2.56	$ .21
February 19	Short @	2.16	Long @	2.30	.14
Result		−$0.19		+$0.26	+$0.07

between the two contracts will become greater because of rising interest rates or storage costs.

Spreading in financial futures is similar to that just described for commodities. Interdelivery spreads depend on expected changes in the cost of carry for a financial asset between different delivery months. For a long-term bond, the cost of carry involves two components: First, the cost of financing the purchase of the bond for the carry period, generally taken to be the short-term borrowing rate; and second, the coupon income earned on the bond. If the short-term rate is less than the coupon interest on the bond, the holder of the bond during the carry period receives a positive cash flow, the difference between the lower borrowing cost and the higher coupon income received. This positive cash flow is reflected in the price of the nearby and deferred delivery contracts, and the deferred is priced at a discount to the spot price and to the nearby futures contract. Similarly, if short-term rates are higher than long-term rates, the holder of the bond pays a higher borrowing rate while receiving a lower yield on the bond. In this case, the futures price of the deferred contract is greater than the nearby contract, reflecting the negative cash flow from the bondholder.

Spread strategies depend on changes in the cost of carry between contracts, or changes in the shape of the yield curve. For instance, assume the yield curve is negatively sloped, futures prices reflect a negative carry market—the deferred futures price is greater than nearby futures price—and the curve is expected to flatten as short-term rates fall. In this case, the borrowing cost relative to the coupon income received has diminished: It costs less to borrow, while the coupon income remains the same. Because the cost of carry has decreased in dollar terms, the premium or carry on the deferred contracts is smaller, and the price of the deferred contracts falls relative to the nearby contracts. If this is expected to occur, the trader should sell the deferred contract, as the largest price decrease is expected there. To complete the spread, the trader should also simultaneously buy the nearby contract; if prices do not move as expected, one of the legs of the spread still increases in value to offset any losses that occur. Buying the nearby contract and selling the deferred is a bull spread.

In other situations selling the nearby contract and buying the deferred contract, a bear spread, is appropriate. Assume again that the yield curve is negatively sloped, but that the curve is expected to become steeper as short-term rates rise. Because the short-term borrowing rate has become higher relative to the long-term coupon income received on the bond, the premium is higher on the deferred contracts reflecting the now higher cost of carry for the period. The deferred contract should be expected to rise, and buying the deferred while selling the nearby is then profitable.

Even though interdelivery spreads in financial asset futures depend on expected changes in the shape of the yield curve, intercommodity spreads—like those in agricultural commodities—depend on changing relations between related assets. A commot set of spread strategies involves changes in relative risk premiums between financial assets of similar maturities but different issuers. For instance, at the beginning of a recession, the spread in rates between T-bills issued by the U.S. government and Eurodollars issued by banks usually widens as investors prefer to acquire the relatively safer T-bills. Eurodollar rates can be expected to rise relative to T-bill rates to attract investors by offering a higher risk premium. Futures prices also adjust to reflect the movement in rates, with Eurodollar futures prices falling relative to T-bill futures prices. Thus, selling Eurodollar futures while buying T-bill futures may be profitable. This is a TED (T-bill–Eurodollar) spread. Other common spreads involve municipal bond futures versus Treasury bond futures, or over-the-counter stock indexes versus NYSE-listed stock indexes.

Other spreads between assets of similar risk but different maturity involve the differential price volatility of long-term and short-term securities as rates change. A very common spread involves Treasury note futures and Treasury bond futures (called a NOB, notes over bonds). For instance, if rates are expected to rise uniformly across maturity the yield curve is expected to rise but maintain its current shape. Then the price of a T-bond and T-bond futures with a fifteen-year maturity can be expected to fall by more than the price of a T-note and T-note futures with a ten-year maturity. The spread between T-bond and T-note futures prices can be expected to widen, and selling the bond futures while buying the note futures may be profitable.

Finally, an intermarket spread involves trading in two futures contracts for the same commodity but on different exchanges. Few opportunities of this kind are available in financial futures. There are few exchanges outside the United States trading financial asset futures similar to those in the United States, and few U.S. futures exchanges offer contracts trading on the same financial asset. A U.S. T-bond contract is traded on both the LIFFE (London International Financial Futures Exchange) and the CBOT, although trading times do not overlap significantly. Similarly, a Eurodollar contract is offered by the LIFFE and the CME, but delivery terms differ.

In agriculture, common intercommodity spreads are cattle and hogs, corn and wheat, and corn and soybeans. Usually, these spreads depend on changing production conditions of the paired commodities. A common spread in metals is between gold and silver, each affected differently by inflation and changing monetary conditions.

Intermarket spreads involve buying futures contracts on one exchange, selling contracts for the same commodity or instrument and delivery month on another exchange. Few opportunities for this spread exist among financial futures because usually two exchanges in the United States do not offer contracts for similar instruments. However, this spread is popular in wheat where similar contracts exist in

Chicago, Kansas City, and Minneapolis. The contracts call for different types of wheat, those produced in the region of the market. Nonetheless, the Kansas City and Minneapolis wheat markets have insufficient levels of speculation to absorb the hedging positions placed on those markets.[1] Thus, speculation comes from the more active Chicago market through spread trading between markets. The spreading between markets responds to relative hedging pressures.

Finally, commodity-product spreads involve commodities where one is produced from another. Examples include spreading soybeans against soybean oil and soybean meal, corn and feeder cattle against live cattle, and crude oil against gasoline and gas oil. In chapter 8 we discuss the first two examples in more detail.

A primary objective of arbitrage, spreading, straddling in options markets, and hedging is to trade in price differentials rather than flat price trading that is the case with speculation. Speculation usually brings much higher risk along with higher expected returns than the price differential activities.

HEDGING

Hedging is more of a market action than a precise, technical act. It is not possible to define hedging as a unique action. Hedging means different things to different people, so there is more than one definition.

Hieronymus gave three definitions in his text: First, the technical process of hedging is "to take a position in futures equal and opposite to an existing cash position."[2] Equal here means equal in size, and opposite means that if the trader is long or short in the spot market, a corresponding short or long position is taken in the futures market.

To illustrate this statement, consider the case of an inventory holder buying grain in the spot market at time $t + 0$ at a price S_0 and at the same time selling a futures contract at a price F_0. The trader is long in the spot market and short in the futures market, a hedged position. At time $t + 1$ the trader sells the cash grain at spot price S_1 and liquidates or purchases the futures contract at futures price F_1.

The result (R), profit or loss, of the hedged transaction is represented by the relative change in the two prices, spot and futures, or the change in the basis as:

$$
\begin{aligned}
R &= (S_1 - S_0) + (F_0 - F_1) \\
&= (S_1 - F_1) - (S_0 - F_0) \\
&= B_1 - B_0 = \Delta B
\end{aligned}
$$

with $B_1 = S_1 - F_1$; $B_0 = S_0 - F_0$; and where B represents the basis, and ΔB the change in the basis.

The objective of the hedger is to pass flat price risks on to someone else, leaving the hedger with a smaller basis variation. As we show in chapter 7, basis risks or variations are typically much smaller than spot market price risks or variations. Hedging is the search for this technical result.

Hieronymus's second definition relates to the result of this technical process. "To hedge is to insulate one's business activities from price level speculation while retaining the opportunity to speculate in basis variation."[3] This definition presents the consequences of the hedging activity as just demonstrated. It is to avoid the highly risky spot or flat price positions and accept the lower risk basis or premium positions obtained with opposite long and short positions in the spot and futures markets. The restrictive constraint of equal and opposite positions is not a part of this second definition.

The international grain trade is composed of literally millions of flat price suppliers (farmers) and billions of flat price consumers (every human being on earth). As the grain moves from supplier to consumer it funnels through various concentrated markets. This concentration is most evident where a few international exporters ship several million tons annually. This temporary concentration of ownership forces too much flat price risk on the firms and leads to various hedging techniques to reduce the impact of flat price movement.

The concept of hedging in this scenario goes well beyond the utilization of an established futures market. For instance, when making a trade a grain merchant may identify a hedge position in the futures market, but may also identify a position in a cash grain of different origin, a completely different grain, or a freight rate that may serve as a hedge. However, the most liquid and commonly used hedge against a spot position is the futures market.

Once a trader establishes a futures hedge, a basis or premium exists. Like the flat price, the basis also moves up or down, but within a much narrower range. Consequently, trading the basis allows grain merchants to carry a much larger book of business than would be the case when trading only on flat prices. This example of the grain merchant's business introduces the third definition of hedging.

The third definition is broader and develops the crucial objective of hedging for a firm. "To hedge is to use futures contracts in managing risk exposure associated with commodity ownership and commitment and with variable price relationships among commodities and related commodity products to levels consistent with profit maximization and/or profit regularization and with capital preservation and expansion."[4] This describes the commercial use of futures emphasizing that capital (inventories in particular) and earnings are subject to risk exposure resulting from variation in prices and price relationships.

These definitions are acceptable within a given context. The most important factor is the risk exposure of the trader. Hedging is a risk-management procedure which usually decreases the flat price risk to a basis risk. As we describe in chapter 5, the decreasing risk effect of hedging is based on the principle of risk diversification. This principle is the basis of portfolio management.

The concepts of the preceding definitions are present in Working's notion of hedging; he defined it as "use of futures contracts as a *temporary substitute* for contracts intended to transfer ownership of a quantity of the commodity, in the normal course of business."[5] Emphasized here is that in the risk reduction process of opposing positions in two markets, the futures contract stands as a temporary substitute in time and place for a later spot transaction.

Finally, the Congress of the United States obligated the Commodity Futures Trading Commission (CFTC) to define hedging. This requirement resulted from the imposition of legal limits on the number of contracts speculators can hold; hedgers, however, are exempt. Thus, administrative authorities must determine who is eligible for the exemption. The effort by the CFTC resulted in a long and conceptual definition in 1977 based on economic context. Unfortunately, there is no succinct phrase to quote. Basically, the CFTC provides an economic definition of hedging, broadened it to include cross hedging, setting specific requirements for anticipatory hedges, and allowing for transactions and positions to be recognized as hedging on a case-by-case basis.[6] For bona fide hedging: (*a*) it must be economically appropriate to reduce risks; (*b*) risks must arise from operating the commercial enterprise; (*c*) the futures positions normally represent a substitute for transactions to be made later in the physical market; and (*d*) price fluctuations of futures contracts must closely relate to fluctuations of cash market value of assets, liabilities, or services hedged. Thus, hedging is more than just enumeration of specific transactions and positions—it is a process of risk reduction. Prior to this definition, several legitimate hedging operations, especially cross and anticipatory hedges, were not recognized as hedges because futures positions did not meet the approximate equal and opposite requirement to the cash position.

Thus, this conceptual definition is preferred over the limited operational definitions. However, more recent definitions place hedging within a portfolio management content, a topic outlined in the next section and discussed in detail in chapter 5.

MOTIVATION FOR HEDGING

As we have shown, the definition of hedging has changed over the years. More important, however, is understanding the perceived motivations for hedging and how they have changed over the years.

The traditional theory of hedging corresponds with the first definition—that futures positions are equal and opposite to spot positions. This theory puts the emphasis of hedging on risk avoidance and assumes that market participants generate returns solely from spot market activities. Inventory holders hedge the risk of their inventory changing value regardless of whether they believe prices will increase or decrease or whether they expect the basis to change. For producers, routine hedging is not likely to change the pattern of returns or return variability from not hedging over the long run.

Traditional hedging theory is often associated with the writings of John Maynard Keynes[7] and John Hicks[8] who characterized hedging as the act of transferring risk from risk-averse hedgers to more risk-tolerant speculators. Risk reduction and transfer was a principal motivation for hedging.

A second theory of hedging corresponds to the second defintion where hedgers take futures positions to profit from expected basis changes. Traders hedge selectively rather than routinely depending on expected basis changes. Working was the first to offer this alternative concept of hedging.[9] He argued there are several reasons a trader may want to hedge, including assuring profits, facilitating business decisions, obtaining financial collateral, and maximizing profits from basis moves. The trader may reduce risks in the process, but it is incidental to the other motivations for hedging. These new ideas, and especially the profit maximization concept integrated with the traditional theory of risk reduction, led to considering hedging in the context of portfolio management.

This third theory, the portfolio approach, treats the futures contract as an asset that a trader can potentially include in a portfolio along with the underlying cash instrument. Leland Johnson[10] and Jerome Stein[11] were the first to argue within this theoretical framework that hedgers enter the futures market for the same reason an investor enters any market—to attain the highest return for a given risk level. The quantity of futures contracts included in the portfolio becomes a variable to adjust when maximizing portfolio returns or minimizing the variance or risk of returns of the portfolio.[12] This approach reconciles differences between Keynes's and Working's theories by combining return maximization with risk maximization.

In addition, some firms hedge to enhance their opportunity to obtain additional financial equity. Futures trading involves no direct transfer of funds to the hedger, but does play a risk transfer role which can be important in financial planning. Speculators who accept the transfer of price risks from hedgers provide a risk-bearing service, but no purchasing power is exchanged between speculators and hedgers.

Financial risk refers to the hedger's ability to repay debts. When hedgers establish a forward price, they have improved their ability to pay back loans associated with hedged collateral. The probability of default declines with hedging. Leaders stand to gain from this reduced chance of default, so they should be willing to increase the loan size.

That is, loan size from lenders to hedgers should be positively related to the act of hedging because of reduced default risk. Hence, the futures market facilitates the possibility of hedgers obtaining additional financial equity. This equity would be virtually impossible to obtain in any way other than with the existence of a futures market. Also, hedgers and speculators post margin money rather than full contract funding to facilitate this process. Of course, this analysis assumes that the lender has resources available to lend, that the hedging customer is creditworthy and not already overextended, and that the lender can see additional benefits that exceed costs from writing a larger loan. This additional credit should exceed the amount needed to just meet margin calls. Nevertheless, the financial potential offered because of the existence of the futures market is substantial. This analysis demonstrates how the futures markets play an indirect financing role, and the importance of speculators in assuring the role.

SPECULATION

Simply put, success for speculators is measured by being long when prices rise and short when prices fall. This success involves market analysis and price forecasting, divided into two distinct categories: the fundamental approach and the technical approach. The fundamental approach relies on analysis of underlying demand and supply factors, while the technical approach assumes that one can forecast futures prices by analyzing current and past price behavior.

However, there is more than forecasting and analysis to successful speculation. It also involves understanding one's motivations and managing money. All traders lose money on some trades, so self-discipline is an important element for success. Traders must remain objective about their decisions and not become emotionally involved in defending losing positions. Self-discipline is easier to maintain when traders have a plan with clearly specified goals.

A major element of this plan is money management, or the management of risk capital. Sufficient risk capital is needed when a margin call occurs so a trader is not forced to liquidate a position due to a temporary adverse price move. On a single trade a trader should risk only a small proportion of the capital set aside for futures market speculation. Also, the risk capital set aside for commodity trading should be only that amount the trader can afford to lose, extra money well above the amount needed for normal living expenses. Then the trader must decide on the desired rate of return on the risk capital, the ratio of potential profit to potential loss for each trade, and the price objective.[13] The latter comes from forecasting prices. Finally, speculators need to remain flexible as market and financial conditions can change rapidly.

FUNDAMENTAL APPROACH. The fundamental forces in the market are those that deal with the basic concepts of supply and demand conditions. Traders using fundamental analysis have an understanding of the interaction between the demand for and supply of a commodity or instrument; they base their forecasts on potential shifts in demand and/or supply and analyze how such shifts affect price. These traders can reason how certain changes in the economy affect the price of their commodity. An early, very practical approach to this reasoning is a balance sheet where inventories, inflows, and outflows are balanced each period; then the analyst can assess how any changes impact on price.

Another common approach is to develop an economic forecasting model to approximate the major forces affecting price. Presumably, most of these forces are inherent to demand or supply. An in-depth understanding of model building requires basic knowledge of the industry and the marketing of the commodity.

Studying supply amounts to analyzing the factors of production of a commodity. The interaction of these input factors and their relative prices determines the level of output. Some products are produced seasonally and some continuously. Weather affects some, but not others. Analyzing quantity supplied also involves knowing inventory levels, carryover, projected usage, imports or exports, likely government programs, and production levels in other countries.

Demand for many commodities depends on analyzing both domestic and foreign factors. Consumer purchases are affected by price levels, prices of complements and substitutes, and their income levels. Exports are influenced by world economic conditions, weather, exchange rates, and trade agreements, all factors that affect price relationships.

Representing all these factors in an economic price forecasting model is not easy, but usually useful. The forecaster must continually update and review the model because price interrelationships are never constant.

TECHNICAL APPROACH. Technical analysts have little or no concern about underlying economic conditions and their influence on price, but instead attempt to infer from the patterns of past price movements how that same price series will behave in the future. Most technical analysis schemes are subjective in nature and not tested by standard statistical reliability tests. Technicians do not believe prices fluctuate randomly or are unpredictable. There is little doubt that technical analysts have substantial influence on the market and that some of these traders are very successful.

Traders in almost all financial markets use various technical analysis techniques. The main tool analysts use is charts that graphically record past prices and from which they make inferences about expected future price patterns. That is, chartists believe certain price movements creating a particular formation can foretell subsequent price movements. Technicians must find this pattern, identify it, and use that information to suggest a profitable trading strategy. The most common charts are bar charts, point and figure charts, and moving average charts.

Many technical trading schemes exist. Some go further than just analyzing price, by combining information about prices, volume, and open interest. The success of any scheme in signaling profitable trades depends on the skills of the traders correctly identifying and interpreting the signals in the data. Also, each commodity usually has its own successful technical schemes that cannot be generalized to other futures contracts.

OVERVIEW. The real question is: Which works better, fundamental analysis or technical analysis? The answer may be that neither of them work well, or both work well. Formerly, fundamental traders had little tolerance for technical analysts and vice versa. However, today fewer traders probably rely on only one technique. With the convenience of computers, signals from both methods are quickly available. A general rule of thumb is that traders should use fundamental analysis to determine if their basic position should be long or short, and technical analysis to determine when to take those positions.

That is, if November soybeans are trading at $6 per bushel in March, technical analysis has nothing to offer concerning whether they might reach $9 per bushel by November. Whether soybeans get to $9 or not depends on supply and demand conditions and the information released between March and November. The level prices reach several months in the future is determined by economic fundamentals relating to the underlying cash commodity, and not to particular price patterns. Remember, futures contracts are economically viable contracts reflecting some cash commodity or instrument, and these contracts are substitutable for the cash commodity during the delivery period. In the long-run, fundamentals dictate price levels.

The pattern those prices might take in going from $6 to $9, however, could be heavily influenced by technical traders. Following the technical signals could be very important in deciding exactly when to enter or leave the market. Fundamental analysis may be right in the long run, but prices may move in the opposite direction in the short run. Many traders postpone taking market positions until the signals from both technical and fundamental analysis are the same.

Finally, technical analysis works best when prices are characterized by systematic components, patterns, or trends.[14] If prices move randomly, components or trends are much more difficult to identify. As we discuss in chapter 6, prices in an efficient market may resemble a random walk which implies the best forecast for tomorrow's price is today's price. However, even prices following a random walk can have trends and some technical analysis scheme can possibly be profitable.[15] That is, due to the large number of markets, contracts and decision rules, chance alone indicates that some schemes will be successful even when prices are random, but there is no guarantee that the scheme will continue to work in the future. The chances of identifying profitable schemes increase if the prices contain systematic components.

Fundamental forecasts are not perfect either. They usually perform poorly in forecasting aberrations from the data set. Also, they are heavily dependent on the timely release of accurate information about variables that influence prices. Nevertheless, fundamental forecasts are based on established theoretical economic relationships; and often one can make probabilistic statements about their accuracy. In the end, most successful traders probably rely on both fundamental and technical analysis for most trading decisions; fundamental to identify long-run changes resulting from changing economic conditions and technical to identify short-run patterns and movements in prices.

NOTES

1. R.W. Gray, "Price Effects of a Lack of Speculation," *Food Research Institute Studies*, supplement to 7 (1967): 177–94.
2. Hieronymus, *Economics of Futures Trading*, 107.
3. Ibid., 150.
4. Ibid., 328–29.
5. H. Working, "Speculation on Hedging Markets," *Food Research Institute Studies* 1 (1960): 187. This definition is slightly reworded from the original version in H. Working. "Hedging Reconsidered," *Journal of Farm Economics* 35 (1953): 560.
6. These specific hedges are defined in chapter 8.
7. J.M. Keynes, *A Treatise on Money*, vol 2. (New York: Harcourt Brace Jovanovich, 1930).
8. J.R. Hicks, *Value and Capital*, 2d ed. (London: Oxford University Press, 1946).

9. Working, "Speculation on Hedging Markets."
10. L.L. Johnson, "The Theory of Hedging and Speculation in Commodity Futures," *Review of Economic Studies* 27 (1960): 139–51.
11. J.L. Stein, "The Simultaneous Determination of Spot and Futures Prices," *American Economic Review* 51 (1961): 1012–25.
12. An excellent review of the development and modification of the concept of hedging over the years along with an evolutionary listing of hedger motivation is provided in: R.W. Gray and D.J.S. Rutledge, "The Economics of Commodity Futures Markets: A Survey," *Review of Marketing and Agricultural Economics* 39 (1971): 57–108.
13. For more on money management with futures market trading, see R.J. Teweles, C.V. Harlow, and H.L. Stone, *The Commodity Futures Game.* Chapter 10.
14. Empirical tests seem to confirm this as simulation tests of technical rules generate profits over certain sets of data. See: S.H. Irwin and J.W. Uhrig, "Do Technical Analysts Have Holes in Their Shoes?" *Review of Research in Futures Markets* 3 (1984): 264–77; and S.N. Neftci and A.J. Policano, "Can Chartists Outperform the Market? Market Efficiency Tests for 'Technical Analysis'," *Journal of Futures Markets* 4 (1984): 465–78.
15. W.G. Tomek and S.F. Querin, "Random Processes in Prices and 'Technical Analysis'," *Journal of Futures Markets* 4 (1984): 15–23.

INDIVIDUAL TRADING BEHAVIOR

5

Individuals trade for their own or for their business interests. They trade in various markets; each trader has specific objectives and constraints, a different level of expertise, and an individual attitude toward risk. Nevertheless, in the end we presume that they behave rationally with respect to the mix among expected return on investment, risk, and capital growth.

In a certain world, one with full information and no risk on outcomes, everybody would use markets once to trade excess capacities against necessary goods and services. Prices would be fixed for each product and each future time period. Indifference curves in microeconomic theory would then be used to choose, in a multiperiod program, returns, and growth paths. Such a simple model is not compatible with the real world characterized by uncertainty and a limited number of markets.

Traders are using more and more sophisticated marketing tools and techniques to adjust their financial and commercial positions to the risky perspectives of world markets. Lack of perfect markets creates the need for futures markets.

This chapter analyzes ways to describe consistent use of the futures market by firm managers and traders, with or without a cash position in the related commodities or instruments. To begin, we review the concept of risk management through diversification. Following that, we develop a model of individual optimization using two markets, cash and futures. We then extend this basic model to several markets and the whole class of traders, speculators and hedgers.

INVESTOR DECISION MAKING

Most market participants are investors. They assume buying or selling commitments to receive a return from their investment. Under conditions of certainty, rational investors choose assets with the highest returns. However, in the real world where investors make decisions under uncertainty, they must consider alternative rules of rational choice.

Any investment decision or market commitment implies a forecast of future events which brings probabilities of occurrence of different states of the world with their consequences. The expected return and related risk of operational activities—such as producing a commodity, dealing in financial instruments, or purchasing raw materials—assuming optimal firm size, may not be consistent with the preference goals and the objectives of the investor as a decision maker. Thus, investors need to manage their individual activity as well as the marketing positions of the firm with respect to alternative markets and opportunities. The investor manages this problem through a risk-return balance among alternatives by using a risk-shifting approach, such as an insurance policy, or a risk-spreading approach based on the diversification principle. Both are a means of risk management, and they are a normal use of markets.

UTILITY ANALYSIS

To solve a decision problem, such as optimal market commitments, traders must know the market opportunities and their own preference functions. The problem is to develop an explicit and rational method for decision making in uncertain situations where the decisions reflect individual objectives, preferences, and instantaneous information review. That is the domain of utility analysis.

Utility functions can characterize individual preferences toward risk. The origins of utility and concepts of expected utility date back to Bernoulli's analysis of the St. Petersburg Paradox. Suppose one asks a gambler how much he or she is willing to pay for an opportunity to play a game in which a coin is tossed until it comes up heads. If it is heads on the first toss, the player receives two ducats; tails means a new toss. On the second toss, the player receives $2^2 = 4$ ducats for a head;

tails means a new play, and so on. With the probability of a head on the first toss being 1/2, on the second toss 1/4, and so on, the expected value of this game is 1/2 (2 ducats) + 1/4 (4 ducats) + 1/8 (8 ducats) = 1 + 1 + 1 + ... A gambler should be willing to pay an infinite amount for the opportunity to play this game, but that is unlikely since most people are risk averse. The paradox is that people reject fair gambles.

John von Neumann and Oskar Morgenstern provided a solution to this paradox by proposing a system for numerically calculating an individual's utility function.[1] Their contribution led to the theory of rational decision making under uncertainty. Constrained by the limits of the axioms of rationality (e.g., transitivity, continuity, and independence) we assume that a utility function exists for an individual, and that a rational decision maker can maximize expected utility. Thus, in economic analysis we assume that the individual chooses that course of action maximizing expected utility.

It is often convenient to have utility functions expressed in polynomial or exponential form. The essential aspect is to obtain an estimate that is subjectively judged to fit the elicited utility point satisfactorily over the relevant range of gains and losses. A variety of different functional forms may be suitable to fit the elicited individual utility function. For empirical purposes we keep the number of distributional moments low. Usually, mean and variance are all that a decision maker considers. In this case, we limit utility surfaces to three dimensions, level of utility (U), mean or expected utility ($E(X)$), and variance of utility ($V(X)$). For a constant value of U, the function can be represented by a series of indifference curves, or iso-utility curves, in mean-variance (E-V) space.

Figure 5–1 shows two indifference maps of utility functions. Every point on an indifference curve is equally satisfying to the decision maker. The iso-utility curve intersects the $E(X)$ axis when $V(X) = 0$, or the expected mean utility is known with certainty. Indifference curves are drawn so that $U_4 > U_3 > U_2 > U_1$.

The slope of the iso-utility curve indicates the decision maker's tradeoff, or substitution rate, between mean and variance. Panel A shows the situation for a risk averter where the curves have an increasing slope as V increases. Panel B demonstrates a risk seeker where the indifference curves have negative slopes as V increases. The steeper the slopes, the greater is the degree of risk aversion or preference.

PORTFOLIO ANALYSIS

Investment activity affects utility through its effects on wealth. The rate of return on investment is a measure of the rate at which wealth accumulates, thus the utility gained from an investment is a function of the rate of return.

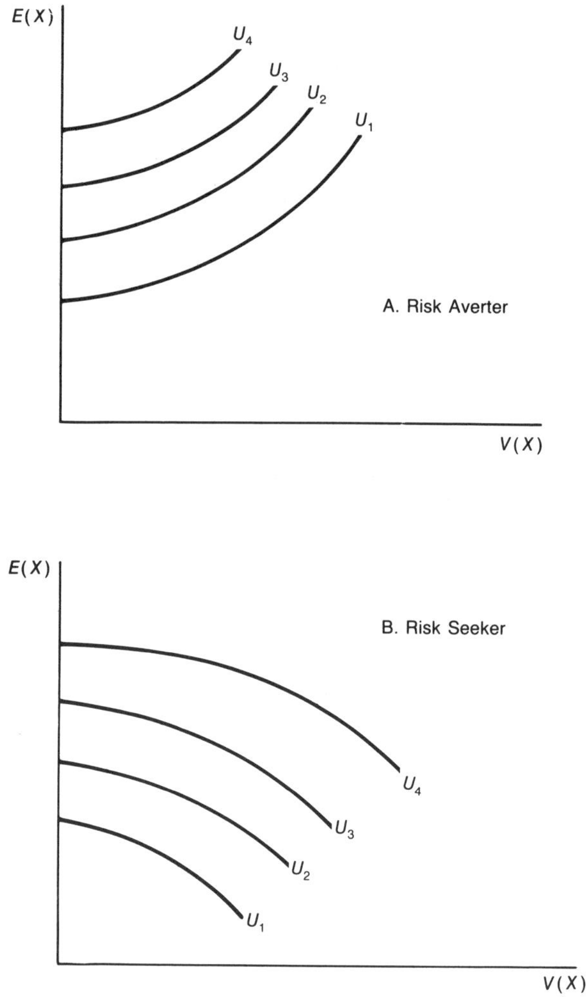

Figure 5-1. Utility Difference Maps in Mean-Variance (E, V) Space

If the world were certain and all outcomes known in advance, persons maximizing utility would simply invest their wealth in that asset with the highest rate of return. However, the world is uncertain, so decision makers can act only to maximize expected utility adjusted by preferences for risk. The investor allocates financial resources into some combination of risky alternatives from among the set of all available assets exchanged in markets. In searching for an optimal position, one must adapt for constraints on fixed initial investments.

The appropriate combination of risky assets constitutes the field of portfolio analysis. Each asset i has a probability distribution of returns, $E(\tilde{R}_i)$, represented by the mathematical expectation of various possible rates of return. It can be defined as:

$$E(\tilde{R}_i) = \sum_j P_{ij} R_{ij}$$

where P_j is the probability of the jth rate of return, R_j, and "$\tilde{}$" means it is a random variable.

The probability distribution of these returns represents the investor's chances of gains and losses, or risk. The dispersion measure commonly used to measure this risk is the variance of returns. Variance has some convenient properties, and regardless of the investor's utility function, if returns are normally distributed the mean and variance contain all the relevant information about the distribution. The formula for the variance of the probability distribution of returns for the ith asset is

$$\sigma_i^2 = \sum_j P_{ij}(R_{ij} - \bar{R}_{ij})^2$$

where $\bar{R}_{ij}$ presents the mean returns for asset i. It is these two measures which are of interest in portfolio analysis.[2]

THE DIVERSIFICATION PRINCIPLE

A portfolio is a combination or group of assets. Portfolio theory, developed by Harry Markowitz, is concerned with the selection and combination of individual investments so, for some level of risk aversion, when taken as a group they maximize return subject to some level of total risk.[3] Conversely, that same group also minimizes total risk subject to some level of total return.

For any set of investments, varying the percentage of each individual investment in the portfolio from 0 to 100 percent results in an infinite number of possible portfolios. These portfolios can then be ranked by their portfolio returns (means) and risks (variances); for each level of risk, the portfolio with the highest return dominates all others in that risk class. Likewise, for each level of return the portfolio with the lowest risk dominates all others in that return class. The locus of points formed by these dominant portfolios traces out a curve known as the efficient (E-V) frontier. The portfolios lying on the efficient frontier are desirable portfolios, and they dominate portfolios lying below the curve. Figure 5–2 shows this efficient frontier; it is curved due to the covariance effect among the multiple assets.

Portfolio analysis is a mathematical procedure used to determine the set of risk efficient portfolios of assets on the E-V frontier. Markowitz's concept of portfolio analysis involved the principle of diversification which is the combining of invest-

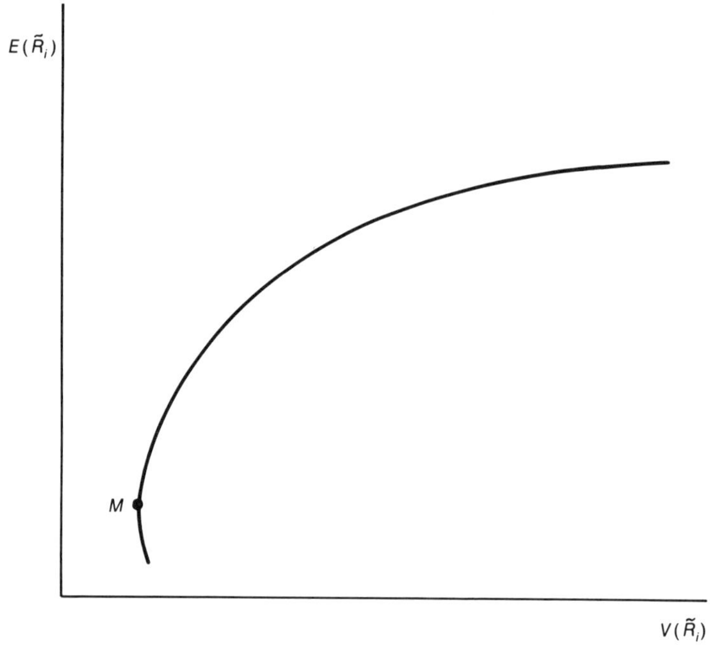

Figure 5-2. Efficient E-V Frontier

ments with less than perfect positive correlation to reduce risk in the portfolio without sacrificing any of the portfolio's return. In general, the higher or lower the correlation of assets in a portfolio, the more or less risky the portfolio.

Consider a two-asset portfolio as an illustration of the diversification principle. Let A and B be two risky assets with expected returns of $E(\tilde{R}_A)$ and $E(\tilde{R}_B)$ and standard deviations σ_A and σ_B, respectively.[4] The covariance of expected returns is designated as σ_{AB}. By definition the correlation, r_{AB}, between the two assets is:

$$r_{AB} = \frac{\sigma_{AB}}{\sigma_A \sigma_B}.$$

We assume the investor is fully invested, so the fraction invested in A plus the fraction in B is one. That is,

$$X_A + X_B = 1$$

where X represents the proportion invested in an asset. This can be rewritten as:

$$X_B = 1 - X_A.$$

Thus, the expected return of this portfolio, $E(\tilde{R}_P)$, is:

$$E(\tilde{R}_P) = X_A E(\tilde{R}_A) + (1 - X_A)\, E(\tilde{R}_B).$$

The expected return of a portfolio is a simple-weighted average of the expected returns of the individual securities, and the weights add to one.

The standard deviation or risk of the return on this portfolio can be written as:[5]

$$\sigma_p = [X_A^2 \sigma_A^2 + (1 - X_A)^2 \sigma_B^2 + 2X_A(1 - X_A)\sigma_{AB}]^{1/2}$$

or alternatively with the correlation coefficient as

$$\sigma_p = [X_A^2 \sigma_A^2 + (1 - X_A)^2 \sigma_B^2 + 2X_A(1 - X_A) r_{AB} \sigma_A \sigma_B]^{1/2}.$$

The expected return is a linear function of X, but the standard deviation is more complex.

PERFECT POSITIVE CORRELATION. Various extreme cases are of interest. Let $r_{AB} = +1$, or perfect positive correlation. In the context of futures markets, this approximates the situation where cash and futures prices move parallel. The preceding standard deviation can be written as:

$$\sigma_p = X_A \sigma_A + (1 - X_A)\sigma_B$$

or a linear function of X. That is, both risk and return of the portfolio are simple linear combinations of the risk and return of each asset. Thus, all combinations of these two perfectly correlated assets lie on a straight line in risk and return space. This line is represented as AC in figure 5–3. There is no reduction in risk from purchasing both assets. Nothing is gained by diversifying as opposed to purchasing individual assets.

Consider the example where two assets have the following characteristics:

	Percentage	
	Expected Return	Standard Deviation
Asset A	20	9
Asset B	14	3

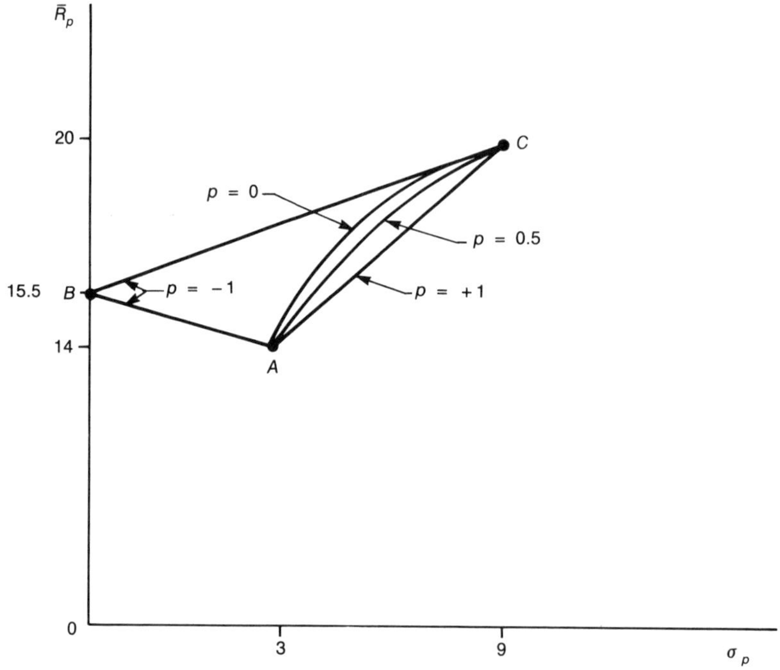

Adapted from Edwin J. Elton and Martin J. Gruber. *Modern Portfolio Theory and Investment Analysis*, 2d ed. New York: John Wiley & Sons, 1984, p. 53.

Figure 5-3. Relationship between Expected Returns and Their Standard Deviation for Various Correlation Coefficients, Showing the Effects of Diversification

The expected return and standard deviation of the portfolio are, when $r_{AB} = 1$:

$$E(\tilde{R}_P) = 20X_A + 14(1 - X_A) = 14 + 6X_A \tag{5-1}$$

$$\sigma_p = 9X_A + 3(1 - X_A) = 3 + 6X_A. \tag{5-2}$$

Taking equation 5-2 and solving for X_A yields

$$X_A = 1/6\sigma_p - 1/2. \tag{5-3}$$

Substituting expression 5-3 into equation 5-1 yields

$$E(\tilde{R}_p) = 14 + 6(1/6\sigma_p - 1/2) = 11 + \sigma_p.$$

The expected return is a linear function of the standard deviation. The portfolio return and standard deviation (risk) for selected values of X_A shown in table 5-1 correspond to the *AC* line segment in figure 5-3. Risks are not reduced through diversification in this case.[6]

Table 5-1. Portfolio Returns and Standard Deviation when $r_{AB} = +1$

X_A	0	0.2	0.4	0.6	0.8	1.0
$E(\tilde{R}_p)$	14	15.2	16.4	17.6	18.8	20
σ_p	3	4.2	5.4	6.6	7.8	9

PERFECT NEGATIVE CORRELATION. When $r_{AB} = -1$, there is perfect negative correlation. This approaches the situation where the trader is long in the cash market and short in the futures market and the two prices move very close together. The expected return expression is the same as for the case just presented, but now the variance of the portfolio is:

$$\sigma_p^2 = (X_A\sigma_A - (1 - X_A)\sigma_B)^2.$$

The standard deviation can be either:

$$\sigma_p = X_A\sigma_A - (1 - X_A)\sigma_B \tag{5-4}$$

or

$$\sigma_p = -X_A\sigma_A + (1 - X_A)\sigma_B. \tag{5-5}$$

Either outcome is valid. σ_p is a broken linear function in X, and we are interested in only those cases when $\sigma_p \geq 0$. This function is represented by ABC in figure 5-3, with the minimum variance at B, the combination point of zero risk. Segment AB becomes irrelevant because it is dominated by segment BC.

Considering the above numerical example, table 5-2 presents the portfolio of expected returns and standard deviation. Solving either equation 5-4 or 5-5, the minimum risk occurs when $\sigma_p = 0$, or $12X_A = 3$, $X_A = 1/4$. That is, there is a combination of these risky assets, or a portfolio, with zero risk.[7]

For any combination of the two risky assets in this latter case, except at the very extremes, the risk is less than in the case where $r_{AB} = +1$. That is, it is possible for the combination of two assets to have less risk than either individual asset. Or, the

Table 5-2. Portfolio Returns and Standard Deviation when $r_{AB} = -1$

X_A	0	0.2	0.25	0.4	0.6	0.8	1.0
$E(\tilde{R}_p)$	14	15.2	15.5	16.4	17.6	18.8	20
σ_p	3	0.6	0.0	1.8	4.2	6.6	9

risk of a portfolio is always smaller when the correlation coefficient between assets is -1 compared with $+1$. Diversification demonstrates the ability to combine assets to reduce risks.

Figure 5-3 also shows results for other cases, namely when $r_{AB} = 0$ and $r_{AB} = 0.5$. Numerical examples for these can be found in Edwin Elton and Martin Gruber.[8] These cases are more complex as the relationship between expected return and standard deviation is no longer linear. These intermediate situations, however, along with generalizing the portfolio to multiple assets with various correlation coefficients, generate the efficient frontier seen in figure 5-2.

That is, portfolio theory extends this two-case example to state that the addition of a risky asset to a portfolio may decrease its risk, so the relevant risk of an asset is not absolute individual risk as reported in σ_i^2, but its marginal risk, σ_{ip}, which is the covariance between the asset and the portfolio. This marginal risk may be positive, null, or negative. Portfolio theory is based on the principle of diversification that combinations of risky assets may be less risky than the weighted average of the risks on individual investments. In general, the greater the departure of the correlation of returns in the portfolio from the value of one, the less risky the portfolio is. The well-diversified portfolio defines that efficient frontier.

This model can also be extended to include lending and borrowing so the investor can buy or sell assets in quantity greater than that allowed by the initial endowment. Still, the efficient frontier is concave as shown in figure 5-2, bounded by a minimum variance portfolio (point M), but with no upper limit bound. This corresponds to the investment opportunities in cash and futures markets as we explain later in this chapter. A point in the lower-left corner of figure 5-2 indicates a minimum variance hedge, and portfolios in the upper-right part of the curve signal more speculation than hedging.

OPTIMAL PORTFOLIO

The question facing the individual decision maker is which portfolio to accept. The efficient frontier in figure 5-2 represents the opportunity set of well-diversified portfolios. Those portfolios on the curve are efficient because the variance of these combinations of assets is minimum for each level of expected return, or conversely, the expected return is maximum for each level of variance. Points on the E-V frontier dominate those points below it, and no point above the frontier is attainable given the constraints of the available assets and their characteristics.

The optimal portfolio of assets to the individual is that member of the set yielding the highest utility. Figure 5-4 combines the information diagrammed in figures 5-1 and 5-2 and demonstrates the optimal portfolio selection for two risk-averse inves-

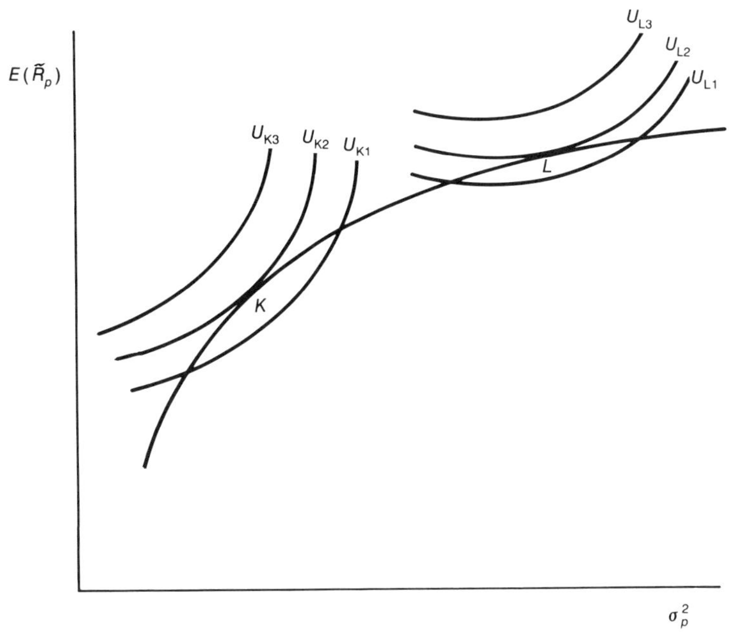

Figure 5-4. Optimal Portfolio Selection by Investors K and L

tors, K and L. The tangency points K and L demonstrate the highest achievable levels of utility. This analysis assumes, as we argued previously, that investors can base their decisions on the first two statistical moments of a probability distribution, expected return ($E(\tilde{R}_p)$) and variance (σ_p^2). The utility curve maps all combinations of returns and variances of the portfolio which yield the same expected utility with $U_3 > U_2 > U_1$.

The two investors, K and L, have different attitudes toward risk. In each case they want to find that set of investment proportions, X_i, that maximizes their utility function. Investor K is more risk averse than investor L; investor L is willing to take on greater risk for the possibility of greater return.

The previous discussion of utility functions, risk preferences, and portfolios expressed in means and variances is now combined. The investor wants to find that portfolio of assets that maximizes the utility function.

Using a quadratic utility function, or negative exponential utility function and assuming a normal distribution of returns, the maximization of expected utility is equivalent to the maximization of expected returns adjusted for risks (i.e., relying on just the first two moments of the distribution), or:[9]

$$\text{Max } E(U) = E(\tilde{R}_p) - \lambda/2 \text{ Var}(\tilde{R}_p).$$

Mathematically, this can be expressed in terms of the familiar portfolio problem as:

$$\text{Max } E(U) = Max \sum_i X_i R_i - \lambda/2 \sum_i \sum_j X_i X_j \sigma_{ij} \tag{5-6}$$

where R_i is the mean of returns on the ith asset;

X_i is the proportion of the portfolio invested in i such that $\Sigma X_i = 1$;

σ_{ij} is the variance of returns on the ith investment, $i = j$, or covariance of returns on the ith and jth investments, $i \neq j$;

λ is the risk aversion parameter, $0 \leq \lambda < \infty$.

This expression indicates that the investor maximizes returns subject to some level of risks. An equivalent expression is to minimize the risk given a certain level of returns. Lambda (λ) indicates the investor's degree of relative risk aversion, or the trade-off for the individual between returns and risks. Each point on the efficient frontier in figure 5-4 would reflect an alternative λ. As λ approaches zero, the investor is less risk averse.

Hence, every combination of risky assets has a corresponding risk and return. Those on the efficient frontier are the most efficient portfolios. Given some value for the risk aversion coefficient, it is possible to find that portfolio on the frontier which maximizes the hypothesized quadratic or exponential utility function.

OPTIMIZATION PROCEDURE WITHIN A PORTFOLIO MODEL

SIMPLIFIED CASE

Consider the case of a firm manager with a cash position in a physical market. This position can be either long or short. The position is risky due to price fluctuations. The manager needs a return on the cash position to cover variable costs as well as the fixed investment in facilities. It is unlikely that the position in the physical market will lead to an optimal expected return with respect to the risk involved. In general, the return is low in a competitive market and risks measured with volatility statistics such as variances, are often high.

To adjust the investments or commitments into an optimal portfolio given market knowledge and preferences, the manager may use the futures market as one of several alternatives. Using the futures market in this fashion is optimal hedging. Optimal hedging is that level of the futures position relative to the cash position resulting in the highest utility relative to returns and risk for a particular individual.

The expected portfolio return of a twofold position in cash and futures markets is:

$$E(\tilde{R}_p) = X_s E(\tilde{R}_s) + X_f E(\tilde{R}_f)$$

where X_s is the amount of the cash position;

X_f is the amount of the futures position;

$E(\tilde{R}_s)$ is the expected return on the cash position, or $E(\tilde{S}_1) - S_0$;

$E(\tilde{R}_f)$ is the expected return of the futures position, or $E(\tilde{F}_1) - F_0$;

and the risk of holding these units can be expressed as the variance of returns:

$$V(\tilde{R}_P) = X_s^2 \sigma_s^2 + X_f^2 \sigma_f^2 + 2X_s X_f \sigma_{sf} \tag{5-7}$$

where σ_s^2 is the variance of the cash returns (price change);

σ_f^2 is the variance of the futures returns (price change);

σ_{sf} is the covariance of the changes in futures and cash prices (returns).

As explained above, maximizing utility is equivalent to maximizing the expression:

$$E(\tilde{R}_p) - \lambda/2 \ \mathrm{Var}(\tilde{R}_p)$$

which in a two-asset framework can be written as:

$$X_s E(\tilde{R}_s) + X_f E(\tilde{R}_f) - \lambda/2(X_s^2 \sigma_s^2 + X_f^2 \sigma_f^2 + 2X_s X_f \sigma_{sf}). \tag{5-8}$$

Normally, we assume the cash position is given and the investor must then determine the optimal size of the futures position, X_f. Traditional literature cited in chapter 4 assumes that the cash and futures positions are equal in size, but opposite in the market. Equal positions in the two markets are appropriate when the cash and futures prices are perfectly positively correlated, or their variances equal, but that is usually not the case due to carry charges and basis risks.

When the cash position X_s is given, the optimal futures position, X_f^*, can be expressed as (see the appendix for a derivation):

$$X_f^* = \frac{E(\tilde{F}_1) - F_0}{\lambda \sigma_f^2} - X_s \frac{\sigma_{sf}}{\sigma_f^2}. \tag{5-9}$$

This expression is the sum of two components.[10] The first,

$$H_1 = \frac{E(\tilde{F}_1) - F_0}{\lambda \sigma_f^2}$$

is known as the speculative component. The second,

$$H_2 = -X_s \frac{\sigma_{sf}}{\sigma_f^2} = -X_s r \frac{\sigma_s}{\sigma_f}$$

is the pure hedging or hedge ratio component where r denotes the correlation coefficient between cash and futures prices. We discuss each of these in turn.

HEDGE RATIO COMPONENT. The pure hedging component H_2 can be expressed in absolute or relative forms. The former accounts for the actual size of the cash position and indicates a quantity to hedge. The relative form assumes the cash position is equal to the unit value of 1, and the hedge position becomes some proportion of the cash position.

Fluctuations between cash and futures prices are usually positively correlated ($r > 0$), so $-r\, \sigma_s/\sigma_f$ is negative. Thus, the hedging component of the optimal hedged position consists of taking an opposite position in the futures market as opposed to the existing cash position.

This hedging component corresponds to the minimum of risk for the portfolio, independently of the expected return. The variance of the portfolio is expressed in equation 5–7. Utilizing the calculus in the appendix, the minimum risk hedge ratio can be expressed as:

$$X_f^* = -X_s \frac{\sigma_{sf}}{\sigma_f^2}.$$

For relative terms, set $X_s = 1$ and let $b = -X_f/X_s$, then b^*, the minimum risk hedge ratio, can be expressed as:

$$b^* = \sigma_{sf}/\sigma_f^2. \tag{5–10}$$

Since in a regression context the coefficient $\beta = \sigma_{sf}/\sigma_f^2$, the value for this hedge ratio can be estimated from the following regression:

$$\Delta S_t = \alpha + \beta \, \Delta F_t \tag{5–11}$$

where S represents spot prices;

F represents futures prices;

α, β are parameters to be estimated;

Δ represents the change (first difference) in prices.[11]

That is, the coefficient from regressing the change in spot prices on the change in futures prices gives the pure hedging component that minimizes the portfolio risk. The more highly correlated the two prices, the nearer the ratio is to 1—the notion of a 100 percent hedge. This risk minimization ratio is usually less than one, but can be greater. Typically cash and futures prices are imperfectly correlated due to basis changes resulting from location, quality, and timing differences.

The hedge ratio concept was developed by Johnson who applied modern portfolio theory to the hedging problem.[12] This approach, often used in the literature, represents the position for a risk averse hedger who wants only to minimize risk, ignoring expected returns and any trade-off between risk and return as noted by the risk aversion coefficient λ.[13] That is, the hedge ratio or pure hedging component, can be determined without reference to a utility function or trader risk preferences.[14] This hedge ratio corresponds to the minimum variance portfolio (point M) in figure 5-2.

Finally, the results of the preceding regression equation can also tell us how effective the hedge is. Since b^* does not necessarily equal 1, the risk reduction achieved from the portfolio model is not measured by comparing the variance of the change in the basis to the variance of the change in the cash price, the traditional approach. Instead, hedging effectiveness is measured by comparing the variance of return in an unhedged position to the variance of return from a hedged position. That is, the minimal obtainable risk is the variance of the portfolio when $b = b^*$. The measure of hedging effectiveness, E^*, is thus defined as the percentage reduction in variance,[15] or

$$E^* = \frac{\mathrm{Var}(S) - \mathrm{Var}(R^*)}{\mathrm{Var}(S)} = 1 - \frac{\mathrm{Var}(R^*)}{\mathrm{Var}(S)} \qquad (5\text{-}12)$$

where $\mathrm{Var}(R^*)$ is the variance of the minimum risk portfolio and $\mathrm{Var}(S)$ represents the variance associated with the unhedged position.

Again assuming $X_s = 1$, we can substitute equation 5-10 into equation 5-7, replace X_f with b, and obtain the following expression for the variance of the optimal portfolio:

$$\mathrm{Var}(R^*) = \sigma_s^2 - \frac{\sigma_{sf}^2}{\sigma_f^2}. \qquad (5\text{-}13)$$

Substituting equation 5–13 into equation 5–12 yields:

$$E^* = \frac{\sigma_{sf}^2}{\sigma_s^2 \sigma_f^2}.$$

This measure of hedging effectiveness is the same as the coefficient of determination, or R^2, from the regression expressed in equation 5–11. Thus, hedging effectiveness refers to the reduction in variance as a proportion of total variance that results from maintaining a hedged position rather than an unhedged position.

SPECULATIVE COMPONENT. The speculative component of the optimal hedge position H_1 contains two key terms, the expected futures price $E(\tilde{F}_1)$ and the risk aversion coefficient λ.

The speculative may be null in two circumstances: First, if the expected futures price $E(\tilde{F}_1)$ equals the current futures price F_0, then H_1 is null. Without a personal anticipation that the futures price will move away from the current price level, there is no speculative expected gain, so the speculative component is zero. Second, a trader with a high aversion to risk can strongly discount the expected gain from a speculative position on the futures market. As λ tends to infinity, H_1 tends to zero. When either of these two circumstances occurs, the optimal hedged position X_f^* is equal to the hedge ratio H_2, which reflects the minimum variance position of a risk-averse manager.

The absolute value of the speculative component is a positive function of the expected speculative gain on the futures market, $E(\tilde{F}_1) - F_0$, an inverse function of the futures price volatility, Var(F), and finally an inverse function of the risk aversion coefficient of the decision maker. The greater the expected speculative gain is, the greater the value of H_1. This counteracts the negative H_2, reducing the size of the short optimal hedge, as expected. However, increased futures price volatility reduces the chance of successful speculation. The higher are the random moves of the futures price, the lower are the chances to have a systematic good forecast. If the futures price is a pure expectation of what the futures cash price will be, the futures price should have no seasonal or systematic pattern. Then the variance of the futures price is a good proxy of the random price volatility. Higher variances lead to a smaller H_1.

Finally, the speculative component is inversely related to the manager's degree of risk aversion. That is, as λ increases, reflecting more risk aversion, H_1 decreases in absolute value. The speculative component decreases relative to the hedge component, putting more weight on H_2 for the risk averse hedger. Or, as risk aversion increases and since H_1 and H_2 are likely of opposite signs, the individual hedges more, or speculates less, relative to the cash position.

Alternatively, the smaller the risk aversion coefficient, the further out the investor moves on the efficient frontier (upper right portion) in figure 5-2 to find the optimal portfolio. The speculative component carries relatively more weight.

Thus, optimal hedge is the sum of the two components, H_1 and H_2. They may work in the same direction or in opposite directions. The following two examples illustrate the concept:

A trader with a long position in the cash market considers using the futures market to diversify the risk of the cash position. The pure hedging component which minimizes risk may indicate selling futures contracts equivalent to 85 percent of the cash position. H_2 is negative. Now, the price forecasting system may give a 95 percent chance of rising market prices; $E(\tilde{F}_1)$ is greater than F_0. Thus, the speculative component is positive and opposite in terms of sign to the pure hedging component. The sales on the futures market will be a losing position. Consequently, the speculative component H_1 reduces the short futures position and the optimal hedge could then be a 75 percent sale of the cash position in the futures market.

A trader with a short cash position at the present date wants to price forward the expected future purchase. The hedge ratio may indicate a 90 percent of the cash position purchase of futures contracts. H_2 is positive. Again, the trader may anticipate a price increase, $E(\tilde{F}_1)$ is greater than F_0. The speculative component is positive and of the same sign as the pure hedging component. Purchases on the futures market are a profitable position. Thus, the speculative component increases the size of the long futures position. The optimal hedge could then be a 110 percent purchase of the cash position in the futures market.

The optimal hedge position considers simultaneously the risk reduction effect and the expected return from the commitments in the cash and futures positions. Theoretically, it is possible for the futures position to be equal and opposite to the cash position as in the traditional hedge. Alternatively, the sum of H_1 and H_2 may be null, so the optimal hedging position is to take no position in the futures market. Doing nothing is sometimes the best position. Finally, it is plausible for futures positions to be on the same side of the market as the cash position. For instance, a cash producer may have a long position in the futures market, or a future cash buyer may have a short position in the futures market. This situation is commonly termed a "Texas hedge."

CROSS HEDGING

The preceding discussion implies that the cash position and futures market contract are for the same commodity or instrument, and the only differences are due to quality, location, and time. However, for many cash commodities and instruments managers have market positions and need to manage the risks, but lack a corresponding futures contract. Hence, to use the futures market these managers must cross hedge, or take a position in a related futures contract. For the hedge to be effective, the cash and futures price movements must be highly correlated.

The optimal hedge relationship is identical to that expressed in equation 5-9.[16] The effectiveness of this hedge is a direct function of the correlation, or covariance, between the cash and futures price series. The higher they are correlated, the more the cash price risk can be diversified through the futures market; that is, the higher the price correlation the more effective the hedge is.

GENERALIZED CASE

Some managers have multiple cash market positions that need to be hedged in multiple futures market contracts. The most straightforward way to handle this is to refer back to the familiar portfolio problem in equation 5-6 as

$$\text{Max } E(U) = \text{Max } \sum_i X_i R_i - \lambda/2 \sum_i \sum_j X_i X_j \sigma_{ij}$$

where i can range from 1 to n, R_i refers to the returns of each cash and futures position and X_i is the proportion of that position relative to the total portfolio. A key item in this relationship is σ_{ij}, the variance-covariance matrix. The variance (diagonal) terms ($i = j$) represent price risks. Certain covariance (off-diagonal) terms ($i \neq j$) terms represent basis risk when i and j refer to cash and futures contracts for the same commodity or instrument. These covariances are the relationships between the variation in returns of the two respective commodities or instruments and contracts. All remaining covariance terms represent variations in returns on all pairs of cash positions, all pairs of futures contracts, and all pairs of cash positions and noncorresponding futures contracts. For many firms with multiple cash position risks—such as soybean processors, cattle feeders, oil refiners, and financial institutions—many of these covariances are highly positive, thereby reducing the number of futures contracts needed for optimal hedging positions. That is, alternative cash positions themselves provide risk diversification. For other firms or countries, particularly those involved in international trade where there is commodity, financial, and exchange rate risk, a lesser number of covariance terms are likely to be positive, leading to more complex optimal hedging outcomes. Still, despite the complexities of multiple futures contracts, optimal hedges can be determined in part from a series of simple regressions as in equation 5-11. Multiple optimal hedges are also still composed of speculative and pure hedging components.[17] We review some empirical studies in this area in chapter 8.

OPTIMAL CASH POSITION

The previous optimal hedge development assumes a predetermined or fixed-cash position. From that, an optimal number of futures contracts can be determined. However, under certain conditions this predetermined cash position may be suboptimal. Ronald Anderson and Jean-Pierre Danthine allow for the possibility of jointly determining cash and futures positions with the incorporation of a production cost function.[18] This allows for the cash activities to be a consequence of the diversification principle.

Introducing the cost component into the portfolio model and doing the necessary calculus (partial derivative) with respect to the cash position X_s, the optimal cash position is expressed as:

$$E(\tilde{R}_s) - E(\tilde{R}_f) r \frac{\sigma_s}{\sigma_f} = c'(X_s) + \lambda X_s^* \sigma_s^2 (1 - r^2)$$

where $c'(X_s)$ is the marginal cost function and all other items are as previously defined. The left side of the equation reflects marginal returns of a diversified position with risk minimization. The firm's optimal cash position is when marginal revenue equals marginal cost corrected for a risk premium. The last term on the right side is the risk premium, a function of the degree of risk aversion, λ, size of cash position, X_s^*, variability of cash prices, σ_s^2, and the proportion of that variability which cannot be eliminated through optimal hedging $(1 - r^2)$. This latter item reflects basis risk.[19] If cash prices are highly variable, the risk of loss is more important, so the risk premium has a higher value. Also, the more risk averse a trader, the larger the risk premium. Without a futures market or opportunity for diversification, the risk premium is at a maximum. In this case, a large risk premium reduces cash market activities, production, and cash trading, all of which lead to decreased market efficiency.

The influence of the risk premium on the cash position can be illustrated using classical microeconomic theory. The risk premium may be either added to the marginal cost or deducted from the marginal revenue. As shown in figure 5-5, the risk premium shifts the marginal revenue curve from *MR* to *MR'* which reduces cash market production and prices. Thus, hedging and cross hedging through the futures market reduces risk and provides an incentive to develop cash activities.

This finding relates to other literature. First, the theory of storage, as modeled in chapter 3, is based on the familiar condition that marginal revenue equals marginal costs. The return from holding a storage position is equal to the net cost of storage, including a risk premium and convenience yield. However, the appraisal of the risk premium there is very subjective.

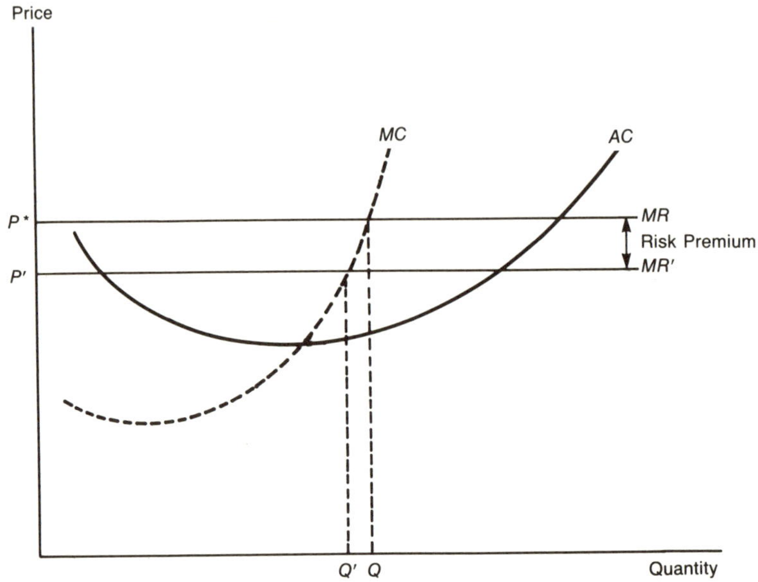

Figure 5–5. Effect of Risk on Production

Second, in very similar articles, Duncan Holthausen[20] and Gershon Feder, Richard Just, and Andrew Schmitz,[21] incorporate hedging decisions into the competitive theory of the firm under uncertainty. The producer maximizes an expected utility or profit function. The models show that the production decision by a risk-averse, competitive firm facing an uncertain price is independent of the subjective distribution of future spot prices and the firm's degree of risk aversion. Output positively relates to the prevailing futures price; production occurs where marginal cost equals the forward price. Holthausen shows that the existence of the futures market induces a firm to increase output relative to there not being a market.

OVERVIEW

Traders who use many markets may find several diversification possibilities. An example of multiple-risk optimal hedging could be a firm buying inputs and cross hedging them, financing these purchases with financial instruments that can be hedged, producing outputs and hedging them, and finally hedging the exchange rates in international trade. The optimal positions depend on the covariances between all sets of cash and futures prices as well as covariances with the original trader's financial portfolio. Using both commodity and financial futures markets at the same time allows firm managers to improve risk management procedures and to utilize more information for improving cash market decision making. This results in increased expected utility and an improved efficient frontier with additional diversification opportunities. Firm managers who hedge are managing a portfolio in much the same manner as speculators. Thus, there is no practical need to distinguish between speculators and hedgers.

APPENDIX: CALCULUS FORMULAS

OPTIMAL HEDGE FORMULA

The optimal hedge formula can be derived by taking the first derivative of the expected utility function with respect to X_f and setting that equal to zero. Restating equation 5–8:

$$\text{Max } E(U) = X_s E(\tilde{R}_s) + X_f E(\tilde{R}_f) - \lambda/2(X_s^2 \sigma_s^2 + X_f^2 \sigma_f^2 + 2X_f X_s \sigma_{sf}),$$

this can be rewritten as (assuming Max $E(U) \equiv$ Max Z):

$$\text{Max } Z = X_s(E(\tilde{S}_1) - S_0) + X_f(E(\tilde{F}_1) - F_0) - \lambda/2(X_s^2 \sigma_s^2 + X_f^2 \sigma_f^2 + 2X_f X_s \sigma_{sf}).$$

Taking the first derivative of this with respect to X_f yields:

$$\frac{\partial Z}{\partial X_f} = E(\tilde{F}_1) - F_0 - \lambda X_f \sigma_f^2 - \lambda X_s \sigma_{sf} = 0.$$

Rearranging the above expression yields:

$$X_f = \frac{E(\tilde{F}_1) - F_0}{\lambda \sigma_f^2} - X_s \frac{\sigma_{sf}}{\sigma_f^2}$$

which is the same as equation 5–9.

The second derivative with respect to X_f is $(-\lambda\sigma_f^2)$, which is negative and indicates that the optimum level is actually a maximum.

MINIMUM RISK FORMULA

With respect to finding minimum risk, equation 5–7 is:

$$\text{Var}(\tilde{R}_p) = X_s \sigma_s^2 + X_f^2 \sigma_f^2 + 2X_s X_f \sigma_{sf}.$$

Taking the derivation of equation 5–7 with respect to X_f and setting it equal to zero yields:

$$\frac{\partial \text{ Var}(\tilde{R}_p)}{\partial X_f} = 2 X_f \sigma_f^2 + 2 X_s \sigma_{sf} = 0.$$

Solving for the minimum risk hedge ratio X_f, yields

$$X_f = -X_s \frac{\sigma_{sf}}{\sigma_f^2}.$$

The second derivative, $2\sigma_f^2$, is positive. The optimum computed level is a minimum.

NOTES

1. J. von Neumann and O. Morgenstern, *Theory of Games and Economic Behavior* (Princeton, N.J.: Princeton University Press, 1944).
2. More detailed developments of these concepts can be found in J.C. Francis and S.H. Archer, *Portfolio Analysis* (Englewood Cliffs, N.J.: Prentice-Hall, 1971); and E.J. Elton and M.J. Gruber, *Modern Portfolio Theory and Investment Analysis*, 2d ed. (New York: John Wiley & Sons, 1984).
3. H. Markowitz, "Portfolio Selection," *Journal of Finance* 7 (1952): 77–91; H. Markowitz, *Portfolio Selection: Efficient Diversification of Investments* (New York: John Wiley & Sons, 1959).
4. See Elton and Gruber, *Modern Portfolio Theory*, for similar, but more detailed, development of these arguments.
5. Standard deviation is the square root of variance and can also be used as a proxy measure for risk, although these two measures are not interchangeable and have different implications.
6. This assumes that it is just possible to buy these two assets. In the case of futures markets where a trader buys an asset and sells a related contract, there is full diversification and total risk reduction if cash and futures prices move parallel (perfect positive correlation).
7. This numerical example does not reflect the case where cash and futures prices move very closely together. In that situation, returns and standard deviations between the two markets would be nearly identical, and risk would be minimized near where $X_A = 0.5$, the naive hedge.
8. Elton and Gruber, *Modern Portfolio Theory*, 51–54. These examples are indications of more realistic market positions. When correlation coefficients between prices are positive, the positions should be opposite; long asset A and short asset B. When correlation coefficients are negative, the positions should be the same sign, either positive or negative. Because cash and futures prices are positively correlated, traders in the search for diversification need to usually take opposite positions in the cash and the futures markets.
9. Francis and Archer, *Portfolio Analysis*.
10. This notion of two components was first introduced by: R.W. Anderson and J.P. Danthine, "Hedging and Joint Production: Theory and Illustrations," *Journal of Finance* 35 (1980): 487–98.
11. Using price differences is appropriate when there is no basis risk. For a discussion of the appropriate specification of this equation under alternative price expectation processes, see: G.E. Bond, S.R. Thompson, and B.M.S. Lee, "Application of a Simplified Hedging Rule," *Journal of Futures Markets* 7 (1987): 65–72.

12. L.L. Johnson, "Theory of Hedging and Speculation in Commodity Futures," *Review of Economic Studies* 27 (1960): 139–51. See also J.L. Stein, "Simultaneous Determination of Spot and Futures Prices," *American Economic Review* 51 (1961): 1012–25.
13. For the first empirical application, see: L. Ederington, "The Hedging Performance of the New Futures Markets," *Journal of Finance* 34 (1979): 157–70.
14. See K.M. Kahl. "Determination of the Recommended Hedging Ratio," *American Journal of Agricultural Economics* 65 (1983): 603–5 for a review of alternative approaches taken to determining the hedge ratio. Kahl points out that most of these approaches are essentially the same. Usually, risk aversion affects the optimal size of the cash and futures positions which may be determined simultaneously, but the optimal hedging ratio is independent of risk aversion. However, when one assumes the level of the cash commodity as given, as in the previous model, the risk aversion parameter may play a role in the determination of the optimal hedge through the speculative component as discussed in the following subsection.
15. Johnson, "Theory of Hedging."
16. Similar to equation 5 in R.W. Anderson and J.P. Danthine, "Cross Hedging," *Journal of Political Economy* 89 (1981): 1182–91.
17. G.F. Sarassoro and R.M. Leuthold, "Offshore Commodity Hedging under Floating Exchange Rates: Comment," *American Journal of Agricultural Economics* 70 (1988): 724–6.
18. Anderson and Danthine, "Hedging and Joint Production."
19. This whole expression is an expanded version of the equilibrium equation in chapter 3 with the inclusion of costs and an explicit risk premium.
20. D.M. Holthausen, "Hedging and the Competitive Firm under Price Uncertainty," *American Economic Review* 69 (1979): 989–95.
21. G.Feder, R.E. Just, and A. Schmitz, "Futures Markets and the Theory of the Firm under Price Uncertainty," *Quarterly Journal of Economics* 94 (1980): 317–28.

MARKET EQUILIBRIUM AND PERFORMANCE

6

Traders use the futures market for different motivations and through multiple practices. Heterogeneous cash market positions, varying initial wealth portfolios, heterogeneous anticipations, and risk-aversion attitudes are at the origin of alternative futures positions. The willingness to buy and sell futures contracts induces a volume of trading and a set of futures prices publicized throughout the world.

For many participants futures prices are unambiguous information. They are the indicator of what will be the spot price in the future. Using that information, producers, merchants, and users initiate specific programs of action. These actions have a feedback on the market evolution through information creation. Futures markets are places where traders exchange information on future states of nature.

Markets are price discovery systems, and if traders use the futures price as a source of information for resource allocation, the question of its quality and accuracy arises. Are futures markets rational and efficient? Do they reflect all available information? If the futures price is a forecast of a future spot price, is it accurate given the information available? Every day brings new information to the market making old prices look inaccurate, but the market may be responding rationally to the new information. This response is a test of market efficiency and performance. Futures market prices reflect a culmination of trader expectations about the future price, but maybe not each individual trader's expectation. Some argue that futures prices are biased due to a risk premium, called normal backwardation. Recently, the capital asset pricing model developed in finance theory has been a useful way to analyze risky assets, portfolios, and market performance.

In this chapter we emphasize price behavior, market equilibrium, and firm strategy. We begin by relating the futures market to the competitive model. This model serves as a norm for evaluating market performance. In a second part we discuss pricing efficiency and then broaden to the question of the risk premium in the third part. We describe in the fourth section the role of information in the functioning of markets along with assessing market performance. The final section discusses the effect futures markets have had on cash price behavior.

FUTURES MARKETS AS COMPETITIVE MARKETS

Futures markets are multiple auctions with both bids and offers available simultaneously. The prices adjust in accordance to demand and supply pressures, often resulting from new information. These demands and supplies and trader price commitments are for some future time period.

Competitive markets are characterized by four conditions: (a) atomicity of participants; (b) homogeneity of product; (c) free mobility of resources; and (d) perfect information. Futures markets come close to meeting these conditions. They provide a base for evaluating market efficiency.

ATOMICITY OF PARTICIPANTS

Atomicity implies so many buyers and sellers that the activity of any one participant is unnoticed or marginal within the whole set of transactions on the market. Market participants are price takers and consider prices as given.

In general, futures markets satisfy this condition, especially for the liquid, active contracts. The large number of floor traders and outside participants virtually assures that at a given price (bid-ask spread) there are always available buyers and sellers of futures contracts. Most market orders of modest size can be filled at little or no price concession.

The number of contracts traded in various markets range from under 100 contracts per hour for relatively inactive markets to over 50,000 contracts per hour for active markets. The more liquid and active the market, the more closely the atomicity condition is fulfilled. This atomistic atmosphere helps assure an efficient market not subject to manipulative pressures.

HOMOGENEITY OF PRODUCT

Homogeneity of product is necessary for a buyer to be indifferent about the supplier from which to buy. Homogeneous means that one product is identical to another. Traders can then buy and sell on a descriptive basis without visual inspection. This increases the geographic size of the market and the number of traders, which leads to greater atomicity. Homogeneity is necessary for the impersonal aspect of futures trading.

Homogeneity condition is well satisfied on the futures market as each contract is standardized except for maturity month and price. One contract for a commodity or instrument is identical to every other contract for that commodity or instrument.

FREE MOBILITY OF RESOURCES

A third condition for perfect competition is that all resources are perfectly mobile, meaning that resources can move in and out of markets readily in response to pecuniary signals. Free mobility of resources requires free exit and entry of firms or buyers and sellers, a condition very difficult to achieve.

Futures markets allow trading on the margin; this becomes the cost of entry. Initial margins seldom amount to more than 10 percent of the value of the contract. This means that the cost of entering the futures market is considerably less than acquiring the same physical commodity in the cash market. There are no barriers to exit, and transaction costs are relatively low. Hence, traders have considerable freedom of mobility in taking future market positions with only minimal capital requirements. Futures markets come closer to free exit and entry than most other markets and still maintain the integrity of their contracts, thereby nearly fulfilling this condition of perfect competition.

PERFECT INFORMATION

Traders must have perfect knowledge if a market is to be perfectly competitive. Perfect knowledge requires complex knowledge of the future as well as the present. This is a purely theoretical concept because perfect knowledge would eliminate the need for futures markets. However, traders develop expectations of future price levels. Futures market participants trade in response to probabilities attached to the occurrence of potential political and economic events around the world. Thus, futures prices represent a composite of the traders' interpretation of the information available and an aggregate weighting of the probability of future events.[1]

Because futures prices are the result of public and private processing of information by many traders, there is a tremendous demand for information about current and future economic activities. Considerable money is at stake and some traders are willing to pay substantial prices for information. Consequently, volumes of information are supplied, both publicly and privately. Private information systems and data vendors are available. In addition, considerable agricultural information about production, storage stocks, and consumption patterns is publicly available virtually free of charge. Much information is transmitted worldwide through modern, computerized communication networks. This deluge of information impacts on the markets and improves their efficient performance. The public nature of futures markets along with the large volumes of market information allow them to approach the theoretical state of perfect knowledge closer than any other market.

Thus, futures markets are a close approximation to the concept of perfectly competitive markets: There are many traders, trading homogeneous contracts with very low entry requirements in a market atmosphere containing voluminous information. All markets can demonstrate potential inefficiencies due to costs of entry, transaction, and gathering and processing of information, but these costs seem lower in futures markets than in most other markets. Thus, futures markets come closer to approximating perfectly competitive markets than any other, which should lead to highly efficient, forward-pricing markets.

FORWARD-PRICING EFFICIENCY

When looking at a cash-futures market environment, there exists at each time period t two prices, the spot price, S_t, and the futures price, $F_{t,T}$. The futures price quotes the spot product for delivery at future date T. Of course, there may exist many spot prices due to location or quality differences, but they are all linked through arbitrage transactions. Futures prices are quoted for several contract maturity months, simultaneously. However, for price efficiency analysis two quoted prices are sufficient, a reference spot price, S_t, and any futures price, $F_{t,T}$.

The analysis of price relationships between current spot, current futures, future spot, and future futures prices are the domain of research on pricing efficiency. Important concepts of market performance can be described using three approaches; first, forward-pricing efficiency; second, risk premium; and third, the efficient market hypothesis. In this section we discuss the first concept.

Forward-pricing efficiency refers to the ability of the futures market to forecast the future spot price at the maturity date. Because many agents use the futures price as a forecast or expectation of the subsequent spot price, there is concern about its accuracy.

Futures prices are not forecasts in the same sense as a weather forecast because traders can respond to them in a production sense, and traders can buy and sell at those prices. Futures prices are a market determined price, and they functionally relate to cash prices in the case of storable commodities and instruments. Futures prices may look like a forecast, but technically they are more—they reflect expectations, are determined in the marketplace, and represent instant interpretation of information. As guides for allocating inventory, futures prices as forecasts may be self-fulfilling, but in guiding long-run production they may be self-defeating.[2] Nevertheless, it is popular when assessing forward-pricing efficiency to refer to futures prices as forecasts, broadly interpreted.

The forward-pricing role of the futures markets relates to the theory of storage. The relationship between cash and futures prices guides the accumulation and decumulation of inventories. Adjustments in inventories, along with the purchase and sale of futures contracts, are associated with the cash-futures price difference.

Because of the functional relationship between cash and futures prices for storable commodities and instruments, both prices are equally valid expectations of the subsequent spot price because they reflect and contain the same information. The futures price is a premium or discount to the current spot price because of the estimated carrying charge. Spot and futures prices are rationally formed prices relating to specific delivery dates, and expectations are imparted to the whole temporal constellation of price quotations.

With the introduction of discontinuous inventory (e.g. potatoes) futures contracts and noninventory (e.g. livestock, short-term financial instruments) contracts, the forward-pricing function of the futures market took on added importance. For these items there is no inventory allocation role. However, through its discovery mechanism futures prices for nonstorables are a useful forecast or expectation of future spot prices.

A common model used to test forward-pricing ability is

$$S_T = \alpha + \beta F_{T-i} + e_T$$

where S_T is the spot price at delivery (or futures if no basis), F_{T-i} is the futures price i months before maturity, and e_T is a random error term. For an efficient, forward-pricing market we hypothesize that $\alpha = 0$ and $\beta = 1$ in an empirical test.[3] Acceptance of this hypothesis means the futures price is an unbiased predictor of the future spot price. The evidence with this model is mixed in tests on corn, soybeans, coffee, live cattle, live hogs, wool, and London metals, to mention a few. In reviewing these studies, Barry Goss indicates that discontinuous inventory and noninventory commodities often fail the hypothesis tests, meaning that futures prices are not unbiased predictors.[4] Continuous inventory commodities usually fail to reject the hypotheses. Goss mentions that the absence of inventories may bring gaps in the flow of information or increase errors in expectations because of the lack of close ties between spot and futures prices.[5]

The preceding model is not a rigorous test of forward-pricing efficiency because one does not know if the reported errors are due to a bias in the market or due to the receipt of new information. New information about demand and supply conditions can cause prices to change, and although the futures market may adjust rapidly and efficiently, the common model cannot incorporate such news. The model cannot measure the influence of new information on changes in prices, nor can it analyze trader behavior. We discuss these topics in the following sections on the risk premium and the efficient market hypothesis.

RISK PREMIUM

The concept of a risk premium in futures markets traditionally relates to the search for a biased futures price with respect to some expected future spot price. A bias is a systematic difference between two prices. The concept of a risk premium, or bias, in futures markets originally rose from the notion of a risk transfer from hedgers to speculators.

More recently, experts consider the futures market as a diversifying alternative, and risk is more than a result of price change; rather it is the contribution of the futures contract to a well-diversified portfolio. One examines risks by measuring how highly correlated the futures contracts are with other portfolio assets. This is a direct outcome of finance theory relating to optimal hedging discussed in chapter 5, and to the capital asset pricing model to be discussed momentarily. First, we examine the traditional notion.

ISOLATED MARKET

One standard of pricing efficiency has been that the futures price is an unbiased estimate of the unobservable expected spot price, or $E_t(S_T) = F_{t,T}$. If this condition does not hold, then there must be a bias in the movement of the futures price. For instance, imagine $E_t(S_T) = F_{t,T} + r$; that is, the expected spot price is a premium with respect to the futures price. If we expect $E_t(S_T)$ not to move without additional

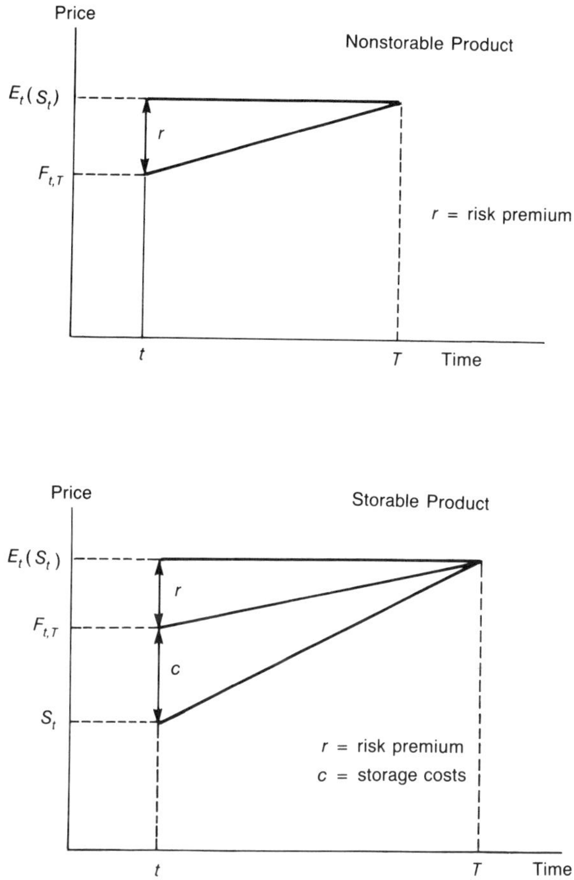

Figure 6-1. The Risk Premium as Described in the Normal Backwardation Theory

information, then $F_{t,T}$ has to increase by an increment equal to r to reach S_T at the maturity date. We call the quantity r, illustrated in figure 6-1, the market bias.

Keynes was the first to discuss risk premium in futures markets, and his concept became known as the theory of normal backwardation.[6] Hicks provided further elaboration.[7] Keynes and Hicks advocated that hedgers, primarily short in the futures market, pay a premium to speculators, primarily long in the market, for assuming the price risk. That is, holders of inventory, desiring to reduce the risk of loss occurring from adverse changes in price, pay a risk premium to speculators to absorb that risk. Also, speculators acting as insurers demand a risk premium as compensation for taking risks. The risk premium is paid through the market by the expected spot price exceeding the futures price by the premium. That is, futures prices are downward biased estimates of the expected spot price and have a tendency to rise as the contract approaches maturity. The market exhibits normal backwardation as futures prices rise. Thus, any speculator long in a futures contract can expect to receive payment for assuming the risk of price change transferred by the hedger. This particular hypothesis assumes, of course, that hedgers are consistently net short.

Working did not accept the notion of normal backwardation and offered an alternative hypothesis that hedgers do not seek to avoid risks, but they hedge because of the expected return arising from anticipated favorable changes in the spot-futures price relations.[8] As we discussed in chapter 4 hedging is a complex commercial commitment in cash and futures markets involving both risk reduction and expected profit. Working argued there are many reasons to hedge, including maximizing basis profits, and to hedge to curtail risks may be incidental to the other incentives for hedging.[9] We noted in chapter 5 how portfolio theory has reconciled these opposing views.

This concept of risk premium spawned many empirical studies that are of historical interest. Brennan found premium levels of 6.6 to 9.5 percent, measuring it as a residual after accounting for expected prices, storage costs, and convenience yield.[10] Lester Telser examined futures markets for cotton and wheat during the stable price years of 1926-1954 and found that futures price changes were not significantly positive. He concluded that futures prices do not exhibit upward trends and, therefore, are not downward biased estimates of expected spot prices.[11] This paper led to a famous exchange between Paul Cootner and Telser concerning the existence of a risk premium in futures markets.[12] Cootner argued there is a seasonal pattern to hedging and hence a risk premium follows the period of peak hedging. Telser modified his position somewhat, but they remained on opposite sides of the risk premium controversy.

Roger Gray refuted much of the previous analysis and tested for the premium directly by assuming a consistently long position in wheat and corn over several stable years.[13] He did not find any consistent profits and concluded futures markets do not possess a risk premium. Most subsequent studies using this approach failed to find normal backwardation or bias in futures markets. Elsewhere, Gray argued that the existence of any risk premium is most likely the result of imbalance among traders and the lack of liquidity in that market.[14]

Other authors have approached the question of risk premium to speculators by examining the actual flow of profits among large hedgers and speculators. Avraham Kamara reviews these and other studies and concludes that in general small speculators do not make substantial profits; in fact, any profits are more than offset by commissions paid.[15] Large speculator profits appear to result from superior forecasting skills. Thus, the notion of a risk premium based on the concept of normal backwardation is not well supported empirically. Kamara concluded from numerous studies that "while it is widely accepted that futures markets are used by risk-averse hedgers, the evidence suggests that they have been able to purchase the insurance very cheaply, so that on average futures prices do not contain a significant risk premium."

Most of these studies were conducted before the introduction of modern finance theory. We now examine how these concepts have altered the notion and search for a risk premium.

INTEGRATED MARKET

Rather than evaluating the price of a futures contract in relation to the spot price and return to storage, and measuring its riskiness through price fluctuations in isolated market situations, an alternative approach is to model the pricing of futures contracts in an equilibrium situation within a larger capital market framework. By broadening the number of financial instruments analyzed to include essentially the entire capital market, these models abstract from the characteristics peculiar to specific futures markets. Futures markets are subsumed under a more general market for financial assets.

This portfolio approach, as we discussed in chapter 5, can be of use to both hedgers and speculators. Both are managing portfolios of assets, and a futures contract can be evaluated by its contribution to a well-diversified portfolio. Speculators examine the characteristics of their investment portfolio and decide how to balance investments among futures contracts and other investment alternatives. Hedgers with actual or anticipatory cash positions use portfolio theory to suggest whether or not to hedge in the futures market, and subsequently, the size of the optimal hedge.

The model of interest here is the Capital Asset Price Model (CAPM), a well-developed model in the finance literature based on concepts similar to the portfolio framework. Katherine Dusak was the first to apply the standard Sharpe-Lintner CAPM to commodity futures markets and we pattern our approach after hers.[16]

The model says that, in equilibrium, the expected rate of return on any asset *i* will be equal to the riskless rate of interest plus a risk premium proportional to the contribution of the asset to the risk of the return on total wealth. An expression representing this is

$$E(\tilde{R}_i) - R_f = [E(\tilde{R}_w) - R_f]\beta_i$$

where $\tilde{R}_i$ is the random rate of return on asset i, R_f is the riskless rate of return, $\tilde{R}_w$ is the random rate of return on a portfolio containing all assets, and β_i is a regression coefficient equaling $Cov(\tilde{R}_i, \tilde{R}_w)/\sigma^2(\tilde{R}_w)$. β_i is the systematic risk, or the risk of asset *i* relative to that of total wealth. This model defines asset risk as the contribution the asset makes to the variability of return on the diversified portfolio. To estimate relative risk, the following linear regression model is often used:

$$\tilde{R}_i = \alpha_i + \beta_i \tilde{R}_w + \tilde{\epsilon}_i$$

where returns are measured by $(P_{t+1} - P_t)/P_t$, with P_t representing the price of the asset, or value of the portfolio, and β_i measuring the degree to which returns on the asset are systematically related to the nominal return on the market portfolio.

Substituting in relative price changes of a futures contract for R_i, the β, beta, which measures the systematic risk, or risk premium, of that contract relative to the portfolio, can be positive, negative, or equal to zero. A beta near one indicates adding that asset or contract to the portfolio does not diversify portfolio risk, while a small beta indicates unsystematic risk and the addition of that asset provides diversification. What is governing the riskiness of an asset is not merely its own variance as often used in isolated market analysis, but its weighted covariance with all other assets comprising total wealth. That is, this risk premium, if it exists, does not depend on a systematic difference between futures price, $F_{t,T}$, and expected spot price, $E_t(S_t)$. In fact, this risk premium is independent of the net long or short positions of hedgers and speculators if $E_t(S_t) = F_{t,T}$; that is, there is no bias in the market. In other words, risk premium may exist, but not necessarily as a systematic downward bias in the futures price. The cash position may be a very small part of the portfolio, having no influence on the covariance sign or sign of the beta, meaning the hedger may pay or receive this risk premium.

Dusak utilized the CAPM to empirically test for a risk premium with futures contracts for wheat, corn, and soybeans during 1952–1967. Measuring returns as percentage changes of futures prices, which assumes full value of the contract in the portfolio, and using Standard and Poor's Composite Index of 500 stocks as a measure of total wealth, she found that for routine long positions systematic risk and average realized returns were close to zero. This provides evidence against the Keynes-Hicks theory of normal backwardation. However, results from this model can be highly sensitive to the index of wealth selected to represent the portfolio.[17]

Dusak's paper became a standard in the literature to which others compare their results. Her model and results have stood the test of time well as most researchers probably doubt that a risk premium in the normal backwardation context exists in the futures market. Nevertheless, model variations and attempted improvements continue. Due to the mark-to-market provision, Fischer Black argued that futures markets should not have a risk premium nor be biased.[18] Because of the statistical properties of futures returns, E.C. Chang questions the reliability of CAPM-based tests.[19] Stoll modeled futures prices in a capital equilibrium framework that included stocks, bonds, and a futures market by hedgers only.[20] Douglas Breeden approached the pricing of commodity futures through a general equilibrium model, defining risk in terms of real consumption, and found significant betas.[21]

Each model imposes different apriori assumptions when estimating the risk premium; researchers debate their appropriateness. This debate continues with new theoretical models and alternative empirical results. New studies will increase our understanding of the market, but probably not change its operation. Nevertheless, the risk premium issue cannot be treated separately from the following topic, forward-pricing performance and the efficient market hypothesis.

PERFORMANCE OF FUTURES MARKETS

Futures markets are competitive markets. Many researchers have examined whether a systematic difference exists between the futures price and the expected subsequent spot price, but few studies empirically test the performance of futures markets against alternative market organizations. That is, even if some unexplained bias or inefficiency exists, is there a more efficient market alternative? Probably not, given the competitive organization of futures markets. Furthermore, forward-pricing efficiency is only one role of futures markets and its assessment is only one aspect of the performance of the markets. No researcher has tested the overall performance of futures markets, assessing simultaneously the efficiency of the market to transfer risks, forward price, transmit information, aid firms in obtaining capital, and allocate resources and inventory. Such an assessment would probably find futures markets are very effective. Nevertheless, in this section we concentrate on examining the abilities of traders to efficiently use new information to form accurate futures prices through trading activities, or the forward-pricing performance.

This latter criteria of market performance relates to the efficient market hypothesis. The combination of an efficient market where traders use all of the available information and the random generation of information implies that the difference between the futures price in t and the subsequent futures price in $t + 1$ is a random number reflecting the receipt of new information. This hypothesis, or model, might be tested with the random walk model, which is:

$$F_{t+1,T} - F_{t,T} = U_{t+1} \qquad (6\text{–}1)$$

where U_{t+1} is a random variable with zero mean in independent drawings.

Researchers often examine the random walk hypothesis with various tests on the first differences of prices. A more precise statement of the requirement for an efficient market is the Martingale hypothesis where the market takes all currently available information into account in establishing price. An expression for this hypothesis is $E(F_{t+i,T}|\Phi_t) = F_{t,T}$ where Φ is current information. This is termed a *fair game* in the sense of there being unbiased price changes. That is, knowledge of current and past price changes contains no information useful for predicting subsequent price changes. Successive price changes are independent and there is no way to use current information on past prices to earn a return above normal (expected returns can exceed zero). Futures prices are a fair game.

Both the random walk hypothesis and the Martingale hypothesis require expected price changes to be serially independent (i.e., no autocorrelation). However, the Martingale hypothesis does not require drawing successive price changes from the same distribution (i.e., identically distributed). That is, the price generating mechanism can have changing variances. Prices following a random walk satisfy the requirements for Martingale, but not vice versa. Most empirical studies test for a random walk when in fact the Martingale model is of interest. This may not always be a serious problem because studies usually test for serial independence which indicates that the expected price change is zero, or there is no bias.

It is possible that the Martingale model can be theoretically true even if cash prices exhibit regular patterns or trends.[22] Important is what happens to prices on the average. An implication of Martingale price movements is that mechanical trading rules advocated by technical analysts cannot be used to enhance profits. Tests of the random walk model or Martingale process are weak form tests, a subject discussed in the next section. We also mention several caveats needed when interpreting the results of these tests.

EFFICIENT MARKET HYPOTHESIS TESTS

Eugene Fama stated that an efficient market is one in which prices "fully reflect" available information.[23] He classified empirical tests of market efficiency as weak, semi-strong, and strong. Weak form tests examine whether current prices fully reflect the information contained in historical prices. The test usually reduces to a test of randomness as discussed earlier, examining for serial correlation to use in forecasts. This test determines if the market correctly uses past prices in forming expectations, and is thereby efficient. The semi-strong form test examines if prices reflect all publicly available information as released. This test usually relies on an econometric forecasting model. A strong form test examines if a private group in the market has monopolistic access to information used in the pricing process. That is, it is a test of whether all information, public and private, is fully reflected in current prices and if traders can make excess profit on the information. Because this has not been an important test in the empirical literature for futures markets, we do not discuss it further.

WEAK FORM EFFICIENCY. Weak form tests usually use equations similar to equation 6–1 as the underlying model. Randomness is often tested specifically, or some specific statistical characteristic or distribution moment is examined. Many tests deal with serial correlation because both the random walk model and Martingale process require uncorrelated price changes. The empirical evidence on the efficient market hypothesis for futures prices using weak form tests is very mixed.[24] The results depend heavily on the sample period, commodity tested, type of data, and technique used in the study.[25]

The random walk and Martingale models are restrictive tests of the weak form efficiency model and fair game because they imply returns are independent over time. Acceptance of the random walk or Martingale hypothesis means the weak form of the efficient market hypothesis must hold, but not vice versa. That is, failure of the Martingale is not evidence of market inefficiency. Market efficiency does not require random walk prices.[26]

Finding a bias in the data is not necessarily inconsistent with market efficiency. Unbiasedness is not a property required for prices to reflect fully all information. Biased prices may exist because of risk premium, costs of information, risk aversion, irrational participants, imperfect capital markets, and alternative transaction and information costs.[27] Thus, the test for efficiency is not necessarily that of a bias or not, but whether prices contain all information from some existing source.

Finally, the existence of nonrandom components does not necessarily mean there exists unexploited opportunities for above-normal profits. Even in a random series short-term trends and cycles may exist, but such price behavior may not cover transaction costs. Probability suggests that profitable technical trading rules and randomly generated prices can coexist for a short time, but such rules have no predictive power for continued success.[28]

SEMI-STRONG FORM EFFICIENCY. Despite the popularity of weak form tests for examining forward pricing efficiency, these tests lack robustness in reflecting all currently available public information. Weak form tests are based on the information contained in past prices. It is possible that new information could arise, causing markets to adjust rapidly, and the "forecast" error observed is entirely forgivable. Semi-strong form tests are a more powerful test of forward-pricing efficiency of markets.

An efficient market contains necessary inaccuracy, that is, price changes due to new information. This is a forgivable error. Any error beyond that, termed *speculative error*, can result from bad trader judgment or noncompetitive market environments. Price changes from these errors may be predictable. Unpredictable price changes imply an efficient market.

Empirical semi-strong form tests of market efficiency usually compare the forward-pricing accuracy of futures prices, acting as expected prices, to econometric price forecasting models using available public information. The latter is a norm to evaluate if the futures market reflects available information or if price changes can be predicted. The same information must be available to both the model and futures market at the same time. Of course, one cannot prove that markets are efficient by this method, only fail to disprove it.

Semi-strong form tests for market efficiency have been conducted on livestock futures markets,[29] Treasury bill forward markets,[30] London metal futures,[31] and soybeans,[32] to name a few, using alternative approaches. Usually by comparing mean squared forecasting errors of the estimated models to futures prices, these tests have found subperiods of time, or certain test procedures, that show the markets are not efficient in a semi-strong form sense. Yet, alternative time periods or tests procedures support the notion. Thus, results can be sensitive to the data and techniques of analysis. In comparing several futures contracts to commercial forecasting agencies, Richard Just and Gordon Rausser found forecast differences small, concluding that futures markets are relatively efficient.[33]

However, comparison of relative forecasting abilities using mean squared errors is only a necessary condition and not a sufficient condition. This test is not sufficient because it does not examine if risk-adjusted profits resulting from using the model exceed the cost of model construction and application. A model that outforecasts, or has a smaller mean squared error than the futures market is not sufficient to conclude that the futures market is inefficient.[34] The sufficient condition for semi-strong form efficiency is that an agent can use the forecasting model to earn risk-adjusted profits beyond the modeling costs. Recent empirical tests on cattle and hog futures markets found significantly lower mean squared errors for forecasting models compared with the futures markets, indicating inefficiency under the necessary condition.[35,36] However, the risk-return ratios on simulated trading strategies using cattle forecasting models were very high, indicating there is not strong evidence of inefficiency in the live cattle futures market. Meanwhile, simulated trading for hogs generated high profits, suggesting potential forward-pricing inefficiency for that market.

The preceding weak and semi-strong form test evidence ignores recent theoretical developments of equilibrium capital market pricing models which include the futures market as one component and often show that the futures price cannot be an unbiased estimate of the expected spot price. Even in an efficient market with rational, risk-averse traders, biased futures prices can arise from a lack of coordination of production plans.[37] Nevertheless, none of these developments have shown an alternative marketing mechanism that provides prices of any less biased nature than the futures market. No one has devised a more efficient marketing alternative.

INFORMATION

When doing comparative efficiency studies, one must account for the costs and benefits of additional information. Compared to some norm like an econometric model, futures markets may appear inefficient. Yet, traders invest in knowledge and it may be costly to collect and analyze the required information.

If futures prices reflect available information, traders have no incentive to acquire costly information. In equilibrium, any excess return from acquiring information is equal to the marginal cost of information, so any trader is indifferent between acquiring information or not.[38] Hence, if information is costly, prices do not reflect all available information and the market does not appear efficient, even though traders act rationally. That is, futures prices will not be unbiased estimates of the spot price. From this perspective, an informationally efficient market is incompatible with costly information.

Regardless, all markets need information to operate. This information may be costly for any market organization. Many commercial decision makers, whether they trade futures contracts or not, rely on futures prices for their marketing and pricing decisions. They expect and trust these markets to transmit useful and accurate information. Futures markets are probably used more than any other market by commercial decision makers for gathering information about expected prices, which speaks to their relative efficiency and low costs from the commercial trader's point of view. Futures markets may be about as efficient as any markets that can be designed. This characteristic may be due to the markets' close approximation to the conditions of perfect competition outlined at the beginning of this chapter.

EFFECTS ON CASH PRICES

Related to the issues of risk premium and forward-pricing efficiency is the influence of futures trading on cash price variation or stability. The connecting link between these concepts is the role of information. Futures markets bring considerable information to the forefront, thus affecting cash price variability.

The traditional belief of many people has been that futures trading destabilizes cash prices. Futures markets have been blamed for causing prices to be too high as well as too low. Only the protestors change. The scenario often presented is that futures trading brings new speculators to the market, some skilled and some unskilled. Presumably, skilled speculators can either forecast better, or have more market power, and can profit from the unskilled speculators who are constantly changing. The activities of skilled speculators destabilize the market and cause prices to be too high or too low. Therefore, adding speculators to a market is undesirable.

Literally hundreds of bills have been introduced in the U.S. Congress to ban various futures contracts, and the only successful one prohibited futures trading of onions in 1958. Testimony suggested there were severe and unwarranted fluctuations in the cash price of onions, and the futures market was the principal contributing factor.

To store a commodity like onions is risky and these risks transfer into additional costs for the storer. Consequently, storers demand a larger price margin between their purchase and sales prices of the product as compensation. However, the futures market allows storers to manage these risks by hedging. They can reduce storer's costs, meaning that they can operate on a smaller marketing (buying-selling) margin.

This theoretical argument suggests that the presence of a futures market should result in a smaller cash price range during the storage season than if no risk-transferring market existed. Holding everything else constant and assuming that markets are competitive, this argument suggests that cash prices received by producers would be higher with, than without, the futures market; and that consumers would enjoy paying lower prices with the futures market.

The case of onions has allowed examination of seasonal cash price variations in the years with and without futures trading. Contrary to the testimony, Working found both the intramonth and intraseasonal variances reduced in years where there was considerable hedging activity in onions.[39] Gray confirmed this by computing alternative seasonal spot price index ranges.[40] The range of cash prices within the storage season narrowed after futures trading began, and after onion futures trading was banned, the index range reverted to the same range that existed before futures trading. These results support the earlier theoretical argument that managing price risks through futures markets can reduce the storer's costs, thus, reducing the seasonal range in cash prices.[41]

With the introduction of numerous futures contracts from the mid-1960s and beyond, the effect of futures trading on cash price variability has received considerable attention. Studies have examined potatoes, pork bellies, livestock, and financial instruments among others, all adequately reviewed in Kamara.[42] The vast majority of these studies either demonstrate that futures markets have a stabilizing influence on cash prices, or no significant effect on cash price variability. In fact, Kamara does not cite any literature showing cash prices being destabilized as a result of futures trading.[43]

Besides the lowering of costs discussed previously, there are several additional theoretical arguments as to why futures trading should lead to more stable cash prices. Speculators are willing to assume ownership of a storable commodity which may create higher prices than would otherwise be the case. This storage activity may prevent prices from rising as high as they might otherwise have done later in the season, bringing stability. In addition, speculators with better than average forecasting skill can moderate price fluctuations by buying and selling to compress rising prices and cushion falling prices. These actions can reduce the seasonal price range.

For all commodities and instruments, the existence of the futures market increases the amount and quality of information and disseminates it faster than otherwise would be the case. Thus, all cash market participants can make more informed decisions, and prices more closely represent basic demand and supply conditions. There are two reasons why futures trading alter the information reflected in expected spot prices.[44] First, futures trading attracts new traders to the market who would not otherwise deal in uncertain commodity prices. These speculators bring new information to the market. Second, futures trading reduces the cost of transacting because the market is centralized; the cost and time involved in finding someone to take an opposite position is relatively small. Lower transaction costs attract more traders to the market to communicate their information. Linking market information to price behavior, Charles Cox and others have found that cash prices provide more accurate signals for resource allocation when the commodity has a futures contract.[45]

Despite the theoretical and empirical evidence of the futures market providing benefits through low cost risk insurance, more stable prices, and possibly even higher prices, agricultural producers continue to vent their frustrations caused by low farm prices in the form of protests at the commodity exchanges. Kamara summarizes the role of information on futures markets by stating, "contrary to the claims by producers and farmers, the economic theory and the empirical evidence have solidly shown that under normal conditions futures trading tends to stablize cash prices and to improve the profitability of the producers and farmers."[46]

NOTES

1. In a broader sense, futures prices are a weighted average of, or influenced by, traders' expectations, hedge ratios, risk aversion, relative wealth and predictive ability related to market positions, and the costs of trading and gathering information.
2. W.G. Tomek and R.W. Gray, "Temporal Relationships among Prices on Commodity Futures Markets: Their Allocative and Stabilizing Roles," *American Journal of Agricultural Economics* 52 (1970): 372–80.
3. Martin and Garcia show that if $\beta \neq 1$, then the test for $\alpha = 0$ is no longer appropriate. See: L.R. Martin and P. Garcia, "The Price-Forecasting Performance of Futures Markets for Live Cattle and Hogs: A Disaggregated Analysis," *American Journal of Agricultural Economics* 63 (1981): 209–15.
4. B.A. Goss, "The Forward Pricing Function of the London Metal Exchange," *Applied Ecoomics* 13 (1981): 133–50.
5. Kahl and Tomek provide a variant of this equation, but more importantly discuss several

noteworthy problems related to pooling of observations, autocorrelation, and regression technique. See K.H. Kahl and W.G. Tomek, "Forward-Pricing Models for Futures Markets, Some Statistical and Interpretative Issues," *Food Research Institute Studies* 20 (1986): 71–85.

6. J.M. Keynes, *A Treatise on Money*, vol. 2. (New York: Harcourt Brace Jovanovich, 1930).
7. J.R. Hicks, *Value and Capital*, 2d ed. (London: Oxford University Press, 1946).
8. H. Working, "Futures Trading and Hedging," *American Economic Review* 43 (1953): 314–43.
9. H. Working, "Hedging Reconsidered," *Journal of Farm Economics* 35 (1953): 544–61.
10. M.J. Brennan, "The Supply of Storage," *American Economic Review* 48 (1958): 50–72.
11. L.G. Telser, "Futures Trading and the Storage of Cotton and Wheat," *Journal of Political Economy* 66 (1958): 233–58.
12. P.H. Cootner, "Returns to Speculators: Telser versus Kenyes"; L.G. Telser, "Reply"; P.H. Cootner, "Rejoinder," *Journal of Political Economy* 68 (1960): 396–418.
13. R.W. Gray, "The Search for a Risk Premium," *Journal of Political Economy* 69 (1961): 250–60.
14. R.W. Gray, "The Characteristic Bias in Some Thin Futures Markets," *Food Research Institute Studies* 1 (1960): 296–312.
15. A. Kamara, "Issues in Futures Markets: A Survey," *Journal of Futures Markets* 2 (1982): 261–94.
16. K. Dusak, "Futures Trading and Investor Returns: An Investigation of Commodity Market Risk Premiums," *Journal of Political Economy* 81 (1973): 1387–1406.
17. See C.A. Carter, G.C. Rausser, and A. Schmitz, "Efficient Asset Portfolios and the Theory of Normal Backwardation," *Journal of Political Economy* 91 (1983): 319–31; A.J. Marcus, "Efficient Asset Portfolios and the Theory of Normal Backwardation: A Comment," *Journal of Political Economy* 92 (1984): 162–64; J.Baxter; T.E. Conine, Jr.; and M. Tamarkin, "On Commodity Market Risk Premiums: Additional Evidence," *Journal of Futures Markets* 5 (1985): 121–25; and C.-F. Lee and R.M. Leuthold, "An Analysis of Investment Horizon and Alternative Risk-Return Measures for Commodity Futures Markets," in *Futures Markets: Their Establishment and Performance*, ed. B.A. Goss (London: Croom Helm, 1986), pp. 119–36.
18. F. Black, "The Pricing of Commodity Contracts," *Journal of Financial Economics* 3 (1976): 167–79.
19. E.C. Chang, "Returns to Speculators and the Theory of Normal Backwardation," *Journal of Finance* 40 (1985): 193–208.
20. H.R. Stoll, "Commodity Futures and Spot Price Determination and Hedging in Capital Market Equilibrium," *Journal of Financial and Quantitative Analysis* 14 (1979): 873–94.
21. D.T. Breeden, "Consumption Risk in Futures Markets," *Journal of Finance* 35 (1980): 503–20.
22. P.A. Samuelson, "Proof that Properly Anticipated Prices Fluctuate Randomly," *Industrial Management Review* 6 (1965): 41–9.
23. E.F. Fama, "Efficient Capital Markets: A Review of Theory and Empirical Works," *Journal of Finance* 25 (1970): 383–417.
24. For adequate reviews of the literature, see: Kamara, "Issues in Futures Markets"; and R.M. Leuthold and W.G. Tomek, "Developments in the Livestock Futures Literature," in *Livestock Futures Research Symposium*, eds. R.M. Leuthold and P. Dixon. (Chicago Mer-

cantile Exchange, 1980), pp. 39–67. For a large set of tests, see: S.J. Taylor, "The Behaviour of Futures Prices over Time," *Applied Economics* 17 (1985): 713–34.

25. P.Garcia, M.A. Hudson, and M.L. Waller, "The Pricing Efficiency of Agricultural Futures Markets: An Analysis of Previous Research Results" *Southern Journal of Agricultural Economics* 20 (1988): forthcoming.
26. J.P. Danthine, "Martingale, Market Efficiency, and Commodity Prices," *European Economic Review* 10 (1977): 1–17.
27. G.C. Rausser and C. Carter, "Futures Market Efficiency in the Soybean Complex," *Review of Economics and Statistics* 65 (1983): 469–78.
28. W.G. Tomek and S.F. Querin, "Random Processes in Prices and Technical Analysis," *Journal of Futures Markets* 4 (1984): 15–23.
29. R.M. Leuthold and P.A. Hartmann, "A Semi-Strong Form Evaluation of the Efficiency of the Hog Futures Market," *American Journal of Agricultural Economics* 61 (1979): 482–89; R.M. Leuthold and P.A. Hartmann, "An Evaluation of the Forward-Pricing Efficiency of Livestock Futures Markets," *North Central Journal of Agricultural Economics* 3 (1981): 71–80.
30. M.J. Hamburger and E.N. Platt, "The Expectations Hypothesis and the Efficiency of the Treasury Bill Market," *Review of the Economics and Statistics* 57 (1975): 190–99.
31. B.A. Goss, "The Semi-Strong Form Efficiency of the London Metal Exchange," *Applied Economics* 15 (1983): 681–98.
32. Rausser and Carter, "Futures Market Efficiency."
33. R.E. Just and G.C. Rausser, "Commodity Price Forecasting with Large-Scale Econometric Models and Futures Markets," *American Journal of Agricultural Economics* 63 (1981): 197–208.
34. W. Joerding, "The Model Dependence of Relative Mean-Squared Error Tests for Market Efficiency," *Journal of Economics and Business* 38 (1986): 227–36.
35. P. Garcia, R.M. Leuthold, T.R. Fortenbery, G.F. Sarassoro, "Pricing Efficiency in the Live Cattle Futures Market: Further Interpretation and Measurement," *American Journal of Agricultural Economics* 70 (1988): 162–9.
36. R.M. Leuthold, P. Garcia, B.D. Adam, W.I. Park, "An Examination of the Necessary and Sufficient Conditions for Market Efficiency: The Case of Hogs," *Applied Economics* 20 (1988).
37. Kamara, "Issues in Futures Markets," 270.
38. S.J. Grossman and J.E. Stiglitz, "On the Impossibility of Informationally Efficient Markets," *American Economic Review* 70 (1980): 393–408.
39. H. Working, "Price Effects of Futures Trading," *Food Research Institute Studies* 1 (1960): 3–31.
40. R.W. Gray, "Onions Revisited," *Journal of Farm Economics* 45 (1963): 273–76.
41. In a later study using more years of analysis, Johnson found that there was no significant change in the seasonal cash price pattern before, during, or after futures trading of onions. He excluded some abnormal years from the analysis. See A.C. Johnson, "Effects of Futures Trading on Price Performance in the Cash Onion Market, 1930–68," in *Selected Writings on Futures Markets*, vol. II, ed. A.E. Peck (Chicago Board of Trade, 1977), pp. 329–36.
42. Kamara, "Issues in Futures Markets."
43. Only one known study has found evidence of the futures market destabilizing cash prices and the evidence is weak. See: S. Figlewski, "Futures Trading and Volatility in the GNMA

Market," *Journal of Finance* 36 (1981): 445–56. Other tests on the same market, GNMA, do not support Figlewski's results. See: W.G. Simpson and T.C. Ireland, "The Effect of Futures Trading on the Price Volatility of GNMA Securities," *Journal of Futures Markets* 2 (1982): 357–66. A recent test on Treasury bonds found no evidence of destabilization. See: G.E. Bortz, "Does the Treasury Bond Futures Market Destabilize the Treasury Bond Cash Market?" *Journal of Futures Markets* 4 (1984): 25–38. Finally, a recent study reports financial futures contracts have not been destabilizing. See: F.R. Edwards, "Futures Trading and Cash Market Volatility: Stock Index and Interest Rate Futures," *Journal of Futures Markets* 8 (1988): 421–39.

44. C.C. Cox, "Futures Trading and Information," *Journal of Political Economy* 84 (1976): 1215–37.
45. S.J. Turnovsky, "Futures Markets, Private Storage, and Price Stabilization," *Journal of Public Economics* 12 (1979): 301–27.
46. Kamara, "Issues in Futures Markets," 288.

COMMODITY FUTURES: PRICING

7

We presented the theoretical background essential to understanding basis and price relationships for all types of futures contracts in chapter 3. We kept that discussion general to apply to commodity and financial instrument futures alike. This chapter specifically applies those theories to agricultural commodity futures contracts and relates the implications from the theoretical models to the price relationships observed daily in actual markets. We discuss basis patterns and behavior for both storable and nonstorable commodities.

STORABLES

PRICE DISCOVERY

Agricultural prices are discovered in the marketplace through the interaction of current supply and demand. Supply of major food and feed grains is the production in a current year plus carryover stocks from previous years. Demand sources include storage, feed use for livestock, food use for humans, industrial uses, and exports to other countries. Similarly for livestock, prices are discovered daily in the marketplace by the interaction of the number of slaughter animals supplied by livestock producers and the demand for meat consumption by humans. Obviously, the demand and supply of food and feed grains are highly interrelated with the demand and supply of livestock and their products.

The discovery of prices for many agricultural products occurs together in both the cash and futures markets. Traders look at information about current market conditions as well as expected demand and supply conditions for the future in making decisions about whether to act in the market today or wait until later. The topic of price discovery is interesting and important, and the literature discusses whether futures or cash markets are the primary location for price discovery.[1] However, detailed discussion of factors determining price levels is beyond the scope of this book, and we refer readers elsewhere.[2]

In this chapter we describe *price relationships* between spot and futures prices, relying on the theory presented previously, and discuss how these price relationships are important to and used by commercial enterprises. We emphasize relative prices, not price levels.

BASIS PATTERNS

The theory of the carrying charge in chapter 3 explains the observed relationship between storable agricultural cash and futures prices. The existence of inventory forces a carry charge because it costs to hold cash commodity, but not futures contracts. Hence, the cash price is discounted below the futures price by the cost of storage, and the size of the discount, or storage cost, is positively related to the size of the inventory.

Storage costs do not change noticeably from day to day. Thus, in the short run cash and futures prices maintain their relative positions, and the basis remains fairly contant. This stability is what makes the market so useful to commercial firms. Over the long run, however, cash prices rise relative to futures, or the basis gradually gets smaller as the futures contract nears maturity. The remaining storage costs become less over time. This gives the basis a distinct seasonal pattern. By delivery month the basis narrows to the point that at the par-delivery location cash and futures prices must be nearly the same. Theoretically, the basis should be zero during delivery month except for marketing costs. If spot and futures prices are not equal, arbitrageurs (traders) simultaneously buy in the low-priced market and sell in the high-priced market to profit from the price discrepancy. This buying and selling or arbitrage action forces the two prices together as the spot commodity is interchangeable in the two markets.

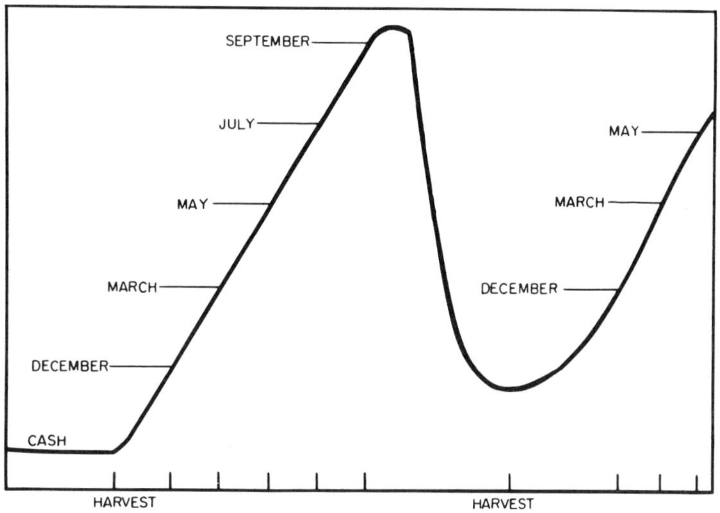

Figure 7-1. Theoretical Relationships between Cash and Futures Prices (Basis) for Corn during Two Crop Years

Figure 7-1 illustrates a theoretical basis pattern for corn. Chicago is assumed as the delivery point. During the planting, growing, and harvest seasons the spot price in Chicago for new-crop corn is below the price for December futures. After harvest the spot price begins to rise relative to the futures price because of mounting storage costs. By December the two prices are equal, and the basis is zero. This pattern repeats for each succeeding delivery month; the spot price rises relative to the futures price until they are equal during the delivery month.

Do not interpret figure 7-1 as implying that the futures price remains constant or that the spot price always increases during the crop year. The figure simply demonstrates how one price behaves relative to the other. Actually, both spot and futures prices fluctuate every day as traders respond to new information. Because of short-run basis stability and the strong functional interrelationship among these prices, spot and futures prices often change nearly identically from one day to the next. The whole set of cash and futures prices fluctuate as a constellation; that is, they move nearly parallel in the short run, but less so in the long run as the basis changes.

At harvest time when a new crop year begins, the current cash price usually drops sharply relative to the futures price. The sudden increased supply of grain drives down the cash price in the new crop year. The futures price may not undergo a corresponding change since it began forward pricing this new crop long before harvest and is not influenced by the sudden change in cash market conditions.

During the following year, the price level of both the cash and futures prices may be higher or lower than the price level of the current year, depending on the supply and demand for grain and other conditions that affect prices that year. To observe the theoretical relationships just described, we refer the reader to the prices displayed in table 2–1.

Due to technical considerations, the actual basis at delivery may not equal zero. Spot prices may be a slight premium to futures because the long traders do not know the precise day, location, commodity grade, and cost of delivery, resulting in a preference by buyers for the spot market. On the other hand, demand and supply considerations caused by storage or transportation problems at the par-delivery point may result in the spot price being discounted relative to futures. Minor differences are common, and the size of the spot premium or discount relative to futures depends on costs and risks of arbitrage between the two markets.

Also, the basis can change abruptly any day due to economic events that affect either the spot or futures market but not both. This is especially true in local markets where storage capacity constraint, labor, or transportation problems may occur but do not influence the national market. Nevertheless, basis variability usually remains much smaller than price level variability, and the basis usually follows a predictable seasonal pattern.

The basis varies in size from year to year due to changes in the size of the inventory, or the crop size, and demand for storage. Large crops result in a larger basis than do small crops. (See figure 3–1.) Another major factor influencing basis size is interest rates, the largest component in the cost of storage. Actual basis is often simply a reflection of interest costs on storage. This feature is especially true for spreads among futures contracts.

Thus, the basis along with price spreads among futures contracts indicate the availability of commodity stocks. Large bases and price spreads represent either an abundance of stocks, or that the futures market is providing an incentive to store the commodity for later release. Small or negative bases and price spreads associate with a shortage of stocks. The market is signaling for the release of stocks from storage. However, a low or negative price for storage (basis) reflects that the convenience yield may exceed the physical cost of storage. Convenience yield reflects the value commercial users place on holding stocks, and a negative price, or the spot above futures, reflects those benefits.

PRICE OF STORAGE LIMITS. Figure 3–1 implies that no theoretical limit exists to the size of the negative price of storage, or how far the spot price may become a premium to futures, because there is no upper boundary to the potential value to the merchant for ownership. Inverse carrying charges relate to the convenience yield. Warehouses and processors may be willing to store grain at a negative price of storage because of the convenience of possessing inventory. Warehouses are multienterprise firms, and profits made on merchandising, blending, and servicing grain, in addition to selling other merchandise to customers, may compensate for the storage losses. They wish to maintain a clientele and to meet unexpected demand. Storage is adjunct to other firm activities. Likewise, processors know that stopping and restarting operations is very costly, so they demand commodity for storage, even at a negative price, to keep plants operating.

Alternatively, government pricing and storage programs may encourage producers and others to hold grain in storage causing current grain users to bid cash prices above the futures prices, resulting in an inverse carrying charge market. Quality and transportation problems may have similar impacts. The critical factor may not be total grain inventory, but the "free," deliverable stock available to the market. Regardless of the cause, merchants carry and hedge stocks on an inverted market when the basis is negative.

On the other hand, an upper limit exists regarding how much the futures contract price can exceed the spot price of the commodity. The maximum basis is the marginal physical cost of holding a unit of the commodity from the present date until maturity of the futures contract. This price is the full cost of storage or "full carry" in industry parlance. Any basis larger than this marginal cost offers arbitrageurs or storers the opportunity for riskless profit by buying spot commodity and simultaneously selling futures contracts. During such times grain can be found stored on the open ground if warehouse capacity is full. This buying and selling action prevents spot and futures price differences (basis) from exceeding the full cost of carry. The appendix to this chapter illustrates computing full carry costs for grain.

Sometimes the market or basis reflects the full cost of storage during harvesttime when a glut of grain exists and local merchants need to discourage farmer marketings by dropping the cash bids relative to futures, thereby widening the basis. Also, because a high proportion of commercial warehouse storage costs are fixed, merchants can cover these once-and-for-all costs early in the crop year at harvest. Thus, cash prices often drop quickly relative to futures prices during harvest, followed by a rapid postharvest narrowing of the basis for about a month, after which the basis closes gradually the remainder of the crop year. Beyond the harvest period the basis is usually less than full carry costs.

The prices for two futures contracts of differing maturities are also highly interrelated. Within a crop year, the price of the more distant contract should be higher than the nearby contract by the cost of carry between the two periods. For example, the price of the May delivery contract for corn is normally at a premium to the price of the previous December corn contract by the expected carry costs from December to May. In practice, this price spread often reflects the interest cost for carrying inventory during the specified time. For the reasons explained earlier, spreads among futures contracts can be negative or inverted.

International traders of grain sometimes deal exclusively in premium markets. That is, cash prices in some countries remain at a premium to the futures prices on the Chicago Board of Trade. This premium may be due to transportation costs; we discuss these markets more fully in the next chapter. In addition, merchants of certain high-protein wheat varieties in the northern plains of the United States confront constant premium markets due to differences in product quality. Nevertheless, the cash and futures prices still behave similarly; basis patterns follow predictable seasonal patterns as cash prices rise relative to futures prices. Of course, in markets separated by location and product quality, the basis does not close to zero at contract maturity. Regardless, price relationships between cash and futures markets respond to and reflect identifiable economic factors.

In summary, cash and futures prices for storable commodities are always intimately related; they move up and down in a constellation. This is true whether the cash price is at a premium or a discount to futures. Both prices respond similarly to changing economic conditions and the bases and spreads reflect logical economic factors. And, regardless of their relationship before contract maturity, spot and futures prices ought to be nearly the same during the delivery period at a par-delivery point.

BASIS EXAMPLES. Figure 7–2 presents a textbook example of the basis pattern just described. The upper half of the figure shows actual prices while the bottom half shows first the December basis on the left vertical axis, and then later the July basis on the right vertical axis. The December basis remains quite constant throughout the planting and growing seasons despite the large fluctuations in cash and futures prices. The cash prices before harvest represent forward cash contract bids for delivery of new-crop grain at harvest. The cash prices after harvest represent actual cash market prices. In late October and early November the basis widens temporarily before closing rapidly in late November. From December and beyond, the cash price gradually rises relative to the July futures price. This narrowing of the basis reflects the reduction in the price of storage as the delivery month approaches. In July 1981 the cash price is below the July futures price by about $0.15, the approximate cost of transporting corn to the delivery point from this particular market in east central Illinois. The basis narrows unevenly reflecting its stochastic nature caused by changing local market conditions and market imperfections. However, the basis variability is less than the price level variability as cash and futures prices fluctuate together.

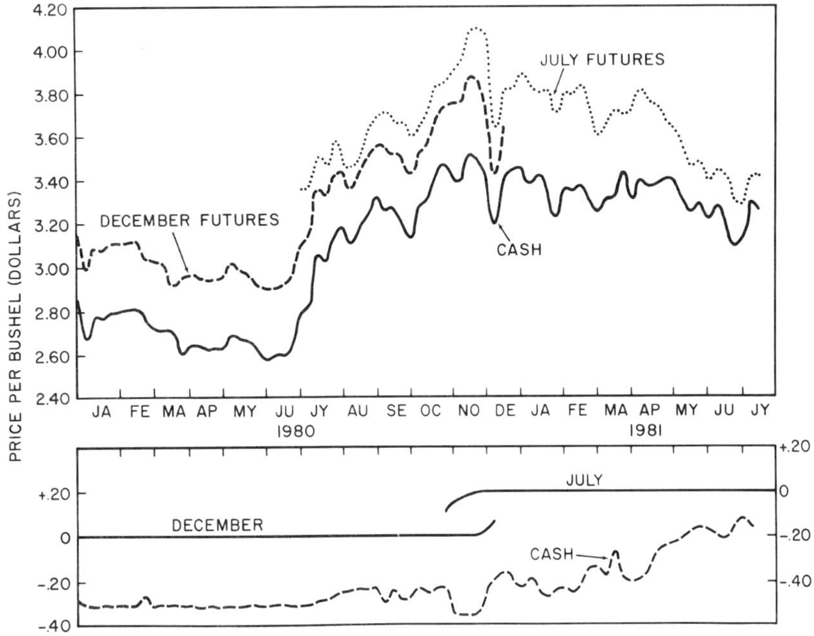

Figure 7-2. Corn Prices and Basis for Crop Year 1980, East Central Illinois

Figure 7-3 shows an alternative example with an inverted basis for corn. There was a record supply of corn in 1982, but government programs and tight farmer holding of inventories kept the free or available stocks of corn low, causing users to bid cash prices above futures prices. Despite the cash price of corn falling from about $2.80 per bushel in February to nearly $2.00 per bushel in the late summer, and rising to well over $3.20 per bushel by the following summer, the basis remains relatively stable, rising seasonally as expected. This repeated annual pattern of the basis makes the futures market an attractive place for commercial operators to manage their price level risks.

NONSEASONAL STORABLE COMMODITIES

The previous discussion dealt with seasonal storable agricultural commodities. However, some storable commodities, most particularly metals, are continuously produced and have a different pattern in spot-future price relationships than that just described. Metals have no new production season each year to force the spot price back to some beginning point as shown in figure 7-1. Continuous production prevents a seasonal pattern to inventories. The existence of inventories, nevertheless,

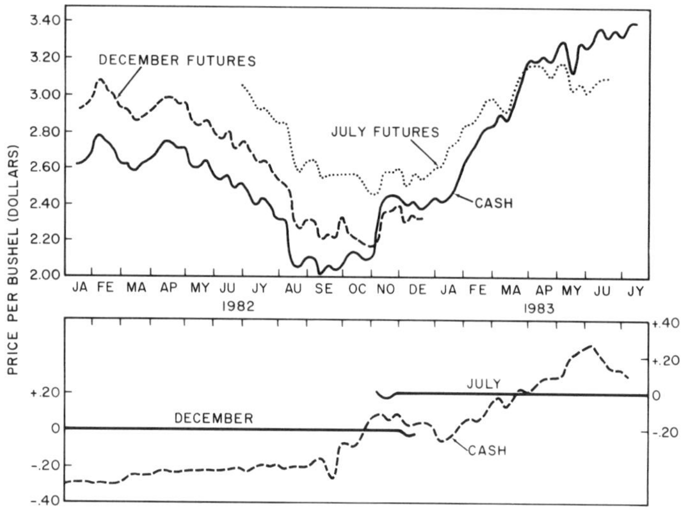

Figure 7-3. Corn Prices and Basis for Crop Year 1982, East Central Illinois

forces a carrying charge to the market. The inventories are usually in such ample supply that a positive carry almost always exists in the market. That is, futures are a premium to spot, and distant futures a premium to nearby futures. Therefore, the theory of storage is applicable to nonseasonal storable commodities.

In table 2-1 each more distant futures contract for metals is higher priced than the preceding contracts. The basis and intertemporal price spreads primarily reflect interest costs for holding the metal as warehousing costs are relatively small. The basis closes toward zero as the futures contract approaches maturity.

BASIS STUDIES

Central to understanding futures markets is knowing and explaining the basis. Ronald Ward and Frank Dasse state, "If the basis cannot be explained, then there is reason to question both the market's performance and economic usefulness."[3] Traders take basis positions, and they must know the fundamental economic composition of the basis, anticipate its changes, and manage its risk like any other market position.

Few empirical studies of the basis for storable commodities exist, but one interesting study focused on frozen concentrated orange juice (FCOJ).[4] Utilizing the theory outlined previously, the authors found that the FCOJ basis reflects the marginal cost of physical product less a convenience yield. However, they also found that unique market characteristics cause the actual basis to deviate from that suggested by the supply of storage theory. Specifically, a bias exists in the FCOJ basis because the market anticipates the additional risk of a freeze.

In an examination of corn basis patterns in Illinois, Philip Garcia and Darrel Good found the important explanatory variables to be (1) ending grain stocks relative to commercial storage capacity; (2) grain production relative to commercial storage capacity; (3) barge rates; (4) interest charges; (5) corn price levels; and (6) regional and seasonal variable shifters.[5] The basis patterns were systematic, explained in large part by the hypothesized variables and were consistent with the reported grain flow direction in the state.

Successful commercial traders who rely extensively on the futures market to manage price risks have a thorough understanding of basis relationships and patterns over time and space.

NONSTORABLES

Chapter 3 emphasized that in general the cost of carry paradigm does not apply to nonstorable commodities such as cattle and hogs, but that varying production patterns are the primary influence on price relationships. The cash price may be higher or lower than the futures price depending on future demand and supply conditions relative to current demand and supply conditions. That is, the basis may be positive or negative, governed by how traders expect cash prices to change over time relative to futures prices. Research discussed in chapter 3 showed that the primary factors affecting the basis for livestock are changing supply patterns or expected animal slaughter numbers. There exists no theoretical limit to the maximum or minimum size of the basis for nonstorable commodities.

The effect of an expected seasonal supply can often be observed in the hog futures contract price relationships. Hog production is very seasonal with more marketings in the spring and fall than in the winter and summer. Thus, prices are usually relatively lower in April and October, relatively higher in February and July. Table 2–1 shows such a pattern with April and October hog contracts priced lower than the immediately preceding and following contracts, and the June and July contracts having the highest prices. These contracts reflect the expected seasonal and cyclical patterns of cash prices. Consequently, basis patterns are different for each contract. The live cattle and feeder cattle futures prices also reflect the market's expectation of future cash prices, but because production is not especially seasonal for fat cattle, seasonal patterns in their futures prices are not as common as just decribed for hogs.

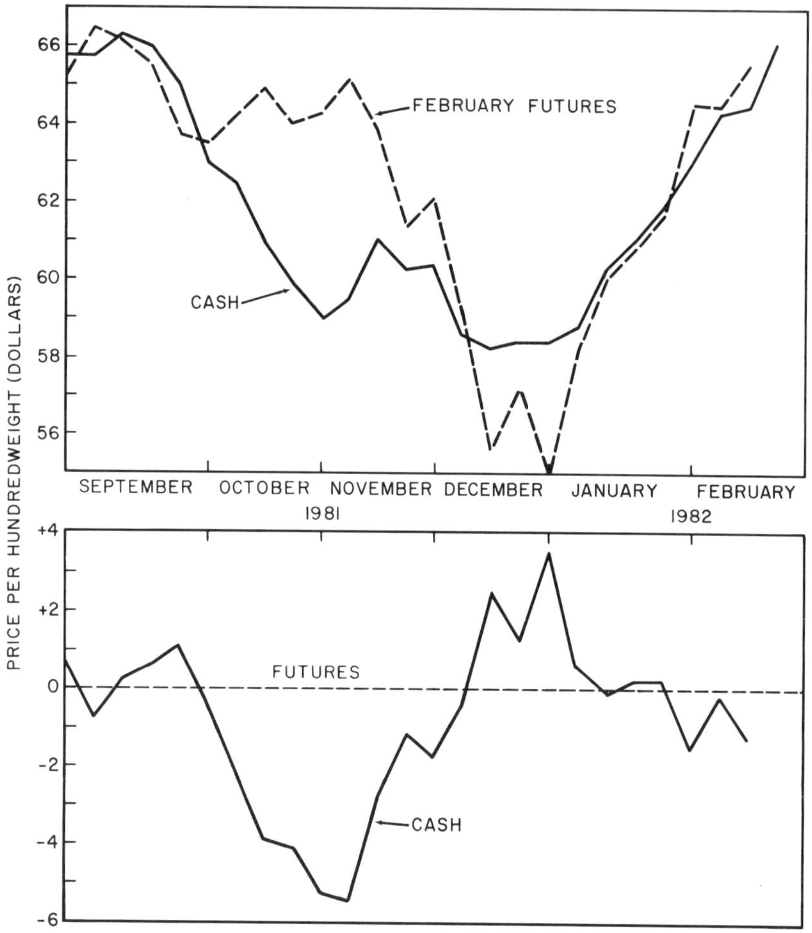

Figure 7-4. Cattle Prices and Basis, September 1981 through February 1982 *(Joliet, Illinois)*

BASIS EXAMPLES

To demonstrate the preceding discussion, figures 7-4 and 7-5 show two examples of nonstorable basis patterns. Figure 7-4 compares February 1982 live cattle futures with the cash price at Joliet, Illinois. Figure 7-5 shows the October 1982 live hog futures compared with cash hog prices at Peoria, Illinois. The basis can vary significantly; it can be either positive or negative. Yet, most of the time, basis variabil-

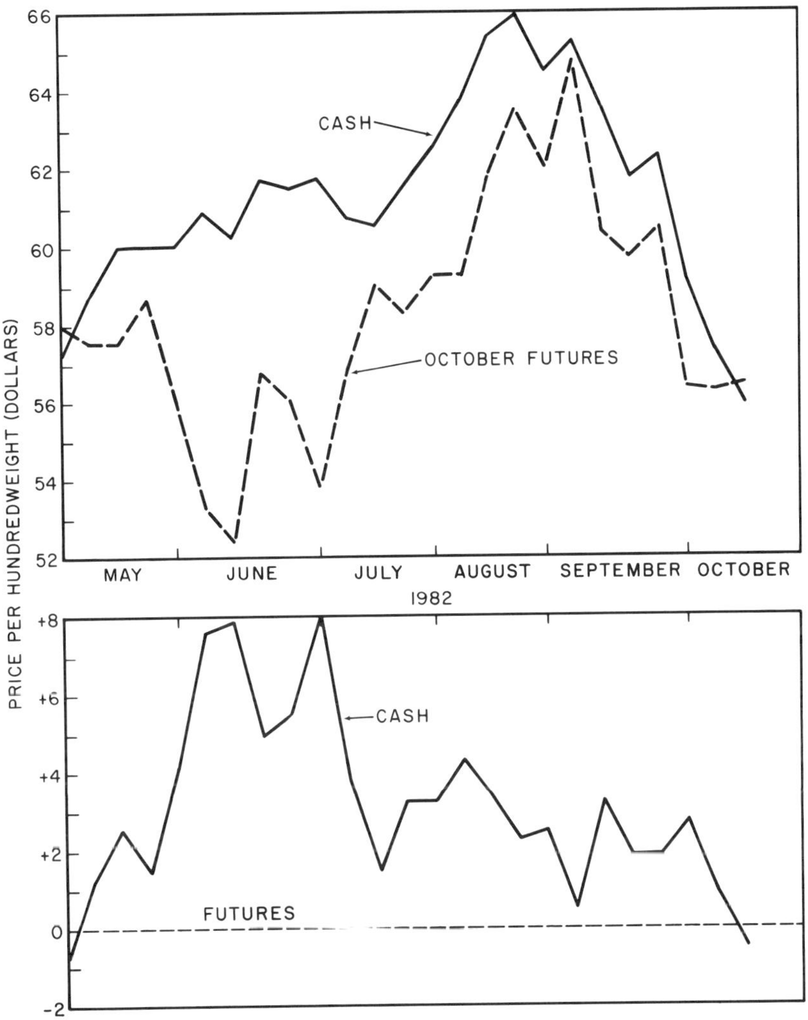

Figure 7-5. Hog Prices and Basis, May through October 1982
(Peoria, Illinois)

ity or risk is less than price level variability or risk. The figures also demonstrate a tendency for cash and futures to move together, and the basis approaching zero during the delivery month as expected.

APPENDIX: COMPUTATION OF FULL CARRY COSTS FOR GRAIN

In this example we compute full carry costs for corn; then we use these costs to determine a full carry basis. The example uses 1985 data.

Normal commercial storage costs are $0.12 per bushel from October 1 to January 1 or $0.04 a bushel per month, and $0.015 a bushel per month thereafter. We assume the interest rate is 12 percent per year (1 percent each month) and insurance costs are $0.001 a bushel per month. The contract months are December, March, May, and July.

If on October 1 the cash price is $2.08 per bushel, then interest costs are approximately $0.021 a month. With a cash price of $2.08 per bushel, the December 1 full carry price should be $2.204 per bushel ($0.08 storage, $0.042 interest and $0.002 insurance). The March 1 full carry price would be $2.34 per bushel (beyond December add $0.07 storage, $0.063 interest and $0.003 insurance). Using this procedure, the table shows the full carry values and actual futures prices on October 1, 1985:

	Dollars per Bushel	
Contract Month	**Full Carry Value**	**Futures Price**
December	$2.20 4/10	$2.15 1/4
March	2.34	2.25 1/4
May	2.41 4/10	2.32 1/4
July	2.48 8/10	2.35 1/4

From October 1 to July 1, full carry costs are $0.408 per bushel, the maximum the July futures price can be a premium to the October 1 cash price. The actual July basis is $0.2725 per bushel, or 67 percent of full carry. The actual December–July spread of $0.20 per bushel is somewhat more than the expected $0.147 per bushel interest costs during that time period. The December–July spread is 70 percent of the full carry spread of $0.284 per bushel. These relationships are fairly typical for the grain markets using Midwest cash prices.

NOTES

1. See, for example C.M. Oellermann and P.L. Farris, "Futures or Cash: Which Market Leads Live Beef Cattle Prices?" *Journal of Futures Markets* 5 (1985): 529–38; and W.D. Purcell and M.A. Hudson, "The Economic Roles and Implications of Trade in Live-

stock Futures," in *Futures Markets: Regulatory Issues,* ed. A.E. Peck (Washington, D.C.: American Enterprise Institute for Public Policy Research, 1985), pp. 329–76.

2. For example, W.G. Tomek and K.L. Robinson, *Agricultural Product Prices,* 2d ed. (Ithaca, N.Y.: Cornell University Press, 1981); and D.L. Good, T.A. Hieronymus, and R.A. Hinton, *Price Forecasting and Sales Management* (Urbana: University of Illinois, 1980).
3. R.W. Ward and F.A. Dasse, "Empirical Contributions to Basis Theory: The Case of Citrus Fruit," *American Journal of Agricultural Economics* 59 (1977): 71.
4. Ibid, 71–80.
5. P.Garcia and D.L. Good, "An Analysis of the Factors Influencing the Illinois Corn Basis, 1971–1981." Proceedings of Applied Commodity Price Analysis, Forecasting, and Market Risk Management Conference, April 1983, 306–26.

COMMODITY FUTURES: HEDGING

8

Futures and associated options markets exist because commercial firms are able to use them to manage their risks and portfolio of assets. Sound management of the purchasing and financing of inputs and sales of outputs is a necessary condition for firm survival. The futures market is only one of many tools decision makers can employ in this management process.

The futures market allows hedgers to manage risk by diversifying commercially risky positions. The market does not necessarily assure hedgers of making a profit. A mismanaged grain elevator remains just that whether it uses the futures market or not. Skilled users do not always make money on the futures market. Giving careful attention to the market and implementing decisions appropriately, however, can assist a manager in reaching goals for profit level, income stability, or financial returns.

Using the futures market effectively requires skill and practice. Many factors affect prices and price relationships; their uncertainty makes it impossible to give examples for all situations. Despite this complexity and the individual nature of each commodity, general trading principles exist to guide practitioners in formulating their own procedures. Faced with many speculative decisions, hedgers learn to use the market some of the time and ignore it at other times. Training and experience are crucial for developing appropriate skills.

This chapter outlines the practical use of agricultural commodity futures markets in managing risks. The chapter begins with a general discussion of risk management, characterizing types of firms and outlining strategies for managing risks through the futures markets. Next, we present several examples, first using one commodity, then several commodities. The discussion ends with a description of how foreign entities can use U.S. futures markets.

BUSINESS AND FINANCIAL RISK

Defining risk as the probability of receiving a stated favorable or unfavorable return, business firms face two principal risks, namely business risk and financial risk. The former refers to the variation in income that a firm experiences, and the latter to a firm's ability to repay its debts.

Business risk for most firms results from the inability to predict accurately quantity and price outcomes. The quantity or production risk faced by agricultural producers is a function of: (1) the level of operating capital available to purchase necessary production resources; (2) the producer's ability to combine resources efficiently in production; and (3) external conditions, such as weather. All raw material producers, processors, and manufacturers face varying degrees of quantity risks that are difficult to reduce.

The price or market risk firms face depends on their size and the structure of the market in which they deal. If firms are price takers, they face a high degree of price risk. Firms in less competitive market situations with more control over prices may face less price risk. In either case, proper use of the futures market potentially can reduce these risks.

Because firms face business risks, they also face financial risks. Financial risk is the possibility that a firm may not earn enough from its equity capital to pay off its debts. Price fluctuations create varying degrees of financial risks, such as reducing profits below expectations, or below zero. By following forward-pricing strategies, firms can lessen the risk of financial default.

BUSINESS TYPES AND STRATEGIES

This section focuses on descriptive and practical applications of business types and their marketing and pricing strategies in the futures market. We distinguish two types of business firms, a cost price business and a replacement cost business. They are characterized by their production, marketing, and trading activities as well as by their location in the marketing chain. These distinctions are useful for establishing contrasting trading situations outlined here.

Cost price businesses are firms involved in transforming products, often located between an atomistic commodity market and a relatively more branded, noncompetitive product market. Firms in this category are often near primary production or consumption. Examples include agricultural producers, meat packers, investors, and certain international trading firms.

Replacement cost businesses are firms located between two commodity markets; they may be strictly trading firms or they may also transform products. Examples include grain trading firms, banks, financial intermediaries, and soybean processing firms.

COST PRICE BUSINESS

A cost price business usually has flat price risk. That is, their risks relate to changes in price levels and not necessarily price relationships. The producer has a long cash position and the consumer a short cash position. The question for the producer is when to sell and at what price, and for the consumer when to buy and at what price. Their speculative positions are similar, but inverse, so it is not necessary to differentiate their business approach. We concentrate on the producers' side.

Producers, in a cost price business, must manage the margin between the total production expenses and the expected resources of sales derived from speculative management in competitive markets. Each producer must establish individual objectives for the business and sales activity. One possible objective is to receive income of given size in equal amounts over regular intervals. A corresponding sales program could consist of selling a small part of production at many intervals. An alternative objective is to sell at the highest price of the year. This strategy may maximize income, but it involves high risks because to accurately forecast the highest price each year is nearly impossible.

These decisions are necessary and speculative; each manager must decide the appropriate level of speculation for the firm. They must make these decisions every year. To define income objectives and speculation strategies, the producer needs to be well informed about fixed and variable production costs and commodity market conditions. The producer must develop information systems to formulate price and market expectations and integrate these with the firm's production processes, cash flow requirements, and financial constraints. One way to manage price uncertainty or risk is by forward pricing.

Producers vary widely in the appropriate risk level for their business. Capital positions determine leverage, which regulates cash flow. Producers in low debt to equity positions can absorb greater losses and thereby take greater risks in marketing than producers in high debt to equity positions. Also, they have more leverage with lenders in regulating their cash flow requirements.

Flexibility in sales management decisions is available and practiced because producers often separate pricing and product delivery. Pricing may occur before, at the same time, or after delivery of the product. If "unpricing" is recognized as an integral part of the sales program, the alternatives become almost limitless.[1] Forward pricing is part of the speculative decision process, allowing firms to adjust their business risk to their financial structure and objectives.

Speculative decision making and the associated pricing and marketing is a dynamic process. Information gathering, forecasting, and risk management are continuous. Factors affecting prices continually change, and a forecast is good only until new information is received.

REPLACEMENT COST BUSINESS

Firms in this category are characterized by buying and selling products in different markets separated by geographical location, product level or time horizon. They induce the flow of products between excess supply markets to excess demand markets. They are arbitrageurs, but at the same time add space, form, or time utility to the product. Because these firms purchase and sell products in different markets, often instantaneously, they are replacement cost businesses. They stand ready to trade anywhere "at the cost of replacement."

In general, the markets for these firms are competitive, and price spreads are seldom much larger than the cost of transportation, product transformation, or storage. Expected profits may be low, but many firms compensate by handling large volumes. Random shocks from weather, political events, and strikes create large price risks.

Sometimes replacement cost firms hold flat positions, meaning they assume a long or short position in one cash market without offsetting it in another market. This can be rational if the position and its associated risks are compatible with the financial structure, goals, and attitude toward risk of the trading firm. However, the lack of sufficient capital prevents most of these firms from obtaining the necessary financing for large flat positions. So, they usually offset initial positions in another market to diversify risks.[2] The managers become experts at managing risks and anticipating changes in price relationships as they are buyers and sellers of price differentials.

The buying and selling in different markets takes on many forms as firms trade in spot, forward cash delivery, futures and option markets. They become involved in very complex situations. If futures are used, they may be buying one basis and simultaneously selling another basis where the two are separated by factors affecting time, space, and form price relationships. One example is a soybean processor buying soybeans and selling soybean oil and soybean meal in cash, forward, futures or option markets to establish a processing margin. Alternatively, an international grain firm may buy and sell wheat in two countries while using U.S. futures markets to establish basis positions. The firm may purchase and sell wheat cash or forward contract, offset in cash or futures markets, and liquidate positions after the bases have changed, with or without moving the product. These firms reassess and revise positions constantly, often daily.

Risks are high as many trades are done at the cost of replacement or under the cost of replacement. The trading process can involve several intermediary markets. For example, competition may force a trading firm to modify its bid or offer during the negotiation process, causing it to price at a discount to replacement. Also, markets are very dynamic and a firm may not be able to tie down all possible contingencies. Foreign sales may occur in different currencies, under alternative ocean freight situations and financing alternatives, with undetermined quality, and under sets of government trading rules that may change. Large firms attempt to counteract these problems by having multiple positions in many different markets around the world, minimizing the possibility of being obliged to buy or sell in a market at a discount to replacement.

Replacement cost businesses must manage risks in very complex, dynamic situations. They have financial and technological constraints to match with their attitudes toward risk. They continually search for new information and anticipate future price relationships, attempting to take advantage of observed marketing and pricing opportunities while managing the associated risks.

MARKET MANAGEMENT

Market management means a systematic approach to marketing and trading activities in line with a firm's objectives toward profitability, risk adherence, and growth. For their survival, managers rely on marketing expertise, management skills, superior data, and information collection and processing for price forecasting and risk estimation. We discuss some of these here.[3]

INFORMATION SYSTEM

COST OF PRODUCTION. The first thing any manager must know before making a marketing decision is the cost of production, that can include the cost of processing, storing, transporting, and financing. Without good knowledge of these costs the manager cannot accurately calculate break-even prices and, hence, easily evaluate marketing alternatives. Costs are usually subdivided into variable and fixed costs that may or may not include returns to management.[4]

The producer can calculate a range of production costs, depending on the activities considered and different rates of return on investment and management. The producer must continually review what the cash and forward markets are willing to pay for the produced product and compare that to production costs to decide when to sell. Production costs and break-even price are individual to each producer.

INFORMATION SOURCES. All managers must remain aware of changing marketing conditions and have access to the latest information. They must feed this information immediately into their decision making processes.

Considerable information is available daily, and even by the minute, from various market news services to which traders can subscribe. Prices and price charts are available daily from numerous private sources.

However, many decision makers need only weekly, monthly, or quarterly reports put out by governments or trade associations. Many reports release inventory, production, consumption, or trade data obtained by observing and accumulating information from numerous markets, or through scientific survey sampling. The U.S. Department of Agriculture is the prime source for domestic and world agricultural data through their volumes of periodic reports. Other U.S. government agencies provide information on general economic and business conditions. Sometimes trade associations or private agencies are the primary source of information concerning specific commodities.

Each manager needs to decide which information services are critical for individual decision making and subscribe to that source. Decision makers must have current, timely, and reliable information.

INFORMATION PROCESSING. Once managers gather information, they need to process it for useful decision making. Processing varies from mental reasoning to sophisticated modeling on the computer. Whatever the level of sophistication, it is important that the manager interpret the new information correctly relative to its impact on markets and prices. Accurate interpretation and forecasting depends on the expertise of the person involved.

We mentioned several forecasting techniques in chapter 4, ranging from the balance sheet approach, to fundamental analysis, to technical analysis. Many experts combine forecasting techniques. The decision maker must be aware of the data requirements, relative accuracy, forecast time horizon, costs of operation, and speed of adjustment for each technique. Different techniques favor different forecasting needs and budgets. Some managers may simply subscribe to services which supply forecasts. Nevertheless, the final trading decision rests with the firm manager or trader.

RISK MANAGEMENT

The information system and forecasting techniques are prerequisites for operators to develop their marketing strategies and daily trading activities. With good knowledge of the data, how the market behaves, and ability to form accurate expectations, traders and decision makers can confidently take market positions. These are features of a comprehensive risk management program.

The business and financial risks outlined earlier are inherent in any production process where there is a potential for profits. Profits are never certain, and firm managers must take risks to have a chance to make profits. The question is not whether to take risks, but how to manage them. The key to profitability is risk management.

STEPS IN DECISION MAKING. There are usually trade-offs between risks and returns or profits with decisions being choices among risky alternatives. Choices are organized into strategies. Minimum risk strategies may have potential for profits, but this potential may be too small relative to other management objectives. Alternatively, maximum profit strategies may be too risky and create such low returns that the firm cannot survive. Decision makers must choose among those strategies that are consistent with the firm's constraints and objectives. This is not a trivial task, and must be done systematically.

A first step in the risk management process is to develop management objectives. These objectives may be of various types, but should be specific and quantifiable. The most basic of these is survival, a matter of debt management or servicing debt through income or refinancing. A manager must specify the returns needed to cover debt commitments. Other objectives are overall business return, business growth levels, a good family living, or maximum levels of debt and risk.

After establishing the objectives, the second step for the market professional is to identify all reasonable alternative courses of action. Each alternative must be analyzed for profit potential and risk of loss. Each risky outcome has a probability of occurrence. The manager then forms expectations.

The manager's third step is to develop basic plans and strategies within management objectives and acceptance levels of risk. The potential marketing tools available for these strategies are large, including futures markets, option markets, forward contracting, government programs, production diversification, and spreading sales or purchases over time. The manager executes a basic strategy selected according to a marketing schedule for a purchasing or sales management plan. The decision maker also needs built-in flexibility in case of changing marketing and production situations.

The last step of a risk management system is feedback or learning. After the outcome of a marketing decision is known, managers evaluate the results relative to the objectives, keeping in mind the probabilistic nature of the outcome. Not all good decisions have favorable outcomes, nor do all bad decisions have unfavorable outcomes. Good or bad luck can happen. However, a market operator who consistently makes good decisions over time improves the odds for success and survival. Appropriate, logical, and informed decision making is the essence of risk management and the basis of a marketing program.

BASIS RISK. The preceding discussion describes the general steps of risk management. Managers using the futures market must manage basis risk. A hedger arbitrages between cash and futures prices, and since these prices do not move parallel to each other, there is a risk. Hedgers are basis speculators. Nevertheless, for hedging to effectively reduce risk, the basis must have some predictable pattern to it, and at least for storable commodities basis risk should be less than flat price risks. The figures in chapter 7 demonstrated this feature.

For firms located at the par-delivery points, cash and futures prices converge by the maturity month. However, because of location and product quality differences, most agricultural firms do not experience the local basis closing to zero at contract maturity. These operators must adjust the futures price to an expected local cash market price after estimating the expected basis from historical information. This localized price is the *target price;* we present several examples in the next section.

Because the target price is based on historical information, it is unlikely that a hedger will ever receive that exact price. This additional uncertainty in adjusting prices for the hedger at a distant location or with a different quality product adds to the basis risk. In fact, once a manager has hedged, price risk actually becomes the deviation in price from the target price, or basis risk, because the hedger agrees to accept the target price. Some managers establish confidence limits allowing for probability statements on the likelihood of the exact price being within some range around the target price. This gives the decision maker some probabilistic limits when assessing basis risk.

HEDGING EXAMPLES

This section gives several examples of hedging both storable and nonstorable agricultural commodities in the futures market after defining several hedges. Further elaboration of these concepts is available in Working[5] and Hieronymus.[6]

TYPES OF HEDGES

CARRYING-CHARGE HEDGE. A carrying-charge hedge associates with the storage of a commodity. A merchant purchases and stores the commodity, and hedges it to profit from storage. The merchant seeks to profit from changes in price relationships (basis), rather than risk price level changes.

OPERATIONAL HEDGE. An operational hedge facilitates merchandising or processing operations. A merchant hedges to establish the price of an input or output, usually holding it for only a short time, often ignoring changes in the basis. The hedge protects the merchant against a rapid change in price while a product is being processed or transported. Typical examples of an operational hedge include a flour miller buying wheat futures to offset a forward sales contract of flour to a baker, or a shipper, exporter, or importer selling futures against a cash purchase. These hedges act as temporary substitutes and are liquidated as soon as the trader takes a corresponding cash position.

SELECTIVE HEDGE. The trader decides whether to hedge or not according to price expectations. The holder of the commodity hedges if prices are expected to fall, and does not hedge if prices are expected to rise. Selective hedging introduces an additional speculative element to hedging as traders hedge only under certain price expectations. This common hedging procedure is often done to prevent large losses, and it can relate to optimal hedging as described in chapter 5. Obviously, the manager must have skills in anticipating price movements.

ANTICIPATORY HEDGE. An anticipatory hedge is usually not matched or offset by an equivalent stock of goods or merchandising commitment. The anticipatory hedge serves as a temporary substitute for merchandising to be done later, that is, an expected future cash purchase or sale. The anticipatory hedge involves either the purchase of futures contracts against anticipated raw material requirements, or the sale of contracts by producers in advance of the completion of production. For example, flour millers and soybean processors may buy futures contracts in anticipation of subsequent purchases of wheat and soybeans, respectively. Livestock feeders may sell live cattle and live hog futures long before the animals are ready for market. Similarly, grain farmers forward sell their crops before harvest.

Whether this hedge is risk reducing or not depends on the relationship between the buying and selling price. As there is no offsetting cash position, risk exposure may be increased. This is especially true for long hedges if raw material and product prices fluctuate together and the forward purchases are not offset by priced sales. The anticipatory hedge allows the merchant to establish an approximate forward price for the input or later produced product, facilitating the merchant's financial position, cash flow, and determination of potential production profits.

CROSS HEDGE. To cross hedge is to assume a futures position opposite an existing cash position, but in a different commodity. Typically, there is no active futures contract in the commodity corresponding to the cash position, so the trader must select a related commodity for hedging. To be effective, the prices and commodity values of the cash commodity and futures contract must have a fairly high positive correlation. Examples include hedging corporate bonds in the Treasury bond market, grain sorghum in corn, and boneless beef in live cattle. As long as there is a relationship between the two commodities, cross hedging is a bona fide use of the futures market.

Now we turn to specific agricultural hedging examples.

MERCHANT HEDGING

The easiest hedge to understand is the carrying-charge hedge associated with grain in storage. The objective of a replacement cost firm is to purchase grain, reduce the risk by taking a diversifying position in the futures market, and earn a return while storing the commodity. The income earned depends on the seasonal narrowing of the basis. Once hedged, the trader is only concerned about changes in the basis.

Suppose that on November 1 a grain merchant considers buying and storing corn and establishing a forward price for it by selling a July futures contract. The local cash price for corn that day is $2.76 per bushel, and the July futures price is $3.11. From historical records, the merchant projects the local basis to be $0.15 under on July 1.[7] The target price is then $3.11 minus $0.15, or $2.96. Perhaps a 95 percent confidence range for this target price would be $2.87 to $3.05. The $0.20 difference between the current cash price of $2.76 and the target price of $2.96 is what the merchant can expect in return for storing corn until July. The merchant must compare this number with the cost of storage, and decide if prices within the stated range meet the firm's financial goals.[8]

Assume the merchant decides to purchase grain and hedge it on November 1, expecting to receive $0.20 for storage. On July 1 the merchant sells cash grain locally and buys back the July futures.[9] The cash and futures transactions are separate, but performed simultaneously.

Example 1 shows the basis narrowing from $0.35 under on November 1 to $0.13 under on July 1, the latter being narrower than the expected basis of $0.15 under. As a result, the merchant receives $0.02 more than the target price of $2.96: $2.50 (price for cash grain) plus $0.48, the gain from the futures transaction or $2.98. The return for storing corn can be found by subtracting from the current price received the cash price of the previous November: $2.98 less $2.76 equals $0.22. Alternatively, this return can be found by subtracting the basis on July 1, $0.13, from the basis on November 1, $0.35, or by combining the gains and losses of the cash and futures transactions, −$0.26 and $0.48. Because the return is $0.02 higher than expected, it presumably fulfills the original marketing objective.

Example 1

Date	**Cash transaction**		**Futures transaction**		**Basis**
Nov. 1	Stores cash grain	$2.76	Sells July futures	$3.11	$0.35 under
July 1	Sells cash grain	2.50	Buys July futures	2.63	$0.13 under
		−$0.26		+$0.48	

Return from storage and basis change: $0.22

In this example the prices in both the cash and futures markets fell. The merchant diversified the market position, shifted the risk of a price level change to someone else, and retained the opportunity to speculate on the basis. The merchant used the futures market as a temporary substitute for selling cash grain and gained some assurance of making a profit on grain storage.

A short hedger is long the basis. Such traders make money if the basis increases (cash rises relative to futures), and lose if the basis decreases (widens). In example 1, the basis increased or narrowed from $0.35 under to $0.13 under, a gain of $0.22.

This example could easily have turned out differently. Consider example 2 where cash and futures prices rise and the basis narrows from $0.35 under to $0.17 under. As a result, the merchant receives $0.02 less than the target price of $2.96: $3.00, the price of cash corn less $0.06, the loss from futures transaction equals $2.94. The return for storing corn is $0.18 per bushel, the amount the basis closed. Because prices rose, the merchant would have received a larger return by not hedging, but the merchant would not have known on November 1 whether prices were going to rise or fall. The merchant was not able to assume the risk of a sharp price decline with an unhedged position and decided to hedge, knowing that a final price near the target price would cover storage costs. Hedging protects against price level risks, but also prevents attaining large windfall gains from favorable price level moves. Hedging is a speculative decision, allowing traders to selectively exercise judgment about price relationships.

Example 2

Date	Cash transaction		Futures transaction		Basis
Nov. 1	Stores cash grain	$2.76	Sells July futures	$3.11	$0.35 under
July 1	Sells cash grain	3.00	Buys July futures	3.17	$0.17 under
		+$0.24		−$0.06	

Return from storage and basis change: $0.18

PRODUCER HEDGING

Producers may have carrying-charge hedges like that just described, but most of their hedges are anticipatory. Producers use anticipatory hedges to forward price an anticipated cash market transaction; it serves as a temporary substitute for the expected cash sale or purchase. As the next section shows, it may not always be possible to calculate a basis.

PREHARVEST HEDGE. Cost price businesses hedge grain and other commodities during their growing season or even before planting. Suppose, for example, that on May 1 the December corn futures price is $2.90 per bushel and that the cash price on October 15 at the local elevator averages $0.20 below the December futures. The target price for corn in October is $2.90 less $0.20, equaling $2.70. A 95 percent confidence range for that target price could be $2.58 to $2.82. The producer must weigh this target price and its risk against the expected cash price, price level risks, and break-even price. New prices are available every day. If the target price and its range seem reasonable, the farmer sells December futures contracts for the amount of grain desired to be hedged. On October 15 during harvest, the farmer delivers and sells cash corn to the local elevator and simultaneously buys December futures, offsetting the original contract and closing the futures position.

In example 3 the final price received for corn in October is $2.78, the price for cash grain, less $0.07, the loss on the futures market, which equals $2.71. Because the basis on October 15 is $0.19 under instead of the expected $0.20 under, the final price is $0.01 more than the target price. In this situation the farmer would have received a higher price by not hedging. More importantly, on May 1 the farmer accepted a target price of $2.70 with a relatively small risk and received a price very close to that figure. Circumstances on May 1 presumably prevented the farmer from accepting a larger risk.

Example 3

Date	Cash transaction		Futures transaction		Basis
May 1	Plants crop		Sells December futures	$2.90	
Oct. 15	Sells cash grain	$2.78	Buys December futures	2.97	$0.19 under
				−$0.07	

Final price received: $2.71

Example 4 shows a situation where cash prices drop. The final price received is $2.48, the price for cash grain, plus $0.19, the gain on futures market, or $2.67. The farmer received $0.03 less than the target price because the basis on October 15 is $0.23 under, $0.03 larger than expected. By hedging, however, the farmer shifted the risk of a price decline and realized a higher price than by not forward pricing and just selling cash grain in October.

Example 4

Date	Cash transaction		Futures transaction		Basis
May 1	Plants crop		Sells December futures	$2.90	
Oct. 15	Sells cash grain	$2.48	Buys December futures	2.71	$0.23 under
				+$0.19	

Final price received: $2.67

ROLLING A HEDGE. A hedger can combine these procedures in forward pricing. The producer could, for example, establish the price for grain in production by selling December futures in May and then later, perhaps in August, when both the December and July contracts are trading, buy back the December contract and simultaneously sell the July contract. In this way the forward price is simply switched from December to July. The hedge is rolled forward, and the pricing crop year is extended beyond twelve months. Rolling forward hedges is appropriate when the producer has the necessary storage facilities, flexible cash-flow requirements, and sees an opportunity to obtain additional return after storage.

Example 5 illustrates this procedure. Suppose that on May 1 the producer calculates a target price for December of $2.70 with 95 percent confidence that the final price will be within $0.12 of that. Providing that price is satisfactory, the producer sells December futures on May 1. In August the producer notices that the December futures contract is trading at $0.24 below the July futures price. In other words, the market is offering $0.24 for storing grain from December to July. To determine a target price from rolling the hedge forward in August to a July futures contract, the producer subtracts $0.15, the average basis on July 1, from $3.04, the July futures price on August 15, and adds to this the $0.10 made on the futures market from May 1 to August 15. The final target price is $2.99, $0.29 higher than that expected at harvest. A 95 percent confidence range could be $2.90 to $3.08. If this new price is sufficiently attractive, the producer can buy the December contract back on August 15 and simultaneously sell a July contract, rolling forward the hedge. This position is maintained until July 1 when the producer sells the cash grain at the local elevator and closes out the July futures position. The final price received is $2.86, the price for cash grain, plus $0.10, the profit on the December contract, plus $0.06, the profit on the July contract, or $3.02. The final price exceeds the target price by $0.03, reflecting a $0.03 narrower basis in July than anticipated.

Example 5

Date	Cash transaction		Futures transaction		Basis
May 1	Plants crop		Sells December futures	$2.90	
Aug. 15			Buys December futures	2.80	
			Sells July futures	3.04	
July 1 (next year)	Sells cash grain	$2.86	Buys July futures	2.98	$0.12 under
				+$0.16	

Final price received: $3.02

This example demonstrates that to be successful, a hedger speculating on the basis must monitor and interpret all price relationships. Hedgers have the opportunity to roll hedges forward and backwards to take advantage of anticipated changes in price relationships. Such activities have similar effects and results as spread trading between contracts by speculators, a subject discussed later in this chapter. The key element in the decision is understanding the basis and price spreads.

NONSTORABLE COMMODITY HEDGE. The hedging of nonstorable livestock commodities is similar to that for storable commodities, but there may be some additional uncertainties due to the transformation of the animal during the interim. Animal feeding is particularly risky because the firm manager must both buy inputs and sell outputs in highly price variable markets, and there is limited opportunity for varying the final marketing time once the feeding process has started. When purchasing inputs the producer needs to calculate the final break-even price and compare that to the expected selling price. The cost of the feeder animals and feed may comprise 90 percent of the total costs.

Consider a cattle feeder who, on January 2, purchases 650-pound feeder steers at $78 per hundredweight, or $507 per animal, and plans to put on 450 pounds of gain by June 1. If the feeder estimates that the cost of gain is $46 per hundredweight ($207 per animal) including feed, fixed costs, labor, and returns to management, each 1,100-pound fat animal costs $714. The feeder needs $64.91 per hundredweight on June 1 to break even.[10]

The cattle feeder next determines a target price and confidence interval by localizing the futures price for a particular contract month. The feeder should select the futures contract for the month closest to, or immediately following, the time the fat animals will be ready for market. Selection of any other contract could increase basis risks considerably due to variability in nonstorable commodity spread relationships.

For example 6 historical records of the June contract show the local cash market price to average about $1.00 per hundredweight below the futures price in June. Hence, on January 2 the feeder can establish a forward target price for cattle of about $68.50. The feeder needs to compare this target price and basis risk with the expected cash price and its associated or unhedged level of risk to decide whether to hedge or not. This target price suggests a profit potential of $3.59 per hundredweight, or $39.49 per 1,100 pound steer. The feeder must decide if those prices fit with the firm's objectives and constraints.

If the feeder hedges with a June futures contract from January until June, the final price received for cattle is $66.50, the price for cash cattle plus $2, the profit on the futures transaction, or $68.50 per hundredweight.[11] This equals the target price because the basis at marketing time equals the expected basis. Note that on the cash transaction side of the example we enter the break-even price and not a January 2 fat cattle price which is of no relevance to the current decision.

Example 6

Date	**Cash transaction**		**Futures transaction**		**Basis**
Jan. 2	Breakeven price	$64.91	Sells June futures	$69.50	
June 1	Sells cash cattle	66.50	Buys June futures	67.50	$1.00 under
		+$1.59		+$2.00	

Final price received: $68.50

PROCESSOR HEDGING

Most business firms purchase inputs that vary in price, and they often know in advance their input needs. Individual input prices may have very little relationship with output prices because they do not fluctuate together and there is a time lag between purchasing inputs and selling outputs. This means many firms need to establish input prices forward in time. Procurement policies differ widely among firms depending on their size, market power, financial structure, pricing arrangements, inventory policy and program, and attitude toward risk. Thus, the use of futures markets in implementing these policies becomes highly individualized. If these firms are to use the futures markets, they must place long hedges.

Examples of long hedges are grain merchants who have sold forward cash grain, and livestock feeders, flour millers, feed manufacturers, or other processors who need grain in the future because of a commitment to some conversion, merchandising, or manufacturing process. These firms can purchase grain several ways. They can buy cash grain and store it, obtain a forward cash contract, establish a forward price by purchasing a futures contract, or simply wait and purchase the grain later as needed. The first three options give greater certainty of the input price compared to the last option. To buy cash grain and store it assumes the buyer has sufficient storage space and financial leverage to obtain grain inventory. Such may not always be the case.

Example 7 illustrates a long hedge for grain. Assume the buyer determines that the local cash price on July 1 averages about $0.10 under the July futures price; with a 95 percent confidence, the final price will be within $0.07 of the target price. On April 1 the buyer calculates a target price for July after hedging of $2.95 less $0.10, or $2.85. Of course, the target price for an unhedged position may also be $2.85, but its associated 95 percent confidence range may be several times the $0.07 for the hedged position. Assuming that the hedge is placed on April 1, the merchant buys cash grain locally on July 1 for $2.99 and closes the futures position. The final cost for grain is $2.99 less $0.15, the profit in the futures market, or $2.84. Because the basis is $0.01 larger than anticipated, the final price is $0.01 lower than the target price, but well within the risk tolerance. By hedging, the buyer avoided having to pay $2.99 for the grain.

Example 7

Date	**Cash transaction**		**Futures transaction**		**Basis**
Apr. 1	Short cash grain	$2.74	Buys July futures	$2.95	$0.21 under
July 1	Buys cash grain	2.99	Sells July futures	3.10	$0.11 under
		−$0.25		+$0.15	

Basis change: $0.10

The long hedger essentially paid someone else to store the grain until July. The anticipated storage cost is the same as the expected closing of the basis. In this example, with a target price of $2.85 and a cash price on April 1 of $2.74, the buyer expected to pay someone else $0.11 for storage, the same as the expected narrowing or increasing of the basis from $0.21 under to $0.10 under. The buyer in this case paid $0.10 to have the grain stored, $0.01 less than expected because the basis at liquidation was $0.01 larger than expected.

A long hedger is short the basis. This trader makes money if the basis decreases (cash falls relative to futures), and loses if the basis increases. In example 7, the basis increased from $0.21 under to $0.11 under, causing the hedger to lose $0.10 per bushel. However, this was expected because the trader knows grain storage is not free.

OVERVIEW. The positions of long hedgers and short hedgers are mirror images of each other. There is a parallelism between these hedgers regarding the basis, despite their opposite perspectives toward it. Calculation of the target price, its risk, and expected basis changes are identical to both sides. However, an increase in the basis (cash rising relative to futures) represents a return for storage to the short hedger and a cost of storage to the long hedger. Thus, the short hedger prefers the situation when the basis is wider than normal (cash below futures), and expected to increase (narrow), and the long hedger prefers the situation when the basis is narrower than expected and closes a relatively small amount. These incentives and disincentives for trading cause the basis to change as traders constantly search for equilibrium. The trade-offs between long and short hedgers also emphasize the zero-sum nature of the market.

Thus, a trader long the basis gains if cash prices rise relative to futures and loses if cash prices fall relative to futures. Just the opposite is true for a trader short the basis. This person loses if cash prices rise relative to futures and gains if cash prices fall relative to futures.

CONTRACT MONTH SELECTION AND SPREADING

Most merchants place hedges in the nearby contract month or in that contract month that is closest to or immediately following when they expect to enter the cash market. Careful study of price relationships among futures contracts and correct anticipation of their changes could allow the hedger to obtain a better price. That is, hedgers may profit from rolling hedges backward and forward in response to expected changes in price relationships. Such rolling of hedges has the same result as spread trading by speculators.

For example, presume a merchant or producer is hedging corn harvested in October with the plan to store the grain until the next spring. It is reasonable to place the hedge in the May contract. However, if the December-May spread is too narrow, the trader should hedge the corn by selling December futures.[12] If the December-May spread does not widen, the inventory and hedge can be liquidated in December. If the spread widens, the trader can roll the hedge forward before December to the May contract and carry the grain for later sale. This process allows the trader to wait until the spread reflects a reasonable storage return before locking in the return. A short hedger does not want to place hedges in distant contracts until spreads between nearby and distant contracts are as wide as the trader feels they can become.

For example, assume the October-December basis is $0.20 per bushel and the December-May spread is $0.15 per bushel. The market is offering $0.20 for storage until December and $0.35 until May. If the original hedge is placed in December and later rolled forward to the May contract when the December-May spread is $0.32, then the hedger receives $0.52 for storing corn held until May. This additional return of $0.17 from rolling the hedge forward from December to May is also available to a spread trader. The spreader would buy the May contract and sell the December contract at the same time the hedger places the original hedge, and liquidates the spread when the hedger rolls the hedge forward.

Alternatively, a corn merchant could hedge in distant contracts when spreads are very wide and expected to narrow in the near future, even though the cash market will be entered relatively soon. That is, if the December-May spread is very wide and expected to narrow by December, it may be advantageous for the trader to sell May contracts and attempt to profit from not only the normal closing of the basis but also from the narrowing of the December-May spread. Interested readers can work out a numerical example.

Thus, a short hedger desires to hedge in nearby contracts if spreads are narrow and expected to widen before making the final cash transaction, and to hedge in distant contracts if the spreads are wide and expected to narrow. For a long hedger the rules of thumb are just the opposite. If spreads are narrow and expected to widen before the final cash transaction, long hedgers should hedge in distant contracts with the anticipation of rolling backwards. This action attempts to minimize the payments for storage. If spreads are wide and expected to narrow, then the long hedger should hedge in nearby contracts and roll the hedge forward later.

In reality, hedgers have many more alternatives than those just described. For example, they can sign forward contracts at a fixed basis and hedge these contracts.[13] This may give nearly the same effect as rolling hedges. They may also roll hedges both forward and backward to take advantage of short-run situations. For example, merchants may take new-crop November soybean hedges and roll them backwards to the September contract briefly if a September price premium relative to November is expected to decrease soon, and then roll the hedges forward to November again after the price relationship changes.[14] A sharp spread speculator can also trade this anticipated change in price relationships.

PREMIUM TRADING

Under several circumstances, the cash price may be above, or a premium to, the futures price. If this reflects just one factor—the time element—the market is exhibiting an inverse carry charge and there is a negative price or return for storing. That is, at the par-delivery point the price of grain in the future is lower than the current cash price, and because the basis is expected to close to zero, short hedgers long the basis pay for the privilege of storing. In this same situation long hedgers short the basis in essence are paid for not storing, or pay a negative price as the basis narrows. Long hedgers receive grain in the future cheaper than it currently costs, and do not have to pay for storage. Chapter 3 discussed the concept of convenience yield and why such market situations occur.

In other instances, the cash price may exceed or be below the futures price because of quality differences, a second factor. A particular cash commodity may be of higher or lower quality than that priced on the futures market, thus creating a premium or discount relationship. Nevertheless, if the premium remains fairly stable, basis relationships change seasonally in the same fashion as previously discussed, only the cash price may be above the futures price most of the time. Obviously, in such situations the basis at the par-delivery point does not close to zero, but to the size of the quality premium. Long and short hedgers still assume basis positions and risks, and gain or lose according to how the basis changes. These circumstances are not unusual for producers and traders who handle specialty crops or high quality products.

The third factor giving rise to premium cash markets is location; prices vary over space due to transportation costs. In this case, the cash price may be at a discount relative to the futures market, or a premium, depending on the cash market's location relative to the futures market in Chicago, and whether the cash market is in a surplus supply or producing region or a deficit demand or consuming region. For example, on January 5 the March corn contract at the Chicago Board of Trade is worth $2.39 per bushel. On the same day a grain exporter could be buying corn in New Orleans for March export shipment at $2.77 per bushel. The March premium on January 5 for corn in New Orleans is $0.38 per bushel over the March contract. Conversely, trading of corn on railroad tracks in Peoria, Illinois, on the same day for March shipment at $2.29 per bushel implies a negative premium of $0.10 per bushel relative to the March contract. The price differences reflect transportation charges.

Premium relationships are especially visible in international grain trading, where the concept of premium trading originated. Grain moves from one international port to another with prices usually expressed relative to some futures contract in Chicago. Premium trading replaces basis trading in that premiums quoted for two markets can be using the same futures contract and par-delivery point, indicating that time is not a factor. Premiums can be positive or negative; negative reflecting a relatively high supply area or country and positive for a relatively high demand area or country. Any one premium should not exceed full transportation and delivery costs between the futures market par-delivery point and the local physical market. Differences in premiums between any two physical markets or countries compared with transportation costs between them reflect incentives for grain traders to forward contract shipments.

Premiums can and do fluctuate according to: (1) supply and demand conditions in one market relative to other markets and the futures market; (2) availability and cost of transportation; (3) availability and cost of storage; and (4) relative value of substitutes.

Premium trading is a way to exchange products in the future while reducing the risk of flat price trading, much as basis trading described before. Consider the following example. On October 10 an interior grain merchant sells wheat forward for November delivery on the railroad track at $3.65 per bushel, and hedges this commitment long on the nearest futures contract, December, at $3.80. The merchant is short the premium at −$0.15. Next, on October 28 the merchant purchases wheat near the cash delivery point at $3.70 per bushel and liquidates the hedge at $3.87. The merchant immediately delivers the wheat. The premium is now −$0.17, and because the merchant was short the premium, there is a profit of $0.02. The true purchase price of grain was $3.63 per bushel, but the merchant may have some delivery expenses. These transactions are summarized in example 8.

Example 8

Date	Cash transaction		Futures transaction		Premium
Oct. 10	Short November wheat	$3.65	Buys December futures	$3.80	$0.15 under
Oct. 28	Long November wheat	3.70	Sells December futures	3.87	$0.17 under
		−$0.05		+$0.07	

Premium gain: $0.02

Changes in premiums affect the flow of cash products. To attract grain from farther areas, premiums in deficit markets need to appreciate. Conversely, falling premiums slow down the flow of grain. Grain movement can be induced if deficit market premiums associated with nearby contracts appreciate relative to those associated with deferred premiums, or nearby futures contracts appreciate relative to deferred contracts. Both of these events discourage storage.

Cash product movement slows down with the opposite changes in price relationships. That is, widening board spreads encourage storage; nearby deficit market futures premiums fall relative to deferred futures premiums. This latter event is a widening of the premium carrying charge.

OPTIMAL HEDGING

The preceding examples all demonstrate the classical concepts of hedging from a practitioner's point of view, emphasizing the process of hedging and the roles of the basis and premium. These and many similar examples are useful to most commercial firms who use the futures market daily. The main concerns of many merchants are how to manage flat price risks and how to profit from anticipated changes in bases and premiums. They remain almost fully hedged or diversified all the time, and are not especially concerned with risk-return trade-offs and risk preference levels.

However, the principles of optimal hedging outlined in chapter 5 can be applicable to these situations. Two key studies have applied these concepts to single agricultural commodities; they expand the concepts of the earlier eight examples to a more comprehensive, analytical framework.

Anne Peck expanded the basic Markowitz portfolio model to include both basis and price risk and applied it to hedging strategies for eggs.[15] She obtained the expected futures prices needed for the speculative component of the optimal hedge from various forecasting procedures. She allowed the risk parameter to vary over a wide range of values, and found optimal hedges ranging between 75 and 95 percent of production.

Jacques Rolfo applied the portfolio model to hedging strategies of cocoa producers in four countries.[16] He assumed that cocoa producers are subject to both price and quantity uncertainty in production, meaning that their utility function is expressed in income, a product of price times quantity. Allowing the risk parameter to vary, Rolfo found that at high-risk aversion levels optimal hedges range from 60.9 to 93.5 percent of expected output for the four countries. As the correlation between price and quantity distributions approaches zero, the higher is the optimal hedging ratio. At no risk level was an equal and opposite hedge, or a hedge ratio of 1, optimal. When cash and futures positions are jointly determined, the routine equal and opposite hedge is generally suboptimal.[17]

MULTIPLE COMMODITY TRADING

Some firms are in more complex transformation positions than just transportation and storage. Specifically, these firms are involved with a processing transformation allowing them to forward price their major inputs and products simultaneously. Most notable in this area are soybean processors who buy soybeans for processing into soybean oil and soybean meal, cattle feeders who purchase feeder cattle and corn to produce fat cattle, and oil refiners who purchase crude oil to produce gasoline and other products. Futures contracts exist for all of these commodities. These firms basis trade and premium trade, but there are multiple commodity relationships to observe, as well as the price relationships between inputs and outputs relative to the costs of processing. We present examples for soybeans and cattle.

SOYBEAN PROCESSING

The difference between the combined weighted values of the two products, soybean oil and soybean meal, and the value of the input, soybeans, is the soybean processing margin, or the "crush."[18] A typical 60-pound bushel of soybeans produces about 11 pounds of oil (18.33 percent) and about 47 pounds of meal (78.33 percent). The residual is waste occasionally sold to the feed industry. These production numbers and percentages change with varieties, weather conditions, and geographic location.

Soybean processors can buy or sell each of the three commodities in the current cash market, forward cash contract market, or the futures market. This alone presents a minimum of 27 different combinations for buying and selling commodities, or 27 different processing margins. In actuality, there are many more as a trader can introduce different futures contracts for alternative time horizons, or various forward markets for alternative premiums. Traders can roll these positions from contract-to-contract or from market-to-market. They can buy and sell bases and premiums; they need not enter all markets simultaneously. Option contracts are now available for all three products also, and the Chicago Board of Trade indicates that by just using futures and option puts and calls there are 128 crush and reverse crush strategies for each delivery period. Obviously, combining time horizons and other marketing tools can expand this number considerably.

Following are just a few trading plans that illustrate the range of alternatives available to soybean processors.[19] These examples do not include possibilities for using the options market.

SOYBEAN TRADING ALTERNATIVES.

1. Buy soybeans cash and sell soybean oil and soybean meal cash. This accepts the current cash processing margin.
2. Buy soybeans cash and sell soybean oil and soybean meal with cash-forward contracts. This accepts a fixed processing margin based on a particular combination of cash market and forward cash contract prices. Dealing in alternative premium (geographic) markets can introduce flexibility.
3. Buy soybeans cash and sell soybean oil and soybean meal futures; remove the product hedges when selling products in the cash market. This postpones final acceptance of the margin due to basis risks. Hedges can be placed in the months corresponding to soybean processing, or in alternative months, depending on relative prices and spreads.

4. Buy cash soybeans and hedge, sell soybean oil and soybean meal cash when produced, removing the soybean hedges at that time. This accepts future spot margins.
5. Buy soybean futures and sell soybean oil and soybean meal futures. This accepts the margin reflected on the futures market, plus may involve basis risk. This is the "board" crush, reflecting that all three contracts trade at the Chicago Board of Trade.
6. Sell soybean futures and buy soybean oil and soybean meal futures. Processing firms take this reverse crush spread position when they observe unprofitable margins reflected in the futures market and believe the margins must widen before futures contracts mature. This spread can involve many combinations of contract maturities. Obviously, speculators can trade this spread also.
7. Buy soybeans cash and hedge them short, sell soybean oil and soybean meal forward with cash contracts and hedge them long. This is a combination of strategies 2 and 6. In effect, this strategy locks in cash prices, places a reverse spread in the futures market, and postpones the acceptance of the processing margin until the lifting of hedges later. Variations include hedging one or two of the commodities instead of all three.

Obviously, there are a very large number of pricing possibilities and processing margins in the soybean industry. Many margins become known only in the future. The industry is very competitive, plus speculators can play an active role in determining current margins on the futures market, so it is not uncommon to see margins less than processing costs.

Success of a processing firm depends on its ability to select profitable margins and take advantage of them. Soybean firms often vary the level of their operations depending on margins, speeding up or slowing down flows of products and processing activities resulting from changes in price relationships and spreads. Also, the relative shares of the two products toward their joint product value may change due to differing demand and supply conditions. Changing shares could suggest alternative trading activities for the processor in the meal market as opposed to the oil market. The key is for firms to create and lock in profitable margins when they exist.

CATTLE FEEDING

Cattle feeders have opportunities, similar to soybean processors, in forward pricing the cattle feeding margin. They can use the futures market to place long hedges in corn and feeder cattle and short hedges in fat or live cattle contracts. The value of these contracts, appropriately weighted, should reflect the margin necessary to cover the costs of feeding. Feedlot managers usually purchase cash corn and feeder cattle at the same time, but they do not sell fat cattle until nearly six months later, so a biological time lag must be inserted between the maturity dates of the input futures contracts and the fat cattle contracts. Cattle feeders have about the same variety of pricing options as do soybean processors, but the time lag and contract sizes make good matches more difficult. Thus, cattle feeders probably face more basis and unmatched position risks than soybean processors.

The opportunity for using the three futures markets allows the cattle feeder to determine or establish a target profit level long before feeding commences. For example, in the late summer or fall months the feeder could buy December corn futures and December feeder cattle futures, establishing target prices for these inputs for a feeding period expected to begin in late November. At the same time the feeder could sell June live cattle futures establishing a May target price for finished animals. These trades establish a target profit level. In November the feedlot manager liquidates the corn and feeder cattle futures contracts and purchases these inputs in the cash market. The short live cattle contract is not liquidated until May when the manager markets fat cattle. How closely actual profits come to the target profit depends on basis risks, or how close each actual basis is to the expected basis. Buying and selling the appropriate number of contracts and matching them to the cattle feeding operation is very complex.

Whether a cattle feeder should use all three markets or not, and how many contracts, depends on the trade-offs between expected incomes and price level versus basis risks. The manager must consider the interrelationships between all cash and futures prices as reflected in the many combinations of variances and covariances of prices. One partial study of potential opportunities examined means and variances, but not covariances among prices nor levels of risk aversion. Raymond Leuthold and Scott Mokler simulated a cattle feedlot and calculated daily feeding margins (target profit levels) as reflected through the three futures markets beginning three months before feeding commenced.[20] They also calculated expected margins during feeding using the fat cattle futures price. Whenever a margin of a predesignated size appeared, they placed appropriate hedges. They found that a modest positive margin occurred at some time for every lot simulated. That is, profitable margins eventually occur if the feeder has patience. Plotting the resulting means and variances when searching for three commodity hedges produced the near perfect E-V frontier curve as described in chapter 5.[21]

In a more comprehensive study, Paul Peterson and Leuthold applied the Markowitz portfolio model outlined in chapter 5 to a cattle feedlot simulation that included covariances between cash and futures prices in the analysis.[22] The search for optimal hedges took place both before and during feeding. Because of the high level of correlation between prices, it was optimal for the highly risk averse feeder to establish full naive hedges for all three cash positions before feeding began only 24 percent of the time. Partial hedging in one or more commodities was most common in the simulation. Conversely, for producers of low-risk aversion the optimal hedge position was usually to hedge only one, sometimes two, commodities. Thus, because of the high correlation between corn, feeder cattle, and fat cattle, cash and futures prices, it is seldom necessary for a cattle feeder to fully hedge all three commodities at the same time. Optimal hedge strategies suggest partial hedging or hedging only one or two commodities.

FUTURES MARKETS AND INTERNATIONAL TRADE

So far we have emphasized the use of futures markets by commercial firms that trade in regional United States cash markets. However, futures markets are also a useful marketing tool for international trading and processing firms throughout the world. In addition, marketing boards in exporting and importing countries can use these markets.

The problem for firms and countries trading internationally is to find the optimal mix of commercial and futures positions in several markets, such as the basic product, currency, transportation, and interest rate. As an example, we discuss in this section some practical techniques used by traders in importing countries.

IMPORTERS AND FUTURES MARKETS

For importing firms and countries, buying cash products spread over time and establishing long-term bilateral agreements are common approaches to purchasing imports. However, using the futures market allows them to extend their pricing horizons, to fix price levels and to establish basis (premium) price. They can fix prices now or later, establish the basis now or later, and roll futures contracts backwards or forwards. Often, they make cash transactions with no reference to flat prices, only to the basis (premium). That is, a trader buys a product at one location at a fixed basis (premium) and sells it at another location at a different fixed basis (premium), presumably at a price difference exceeding transportation costs. Even though the trader may not enter the futures market, all price quotes and transactions are made in reference to the futures market. Following are three specific uses of futures contracts for pricing and importing often observed in the grain trade.

FIXED (FLAT) PRICE CONTRACT. The exporter and importer agree on the exact flat price, usually based on a futures contract nearest to the shipment date. On the contracting day, the exporter buys futures contracts as a temporary substitute for the cash purchase, assuming the firm does not have cash grain on hand. Before shipment, the exporter buys cash, lifts the futures hedge, and books transportation to the port. The importer pays the price fixed on the contracting date. The exporter's profit is the difference between the basis agreed to on contracting date and the basis when the grain is purchased, adjusted for the costs of relocating the grain from inland points to the agreed on port for export.

FIXED BASIS CONTRACT. Basis contracts separate the time of contracting from the time of pricing, which separates price level from the basis. On contracting day, the parties agree to the basis and the futures contract used for establishing the price. This basis usually includes transportation costs and premiums or discounts for quality variation. After contracting, the exporter buys cash and sells futures to hedge the purchase, and books transportation. The timing of pricing is up to the importer, allowing considerable flexibility but also incorporating risks. When the price becomes acceptable, the importer instructs the exporter to purchase the futures contract or purchase futures contracts for the exporter's account (meaning that the transaction will show on the exporter's accounts). This fixes the futures price, and the importer pays the exporter the price of the futures contracts plus the fixed basis. Here, the importer has gained flexibility.

The exporter is indifferent between these two pricing methods. The sale price and forward basis are the same for the alternatives. In both cases the exporter buys cash grain and books transportation later, establishing profit opportunities between the bases. The major difference is to the importer who has the option to price the grain later, if desired. That is, the pricing dates of the two methods are different. Consequently, the net price to the importer differs, but because the exporter is hedged, any difference in final price among the methods is offset in the futures market, leaving the exporter with just the arbitrage profit or loss. The exporter's job is to get the grain to the export point at a preestablished basis level.

FIXED BASIS AND EX-PIT TRADE. Basically the same as the fixed basis contract, in this contract the basis is fixed on contracting date, followed later by the exporter buying cash, hedging short on the futures market, and booking transportation. The difference is that the importer establishes the flat price later by buying futures on his or her own account. (Obviously, the two traders need not enter the futures market at the same price.) Then on shipment date, the importer and exporter exchange their futures and cash positions at the price for that day. This exchange takes place outside the trading pit. The importer still pays the exporter the futures price plus the basis, but some money transference has already taken place through daily marking-to-market.

Exchanges allow these ex-pit trades—sometimes called cash-futures swaps, or exchange for physicals, or actuals—as long as there is an accompanying equal cash transaction.[23] These transactions occur outside the pit, usually by the hedgers' brokers. They should not affect current market prices, nor the competitive auction process. The advantage of these transactions is that both the buyer and seller trade at the same price. That is, if both hedgers liquidate their futures positions in the trading pit, the transactions might occur at different prices. Thus, the basis trade for the cash commodity would be made at different bases for the two hedgers, losing the effectiveness of the basis trade. This is why many cash commodity dealers who basis trade require the exchange of cash against futures.[24] Also, there is no reason the preceding long hedger (importer) cannot price by taking futures positions, unprice by liquidating those positions, and then price again through new futures positions, repeating the process many times. Pricing and unpricing adds flexibility, but also risk.[25]

OPTIMAL HEDGING

The concepts of optimal hedging also apply to international trade situations. Here, the trading firm or country may need to manage risks simultaneously in commodity price, currency, transportation, and interest rate. And, as discussed earlier for multiple commodity hedging, positive correlation among the various cash and futures prices likely mean the firm or country need not fully hedge all of their price risks. Also, basis risks may be higher for foreign than for domestic entities, decreasing the usefulness of the futures markets for managing risks in international situations.

Applying the principles of optimal hedging to international risk management becomes complex because of multiple risks, determination of several expected prices, alternative currencies available, and basis risks. The literature is growing in this subject matter area with recent theoretical contributions by Simon Benninga, Rafael Eldor, and Itzhak Zilcha,[26] and the derivation and application of optimal hedge ratios for internationally traded commodities and currencies by Stanley Thompson and Gary Bond,[27] and Gboroton Sarassoro and Leuthold.[28] These models are complex and left to the interested reader.

NOTES

1. An example of unpricing is liquidating or canceling a short futures position or forward contract because price forecasts change while maintaining the long cash position.
2. Small flat positions often occur because of the inability to match, buy, and sell trades exactly.
3. For supplemental discussions of many of these items and their use in practical decision-making procedures for producers, see: D.L. Good, T.A. Hieronymus, and R.A. Hinton, *Price Forecasting and Sales Management.* (Urbana: University of Illinois, 1980); and A.B. Paul, R.G. Heifner, J.D. Gordon, *Farmers' Use of Cash Forward Contracts, Futures Contracts, and Commodity Options.* U.S. Department of Agriculture, Economic Research Service, Agricultural Economics Report No. 533, (Washington, D.C., 1985).
4. For an example of establishing production costs for soybeans, see: R.M. Leuthold and P.J. van Blokland, *Using the Futures Market in Financial Planning.* University of Illinois at Urbana-Champaign Cooperative Extension Circular 1194, 1984.

5. H. Working, "New Concepts Concerning Futures Markets and Prices," *American Economic Review* 52 (1962): 432–59.
6. Hieronymus, *Economics of Futures Trading*, 329–33.
7. The grain trade defines basis (B) as $B = S - F$ (i.e., spot (cash) price minus futures price). This results in basis usually being a negative number. Grain traders quote cash prices as "X [cents] under," meaning that the cash price is below some futures contract by X cents. So as not to continually use the word negative, and not to confuse simple mathematics by appearing to incorrectly subtract negative numbers, we express basis levels as positive numbers, but use "under" to reflect cash prices being discounted relative to futures prices. A basis expressed as "over" means the cash price is a premium to the futures price.
8. Hedgers must also consider the cost of using the futures market, about $0.015 per bushel for grains. For simplicity, we ignore this cost in these examples, but it cannot be in practice.
9. To keep these examples straightforward, we assume one-for-one hedges and ignore the optimal hedge ratio developed in chapter 5. The optimal hedge ratio for grains as used in most of these examples would be very near one anyway. After presenting these simpler examples, we discuss the use of optimal hedge ratios later in this chapter.
10. This calculation disregards the additional cost of using the futures market which is about $0.20. Also, animals shipped to market lose weight, called "shrink," typically calculated at 4 percent of the fed weight. Hence, this feeder actually markets animals weighing 1,056 pounds, therefore requiring a higher break-even price of $67.61 per hundredweight. Obviously, the break-even price is very sensitive to the expected sale weight of the animal.
11. Alternatively, the sum of the break-even price ($64.91) + the cash profit ($1.59) + the futures profit ($2.00) equals $68.50.
12. This whole discussion assumes cash price is discounted below futures price, and nearby contracts are discounted below distant contracts.
13. We define and describe basis contracts later in this chapter.
14. For an interesting example of these transactions, see V.A. Wiese, "Use of Commodity Exchanges by Local Grain Marketing Organizations," in *Views from the Trade*, ed. A.E. Peck (Chicago Board of Trade, 1978), pp. 85–90.
15. A.E. Peck, "Hedging and Income Stability: Concepts, Implications, and an Example," *American Journal of Agricultural Economics* 57 (1975): 410–19.
16. J.Rolfo, "Optimal Hedging Under Price and Quantity Uncertainty: The Case of a Cocoa Producer," *Journal of Political Economy* 88 (1980): 110–16.
17. For another study that incorporates production uncertainty for farmers, as well as some financial uncertainty, see V.J. Alexander, W.N. Musser and G. Mason, "Futures Markets and Firm Decisions under Price, Production, and Financial Uncertainty," *Southern Journal of Agricultural Economics* 18 (1986): 39–49. Separately, Tomek warns that the size of optimal hedges for farmers may be overestimated because of the omission of important costs from the objective function. These costs include yield risk, transaction costs, costs of margin calls, costs of managing a position in futures and lumpiness of contracts. See: W.G. Tomek, "Effects of Futures and Options Trading on Farm Incomes," Cornell Agricultural Economics Staff Paper No. 87-9, Cornell University, May 1987.
18. The term *crush* refers to the original process for manufacturing soybean oil and meal where processors literally crushed the soybean to press out the oil. Modern day processing is chemical extraction.

19. For another discussion of these alternatives, See Hieronymus, *Economics of Futures Trading,* 231–32.
20. R.M. Leuthold and R.S. Mokler, "Feeding-Margin Hedging in the Cattle Industry," *International Futures Trading Seminar,* vol. VI. (Chicago Board of Trade, 1980), 56–68.
21. For a similar study applied to hogs, see D. Kenyon and J. Clay, "Analysis of Profit Margin Hedging Strategies for Hog Producers," *Journal of Futures Markets* 7 (1987): 183–202.
22. P.E. Peterson and R.M. Leuthold, "A Portfolio Approach to Optimal Hedging for a Commercial Cattle Feedlot," *Journal of Futures Markets* 7 (1987): 443–57.
23. The grain trade has used ex-pit transactions for some time, and these trades are not limited to importers and exporters. Such trades are expanding quickly to the currency and financial markets. One particular advantage is that these trades can occur when the exchange is closed. As long as ex-pit trades remain a small proportion of the total volume, there is usually no particular problem, although regulators do monitor them closely. The trades are reported to the clearinghouse and are recorded in total futures trading volume figures.
24. *Commodity Trading Manual* (Chicago Board of Trade, 1982), 79–80.
25. Two marketing case examples integrating risk management procedures and practical techniques of futures trading are available on request from the authors. One, "A Farmer, Bob McLauren," demonstrates a marketing program for an Illinois corn farmer, a cost price business. The other, "The Agro Trading Company," illustrates for a replacement cost business an international trade situation in edible oils, emphasizing premium markets.
26. S. Benninga, R. Eldor, and I. Zilcha, "Optimal International Hedging in Commodity and Currency Forward Markets," *Journal of International Money and Finance* 4 (1985): 537–52.
27. S.R. Thompson and G.E. Bond, "Offshore Commodity Hedging under Floating Exchange Rates," *American Journal of Agricultural Economics* 69 (1987): 46–55.
28. G.F. Sarassoro, and R.M. Leuthold, "A Multiple-Risk Optimal Hedging Model: An Example." *NCR Conference on Applied Commodity Price Analysis, Forecasting, and Market Risk Management* 1988, 296–309.

INTEREST RATE FUTURES: PRICING

9

This chapter examines the application of the general futures pricing models to short-term and long-term interest rate futures contracts. A general introduction covers the major features of the more popular interest rate futures contracts. The next section discusses the pricing of nonstorable interest rate futures and the arbitrage arguments related to the proof of the pricing model. The following section covers the pricing of storable bond futures, the cost of carry model, and some of the complexities in pricing related to underlying features of the bond contract. Finally, the last section reviews intercommodity and interdelivery spreads.

INTEREST RATE CONTRACTS

SHORT-TERM INTEREST RATE CONTRACTS

Two major futures are related to movements in short-term interest rates: the Eurodollar and Treasury bill contracts. After each of the underlying assets is discussed, the futures are introduced.[1]

EURODOLLARS. A Eurodollar account is a deposit denominated in dollars and held outside the U.S. Such accounts have fixed maturity and interest rates so that the Eurodollar account closely resembles a domestic certificate of deposit (CD). The primary difference is that there are no reserve requirements against the Eurodollar deposit, and so banks can offer slightly higher rates on these accounts over domestic CDs. The rate on Eurodollars is tied to the LIBOR (London InterBank Offered Rate), a rate on funds placed between major London money center banks. Because domestic U.S. banks can borrow or place funds in Eurodollars for maturities ranging from overnight to six months—and up to five years—rates in the Eurodollar market are closely correlated to such U.S. short-term rates as the Federal funds rate for overnight funds, and CD and commercial paper rates for various maturities. For this and other reasons, the Eurodollar contract has become the most actively traded of the short-term asset contracts.

TREASURY BILL. A U.S. Treasury bill is an obligation of the U.S. government to pay a fixed amount, the face value, at maturity. As discussed in chapter 3, T-bills are priced at a discount from face value; the difference between the price paid for the bill and the maturity face value is called the discount and represents the interest earned on the bill until maturity.

U.S. T-bills are auctioned on a regular schedule by the Treasury. Three- and six-month bills are auctioned every Monday and one-year bills are auctioned once every month.[2]

SHORT-TERM RATE FUTURES. Eurodollar and T-bill contracts are each based on an underlying $1 million face value security with 90 days to maturity as of the delivery date of the contract. Each contract trades on a quarterly March-June-September-December cycle. Although futures prices for short-term assets are based on the expected price as discussed in chapter 3, the actual futures price quoted in the market is in terms of annualized expected yield. This pricing convention reflects the way that cash T-bills are bought and sold. For the T-bill contract, if the expected rate is 8 percent, the futures price is 100 minus 8, or 92. The dollar amount involved is $1 million − ((90/360) × 0.08 × $1,000,000), or $980,000. This index system of pricing ensures that the futures price rises as the dollar value of the contract rises, as is the case with all other futures. For instance, if yields fell to 5 percent in the futures market, the futures price would become 100 minus 5, or 95, and the dollar value of the contract would rise to $1 million − ((90/360) × 0.05 × $1,000,000), or $987,500.

Although the short-term contracts vary in small details, the delivery mechanisms are relatively similar. The delivery procedure for the T-bill contract is used as an illustration. Delivery takes place on one specific day of the delivery month as part of a two-day process. According to Chicago Mercantile Exchange (CME) rules, the second business day following the third auction of the month is notification day, the last trading day of the contract. (Even though the rule for fixing the date sounds somewhat complicated, the third auction is generally the third Monday of the month, and notification day is generally the third Wednesday of the delivery month.) On notification day, those with long and short positions on the contract notify the clearinghouse of their intention to take or make delivery. These long and short positions are matched by the clearinghouse; and the sellers' and buyers' banks are instructed to expect payment and to deliver. The following day, delivery and payment take place.

In the T-bill contract, the commodity delivered is one particular issue, that T-bill currently outstanding that has ninety or ninety-one days to maturity on delivery day. Thus, the T-bill contract is one of the simplest of the interest rate futures in that it involves only one specific asset delivered on only one particular day. For the Eurodollar contract, physical delivery of an account outside the U.S. would be impractical; thus, the Eurodollar contract is settled on a cash basis.

LONG-TERM INTEREST RATE CONTRACTS

The most popular of the long-term interest rate futures are the Treasury bond and Treasury note contracts, both traded on the Chicago Board of Trade. T-bonds and notes are discussed first, then the futures contract characteristics are introduced.

T-bonds and notes are long-term coupon obligations of the U.S. government. T-notes generally have maturities of over one year to ten years; T-bonds currently have maturities of ten to thirty years. Both are auctioned by the Treasury on a relatively regular quarterly basis. The most actively traded and quoted bond tends to be the most recently issued, longest-term bond. For instance, as of this writing, the 8⅞ percent bond maturing in 2017 has the longest term and its yield is a benchmark quoted extensively in discussions of credit market conditions. As discussed in chapter 3, the price of a bond or note is the present value of the coupons and principal repayment, discounted at the market interest rate applicable to cash flows of this risk class.

FUTURES. Because of its extreme popularity, the major features of the T-bond contract are discussed in detail; the note contract is quite similar in delivery and contract specifications. Both bond and note contracts are based on a $100,000 face value, 8 percent coupon standard, with the bond contract referring to a fifteen-year maturity, the note contract to a seven- to ten-year maturity. Like the cash asset, the futures price is denominated in percentage of par or face value. For instance, a futures price of $90^{16}/_{32}$ would be equal to 0.905 of $100,000 face value, or $90,500.

The T-bond contract is not as simple as the bill contract for a variety of reasons. Although the futures price quoted on the bond contract is based on an 8 percent coupon standard, the contract calls for delivery of any T-bond with at least fifteen years to maturity or call. This guarantees a sufficiently large deliverable supply of Treasury bonds. Thus, the actual bond received in delivery can be one of between twelve and twenty outstanding bond issues with the proper maturity.

DELIVERY PROCEDURE. Delivery procedures involve a three-day process. The first day is called position day. On this day, the sellers notify the clearinghouse that they intend to make delivery. The earliest possible position day can occur two business days before the first business day of the contract maturity month. As outlined in chapter 2, the sellers initiate the delivery procedure, and thus choose when delivery takes place and which bond is delivered. These two seller's options, when to deliver and which bond to deliver, are referred to as the timing option and the quality option, respectively. The role of these options in futures pricing is discussed in a later section. The price received by the seller is the futures settlement price on position day.

The second day is notice of intention day. The clearinghouse selects a buyer from the pool of outstanding long contracts to receive delivery. Once chosen, the buyer is invoiced by the seller for the particular bond to be delivered and the amount to be paid.

The third day is delivery day, when delivery and payment take place. The latest that delivery can occur in the month is generally the last business day of the month. However, trading of the contract generally ends seven business days before the month's end. Thus, for approximately seven days at the end of the month the settlement price for delivery is fixed and unchanging.

CONVERSION FACTORS AND CHEAPEST TO DELIVER. Because generally a large number of bonds are eligible for delivery, a means has been devised to allow for payment at delivery for different coupon bonds while maintaining an 8 percent standard for the futures price. The Chicago Board of Trade (CBOT) has calculated conversion factors which adjust the contract futures price, based on an 8 percent standard coupon, to conform to the value of the bond actually delivered. For instance, assume that it is very near delivery of the June futures contract, and the June futures price is currently 100 with a yield of 8 percent. If the seller were to deliver a higher-coupon bond, say a 14 percent, the value of the 14 percent bond would be greater than 100. If yields were 8 percent, the price of a 14 percent, 20-year bond would be 159.38. The seller who delivers, should receive 100 × 1.5938, or 159.38 for the 14 percent bond. This is the idea behind the conversion factor: it is a number that adjusts the futures price to conform to the price of the bond actually delivered. Here, the conversion factor of the 14 percent, twenty-year bond is 1.5938.

Conversion factors are calculated by pricing the delivered cash bond to yield 8 percent. In the preceding example, the 14 percent coupon bond priced at a yield of 8 percent is 159.38. This price is then divided by 100 to give the bond's conversion factor, 1.5938. The value of the bond in the futures market, its invoice amount, is equal to the futures price times the conversion factor, here 100 × 1.5938 = 159.38. If the June futures price were 75 on the delivery day, reflecting a yield in the futures market of 11.1 percent, the 14 percent bond invoice amount would be equal to 75 × 1.5938 = 119.54 which is the price of a 14 percent coupon, twenty-year bond at a yield of 11.1 percent. Each deliverable bond has its own conversion factor for every contract month. For instance, the 14 percent coupon, twenty-year bond discussed earlier would be a 14 percent, 19¾-year bond for the September contract, and the conversion factor for this bond for September delivery is 1.5903.

Many times the invoice amount, calculated using the conversion factor, is not exactly equal to the cash market price for the bond. One reason for the discrepancy reflects the assumptions made by the CBOT in calculating the conversion factors. Delivery is assumed to take place on the first delivery day of the contract month. In addition, the maturity date of the bond is rounded off to the first day of the quarter. For instance, a bond due on March 15, 2010, would be assumed to mature on January 1, 2010, for the conversion factor calculation. Further, the cash price of the bond can vary due to supply considerations, interest rate expectations, and a wide variety of other influences in the cash market. Thus, there is usually a discrepancy between invoice price received for the bond in the futures market (futures price × conversion factor, or FP × CF) and actual cash market price for the bond.

This discrepancy leads to the determination of the cheapest to deliver (CTD) bond. Out of the twelve to twenty bonds eligible for delivery, there is one that has the greatest discrepancy between cash price and invoice amount in the seller's favor. As an illustration of the reasoning involved, assume that the only bonds eligible for the June contract are as shown:

Bond	Conversion Factor	Invoice Amount	Market Price
14% 20-year	1.5938	1.5938 × 100 = 159.38	158
7% 16-year	0.9106	0.9016 × 100 = 90.16	92

The first is a 14 percent, twenty-year bond, with a conversion factor of 1.5938, currently priced in the cash market at 158. The second eligible bond is a 7 percent coupon, sixteen-year bond, with a conversion factor of 0.9106, currently selling in the cash market for 92. With a June futures price of 100, the invoice amount of the 14 percent bond is 100 × 1.5938 = 159.38, or $159,380. Thus, the seller of the June futures contract could deliver the 14 percent into the June futures contract and receive $159,380; however, the seller would be able to acquire the bond in the cash market at its current cash price of $158,000. Similarly, the seller could also deliver the 7 percent coupon bond into the June contract and receive 100 × 0.9106 = 91.06, or $91,060, even though it would cost $92,000 to acquire it in the cash market. The choice is plain, if the seller did not already own a bond conformable for delivery, the bond to deliver would be the 14 percent coupon bond. The futures seller would receive $159,380 less $158,000, or $1,380 profit because of the discrepancy between invoice amount and cash price.

Even before the actual delivery month, the preceding calculation can be made using current futures prices and current cash market prices. Generally, the bond that is cheapest to deliver prior to the delivery month tends to remain so until delivery itself. Buyers and sellers of the contract tend to price the futures based on what is expected to be delivered, the CTD bond. Thus, the futures price, although based on an 8 percent coupon standard, tends to behave in a manner similar to the CTD, here a 14 percent coupon.

In fact, the change in the futures price can be directly related to changes in the price of the CTD. Because the invoice amount, $CF \times FP$, approximates the CTD price, then

$$\Delta FP = \Delta CTD/CF.$$

Further, if the conversion factor of the CTD bond were 2, for instance, this would mean that the futures price would be half as volatile as the cash cheapest to deliver price. This knowledge of relative volatility between futures price and cheapest to deliver is used in the discussion of hedging in chapter 10.

The long-term interest contracts are thus more complex than the short-term interest contracts and as noted contain a variety of seller's options. The seller has the choice of when to deliver on the contract and also which particular bond to deliver. In addition, contract specifications lead to the existence of a cheapest to deliver bond, which underlies the contract and on which the contract price is based.

THE PRICING OF SHORT-TERM INTEREST RATE CONTRACTS

THE YIELD CURVE AND IMPLIED FORWARD RATES

As discussed in chapter 3, the price of a nonstorable financial futures is equal to the expected price—or what is the same thing—the expected yield of the asset at delivery. That is,

$$F_{t,T} = E(S_T)$$

or for financial futures

$$R_{\text{fut}} = E(R_T) \tag{9-1}$$

Under the Pure Expectations Hypothesis (PEH), it was argued in chapter 3 that expected rates for future time periods are reflected in the shape of the yield curve. This can be used in short-term interest rate futures pricing.

The PEH theory can be given a more mathematical content and used to estimate an expected rate for a specific future time period relating to a futures contract delivery time.

It is reasonable to assume under the theory that market participants have no fixed preference for a maturity segment, because investors buy long-term or short-term securities depending only on their expectations of future rate movements as against the current rates available. For instance, expectations of rising rates cause investors to prefer short-term securities initially, until rates have adjusted; falling rates cause investors to favor long-term securities initially.

If it is true that there is no maturity preference, then the reward, or return, for investing in a long-term security should be the same as the return from investing for the same time period in a short-term security and rolling the investment over at expected future short-term rates. In other words, a dollar invested in a long-term security with a three-year maturity should bring the same reward as a dollar invested in a one-year security and reinvested in a one-year security in both the second and third year. Mathematically:

$$\$1(1 + R_3)^3 = \$1(1 + R_1)^1 \times (1 + r_e)^1 \times (1 + r_e)^1$$

where R_1 and R_3 represent the observed market rates for the current one-year and three-year rate, respectively, and r_e the expected one-year rate in the roll-over period. PEH implies that the return on any current long-term security, in this case R_3, should be an unbiased (geometric) average of the current short-term rate (here, R_1) and the short-term rates expected to prevail in succeeding years:

$$(1 + R_3)^3 = (1 + R_1)^1 \times (1 + r_e)^1 \times (1 + r_e)^1$$

Even though it may seem to most investors that the ordinary purchaser of securities is most decidedly not indifferent to the two alternative ways of investing, it can be argued that the result reflects reasonable behavior. For instance, assume that the current two-year rate is 10 percent, the current one-year rate is 5 percent, and the general market truly believes that the one-year rate next year will be 10 percent. Under these assumptions, the two-year rate is not an unbiased average of the current one-year and the expected one-year rates:

$$(1.10)^2 \neq (1.05) \times (1.10).$$

If this is the case, investors and debtors will have differing preferences for short-term and long-term securities. By borrowing short-term at the current 5 percent with an expectation of refinancing next year at 10 percent, debtors expect to secure financing costing an average 7.5 percent over the two-year period:

$$\text{average rate} = (1.05) \times (1.10) = 1.075.$$

Debtors preferentially seek to sell one-year securities, and have to increase the rate on these securities to attract investors to the available (large) supply. Similarly, investors preferentially invest in the long-term security yielding 10 percent rather than in the alternative strategy yielding an expected 7.50 percent. Rates on the two-year security fall as the available supply is sought by a large number of investors. This rate adjustment continues until the two-year security price and yield and the one-year security price and yield have adjusted and there is no longer a differential supply and demand between short-term and long-term securities. This occurs, of course, where the current long-term rate is indeed equal to the unbiased average of the current short-term and successive expected short-term rates.

The above relationship between long-term rates, short-term rates, and expectations can be used to estimate expected rates from directly observable market rates. In general terms, we know that the n period rate is an average of the current one-period rate and succeeding $n - 1$ expected short-term rates:

$$(1 + R_n)^n = \prod_{i=2}^{n} (1 + r_{ei}) \times (1 + R_1)$$

In the same manner, the $n + 1$ period rate is an average of the current one-period rate and succeeding n expected one-period rates:

$$(1 + R_{n+1})^{n+1} = (1 + r_{en+1}) \times \prod_{i=2}^{n} (1 + r_{ei}) \times (1 + R_1)$$

Therefore by substitution:

$$(1 + R_{n+1})^{n+1} = (1 + R_n)^n \times (1 + r_{en+1})$$

or

$$(1 + R_{n+1})^{n+1}/(1 + R_n)^n = (1 + r_{en+1}) \qquad (9\text{–}2)$$

In this way, expected rates for any period in the future can be implied from current observable rates. More particularly, this implied forward rate (IFR) is a function of the rate on an asset maturing immediately before the period in question (here, time n) and the rate on an asset maturing immediately after the period in question (here,

Table 9-1. Calculation of Implied Forward Rates

Example 1: Three-month rate two months from today.

Today = January 18

Rates needed:
T-bill maturing 3/18 (77 days from today) Rate = 5.65%
T-bill maturing 6/18 (168 days from today) Rate = 5.85%

Calculation: $(1.0585)^{168/360} = (1.0565)^{77/360} \times (1 + \text{IFR})^{90/360}$

$$\frac{(1.0585)^{168/360}}{(1.0565)^{77/360}} = (1 + \text{IFR})^{90/360}$$

$$\frac{1.0268}{1.0118} = (1 + \text{IFR})^{90/360}$$

$$1.0148 = (1 + \text{IFR})^{.25}$$

$$1.0606 = (1 + \text{IFR})$$

IFR for period from March 18 to June 18 = 6.06%

Example 2: One-year rate three years from today.

Today = January 18, 1989

Rates needed:
T-note maturing 1/18/92 (3 years from today) Rate = 6.75%
T-note maturing 1/18/93 (4 years from today) Rate = 7.05%

Calculation: $(1.0705)^4 = (1.0675)^3 \times (1 + \text{IFR})^1$

$$\frac{(1.0705)^4}{(1.0675)^3} = (1 + \text{IFR})$$

$$\frac{1.313}{1.216} = (1 + \text{IFR})$$

$$= 1.0797$$

IFR for period from January 18, 1992, to January 18, 1993 = 7.97%

time $n + 1$). Examples of the calculations involved in an expected one-year rate three years from the present and an expected three-month rate two months from the present are given in table 9-1.

Assume the date is January 18. To calculate the IFR for a ninety-day Treasury bill as of March 18—two months from today—two rates are needed: the rate on a security maturing at the beginning of the period (March 18) and the rate on a security maturing at the end of the period (March 18 plus ninety days, or June 18). With rates of 5.65 percent and 5.85 percent, respectively, the IFR is calculated to be 6.06 percent. Note the use of fractions of a year in the calculation of powers: a 168-day investment at 5.85 percent should be equal to an investment for 77 days at 5.65 percent and another 90-day investment at the IFR of 6.06 percent.

Thus, from table 9–1, the IFR, an estimate of the ninety-day T-bill rate expected by the cash market as of March 18, is 6.06 percent. If current yields from the yield curve imply an expected rate, or IFR, of 6.06 percent for the ninety-day period from March through June, then we would expect the price of the March futures contract (which calls for delivery of a 90-day bill running from March through June) to also imply a yield for that period of 6.06 percent.

That is, given the free flow of market participants and information between the cash market for Treasury securities and the futures market, we would expect that the two prices or two rates, cash and futures, on this one asset, a 90-day Treasury bill from March through June, should be the same. The futures rate (R_{fut}) should be equal to the Implied Forward Rate from the yield curve for the same time period:

$$R_{fut} = IFR \tag{9–3}$$

Equation 9–3 is a more specific restatement of the pricing relation for the nonstorable asset futures in equation 9–2: The futures price should be equal to the expected price at delivery. However, the existence of two market consensus forecasts, cash and futures, and two asset markets allows us to offer a much more detailed proof of the accuracy of the pricing of nonstorables in financial futures than is available with agricultural futures. Indeed, the key to the expectational pricing of nonstorables in financial futures is not the pricing model itself, which is easily understandable, but the various cash and futures transactions possible if the relation between expected rates in the two markets does not hold. If the two rates are not equal, it can be shown that there is an opportunity to buy and sell securities to achieve an arbitrage profit; that is, to achieve a certain no risk cash flow with no investment on the part of the market participant. Later we discuss the proof of equation 9–3, these cash and futures transactions, in much greater detail.

QUASI-ARBITRAGE

Perhaps the easiest way to approach the arbitrage possibilities if equation 9–3 does not hold is to consider using the futures market as an alternative way to acquire a cash investment.[3] If an investor can use the futures market as an alternative means to buy a cash investment, rates in the futures market should be closely related to rates in the cash asset market.

For instance, an investor with money in January to invest for a six-month holding period can (*a*) acquire a six-month security maturing in June; (*b*) acquire a shorter-term security, say, one for three months maturing in March, and plan to roll over in March into another three-month security running from March to June; or (*c*) acquire a three-month security maturing in March, as in (*b*) and at the same time acquire the rollover security running from March through June by using the futures market, buying a March futures contract, and actually taking delivery in March. These choices are presented in table 9-2. Under the PEH, alternatives (*a*) and (*b*) should be the same, as has been discussed, and should yield the same rate of return for the six-month holding period. Next we show that alternative (*c*) must also yield that same rate of return for the six-month holding period.

As an example of the reasoning involved, assume that the investor was faced with the choices and rates in table 9-2, example A. The investor could simply buy a June T-bill in the cash market and hold it until June for a yield of 17.5 percent. Alternatively, the investor could buy the March bill yielding 15 percent, hold it until March, and plan to buy another bill in March that matures in June. It has been argued that investment in either alternative should be expected to lead to the same six-month holding period yield. Alternatives *a* and *b* imply a forward rate over the second three-month period of 20 percent, so the investor expects that the rollover in March will be into a security yielding 20 percent from March through June. This is exactly the situation discussed under the PEH.

If a futures market for the financial instrument also exists, however, a third investment alternative available, *c*, should also yield a return for the six-month period of 17.5 percent. The investor could acquire the March T-bill with a yield of 15 percent and buy another bill that runs from March through June using the futures market. Given the 15 percent yield for the first three months available from the March Treasury bill, the futures rate must equal 20 percent, the same as the IFR.

If the futures rate does not equal the IFR, then alternative *b* or *c*, with the higher overall return, will be favored by investors exclusively. In table 9-2, example A, the IFR of 20 percent is less than the futures rate of 25 percent. The investor choosing alternative *c*, using the March futures would have a total yield over the six months of: $(1.15) \times (1.25) = 1.20$, better than the holding period return under alternative *a* or *b* of 17.5 percent. If such an alternative exists, then all investors will prefer to use the futures market (alternative *c*) rather than the cash market alone (alternative *a* or *b*). This exclusive preference by investors for alternative *c* forces the futures price to rise relative to the other investment alternatives, and the futures yield to fall. If the futures rate falls to 20 percent, the return to alternative *c* becomes $(1.15) \times (1.20) = 1.175$, the same as alternative *a* or *b*. Thus, in equilibrium the futures rate should be 20 percent, the same as the IFR. (Of course, the prices and

Table 9–2. Quasi-Arbitrage Transaction: Buying a Strip of Futures

Example A: Date = January 1

Choice *a*: Buy 6-month T-bill (June maturity)
Rate = 17.50%

Choice *b*: Buy 3-month T-bill (March maturity)
Rate = 15%
Roll over into second T-bill (June maturity)
IFR = 20%

Choice *c*: Buy 3-month T-bill (March maturity)
Rate = 15%
Buy a second 3-month T-bill through futures market (March contract)
Rate = 25%

Choice depends on the rate in the futures market versus the Implied Forward Rate:

With *a* or *b*, return $= (1 + R_6)^{180/360} = (1 + R_3)^{90/360} \times (1 + \text{IFR})^{90/360}$

$(1 + .175)^{.5} = (1 + .15)^{.25} \times (1 + .20)^{.25}$

With *c*, return $= (1 + R_3)^{90/360} \times (1 + R_f)^{90/360}$

$= (1 + .15)^{.25} \times (1 + .25)^{.25}$

Choice *a*: Buy June T-bill

(price = \$1,000,000 − (.175 × \$1,000,000 × 180/360)
= \$1,000,000 − \$87,500
= \$912,500)

Get 17.50% return for 6-month holding period.

Choice *b*: Buy March T-bill

(price = \$1,000,000 − (.15 × \$1,000,000 × 90/360)
= \$1,000,000 − \$37,500
= \$962,500)

Buy June T-bill

(price = \$1,000,000 − (.20 × \$1,000,000 × 90/360)
= \$1,000,000 − \$50,000
= \$950,000)

Get $(1.15)^{.25} \times (1.20)^{.25}$ = 17.50% return for 6-month holding period.

Choice *c*: Buy March T-bill

(price = \$962,500)

Buy March futures contract and take delivery

(price = \$1,000,000 − (.25 × \$1,000,000 × 90/360)
= \$1,000,000 − \$62,500
= \$937,500)

Get $(1.15)^{.25} \times (1.25)^{.25}$ = 20% return for 6-month holding period.

Table 9–2. (Continued)

Example B: Date = January 1	
Choice *a*:	Buy 6-month T-bill (June maturity) Rate = 17.50%
Choice *b*:	Buy 3-month T-bill (March maturity) Rate = 15% Roll over into second T-bill (June maturity) IFR = 20%
Choice *c*:	Buy 3-month T-bill (March maturity) Rate = 15% Buy a second 3-month T-bill through futures market (March contract) Rate = 18%
Choice *a*:	Buy June T-bill (price = \$912,500) Get 17.50% return for 6-month holding period.
Choice *b*:	Buy March T-bill (price=\$962,500) Buy June T-bill (price = \$950,000) Get $(1.15)^{.25} \times (1.20)^{.25}$ = 17.50% return for 6-month holding period.
Choice *c*:	Buy March T-bill (price—\$962,500) Buy March futures contract and take delivery (price = \$1,000,000 − (.18 × \$1,000,000 × 90/360) = \$1,000,000 − \$45,000 — \$955,000) Get $(1.15)^{.25} \times (1.18)^{.25}$ = 16.50% return for 6-month holding period.

yields of the three-month security and the six-month security also adjust as well to the differing demand of investors; in the example, only the futures rate is shown as adjusting.) As this example shows, the existence of investors who use the futures market to acquire their rollover security at the lower futures price, or higher futures rate (25 percent), ensures that the IFR indeed equals the futures rate, or that equations 9–2 and 9–3 hold.

What happens if the futures rate is less than the Implied Forward Rate? This situation is shown in table 9–2, Example B. With the futures rate at 18 percent, the return to alternative (*c*) is (1.15) × (1.18) = (1.165) for the six months compared to the 17.50 percent from alternative *a* or *b*. In this case, there is a preference for the cash market securities and little demand for the futures, causing the futures price to fall (and the futures rate to rise) relative to the cash securities. The adjustment in prices will stop when the return on *c* is indeed equal to *a* or *b*, or when the futures rate is 20 percent, the same as the Implied Forward Rate.

This reasoning can be extended into yet more distant futures delivery months. An investor in January can acquire, for instance, the one-year Treasury bill or invest in a three-month bill and buy three futures contracts for March, June, and September deliveries; this set of futures purchases is known as a strip of futures. The return for the one-year bill should be the same as the return from buying the current March bill and buying bills using the March, June, and September futures contracts. Thus, it should be the case that the rates for a series of consecutive futures contracts are equal to their respective IFRs. That is, the June futures contract rate should be equal to the implied forward rate for a security running from June through September. This extention of the buying of futures contracts over the available delivery months compared to investments in the cash market for T-bills lends the quasi-arbitrage strategy its name, buying a strip of futures.

A very similar quasi-arbitrage opportunity using the March futures contract is represented in table 9–3. Here, the holding period is three months, and the choice of available investments is between (*a*) acquiring a three-month treasury bill for the full holding period, or (*b*) acquiring a six-month T-bill, a longer maturity than needed, and at the same time arranging to sell the bill at the end of the holding period in March through the futures market. Again, the choice between *a* and *b* depends on the total return for the three-month holding period. This requires a comparison of the three-month rate (15 percent) with the return from the purchase and eventual sale at the futures price of the six-month bill. In this case, if the futures rate is less than the IFR, the futures price is too high. A better return can be had if the investor uses this too-high futures price to sell off the original six-month bill. Under *b*, the three-month return is 18.6 percent, and all investors with a three-month holding period would favor alternative *b*, selling the futures contract. Again, such differential selling would continue until the futures price declined sufficiently so that the futures rate does indeed equal the IFR. The investment strategy for the three-month holding period and its consequences, if the futures rate is greater than the IFR, is left to the reader as an exercise.

This second quasi-arbitrage is a hedged yield curve ride. The name is derived from a popular strategy, in the cash market alone, of buying a security with a maturity longer than the intended holding period, the six-month security in this example, with the intent of "riding the yield curve" down and selling the now short-term security at the end of the holding period. With a futures market available, the investor does not have to wait for the end of the holding period to see if resale rates are indeed favorable and the yield curve ride a success. With a futures market, the resale price

Table 9-3. Quasi-Arbitrage Transaction: Hedged Yield Curve Ride

Date = January 1

Choice *a*: Buy 3-month T-bill (March maturity)
Rate = 15%

Choice *b*: Buy 6-month T-bill (June maturity)
Rate = 17.50%
Sell bill into futures market in 3 months (March contract)
Rate = 18%

Choice *a*: Buy March T-bill (price = $962,500).
Get 15% return for 3-month holding period.

Choice *b*: Buy June T-bill (price = $912,500).
Sell March futures contract (price = $955,000).
Return on 3-month holding period:

$$= \frac{\Delta \text{Price}}{\text{Amount Invested}} \times 360/90$$

$$= \frac{\$955{,}000 - \$912{,}500}{\$912{,}500} \times 360/90$$

$$= .186$$

Get 18.6% return for 3-month holding period.

of the six-month security can be fixed at the beginning of the holding period, and compared to the direct three-month alternative; hence the name of the quasi-arbitrage, *hedged* yield curve ride. Again, the futures market offers an alternative investment vehicle, and the use of the futures market by investors ensures that equation 9-3 does indeed hold.

In summary, then, the futures rate should equal the Implied Forward Rate. If it does not, then investors can use the futures market to acquire a more favorable rate on their investments whether the futures rate is greater than the IFR, as in table 9-2, example A, or the futures rate is less than the IFR, as in table 9-3. Such quasi-arbitrage opportunities should guarantee that the futures rate is equal to the IFR in equilibrium.

ARBITRAGE

To be effective, quasi-arbitrage transactions require that there be investors with capital to commit for a certain holding period. We can go one step further in the discussion of cash versus futures transactions under equation 9-3 and consider a pure arbitrage. An arbitrage opportunity exists when an asset sells for two different prices in the same market. Arbitrage opportunities by their very nature do not last long.

With the ability to buy at the lower price and simultaneously sell at the higher price producing a riskless, or certain, return on the arbitrage transaction, investors tend to drive the prices to equality by these differential transactions. The arbitrage transactions described next serve to ensure that the price of a three-month Treasury bill should be the same in the cash and futures market, or that futures rate equals the IFR.

IMPLIED FORWARD RATE GREATER THAN FUTURES RATE. If the futures rate is less than the IFR for the ninety-day T-bill deliverable into the futures contract, this implies that the price of that bill in the futures market is too high compared to the cash market price. Consequently, an arbitrageur seeks to sell the T-bill in the futures market while simultaneously acquiring that bill in the cash market. The arrangement to sell the bill for future delivery in the futures market is straightforward (see table 9–4). In the case of the March futures contract, the arbitrageur sells one futures contract at the current price of $955,000 for March delivery. No cash flow on the futures contract takes place at this time, the arbitrageur promising to deliver a 90-day T-bill in March. (Margin on the futures contract, as well as commission costs, are ignored in this example.)

The arbitrageur, in turn, must arrange now to buy that T-bill running from March through June at the implied forward rate. This can be accomplished by transactions (2) and (3) in table 9–4. The arbitrageur buys the Treasury bill deliverable into the March futures, the bill maturing June 15, at a rate of 17.5 percent (price of $912,500). The arbitrageur can acquire the bill without any investment by borrowing the funds, $912,500, for the period the money is needed, the three months until March 15, the maturity of the contract. The two transactions can be considered a means of buying the bill underlying the March futures contract, the June 15 bill, and "storing" it until needed for delivery into the March futures contract.

To see that transactions 2 and 3 do indeed result in the arbitrageur acquiring the March-to-June Treasury bill in the cash market at the Implied Forward Rate, consider the original IFR equation:

$$\$1(1 + R_6)^{180/360} = \$1(1 + R_3)^{90/360} \times (1 + IFR)^{90/360}$$

or

$$\$1/(1 + R_3)^{90/360} \times (1 + R_6)^{180/360} = \$1(1 + IFR)^{90/360}$$

To synthesize an investment of $1 at the Implied Forward Rate (the right side), the arbitrageur must borrow the present value of $1 for 90 days at the 90-day rate ($\$1/(1 + R_3)^{90/360}$) and invest it at the six-month rate for 180 days. With a difference of scale, this is what transactions 2 and 3 accomplish, as the arbitrageur borrows the required sum of money, $912,500, for three months at the three-month rate, and invests it at the six-month rate by buying the six-month Treasury bill. On March

Table 9-4. Arbitrage Transaction, Hedged Yield Curve Ride

Date = January 1

Current market rates:	March T-bill	= 15%	
	(price	= $962,500)	
	June T-bill	= 17.5%	Implied Forward Rate = 20%
	(price	= $912,500)	(March through June)
	March futures	= 18%	
	(price	= $955,000)	

Arbitrage transactions on January 1:

Futures market:

1. Sell March T-bill futures contract.
   (Will receive $955,000 as of March delivery).

Cash T-bill market:

2. Borrow $912,500 at 15% for 3 months.
   (Promise to pay $912,500 × $(1.15)^{.25}$ = $944,946 at end of March.)
3. Buy June T-bill with borrowed proceeds.
   Pay $912,500.

Arbitrage transactions at the end of March:

4. Deliver June T-bill into futures contract.
   Receive $955,000.
5. Pay back initial borrowing of $944,946.
   Arbitrage profit: $955,000 − $944,946 = $10,054.

Implied Repo Rate (IRR) Calculation

Break-even point on arbitrage transactions where:

Amount promised to pay back on initial borrowing	= Proceeds from delivery in futures market
Promise to pay back	= Proceeds from March futures contract
$912,500$(1 + IRR)^{.25}$	= $955,000
$(1 + IRR)^{.25}$	= $955,000/$912,500
	1.0465
(1 + IRR)	= 1.1993
Implied Repo Rate	= 19.9%

---

15 this synthetic bill (the $1 investment at the IFR) can be delivered into the futures market. Because the Treasury bills trade on a discount basis, the price paid for the synthetic IFR bill is less than the price received for it in the futures market (futures rate greater than Implied Forward Rate).

Once the transactions in 1 through 3 are effected at the outset of the arbitrage, all the rates (futures and two cash market rates) have been fixed, and the arbitrage profit is guaranteed no matter what happens to interest rates during the arbitrage period.

We can see this by following the consequences of the three initial transactions. In March, the arbitrageur must deliver a three-month Treasury bill into the futures market. Because a six-month bill was bought three months ago at the onset of the arbitrage, the trader has a three-month Treasury bill conformable for delivery. At delivery, the futures price, $955,000 is received. The only other obligation remaining to the arbitrageur is to pay back the three-month loan plus interest, or $944,946. Using the proceeds from the futures delivery, the arbitrageur can meet the loan obligation and have an arbitrage profit of $10,054 remaining.

The ability to enter both markets simultaneously, selling the March three-month T-bill in the futures market while at the same time synthesizing it in the cash market, as in table 9–4, eventually drives the futures rate to the IFR. Selling futures depresses the futures price and raises the futures rate. Similarly, borrowing short-term and lending long-term also causes the IFR to readjust, in this case downward. The arbitrage transactions, then, serve to ensure that the futures rate equals the IFR, or that equations 9–2 and 9–3 hold for financial futures. As stated at the beginning of the section, the arbitrage transactions are the key to the accuracy of equation 9–3.

Another way to approach the arbitrage transactions in table 9–4 is to compare it to the quasi-arbitrage in table 9–3. In this quasi-arbitrage, the futures rate was less than the IFR. The preferred investment alternative in the quasi-arbitrage (alternative (*b*) in table 9–3) is also transactions 1 and 2 of the arbitrage (table 9–4). The arbitrage differs in that no investment is made by the arbitrageur; instead, the funds needed are acquired through borrowing at the three-month rate. Arbitrage transaction 3 can be considered the reverse of choice *a* in the quasi-arbitrage (table 9–3). That is, the choice not taken in the quasi-arbitrage (investing at the three-month rate) is reversed in the arbitrage (borrowing at the three-month rate). The two transactions, quasi-arbitrage and arbitrage are thus very closely related, in essence differing by one step.

MARKET IMPERFECTIONS: THE IMPLIED REPO RATE. Although accurate in its general outline, the arbitrage transaction just described depends critically on the ability to borrow and invest at the rates used to calculate the initial IFR. These transactions are available theoretically to anyone who can arrange to borrow, invest, and sell in the futures market at these rates. Selling in the futures market and lending or investing at the Treasury rate (buying the six-month T-bill at the six-month cash rate) is certainly possible for any investor. The ability to borrow at the Treasury rate for any period is generally not available. Thus, to be realistic, the arbitrage transactions as calculated in table 9–4 must be modified to take into account the true borrowing rate for these transactions. We can ask the question, at what rate on the three-month borrowing would the arbitrage transaction still be profitable? The IRR calculation in table 9–4 shows that the arbitrage profit is 0 (or negative) at a three-month borrowing rate of 19.9 percent or higher. At 19.9 percent, the arbitrageur would have to repay $955,000, which is the amount received in the futures market at delivery.

This break-even rate is the implied repo rate, and it is the highest rate that still ensures an arbitrage profit allowed on the transaction. Under actual market conditions, then, the arbitrage opportunity is generally analyzed by the break-even or the repo rate implied on the arbitrage compared to the three-month rate actually available to the arbitrageur. If the arbitrageur can borrow at 19.9 percent or lower, then the arbitrage can be performed. If the borrowing rate for the period in question is greater than 19.9 percent, then no profitable arbitrage opportunity exists.

The break-even rate is termed the implied repo rate because it is usually compared to the borrowing cost under a repo, or repurchase, agreement. Most arbitrageurs acquire funds through repurchase agreements, the sale of a security to another with the promise to buy it back at a higher price at the end of some time period. This repurchase agreement creates a collateralized loan: the security is transferred to the other party while the arbitrageur has the use of the money. The repurchase at the higher price results in the return of the collateral and the repayment of principal plus implied interest or the difference in price. Thus, if the arbitrageur can effect a repo agreement at a repo rate lower than the implied repo rate of 19.9 percent, then the arbitrage is profitable.

The pricing relation of equation 9–3 is not exact but results in a range of futures prices over which the implied repo rate, compared to the current repo borrowing rate, is too high to make the arbitrage possible. There is, therefore, a band of possible futures prices and futures rates within which the futures price can vary without resulting in an arbitrage reaction. If the futures price trades beyond this range, however, the arbitrage transactions in table 9–4 become profitable, and the ensuing arbitrage transactions tend to drive the futures price back within the band.

FUTURES RATE GREATER THAN IMPLIED FORWARD RATE. Arbitrage profits are also available if the futures rate is greater than the IFR for the ninety-day bill deliverable into the futures market. As might be expected, the transactions in this arbitrage are closely related to the transactions in the previous arbitrage. If the futures rate is too high (futures price too low) relative to the IFR in the cash market, the arbitrageur wants to acquire the T-bill in the futures market at the too-low price while simultaneously arranging to sell that bill in the cash market at the forward rate. Table 9–5 shows an example of an arbitrage transaction of this sort.

Again, the transaction in the futures market is relatively straightforward: the arbitrageur promises to buy a ninety-day bill for March delivery. At the same time, the arbitrageur completes two transactions in the cash market: (*a*) by arranging to acquire a three-month T-bill, paying a price based on the three-month yield, and (*b*) by borrowing the funds required for six months at the six-month rate. In dollar amounts, the arbitrageur borrows $962,500, the price of the three-month bill, and promises to repay this principal plus 17.5 percent interest in six months (June). The

Table 9–5. Arbitrage Transaction, Strip of Futures

Date = January 1

Current market rates:	March T-bill	= 15%	
	(price	= \$962,500)	
	June T-bill	= 17.5%	Implied Forward Rate = 20%
	(price	= \$912,500)	(March through June)
	March futures	= 25%	
	(price	= \$937,500)	

Arbitrage transactions on January 1:

Futures market:

1. Buy March T-bill futures contract.
   (Promise to pay \$937,500 as of March delivery).

Cash T-bill market:

2. Borrow \$962,500 at 17.5% for 6 months.
   (Promise to pay \$962,500 $(1.175)^{.5}$ = \$1,043,325.14 at end of June.)
3. Buy March T-bill with borrowed proceeds.
   Pay \$962,500.

Arbitrage transactions at the end of March:

4. March T-bill matures; collect \$1,000,000.
5. Take delivery on March futures; receive June T-bill; pay \$937,500. Keep 62,500 difference in price.

Arbitrage transactions at end of June:

6. June T-bill matures; collect \$1,000,000.
7. Use \$1,000,000 + \$62,500 to repay 6-month loan.
   Arbitrage profit: \$1,062,500 − \$1,043,325.14 = \$19,174.86

Implied Repo Rate Calculations

Break-even point on arbitrage transactions where:

Amount promised to pay back = Proceeds from maturing bill plus price difference on initial borrowing

Promise to pay back	= Proceeds plus price difference
$\$962,500(1 + IRR)^{.50}$	= \$1,062,500
$(1 + IRR)^{.50}$	= \$1,062,500/\$962,500
	1.104
(1 + IRR)	= 1.218
Implied Repo Rate	= 21.8%

arbitrageur then uses the proceeds to acquire the three-month cash T-bill. These three arbitrage transactions again set the rates at which the arbitrage takes place, locking in the arbitrage profit. Again, the arbitrageur does not use any personal money, borrowing whatever is needed to set up the transactions.

In March two events occur: first, the three-month T-bill acquired in the cash market now matures, and the arbitrageur collects its $1 million face value. Second, the March futures contract matures, and the arbitrageur takes delivery. With a futures price of $937,500 to pay, the arbitrageur has sufficient funds to acquire the bill and to have an excess of $62,500. To be conservative in the arbitrage, let us assume that the funds are not invested, but are retained at 0 percent interest until the end of the arbitrage.

Finally, in June, the last of the arbitrage transactions unwind: first, the three-month T-bill acquired in the futures market in March matures, and the arbitrageur receives the $1 million face value. Second, the original six-month loan matures, and the arbitrageur must pay the principal plus interest, using the $1 million face value just acquired plus the $62,500 previously received, netting an arbitrage profit of $19,174.86.

This second set of arbitrage transactions, like the first, is a combination of the quasi-arbitrage transactions in table 9–2 discussed previously. In the quasi-arbitrage, the favored choice was *b*, buying a March T-bill and the March futures. This is steps 1 and 2 of the arbitrage. Step 3, borrowing at the six-month rate, can be considered the reverse of choice *a*; rather than investing at the six-month rate by buying a six-month T-bill, the arbitrageur would reverse choice *a* by borrowing at the six-month rate.

There is also an implied repo rate on this arbitrage, the break-even rate on the six-month borrowing that would serve to eliminate the arbitrage profit. Again, the question is, what is the highest rate at which the arbitrageur could borrow for the six-month period and still make an arbitrage profit? Table 9–5 shows the implied repo rate calculation. As before, this indicates that the arbitrageur must be able to arrange repo financing at a rate of 21.8 percent or lower or there will be no profitable arbitrage. Again, the inability to borrow at the Treasury rate leads to a band of futures prices within which the equilibrium futures price can remain.

One of the two arbitrage transactions occurs, then, if the futures rate does not equal the implied forward rate. The purchase and sales transactions discussed earlier change relative prices and drive the two rates to equality. Thus, equation 9–3 can be expected to hold.

OTHER MARKET IMPERFECTIONS

Besides the ability to borrow at the Treasury rate, there are two additional market imperfections to be mentioned in connection with the arbitrage transactions just discussed. First, the examples as presented ignore any margin on the futures position. Margin would have to be posted at the contract's initiation. In both arbitrages, there is a cash T-bill in the possession of the arbitrageur; if we assume part of the T-bill position can be used as original margin, then this consideration is not of major importance to the success of the arbitrage transaction. However, after the posting of initial margin, there is the possibility of cash flow, either positive or negative, arising out of the daily marking-to-market. This is where the arbitrage can break down in the sense of being a certain profit at initiation. If there is a margin call, and additional funds are required during the arbitrage, then these funds must be borrowed at the rate in force at the time of the margin call. This would reduce the arbitrage profit possible. Similarly, a positive cash flow into the margin account could be reinvested at current market rates, and this would serve to increase the overall profit on the arbitrage transaction. Thus, due to this institutional characteristic of the futures market, there is some uncertainty as to the ultimate profitability of the arbitrage transaction. The size of the cash flow (either positive or negative), and the market rates at which the cash flow could be invested or borrowed, are unknown at arbitrage initiation. However, an estimate of the possible size of the futures price movement can be gained from past price volatility. Hence, the arbitrage profit, although no longer certain at initiation, can be reasonably estimated before the transactions are begun.

The second consideration in the success of the arbitrage is tax liability. There are differential tax rates applied to profits or losses on cash versus futures transactions. Thus, the "band" of futures equilibrium values discussed earlier is also determined, in part, by the after-tax cash flows possible on the arbitrage to the marginal arbitrageur.

EMPIRICAL EVIDENCE: TREASURY BILL PRICING EFFICIENCY

The accuracy of equation 9–3, that futures yields should be equal to the corresponding implied forward rate in the cash market, has been tested extensively for the Treasury bill futures contract.

In general, the consensus from the empirical tests seems to be that T-bill futures are efficiently priced and that the futures market rates are indeed equal to expected rates extracted from the cash market. However, the studies vary in their sample period as well as in their treatment of such issues as transaction costs, the use of futures contracts rather than forward contracts, and the uses of nearby or deferred contracts for which no deliverable T-bill would exist. Such differences in method have led to conflicting results that are not easily reconciled. Some studies have concluded there is a definite inefficiency in T-bill futures prices;[4] others, using a similar time period but differing in their treatment of transaction costs and in statistical technique, have concluded that prices are efficient.[5] In addition, almost every study finds some evidence of inefficiency in futures prices, but many conclude that the discrepancy in rates is not sufficient to overcome institutional obstacles to exploit them. For instance, both

D.R. Capozza and B. Cornell[6] and R.J. Rendleman and C.E. Carabini[7] find evidence of consistent profitable arbitrage opportunities but cite the indirect costs of monitoring futures markets, training personnel, and entering into risky transactions (such as borrowing by short-selling Treasury bills) as probably sufficient to prevent profitable exploitation of opportunities of this size by corporations or commercial banks. G. Morgan attributes the seeming inefficiency he found to differences in characteristics of futures relative to forward contracts.[8]

More recently, I.G. Kawaller and J. Koch have shown that the apparent inefficiency in T-bill futures pricing can be explained through the financing of the arbitrage transactions via the repo market.[9] The authors find that the direction and magnitude of the futures rate-implied forward rate difference is attributable to the difference between cash T-bill rates and the rates at which the arbitrage transaction can be accomplished using the current rate on repo financing. In other words, the futures price is efficient when the actual transaction costs, particularly the financing or borrowing cost, is accounted for.

Finally, R.W. Kolb and G.D. Gay approach the question of T-bill futures pricing efficiency in a different way, and find considerable pricing inefficiency.[10] They compare the futures yield on the once-traded one-year T-bill futures contract with the yield on the corresponding strip of three-month T-bill futures. By comparing the yields on two different futures transactions, the one-year versus the three-month strip, this approach can eliminate some of the more ambiguous market imperfections that were mentioned previously as having an impact on efficiency: tax differentials between spot and futures transactions and differences in cash flow due to marking to market. The authors find a large difference between yields on the one-year versus the strip of three-month futures; in addition, such institutional imperfections as transaction costs and margin cash flow are tested for and found insufficient to explain the differential. However, because of the relatively light volume in the one-year contract, and because trading in the contract was eventually discontinued, it is difficult to ascertain if this pricing inefficiency has continued.

The general conclusion seems to be that whatever discrepancy in rates is found is sufficiently small and infrequent to allow a general, qualified conclusion of efficiency. Thus, the empirical evidence suggests that, in T-bills, the futures price reflects the expected spot price.

PRICING OF STORABLE FINANCIALS

COST OF CARRY MODEL

As with agricultural commodity futures, some financial commodities can be delivered into more than one futures maturity, and hence are considered storable.

Because the commodity, such as a Treasury bond, note, or stock index portfolio, can survive unchanged from today through several delivery periods, it serves as a direct link between today's price of the commodity and the price of a distant delivery futures contract on that commodity.

As with agricultural futures, the futures price for a storable financial asset is equal to today's spot price plus the cost of carrying that financial asset from today to future delivery. The cost of carrying a Treasury bond through time consists of two cash flows: the first is related to the current market short-term interest rate. The short-term interest rate can be considered the opportunity cost of investment for the short-term carry period. If funds were not used to purchase and hold the long-term security until futures delivery, they would be invested in another, short-term, financial instrument over this period. Alternatively, it is common for market participants to borrow the long-term asset purchase price for the carry period. In this case, the short-term rate would represent the actual borrowing cost for the holding period. In any event, part of the cost of carry is composed of the current short-term market rate for the carry period, either as opportunity cost or as actual borrowing rate.

The second component of carrying cost is unique to financial futures, and represents the cash flow generated from holding a long-term financial instrument through time. In contrast to the short-term cost of borrowing, the long-term rate represents a positive cash flow to the bondholder of coupon income on the asset for the carry period. Holding a $100,000 face value, 10 percent coupon bond for three months, for instance, will bring to the holder three months of 10 percent coupon income, or $2,500.

In general terms, the futures price is equal to the spot price today, time t, (S_t) plus the net cost of carry, or:

$$F_{t,T} = S_t + (r - y) \times (T - t)/360 \times S_t \qquad (9\text{–}4)$$

Here, r represents the short term borrowing or opportunity cost over the carry period $(T - t)/360$, and y represents the long-term bond coupon income.

As can be seen from equation 9–4, whether the futures price is greater than the current bond spot price (a negative carry market) or the futures price is less than the current bond price (a positive carry market) depends on the relative size of short-term versus long-term rates, or the shape of the yield curve.

If the yield curve is positively sloped, its normal shape, then long-term bond income exceeds the short-term borrowing cost. The bondholder must thus discount the futures price from current bond prices to entice someone to buy the bond in the futures market for a more distant delivery. For instance, if the yield curve is as shown

Table 9-6. Futures Price of a T-bond Futures under Cost of Carry Model

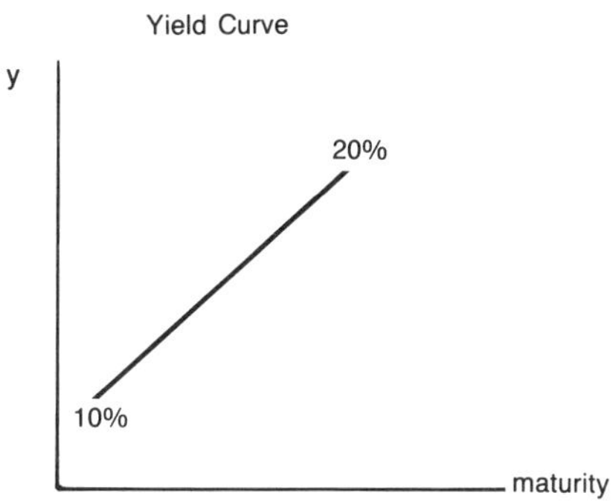

Short-term yield:	10%
Long-term yield:	20%
Spot T-bond price:	100 ($100,000)

Cost of carry:

Three-month carry:

a. Short-term borrowing or opportunity cost:

$0.10 \times \$100{,}000 \times 90/360 = \$2{,}500$

b. Long-term yield:

$0.20 \times \$100{,}000 \times 90/360 = \$5{,}000$

Equilibrium futures price:

$$\begin{aligned} F_{t,T} &= S_t + (r - y) \times (T - t)/360 \times S_t \\ &= \$100{,}000 + (.10 - .20) \\ &\quad \times 90/360 \times \$100{,}000 \\ &= \$100{,}000 + \$2{,}500 - \$5{,}000 \\ &= \$97{,}500 \text{ (or 97.5)} \end{aligned}$$

Six-month carry:

a. Short-term borrowing or opportunity cost:

$0.10 \times \$100{,}000 \times 180/360 = \$5{,}000$

b. Long-term yield:

$0.20 \times \$100{,}000 \times 180/360 = \$10{,}000$

Equilibrium futures price:

$$\begin{aligned} F_{t,T} &= S_t + (r - y) \times (T - t)/360 \times S_t \\ &= \$100{,}000 + (.10 - .20) \\ &\quad \times 180/360 \times \$100{,}000 \\ &= \$100{,}000 + \$5{,}000 - \$10{,}000 \\ &= 95{,}000 \text{ (or 95.0)} \end{aligned}$$

in table 9-6, then the bondholder gains a net positive cash flow from holding the bond through the carry period. Assume the storable bond is priced at par, or $100,000. Over a three-month period, the bondholder must pay a 10 percent borrowing rate on the $100,000 bond, or in dollar terms, a charge of $2,500:

$$\text{short-term carry cost} = \$100{,}000 \times 0.10 \times 90/360 = \$2{,}500.$$

At the same time, the holder receives a long-term yield of 20 percent for three months, or in dollar terms, \$5,000:

long-term income = \$100,000 × 0.20 × 90/360 = \$5,000.

On a net basis, then, the holder of a long-term bond receives a positive cash flow of \$2,500 for holding the bond over the three months. If the bondholder desires to sell the bond forward in the futures market three months from today, the spot price of \$100,000 must be discounted by \$2,500, the net cost of carrying, to arrive at a futures price of \$97,500:

FP = \$100,000 + (0.10 − 0.20) × 90/360 × \$100,000 = \$97,500.

If the seller attempts to set a futures price greater than \$97,500, no one will be willing to take the long side of the contract. With a futures price greater than \$97,500, it would be more profitable to acquire the bond by buying it today and storing it at a net cost of \$97,500, rather than by acquiring it through the futures market and paying more. Thus, the futures price must reflect the current spot price plus the net cost of carry. No other futures price represents an equilibrium.

In the example, the equilibrium futures price for delivery in three months is \$97,500. Similarly, table 9-6 shows that the futures price for six-month delivery would reflect the net cost of carrying for six months, or a positive cash flow to the bondholder of \$5,000. Thus, the equilibrium price for a six-month delivery would be \$95,000. A positive yield curve, then, with short-term rates less than long-term rates, results in an equilibrium structure of futures prices for various maturities representing a positive carry market. With a positively sloping yield curve, futures prices decrease with increasing maturity.

Similar reasoning is involved in the determination of futures prices with a negative yield curve (see table 9-7). In this instance, short-term borrowing rates are 10 percent, while long-term yields are 5 percent. Assume the storable bond is priced at par, or \$100,000. The holder of a \$100,000 long-term bond for three months would be required to pay \$2,500 in financing costs:

short-term carrying cost = \$100,000 × 0.10 × 90/360 = \$2,500.

At the same time, the bondholder would receive \$1,250 in coupon income:

long-term carrying cost = \$100,000 × 0.05 × 90/360 = \$1,250.

Thus, the futures price would have to be high enough to compensate the bondholder for the net cost of carrying of (\$2,500 − \$1,250) or \$1,250. The equilibrium futures price for three-month delivery would be \$101,250. Similarly, the six-month equi-

Table 9–7. Futures Price of a T-bond Futures under Cost of Carry Model

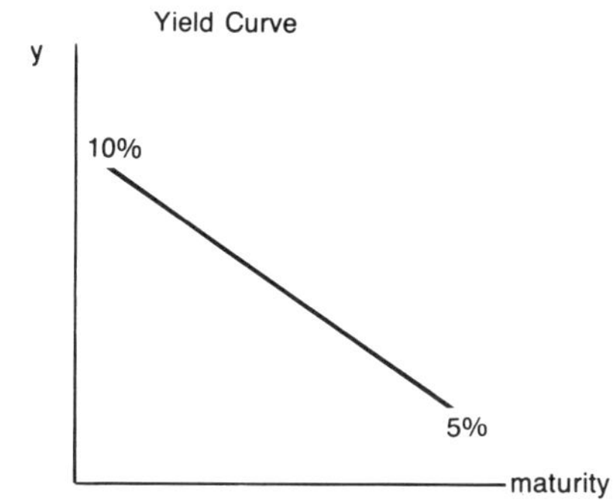

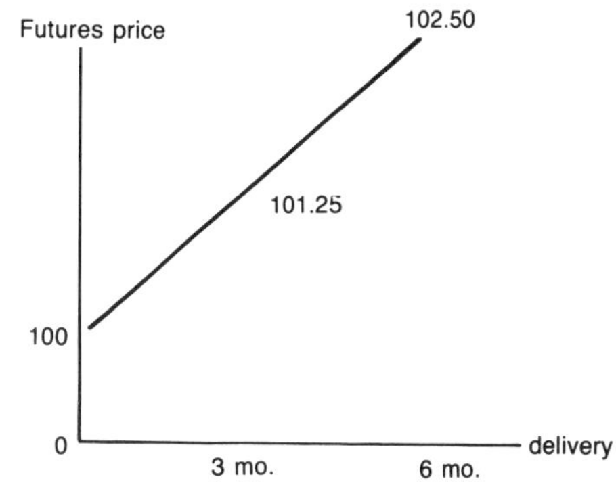

Short-term yield: 10%
Long-term yield: 5%
Spot T-bond price: 100 ($100,000)

Cost of carry:

Three-month carry:

a. Short-term borrowing or opportunity cost:

0.10 × $100,000 × 90/360 = $2,500

b. Long-term income:

0.05 × $100,000 × 90/360 = $1,250

Equilibrium futures price:

$F_{t,T} = S_t + (r - y) \times (T - t)/360 \times S_t$

− $100,000 + (.10   .05)

× 90/360 × $100,000

= $100,000 + $2,500 − $1,250

= $101,250 (or 101.25)

Six-month carry:

a. Short-term borrowing or opportunity cost:

0.10 × $100,000 × 180/360 = $5,000

b. Long-term income:

0.05 × $100,000 × 180/360 = $2,500

Equilibrium futures price:

$F_{t,T} = S_t + (r - y) \times (T - t)/360 \times S_t$

= $100,000 + (.10 − .05)

× 180/360 × $100,000

= $100,000 + $5,000 − $2,500

= 102,500 (or 102.50)

librium futures price would be $102,500. Thus, a negative yield curve results in a negative carry market, with futures prices higher for more distant deliveries.

The general pricing formula, equation 9–4, is valid for any futures contract based on a long-term financial asset, including Treasury bonds, Treasury notes, and a stock portfolio. As in bond futures, the price on a stock index futures represents the net cost of carry on the asset, in this case the portfolio of stocks underlying the stock index. With a stock portfolio, as with a long-term Treasury bond, one cost of carry cash flow reflects the opportunity cost or actual borrowing cost for an investment in the index portfolio over the carry period. The other cash flow represents the yield received from holding a stock portfolio over the carry period. This is the dividend yield on the underlying stock portfolio. Thus, the futures price for a stock index futures depends on the initial index level, I_t, the short-term interest cost on the index portfolio r net of the positive cash flow of the dividend payments d, or:

$$F_{t,T} = I_t + (r - d) \times (T - t)/360 \times I_t \tag{9-5}$$

Again, whether the futures price reflects a positive or negative carry depends on the relative size of the short-term rate, the cash outflow compared to the dividend yield, the cash inflow to the portfolio holder. The pricing of stock index futures is discussed in much greater detail in chapter 11.

ARBITRAGE

The arbitrage arguments supporting pricing equation 9–4 are more direct than was the case with nonstorable financial futures. In either case—a positive or a negative carry market—arbitrage profits can be made whenever the futures price does not equal the current spot price plus the cost of carry.

As an example, it was determined in table 9–6 that the equilibrium futures price for the three-month contract was 97.5, or $97,500. If the futures price were greater, say $99,000, then an arbitrage opportunity would be present. In this case, the futures is overpriced by $1,500 relative to the spot commodity, the Treasury bond. If this is so, then the arbitrageur can make a riskless arbitrage profit by arranging to sell the futures at 99 and simultaneously acquiring the Treasury bond and arranging its financing at the current short-term market rate. In this instance, the arbitrageur can arrange to borrow the required purchase price of $100,000 for three months at the current three-month rate of 10 percent, agreeing to pay $2,500 interest plus $100,000 in principal repayment at the end of the three-month carrying period. The arbitrageur then carries the bond over the three month period, and in doing so gains the long-term yield of 20 percent, or $5,000 on the bond. Finally, at maturity of the futures, the arbitrageur delivers the bond, receives $99,000 in the futures market, repays the $102,500 borrowing (principal plus interest) with the $99,000 proceeds plus the $5,000 in bond income, for a net arbitrage profit of $99,000 + $5,000 less $102,500, or $1,500. This is also the dollar amount by which the futures was originally overpriced at the start of the arbitrage.

A similar arbitrage transaction can be arranged in a negative carry market if the futures price is greater than the theoretical price of 101.25. Again, with the futures overpriced, the arbitrageur can arrange to buy and hold the financial asset at the spot price plus the cost of carry, and simultaneously arrange to sell it and deliver at the futures price. Thus, in either a positive or negative carry market, the arbitrage transactions discussed here serve to exert downward selling pressure on the futures price until it does indeed reflect the current spot price plus the net cost of carry.

INSTITUTIONAL CONSIDERATIONS

Even though the arbitrage transactions relating to storable financial assets are like the simple ones outlined earlier, institutional details affect the equilibrium futures price. Some of these details relate to the design of the bond contract, and others relate to the arrangements used in the spot T-bond market to acquire a cash bond. Because these real life considerations can profoundly affect the equilibrium futures price, they are discussed in greater detail in the context of a particular arbitrage opportunity.

First, the futures contract on T-bonds and notes allows for delivery of a large number of bonds with different coupon and maturity characteristics. As discussed previously, one of the bonds conformable for delivery would be most advantageous for the seller to acquire and deliver into the futures market. This bond is the one with the largest difference between cash market price and futures invoice amount received, the cheapest to deliver (CTD). One bond, then, is generally expected to be the delivered bond. An arbitrageur who is interested in the possibility of a futures disequilibrium compares the cost of acquiring this CTD and the net cost of carrying it against the amount to be received for the bond when it is delivered into the futures market. Thus, the equilibrium futures price depends on the spot price of the CTD plus the net cost of its carry compared to the invoice amount of the CTD bond (FP × CF) received at delivery.

A second complicating factor relates to the determination of the full costs of acquiring any bond in the cash market. The full cost of the bond is composed not only of the price quoted in the market but also any accrued coupon interest on the bond since the last coupon payment. That is, a bond quoted, for instance, at a market price of 100 results in a full purchase price of $100,000 plus any accrued interest up to the purchase date. Thus, when calculating the equilibrium futures price, the cash price or the cost of acquiring the CTD bond must also reflect any cash flow involved in the payment of accrued interest.

As an example, let us calculate the full cash flow required to obtain the CTD bond for delivery into the June futures contract (see table 9–8). Assume the CTD is known and has an 11.5 percent coupon and a twenty-year maturity on November 15. Its current price is 105. If we plan to purchase the bond on January 2, we must pay the seller $105,000, the market quote, plus accrued interest from the last coupon payment date, November 15. This is because the payment of the full semiannual coupon always goes to the current bondholder. If we hold the bond to the next coupon payment date, May 15, we receive a payment of one-half of $11,500, or $5,750, the coupon interest from November 15 through May 15. However, we have not held the bond for the full six months, but purchased it on January 2. Part of the $5,750—47 days of interest—belongs to the previous owner who held the bond from November 15 through January 2. To adjust for this, the purchaser of any bond must pay the seller the value of the accrued interest up to the purchase date. Thus, to acquire the CTD, the purchaser needs to pay the market price of $105,000 plus accrued interest, 47/365 × $11,500 = $1,841.93, for a total of $106,484.93. In calculating the spot price of the bond, an adjustment must be made to reflect not only the quoted market price but also the accrued interest that must be paid.

Table 9-8. Cash and Carry Arbitrage Transactions

Date: January 2	Cheapest to deliver bond: 11.5% due November 15
Futures delivery: June 15	20-year maturity
Carry in days: 165 days	Current price: 105
	June futures price: 77.5
	Cheapest to deliver conversion factor: 1.3869
	Current short term borrowing rate: 7.25%

Coupon payments on cheapest to deliver bond as of January 2:

Last coupon payment date: 11/15 (47 days before January 2)

Next coupon payment date: 5/15 (31 days before June 15)

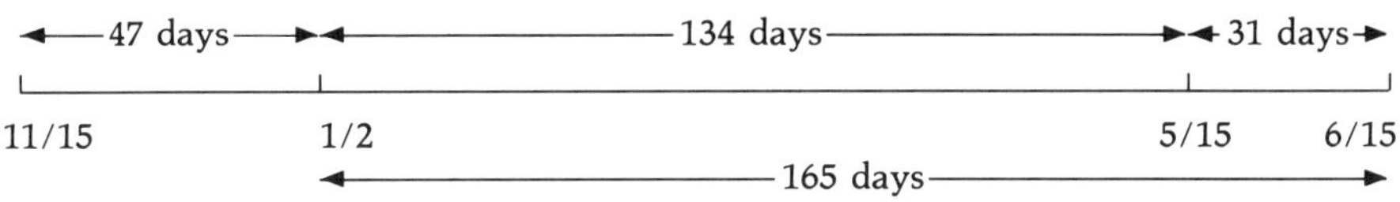

Cost of carry

a. Purchase price of bond: Spot price + accrued interest since last coupon

$105,000 + (47/365 × $11,500) = $105,000 + 1,484.89

= $106,484.89

b. Borrow purchase price of bond for carry period of 165 days at 7.25%:

Cost = $106,484.89 × 0.0725 × 165/365 = $3,489.93

c. Receive coupon payment of $5,750 on May 15

Spot price + cost of carry = $106,484.89 + 3,489.93 − 5,750

= $104,224.82

Receipt in futures market

a. Bond delivery price of cheapest to deliver

FP × CF = 77.5 × 1.3869 = 107.484 or $107,484.00

b. Accrued interest received from buyer since last coupon

Acc int = 31/365 × $11,500 = $979.39

Receipt in futures market: $107,484.00 + 979.39 = $108,463.39

Table 9-8. (Continued)

Arbitrage transactions:

January 2:

a. Borrow \$106,484.89 until June 15 (165 days) at 7.25%
(Promise to repay \$106,484.89$(1.0725)^{165/365}$ = \$109,974.82 on 6/15)

b. Buy cheapest to deliver bond (11.5% of 2015) with borrowed proceeds.

c. Sell June T-bond futures contract at FP = 77.5

May 15:

a. Receive coupon payment of \$5.750

June 15:

a. Deliver bond (11.5% of 2015) into futures and receive FP × CF + accrued interest
Receive (77.5 × 1.3869 = \$107,484) + \$979.39 for a total of \$108,463.39

b. Use borrowed proceeds and coupon payment received on May 15 to repay 165 day loan (from January 2)
Arbitrage profit = (\$108,463.39 + \$5,750 − \$109,974.82)
= \$4,238.57

We have calculated the spot price of the underlying bond. We next need to determine the cost of carry for the bond from purchase date, January 2, to futures delivery, June 15. The first component of the cost of carry is the short-term rate: if we borrow the purchase price necessary to acquire the bond, we must pay the current short-term rate for the period January 2 through June 15 (165 days). If the current short-term rate is 7.25 percent for the period, then the short-term interest carry cost is equal to:

$$.0725 \times 165/365 \times \$106{,}484.89 = \$3489.93$$

However, the second component of the cost of carry is a cash inflow to the bond holder, the coupon payment of \$5,750 received May 15 plus any interest on this sum invested from receipt on May 15 through the delivery of the bond at the end of the carrying period on June 15. To be conservative, let us assume no reinvestment of the \$5,750 coupon received. Thus, the net cost of carry is \$109,974.82 less \$5,750 in coupon income, or \$104,224.82. The net amount necessary, then, to acquire the CTD bond for the June futures contract and hold it until June 15 delivery is \$104,224.82.

To know if an arbitrage possibility is indeed present in the futures market, we need to know what the arbitrageur would receive in the futures market on delivery of the CTD bond. The current futures price is 77.5, and so the arbitrageur would receive the invoice amount on the CTD bond of the FP × CF. In this case, that is 77.5 × 1.3869, or \$107,484. In addition, the arbitrageur would receive accrued interest.

The purchaser of this bond through the futures market would have to compensate the arbitrageur for any accrued interest on the bond from the last coupon payment on May 15 through the purchase date of June 15, or 31 days of accrued interest out of a coupon of $5,750. This amounts to 31/365 × $11,500 = $979.39. Thus, if delivering into the futures market, the arbitrageur would receive a total of $107,484 (FP × CF) plus $979.39 (accrued interest), or $108,463.39.

We can now ascertain if there is an arbitrage profit possible by comparing the spot price plus the net cost of carry with the proceeds from delivery into the futures market. As table 9–8 shows, the arbitrageur must pay $104,224.82 to acquire and carry the bond, but would receive a greater amount, $108,463.39, for delivery in the futures market for the June contract. The arbitrageur would make $108,463.39 less $104,224.82, or $4,238.57 by simultaneously selling the June futures at 77.5 and acquiring the CTD bond at 105. Again, the futures price should reflect the current spot price plus net cost of carry; the calculation of these amounts has been refined here to reflect the institutional constraints and cash flows involved in actually acquiring the cash bond with its accrued interest, holding it, and delivering it into the futures market. The equilibrium futures price, then, would be the spot price of the CTD plus carry costs, adjusted back by the conversion factor, or in this case, it would be (104,224.82 − 979.39)/1.3869, or < 74.44.

As there is indeed an arbitrage profit possible, the arbitrageur arranges to acquire the bond, paying the short-term rate to borrow the funds, and simultaneously selling the bond for delivery into the June futures contract. The cash flows and timing of the payments involved in the arbitrage are detailed in table 9–8.

The arbitrageur enters into the three initial transactions: (1) borrowing the full purchase price of the cheapest to deliver, $106,484.89, until delivery of the futures contract on June 15 (165 days); (2) buying the cheapest to deliver bond, paying with the proceeds from (1); and (3) selling the June T-bond futures contract at a futures price of 77.5.

In May the holder of the cheapest to deliver receives the semiannual coupon payment of $5,750, and keeps this amount until delivery of the futures contract in June.

Finally, on June 15, the arbitrageur delivers the bond into the futures market and receives the invoice amount, $107,484, plus accrued interest on the bond since May 15, $979.39, for a total of $108,463.39. This plus the coupon of $5,750 received in May repays the original borrowing (transaction 1) of $109,974.82, and an arbitrage profit of $4,238.57 remains.

Even though the preceding transactions look complex, they are merely a more detailed example of the basic arbitrage transactions discussed previously. If the futures price is too high, then an arbitrageur is able to make a riskless profit by buying the underlying bond, carrying it, and delivering it into the futures market at the too-high price. This example is more realistic in that the underlying bond is the cheapest to deliver and the cash flows include provisions for accrued interest on the bond.

OTHER IMPERFECTIONS

SUPPLY PROBLEMS. Because the arbitrage transaction and the futures price depend so critically on the CTD bond, on occasion problems with the CTD can cause discrepancies in the pricing relation just discussed.

We have assumed that the CTD bond is known and priced in the spot or cash market. This is not always the case. For instance, in 1981 there were rumors that the Treasury would auction a forty-year bond rather than the usual thirty-year in its quarterly financing. If the Treasury did so, this forty-year bond would most probably be the CTD due to its long maturity.[11] Because there were doubts about which bond would ultimately be the CTD, there was a great deal of uncertainty in futures pricing.

A similar problem exists much more frequently for the T-note contract. There are times when the most likely CTD will be the note to be auctioned near the futures contract maturity. For instance, the most likely CTD for the March contract would be the newest note auctioned in the first quarter. Thus, pricing of the T-note contract before its final quarter is difficult because the spot price component of the futures price must be estimated. This uncertainty in pricing has made the T-note contract less popular and there is usually a relatively small volume in the note contract.

Anticipated supply problems with the CTD can also affect the futures price. In 1986 there was great concern that the current holders of the CTD on the maturing contract would be unwilling to sell the cash bond. Futures prices for the T-bond contract began to drift higher in anticipation of inadequate deliverable supply; again the cost of carry model was inaccurate.

CONTRACT OPTIONS. Because of the way delivery is specified in the T-bond contract, a number of seller's options implied in the delivery procedure can affect the price.

As discussed earlier, the seller of the contract has the option of which specific bond to deliver (the quality option) and which particular day to deliver on the contract within the delivery month (the timing option).

Other options are implied in the T-bond contract as well. For instance, there may an "accrued interest" option in the delivery month. Upon delivery, the seller receives funds that can be invested at the market rate. If, however, delivery is deferred one more day, the funds invested in the CTD bond earn the current T-bond rate or accrued interest. The seller then has a daily option to deliver based on the current short-term rate compared to the long-term coupon yield.

Another option is called a waiting option. This involves the last seven business days of the delivery month after trading in the futures has stopped. If the seller delivers during these seven days, the settlement price used for the invoice amount is fixed on the last day of trading. Thus, in the last seven business days of the delivery month, the seller has a decision process based on something quite similar to an option: a fixed settlement price, or exercise price, against which to evaluate delivery or expiration based on a still changing cash bond price underlying the contract.

Because all of these options are in the seller's favor, the buyer of the futures contract may discount the price to reflect the value of these options transferred to the seller. If the options have value, the futures price may be less than the equilibrium price based on the cost of carry model.

OTHER MARKET IMPERFECTIONS. As with the T-bill futures contract, there may also be discrepancies in price related to the intervening margin cash flow as well as to the computation of arbitrage profits based on after-tax cash flow rather than pretax.

The next section discusses the empirical evidence concerning the accuracy of the cost of carry model for long-term bond futures pricing, and the value, if any of the implied options discussed earlier.

EMPIRICAL EVIDENCE: T-BOND PRICING EFFICIENCY AND IMPLIED OPTIONS

Testing for efficiency in the bond contract is difficult because of the complexities of the contract. Both the specific day of delivery and the specific bond delivered can be difficult to determine in advance. In addition, the timing of price quotations on cash bonds as compared to bond futures prices, and the actual availability of the CTD bond, must be accounted for in some way in any empirical test of the arbitrage transactions. In the few studies of T-bond futures efficiency, the bond contract has been found to be efficient.[12] However, as with the T-bill pricing tests, the approaches used by the different authors vary, and thus comparisons of the findings of one study with another are difficult.

The implicit options on the T-bond contract have also been examined. G.D. Gay and S. Manaster modeled the bond contract as a portfolio of options: the quality option (which bond to deliver), the timing option (accrued interest option—when to deliver within the maturity month), the end-of-month or waiting option (when to deliver within the last seven business days).[13] The authors find that an end-of-month waiting option has value. The other options, particularly the timing option, appear to have no significant value. Recently, however, M. Arak and L.S. Goodman have found that the end-of-month option has too little value to explain the bias in Treasury bond prices.[14] On the other hand, using a simulation study, E. Kane and A.J. Marcus find that the uncertainty involved in the quality option is considerable and should lead to a discount of between 2 and 7 percent from the actual futures price.[15]

SPREADS

As discussed in chapter 4, spreads between financial futures contracts depend on expected changes in carrying cost (interdelivery spreads) or changes in expected yields (intercommodity spreads). The motivation for a spread trade, then, depends strongly on expected changes in the determinants of a futures price. In this section, we examine in more detail the two spread trades.

INTERDELIVERY SPREADS

As discussed in chapter 4, interdelivery spreads involve expected changes in the cost of carry of a storable financial asset, or changes in the short-term yield relative to the long-term yield. Since T-bond futures are the most heavily traded of the storable financial contracts, the following discussion concentrates on T-bond spreads. The analysis is equally applicable to other storable financials such as T-note and municipal bond contracts.

BEAR SPREAD

Assume, for instance, that the yield curve is positively sloping, with short-term rates less than long-term rates. This implies a positive carry market, as illustrated in table 9–6. In table 9–6, the short-term yield is at 10 percent, and the long-term yield is at 20 percent. The price of the three-month contract, at 97.5, is at a discount from the spot price of 100, and the six-month contract, at 95, is at a discount to the three-month contract. If the relative cost of carry is expected to change, then all futures prices must adjust to reflect the change in the dollar amount of the cost of carry. For instance, if the short-term yield is expected to rise from 10 to 15 percent (yield curve flattens), then the prices of the three- and six-month contracts adjust to reflect the smaller short-term borrowing costs of 15 percent relative to the long-term coupon income of 20 percent. Since the positive cash flow accruing to the bondholder is reduced through higher borrowing costs, the discount on all futures prices should now be smaller. Further, changes in the net cost of carry affect the more deferred contracts the most since the discount on the futures price reflects a longer carrying period. If the short-term rate rises to 15 percent, the equilibrium three-month futures price would change from 97.5 to 98.75:

$$F_{t,T} = 100 + (0.15 - 0.20) \times 0.25 \times 100$$
$$= 100 + (3.750 - 5.000) = 98.75$$

an increase of $1,250. Similarly, the six-month futures price would also rise, from 95 to 97.5:

$$F_{t,T} = 100 + (0.15 - 0.20) \times 0.50 \times 100$$
$$= 100 + (7.500 - 10.000) = 97.5$$

an increase of $2,500.

This relative change in prices is the basis of the bear spread: if the short-term rate rises relative to the long-term yield, then the deferred contract should be expected to rise relative to the nearby contract. Buying the deferred while selling the nearby should be profitable. Put another way, if the net cost of carry decreases, as it did here, then the difference in price between the nearby and deferred contracts should decrease as well. If the deferred futures price is less than the nearby, this means that the deferred rises relative to the nearby.

The spread, as constructed, would involve a profit of $1,250, a gain of $2,500 on the long six-month futures versus a loss of $1,250 on the short three-month futures. This is less than the profit from an outright long position on the six-month futures. This illustrates the lower risk and lower return possibilities of the spread. If prices move differently than expected by falling rather than rising, the short futures position would help offset the losses on the long position. For this reduced risk, the possible reward is also reduced.

A similar relative price change occurs under a negatively sloping yield curve (see table 9–7). Assume again that the short-term yield rises relative to the long-term, here from 10 to 15 percent. This implies a higher borrowing cost relative to the long-term coupon interest of 5 percent. Futures prices in a negative carry market should adjust upward to reflect this: the premium on the futures prices should become larger to reflect the higher relative cost of borrowing. For the three-month futures, the price should rise from 101.250 to 102.5

$$F_{t,T} = 100 + (0.15 - 0.10) \times 0.25 \times 100 = 102.5$$

an increase of $1,125. For the six-month futures, the price should rise from 102.50 to 105, an increase of $2,500, reflecting the longer carry period. A bear spread, buying the deferred and selling the nearby, should be profitable. If the net cost of carry increases, then the difference in price between the nearby and deferred should increase as well. If the deferred futures price is greater than the nearby (negative carry market), then the deferred contract must rise relative to the nearby.

BULL SPREAD

A bull spread—buying the nearby and selling the deferred—is appropriate if the short-term yield is expected to fall relative to the long-term yield. Refer back to table 9–6. If the short-term yield is expected to fall to 5 percent relative to the long-term yield of 20 percent, then the net cost of carry would increase in dollar amount. This is because the borrowing rate to be paid has fallen relative to the long-term coupon interest on the bond to be received. If this happens, futures prices should adjust to reflect the larger positive cash flow accruing to the bondholder for the carry period, and the discount on the futures prices should be greater. Also, the longer the carry period, the greater the adjustment in the futures price discount. The three-month futures price should fall from 97.5 to 96.25:

$$F_{t,T} = 100 + (0.05 - 0.20) \times 0.25 \times 100$$
$$= 100 + (1.25 - 5.00) = 96.25$$

a decrease of $1,250. The six-month futures should fall even more in dollar amount, from 95 to 92.5:

$$F_{t,T} = 100 + (0.05 - 0.20) \times 0.50 \times 100$$
$$= 100 + (2.50 - 10.00) = 92.5$$

a decrease of $2,500. Thus, selling the deferred and buying the nearby, a bull spread, should be profitable. If the net cost of carry increases, then the difference between futures prices should increase in dollar amount as well. With the deferred futures price less than the nearby, the deferred futures price should fall relative to the nearby.

A bull spread is also appropriate if the short-term rate falls relative to the long-term rate in a negative carry market. The change in prices expected if the short-term yield becomes 7.5 percent in table 9–7 is left to the reader as an exercise.

TAILING THE SPREAD

The spread between futures prices on the nearby versus deferred contracts is also affected by changes in the spot price of the bond. To see this, note that the futures price is determined by adding or subtracting a percentage of the current spot price, the net cost of carry, from the current spot price. In table 9-6, the net cost of carry for the three-month contract is $(0.10 - 0.20)^{.25}$, or 0.025 of $100,000, or −$2,500. If the spot price fell to 90 and the net cost of carry remained the same in percentage terms, the dollar amount of the premium or discount would change as well (here, the discount would be 0.025 of $90,000, or $2,250). This would occur if the yield curve experienced a parallel shift upward, both the short-term and long-term rate rising by the same amount. The spread between contracts would become smaller ($2,250 rather than $2,500) because the cost of carry is calculated from a smaller spot price. Thus, the spread between futures prices can be affected both by relative changes in the short-term versus long-term rate, and by changes in the long-term rate. In general, if the spot price rises, the spread between futures contracts would increase. The cost of carry would be a percentage of a larger number, and would be larger in dollar amount. Similarly, if the spot price falls, the spread would decrease because the cost of carry would be a percentage of a smaller number.

The effect that the spot price can have on the spread is important because it can negate the effect of changing relative yields. For instance, recall the example of the bear spread in the positive carry market, in which the short-term rate was expected to rise from 10 to 15 percent relative to the long-term yield of 20 percent. This would change the net carry from 10 percent (0.10 − 0.20) to 5 percent (0.15 − 0.20). The three-month futures price was expected to adjust from 97.5 to 98.75, and the six-month from 95 to 97.5, and the bear spread profit (short deferred, long nearby) was expected to be $1,250. The discount between the futures prices would be smaller, reflecting the smaller net cost of carry of 5 percent rather than 10 percent.

However, if the long-term rate shifted downward at the same time, this might affect the potential profit on the spread considerably. For instance, assume the net cost of carry shifted to 5 percent and the short-term and long-term yields shifted as well, to 5 percent and 10 percent, respectively. With the long-term yield falling from 20 to 10 percent, the spot price of the bond would rise from 100 to 176.062 (assuming a 20 percent coupon, 15-year maturity security). The three-month futures price would rise from 97.5 to 173.862:

$$F_{t,T} = 176.062 + (0.05 - 0.10) \times 0.25 \times 176.062$$
$$= 176.062 - 2.200 = 173.862$$

and the six-month futures price would rise from 95 to 171.661:

$$F_{t,T} = 176.062 + (0.05 - 0.10) \times 0.50 \times 176.062$$
$$= 176.062 - 4.401 = 171.661$$

This would mean that the profit on the bear spread would no longer be $1,250, but would change to a gain of only $196. The long three-month contract would rise from

97.5 to 173.862, a gain of $76,362, while the short six-month contract would rise from 95 to 171,661, a loss of $76,166. Here, then, much of the profit expected from the shift in the net cost of carry from 10 to 5 percent was negated by the simultaneous change in the long-term yield from 20 to 10 percent. Even though the changes are an extreme example, it illustrates the effect that a change in the long-term yield can have on the outcome of a spread based on a change in short-term versus long-term rates.

To eliminate the effects of spot price changes on a spread, it is necessary to "tail" the spread. Tailing the spread involves adding more nearby futures contracts to the initial bull or bear spread position to counterbalance changes in the spread relation due only to the rise or fall of the spot price. Doing this allows the spreader to profit only from expected changes in the relative cost of carry, or the relative movements of the short-term and the long-term yields.

When the spot price changes and the carry cost remains the same in percentage terms, both the nearby and deferred contracts prices change. However, the deferred price always changes more due to the longer carrying period. For instance, the change in a three-month futures contract due to a change in the spot price would be:

$$\Delta F_3 = \Delta S + (r - y)^{0.25} \Delta S$$

while the change in the six-month futures contract would be larger:

$$\Delta F_6 = \Delta S + (r = y)^{0.50} \Delta S$$

by $(r - y)^{0.25} \times \Delta S$.

To offset the effect of the spot price change, more nearby futures contracts should be added. A sufficient number should be added so that the change in the value of the total nearby position is equal to the change in the value of the deferred. The extra futures to use in our example is equal to the extra price change of the deferred over the nearby, $(r - y)^{0.25}$. In table 9-6, this would involve $(0.10 - 0.20)^{0.25}$, or 2.5 percent more nearby contracts. (For instance, instead of 100 nearby and 100 deferred contracts, a spreader would use 102 nearby and 100 deferred contracts.) The change in value of the nearby would then be equal to the change in value of the deferred as the spot price changed, and the net effect of the spot price change alone on the value of the spread would be 0. In general, the increase in the number of nearby contracts is equal to the percentage cost of carry over the carry period separating the contracts. That is, the extra contracts would be $(r - y)^{.25}$ for the three- and six-month contract spread separated by a three-month carry period, and $(r - y)^{.50}$ for a three- and nine-month contract spread, separated by a six-month carry period.

TURTLE SPREAD

Another spread involving changes in the cost of carry is the turtle spread. The turtle spread involves a spread in two Treasury bond contracts against a Treasury bill futures contract. The motivation for the spread concerns the short-term component of the cost of carry between a nearby and deferred contract.

Under the cost of carry pricing model, the price of a deferred Treasury bond futures contract should be separated from the price of a nearby by the net cost of carry between the contracts. For instance, for the March and June futures, it should be possible to: (*a*) buy the nearby March contract and take delivery, acquiring a Treasury bond for the nearby March futures price; (*b*) carry the Treasury bond for three months, financing it at the short-term borrowing rate in effect from March through June and also receiving three months of coupon income; and (*c*) sell the June deferred contract and deliver the Treasury bond back into the futures market at the deferred June futures price. Thus, the deferred futures price should be equal to the nearby futures price plus the expected cost of carry for the period March through June between the contracts.

Specifically, the proceeds at delivery of the Treasury bond into the deferred June contract, the invoice price $F_{June} \times CF$ (futures price times conversion factor), should be equal to the cost of the bond under the nearby March contract, $F_{March} \times CF$, plus the cost of carry for the period. The cost of carry is the financing of the purchase price, $(F_{March} \times CF) \times$ expected $r \times N/360$ (with N the number of days in the carry period), less the coupon income, $CPN \times N/360$ (with CPN the yearly coupon payment on the Treasury bond carried):

$$F_{June} \times CF = (F_{March} \times CF) + [(F_{March} \times CF) \times E(r) \times N/360] - (CPN \times N/360)$$

Since the conversion factors and the coupon income are fixed, the two futures prices are determined by the expected short-term rate for the period between the two contracts. For instance, assume the March Treasury Bond futures price is at 100, the March conversion factor for the cheapest to deliver, a 15 percent coupon bond, is 1.5, and the expected short-term yield from March through June is 5 percent. This implies an equilibrium June futures price of 98.75:

$$F_{June} \times 1.5 = 100 \times 1.5 + (100 \times 1.5) \times 0.05 \times 90/360 - .15 \times 90/360 \times 100$$

$$F_{June} = (150 + 1.875 - 3.75)/1.5 = 98.75$$

(assuming the conversion factors for the March and June contracts are approximately 1.5, and expressing the coupon income of $15,000 per year as a percentage of par, .15.)

The preceding equation can be used as well to find the expected short-term rate for the period March through June implied by the two futures prices for the March and June T-bond contracts. If the March and June futures prices are 100 and 98.75, respectively, then the market consensus short-term rate expected from March through June is 5 percent. The turtle spread involves a comparison of this expected rate from the T-bond futures market with another market consensus rate, the expected short-term rate in the T-bill futures market for March through June.

Based on the discussion on expectational pricing of T-bill futures and arbitrage, the March T-bill futures price should reflect the expected rate for the 90-day period from March through June. Also, given free access to the T-bill and T-bond futures markets and the same information available to both, the expected rate for the time period March through June should be the same in both the T-bill futures and the T-bond futures markets.

What if the two rates differ? For instance, what if the March T-bill futures rate is 10 percent while the T-bond futures implied rate is, as the example, 5 percent? This would be a disequilibrium situation, and the rates should adjust toward equality. The 10 percent rate in the March T-bill futures market should adjust downward toward 5 percent, while the 5 percent implied rate in the T-bond futures should adjust upward toward 10 percent. A spread trade can be made between the T-bond and T-bill futures based on this expected movement.

For the T-bill futures, the 10 percent rate should fall toward 5 percent, and the T-bill futures price should adjust upward. A long futures position should be initiated in the T-bill contract. For the two T-bond futures, it is expected that the short-term rate component of the cost of carry should rise from 5 percent toward 10 percent. From the discussion on bull and bear spreads, if the net cost of carry narrows on a long term bond contract from 5 to 15 percent to 10 to 15 percent, the spread between the contracts should decrease as well. With the deferred futures at 98.75, less than the nearby at 100, and the cost of carry narrowing, the June deferred futures price would rise relative to the March nearby, and a bear spread—long the deferred and short the nearby—would be profitable. The complete turtle spread, then, involves a long T-bill futures position against a bear spread in the T-bond futures. Again, the basis of the spread is the fact that both contracts, T-bond and T-bill, imply an expected short-term rate for the same time period. If the two market consensus rates differ, it would be expected that this difference should disappear, and that the futures prices should adjust to bring about this equality in expected short-term rate.

Finally, because the T-bond spread involves $100,000 face value commodities while the T-bill futures involve a $1 million face value commodity, ten nearby and ten deferred T-bond contracts should be used in the turtle for every one T-bill contract.

INTERCOMMODITY SPREADS

Most intercommodity spreads involve differences in quality or price volatility between related commodities. Many intercommodity spreads are based on changing risk premiums for financial assets of the same maturity. One of the most popular intercommodity spreads involves the TED spread, a spread between the T-bill contract and the Eurodollar contract. The underlying commodities are both short-term, ninety-day interest rate assets that differ primarily in credit quality. Treasury bills are issued by the U.S. government and have a lower rate than Eurodollars, which are issued by individual banks and carry the credit risk of that bank. TED spreads arise from expected changes in the risk premium separating T-bill from Eurodollar rates. The risk premium can be affected by many factors, from changes in the general economy (for instance, a flight to quality due to adverse economic news) to more specific developments relating to the banking industry. For instance, the Texas savings and loan crisis induced a higher risk premium in the Eurodollar rate reflecting the increased risk perceived in bank funds. Competition for funds between banks can also serve to increase the Eurodollar rate relative to the T-bill rate.

As an example of the TED spread, assume that a major bank failure is expected to occur. Assume also that the T-bill rate expected in two months, in June, is 8 percent while the expected Eurodollar rate for June is 9 percent. The spread between the two June futures contracts is currently equal to 1.00 (T-bill futures price − Eurodollar futures price = (100 − 8) − (100 − 9), or 1.00). If the risk premium is expected to rise on Eurodollar rates, the futures price for the Eurodollar can be expected to fall relative to the bill contract. For instance, if the risk premium is expected to grow from 100 basis points (9 less 8 percent) to 200 basis points (10 less 8 percent), the spread between the two futures contracts would widen to 2.00 ((100 − 8) − (100 − 10)). A short ED, long T-bill position would be expected to be profitable.

A similar quality spread involves the CBOT municipal bond contract with the Treasury bond contract, the MOB (munis over bonds) spread. The commodities underlying the two contracts both reflect long-term (fifteen-year) rates. Generally, muni rates can be expected to be less than Treasury bond rates, but the difference between the rates can change over time in response to changes in credit quality and tax treatment. For instance, a major default in a municipal bond issue would be expected to increase the risk premium on the muni rate relative to the T-bond rate. If this occurred, the muni futures price could be expected to fall relative to the T-bond futures price, and selling the muni futures while buying the T-bond futures would be expected to be profitable.

Spreads are also possible between different stock index futures contracts. For instance, the S&P500 index differs from the Value Line in the types of stocks covered by the two indexes, with the Value Line reflecting both NYSE-traded and over-the-counter stocks. If these two groups of stocks can be expected to respond differently to economic developments, the two indexes and the two futures should be expected to change as well in relative value, the basis for a spread. Similarly, spreads between foreign currency futures would reflect expected changes in value between the two foreign currencies.

Finally, intercommodity spreads are based on differences in price volatility between financial assets. The longer the maturity of the underlying asset, the larger the price change for a given change in interest rates. If there is a parallel shift in T-note and T-bond rates, T-bond prices should change more than T-note prices. For instance, if the yield curve is expected to shift downward, then the T-bond futures price should rise more than the note futures price. A NOB (Notes over Bonds) spread would involve buying the T-bond futures and selling the T-note futures. Similarly, T-bond prices should be expected to change more than T-bill prices if short-term and long-term rates move by the same amount. If the yield curve is expected to shift upward (short-term and long-term rates rising by the same amount), then selling the T-bond futures while buying the T-bill futures should be profitable.

NOTES

1. For a good introduction to the subject of short-term interest rate assets, see M. Stigum, *The Money Market* (Homewood, Ill.: Dow Jones-Irwin, 1983).
2. For a fuller treatment of the Treasury auction process, see Stigum, *The Money Market.*
3. The framework of the discussion follows F. Jones, "The Integration of the Cash and Futures Markets for Treasury Securities," *Journal of Futures Markets* 1 (1981): 33–57.
4. W. Poole, "Using T-Bill Futures to Gauge Interest Rate Expectations." *Federal Reserve Bank of San Francisco Economic Review,* Spring 1978, 7–19, D.R. Capozza and B. Cornell, "Treasury Bill Pricing in the Spot and Futures Markets," *Review of Economics and Statistics* 61 (1979): 513–20; R.J. Rendleman and C.E. Carabini, "The Efficiency of the Treasury Bill Futures Market," *Journal of Finance* 34 (1979): 937–54; and G. Morgan, "Forward and Futures Pricing of Treasury Bills," *Journal of Banking and Finance* 5 (1981): 483–96.
5. B. Branch, "Testing the Unbiased Expectations Theory of Interest Rates," *The Financial Review* 13 (1978): 51–66; B. Chow and D. Brophy, "The U.S. Treasury Bill Futures Market and Hypotheses Regarding the Term Structure of Interest Rates," *The Financial Review* 13 (1978): 36–50; and R.W. Lang and R.H. Rasche, "A Comparison of Yields on Futures Contracts and Implied Forward Rates,"*Federal Reserve Bank of St. Louis Review,* December 1978, 21–30.
6. Capozza and Cornell, "Treasury Bill Pricing."
7. Rendleman and Carabini, "The Efficiency of the Treasury Bill Futures Market."
8. Morgan, "Forward and Futures Pricing."
9. I.G. Kawaller and J. Koch, "Cash and Carry Trading and the Pricing of Treasury Bill Futures," *Journal of Futures Markets* 4 (1984): 115–24.

10. R.W. Kolb and G.D. Gay, "A Pricing Anomaly in Treasury Bill Futures," *Journal of Financial Research* 8 (1985): 157–67.
11. The general characteristics of the bond that is cheapest to deliver have been examined by M. Livingston, "The Effect of Coupon Level on Treasury Bond Futures Delivery," *Journal of Futures Markets* 7 (1987): 303–9; and J.F. Meisner and J.W. Labuszewski, "Treasury Bond Futures Delivery Bias," *Journal of Futures Markets* 4 (1984): 569–77, among others.
12. R.W. Kolb, G. Gay, and J. Jordan, "Are There Arbitrage Opportunities in the Treasury Bond Futures Markets?" *Journal of Futures Markets* 2 (1982): 217–29; B.G. Resnick and E. Hennigar, "The Relationship between Futures and Cash Prices for U.S. Treasury Bonds," *Review of Research in Futures Markets* 2 (1983): 282–99; and B.G. Resnick, "The Relationship between Futures Prices for U.S. Treasury Bonds," *Review of Research in Futures Markets* 3 (1984): 89–104.
13. G.D. Gay and S. Manaster, "The Quality Option Implicit in Futures Contracts," *Journal of Financial Economics* 13 (1984): 353–70.
14. M. Arak and L.S. Goodman, "Treasury Bond Futures: Valuing the Delivery Option," *Journal of Futures Markets* 7 (1987): 269–86.
15. E. Kane and A.J. Marcus, "The Quality Option in the Treasury Bond Futures Market: An Empirical Assessment," *Journal of Futures Markets* 6 (1986): 230–48.

FINANCIAL ASSET FUTURES: HEDGING

10

One of the primary functions of futures markets is to transfer the risk of price change from one individual, the hedger, to another, the speculator who is more willing or able to take on that risk. The genius of the futures markets, and the source of most of the recent innovations in these markets, has been the realization that financial instruments—both stocks and bonds—experience the same sort of price volatility or price uncertainty that has plagued agricultural commodities for years. From this realization of the similarity of risk arose the current proliferation of interest rate and index futures.

The purchase or sale of a financial asset is similar to buying or selling a physical commodity because it is an asset with a market price that varies. However, an important characteristic of financial assets is that there is an inverse relationship between prices of financial assets and interest rates. This is because the prices of financial assets are determined by discounting by a market rate of return the expected cash flow to the investor holding the instrument. For instance, the price of a bond is equal to the value of the cash flow—in this case, periodic coupon payments and return of principal at maturity—discounted at the bond rate of return. Similarly, the price of a pure discount bond such as a Treasury bill—a bond whose only cash flow is the face value paid at maturity—is equal to the face value discounted back to the present at the appropriate rate of return. Therefore, if the market rate of return rises (i.e., the rate used to discount the cash flows rises), the discounted value of the cash flow, or the price of the bond, falls. Similarly, a decrease in the market rate of return increases the present value of total cash flow, or the price of the financial instrument rises.

Thus, the holder of a financial asset such as a bond or fixed-rate mortgage bears the risk of a decrease in value, or rising interest rates during the holding period. In a similar manner, the holder of a forward commitment to lend funds at a fixed rate (e.g., a forward commitment to buy a promissory note, a mortgage, or a bond at a certain rate) suffers an opportunity loss if interest rates rise. The futures market can help reduce this risk; such positions can be hedged by selling a financial futures contract. If interest rates do rise, futures prices decline. Thus, the increase in value of the short futures position serves to offset the actual or opportunity loss in value of the cash position.

Financial futures can also hedge against falling interest rates. As an example, an individual who has borrowed at a fixed interest rate suffers an opportunity loss should interest rates decline while the borrower is committed to the higher fixed interest payment. Similarly, a potential investor in financial assets, one who anticipates buying a financial asset at a later time, wants to hedge against a possible increase in price or decrease in rates before the actual purchase can be made. These people can hedge against interest rate declines by buying a financial futures contract. If rates do decline, the futures price rises, and the increased value of the futures contract can compensate for the opportunity loss experienced by these two individuals.

Because most firms are subject to some form of interest rate risk, the interest rate futures markets can be of use to a large number of firms, financial and otherwise. For example, mortgage bankers can hedge the mortgages they current hold (short hedge) as well as those they plan to hold (long hedge) using the Treasury bond futures contract. Similarly, builders can protect themselves against higher mortgage rates. Corporations can use futures to protect against higher borrowing costs by hedging short, using a short maturity contract like the Treasury bill or certificate of deposit contract to hedge against short-term borrowing, or using a long-term bond contract to hedge against the issuance of a corporate bond, a long-term borrowing. Portfolio managers for pensions, mutual funds, and insurance companies can hedge short their fixed income securities, or bond portfolios, for protection during times of rising rates, or hedge long anticipated incoming cash flows to protect against potential falling rates. Short and long hedges can be effected to protect against interest rate fluctuations in many different instances varying in both maturity and financial asset.

Because of the large number of financial assets and potential financial commitments that vary according to coupon rate, time to maturity, issuer, risk, and many other characteristics, most financial hedges are cross hedges. Thus, the potential hedger must understand the basis and anticipated basis moves. This implies a knowledge of yield curves in both cash and futures markets. The hedger must anticipate whether the basis will strengthen or weaken, or how yield curves might shift. We discussed the structure of yield curves and their behavior in chapter 3. There are, however, certain adjustments that are commonly made to the hedge ratio to reconcile differences in maturity, coupon, and risk between the particular cash position to be hedged and the financial futures contracts available. We discuss these systematic differences in price volatility between different financial instruments in the next section.

The following section examines the particular models that describe the essential characteristics of the hedger's decision process. As discussed earlier, the procedure for hedging financial instruments, or interest rates, is much the same as for physical commodities. One uses the futures markets as a temporary substitute for a cash market transaction. Each model focuses on the optimal hedge ratio, the proportion of the cash position that must be hedged, to protect the hedger against price volatility. Because the models approach the hedge position and definition of price risk in different ways, the resulting hedge ratios are different, and the ratios are generally expressed as functions of the parameters of the individual models. However, as we point out, all of the theoretical models have as the same underlying objective the transference of price risk through the futures market.

The next section describes the management of the hedged position, including such issues as choice of contract maturity. This section also includes a discussion of the possibilities for hedging interest rate risk using methods other than futures.

Finally, the use of futures contracts can be extended beyond pure risk avoidance to strategies involving differential responses to interest rate changes. We discuss such strategies in the last section.

BOND FUNDAMENTALS

Certain relationships between bond coupon, time to maturity, and bond price volatility are useful to know in using financial futures to hedge long-term bonds of any sort. The fundamental bond rules were first formulated by B. Malkiel and supply useful insights into the hedging process.[1]

Rule 1: Bond prices move inversely to interest rates.

If interest rates rise, bond prices fall, and a bond portfolio manager suffers a loss in the value of the holdings. This occurs because the price or value of any bond is the discounted value of the cash flows expected from holding that bond. Coupon payments (C_t) and the repayment of principal at maturity (m) are discounted back to the present at an appropriate yield (market rate, R) to arrive at a price for the bond in question:

$$\text{Price} = \sum_{t=1}^{m} C_t \,/(1 + R)^t \qquad (10\text{–}1)$$

Thus, when market rates rise, the present value of the coupon and principal decrease in value, and the price of the bond must fall to reflect this.

If a portfolio manager is holding a portfolio of long maturity bonds, those holdings lose value as interest rates rise and bond prices fall. In hedging, the portfolio manager seeks to protect the value of the cash bond portfolio by taking a position in the futures market that offsets this cash loss. Thus, the manager would sell futures to hedge the portfolio. If rates do rise, then spot and also futures prices tend to fall, and the manager is able to gain a profit in the futures position by subsequently buying back, or offsetting, the futures position.

If, on the other hand, a corporate treasurer were expecting to acquire investment funds at some point in the future, the treasurer would want to hedge the investment rate on those anticipated funds by going long in the futures market. If rates do fall, then the corporate treasurer loses money on the anticipated cash position through the lower investment rate. Falling rates mean rising prices in both cash and futures markets, and so the long futures position can offset this cash loss.

In financial futures, then, a loss in value through rising rates can be offset by a short futures hedge, and a loss due to falling rates can be hedged by a long futures position.

Rule 2: For bonds alike in all respects (risk, call characteristics, and maturity) except coupon, a small coupon bond experiences more price volatility than a large coupon bond.

For instance, assume an investor is holding two very similar bonds, one a ten-year,

15 percent coupon bond, the other a ten-year, 5 percent coupon bond. If rates rise, both bonds lose value as bond prices fall, but the price of the 5 percent coupon bond falls more.

The reason for the relatively higher volatility of small coupon bonds derives from the behavior of the two components of bond return, coupon payment and principal repayment, as interest rates change. For a small coupon bond, relatively more of the total return on the bond comes from the principal repayment at the bond's maturity. When rates rise, this portion of the bond return, coming at the end of the bond's life, is affected much more by the higher discount rate than is the coupon portion of return. For a high coupon bond, the effect of higher discount rates is not so pronounced because less of the total return derives from the maturity principal repayment. Thus, the value of low coupon bonds is affected more by changing interest rates and low coupon bonds have a higher price volatility than do high coupon bonds.

The implications of rule 2 for hedging have to do with the relative price volatility of the cash position of the hedger as against the futures position. Ideally, the hedger would like dollar equivalence between the two positions. That is, the hedger would like a gain in dollar value in the futures position that would exactly offset the dollar loss on the cash. If losing $5,000 on the cash position, the hedger would like a futures position that would gain $5,000 in value at the same time.

Achieving this equality of gain and loss, or dollar equivalence, is the goal of a good hedge. To achieve dollar equivalence, the relative volatility of the cash position compared to the futures used must be known and adjusted for. Under rule 2, the relative coupon level between cash bond and the bond underlying the futures must be taken into account in hedging. If, for instance, the hedger held a $100,000 face value, fifteen years to maturity, 4 percent coupon bond, and sought to hedge with the T-bond contract (with an underlying standard of a $100,000 face value, 8 percent coupon, fifteen year bond), then the hedger would know that this cash 4 percent coupon bond would tend to be more price volatile than the futures 8 percent coupon bond. More than one contract might have to be used to achieve dollar equivalence. The specific calculations needed to adjust for dollar equivalence are in the next section. For our purposes, rule 2 tells us that lower coupon instruments tend to be more price volatile.

Rule 2 has another implication for the use of futures in bond portfolio management. If a portfolio manager forecasts a general decline in interest rates, then all bond prices would be expected to rise. Under rule 2, however, we know that small coupon bonds tend to rise more. An active portfolio manager would seek to acquire small coupon bonds and perhaps trade out of high coupon bonds before the rate decline to reap the largest possible gain in value on the bond holdings. As we discuss later, high coupon bond futures may be used instead of actual cash sales of high coupon bonds to adjust the portfolio coupon. In this way, bond futures positions may be used in conjunction with a cash or spot portfolio to enhance portfolio return during a period of falling interest rates.

Rule 3: For bonds alike in all respects (coupon, risk, call characteristics) except maturity, a long-term bond experiences more price volatility than a short-term bond.

If an investor held two very similar 8 percent coupon bonds, one with a five-year maturity, the other with a fifteen-year maturity, the fifteen-year bond would experience a greater increase in value than the five-year if interest rates fall.

The reason for this differential volatility between these two bonds is again related to the effect of discounting on bond value. Long-term bonds have more of their total value in distant payments of coupon and principal at maturity. Any rise in the bond yield, the discount rate in equation 10–1, would affect these distant payments more severely, and the value of the long-term bond changes more with changes in yield or discount rate.

Rule 3 implies that a hedger must adjust the number of contracts used in a hedge to take into account the larger price volatility of long-term investments. For instance, a treasurer trying to hedge a $1 million one-year Treasury bill in a cash portfolio might use the $1 million ninety-day T-bill futures contract. However, rule 3 indicates that the cash one-year bill would be more volatile than the ninety-day T-bill futures. To achieve dollar equivalence, or equal gain and loss on futures versus cash positions, the hedger might need more than one T-bill futures contract. Hedge positions must take into account both differing maturity between cash and futures, as here, and differing coupon, as in rule 2.

Active portfolio managers also make use of rule 3 in adjusting their portfolios for an expected change in interest rates. If rates are expected to rise, all bonds decrease in value. However, long-term bonds decrease in price more than comparable short-term maturity instruments. If rates were expected to rise, managers may wish to sell off the long maturity bonds and acquire short-term maturity investments so that the loss in value is as little as possible. Long-term bond futures may also be used in place of cash long-term bond sales. Again, it may be possible to use bond futures as a substitute for a cash transaction. Here, a bond futures is used to mitigate portfolio loss through sale of long-term bonds and acquisition of short-term bonds.

DURATION

So far we have considered bond price volatility in relation to coupon or to maturity separately. Many times the portfolio manager or hedger needs to compare the volatility of bonds that differ both in coupon and maturity, and it is not always possible to come to a definite conclusion using rule 2 or 3 alone. For instance, a comparison of an 8 percent, twenty-year bond versus a 4 percent, ten-year bond yields no clear conclusions on relative price volatility. Based on coupon alone, the 4 percent should be the more volatile of the two bonds, but based on time to maturity, the 8 percent would be considered the more volatile. A measure of total bond price volatility is needed in order to anticipate the size of possible losses on a cash portfolio containing multiple bonds, and also to construct a hedged position to achieve as close to a dollar equivalence as possible. The duration of a bond is a useful concept and, with an adjustment, can be used to compare the interest rate volatility of bonds.

Duration is the average time to recovery of the cash flows from a bond, with the weights representing the proportion of the bond's present value, or price, received at various times. Duration can be thought of as the average time to receipt of a bond's cash flows, with the weight given to any time dependent on the relative value of the cash flow received at that time.

The formula for a bond's duration is:

$$D = \left[\sum_{t=1}^{m} (t \times C_t)/(1 + R)^t \right] / \text{PRICE} \qquad (10\text{–}2)$$

Equation 10–2 assumes annual compounding, and the duration can be expressed in years.

Duration is calculated for a three-year, 10 3/4 percent coupon bond, and a nine-month discount security in table 10–1. For the three-year bond, the weight for the final coupon payment and repayment of principal represents the significant cash flow from this bond, and the weighting for year 3 is a relatively large 81 percent. The coupons to be received in years 1 and 2 represent a percentage of price of only 9.6 and 8.7, respectively, and the duration of 2.72 for the bond is very close to the maturity of the bond, three years. Small coupon bonds tend to have relatively small weights placed on the early times, and much more on the final repayment of principal. Thus, the duration of a small coupon bond is relatively high. The same is true for long maturity bonds: a longer maturity than three years would decrease the relative weighting of the earlier three coupon payments and extend the calculation to include later time periods, resulting in a higher duration. For the discount security, the only cash flow is received at the maturity, and so the duration of a discount security is always equal to its maturity.

For our purposes, the duration of a security also represents the elasticity of price with respect to interest rates:

$$D = \text{percentage } \Delta \text{ in price/percentage } \Delta \text{ in rates}$$

Table 10-1. Calculation of Duration

Coupon bond duration: 10 3/4% coupon, 3 years to maturity,
$100,000 face value
Current rate: 10%

Year	*Cash Flow*	*Discounted Cash Flow*	*Present Value as Percentage of Price*
1	$ 10,750	$ 9,772.73	.096 × 1.00 = .096
2	10,750	8,884.30	.087 × 2.00 = .174
3	10,750	8,076.63	.079 × 3.00 = .237
3	100,000	75,131.48	.738 × 3.00 = 2.214

Price = $101,865.14 Duration = 2.721
Adjusted Duration = 2.721/(1.10) = 2.47

Duration of 10 3/4% bond at 11%:

1	$ 10,750	$ 9,684.69	.097 × 1.00 = .097
2	10,750	8,724.94	.088 × 2.00 = .176
3	10,750	7,860.31	.079 × 3.00 = .237
3	100,000	73,119.14	.736 × 3.00 = 2.208

Price = $99,389.08 Duration =2.718
Adjusted Duration = 2.718/(1.11) = 2.45

Duration of 270-day T-bill, $1 million face value
Current rate: 11%

Year	*Cash Flow*	*Discounted Cash Flow at 11%*	*PV as % of Price*
1	$1,000,000	$924,714.71	1 × .75 = .75

Duration = .75

Duration of a discount security is always equal to its maturity.
Adjusted duration = 0.75(1.11) = 0.675

$$=dS / S \times 100 / d(1 + R) / (1 + R)$$

or $D = dS / d(1 + R) \times 100 \times (1 + R) / S$

(The 100 scales the change to a percentage.) Taking the derivative of bond price (equation 10-1) and simplifying results in equation 10-2. Duration supplies an approximate measure of bond price volatility with interest rate changes:

$$\Delta S \cong -D/(1 + R) \times S \times \Delta R / 100$$

(It is an approximation to the price change because elasticity is defined for very small changes in rates.) For instance, the three-year bond in table 10–1 has a duration of 2.721. If yields change from 10 to 11 percent, the change in the bond's price is calculated as 2.47 percent, or \$2,519:

$$S = -2.721/(1.10) \times \$101{,}865 \times 1/100$$

$$\text{or} \quad S = -2.47\% \times \$101{,}865 \times .01$$

$$= \$2{,}519$$

which is quite close to the true change of 2.43 percent, or \$2,476 (see table 10–1). Adusted duration:

$$D^* = D/(1 + R) \tag{10–3}$$

provides an approximate measure of the percentage change in value expected of any bond for a percentage change in rates. For the three-year bond in table 10–1, the percentage price change expected is approximately 2.721/(1.10), or 2.47 percent.

For our purposes, the adjusted duration (D^*) is most useful, as it allows portfolio managers to measure the expected loss in the value of their bonds in relation to expected changes in interest rates, the first step in constructing the futures position necessary to offset this expected loss as nearly as possible.

A few additional points need to be made concerning the adjusted duration calculation. First, as an elasticity measure, adjusted duration is accurate only for very small changes in yields. Thus, a hedger needs to be conservative in using the number derived from equation 10–2 if yields are expected to be exceptionally volatile. Second, duration and adjusted duration depend on the market yields used to calculate them: the duration of the bond in table 10–1 changes from 2.721 to 2.718 as yield rises from 10 to 11 percent. Third, duration assumes implicitly that all yields, short- and long-term, change by the same amount across the yield curve; that is, duration assumes a completely parallel shift in the yield curve if interest rates change. It is useful to keep these points in mind when duration is used in a portfolio context.

Bond rules 2 and 3 discussed earlier can be restated in terms of duration. Small coupon and long maturity bonds have higher durations because more of the weighting of the cash flow is at the end of the bond's life. Thus, these bonds exhibit higher price volatility. The hedger must adjust for any volatility or duration differences between cash and futures when choosing how many contracts to use to achieve dollar equivalence.

Finally, our definition of dollar equivalence in a hedge involves the achievement of zero price volatility, or zero duration, of the combined cash and futures position.

Thus, the hedger's goal can also be expressed in terms of duration: the objective of the hedge is to choose the number of futures contracts which result in zero duration of the total position.[2]

USES OF DURATION

Besides giving a measure of price volatility, duration is also useful in a variety of portfolio management applications. Because futures can be used not only to hedge a portfolio but also to improve a portfolio's performance, we discuss duration and its use in portfolio management at some length. This serves as necessary background when we discuss the use of futures in enhancing portfolio return in the last section.

During the time a manager holds a bond portfolio, the portfolio is subject to two opposing interest-rate risks: reinvestment rate risk and risk of principal loss. If interest rates fall, then the coupon income received from the bonds can only be reinvested at a now lower rate, resulting in a loss in coupon yield on the portfolio. This loss in reinvestment income is offset to a degree by the now increased price of the bonds under falling rates. Similarly, if interest rates rise, the prices of the bonds in the portfolio fall, resulting in a loss on any resale of the bonds before maturity. Some of this loss is offset by the now larger income from coupon reinvestment at higher rates. Thus, the portfolio is subject to a possible loss under both rising and falling rates, and it is not certain that the change in value of the coupon reinvestment can exactly offset in dollar amount the corresponding change in bond price.

A popular strategy for dealing with these two risks is to immunize the portfolio. With immunization, managers attempt to adjust the portfolios so that the two competing risks, principal and coupon reinvestment, offset each other exactly in dollar amounts. For instance, a portfolio may lose $1,000 in resale value as rates rise. An immunized portfolio gains at the same time $1,000 in incremental reinvestment if held for the full holding period. With these two risks completely offset in dollar terms, the return on the portfolio should be equal to the yield to maturity in effect at the time of immunization. That is, if rates are currently at 10 percent, and the manager immunizes the portfolio, the yield over the holding period should be 10 percent.

To immunize a portfolio, it is necessary to adjust the portfolio so that its duration is equal to the portfolio manager's holding period or investment horizon. (The duration of a portfolio is simply the weighted average of the durations of the individual bonds held in the portfolio. The weights are the proportion of total portfolio value invested in any particular bond.) If, for instance, a pension fund had a relatively long holding period, say ten years, then to immunize the portfolio and balance the reinvestment rate risk with the principal loss risk, a manager must adjust bond holdings so that the weighted average duration of the portfolio is also ten. If the bonds currently held have a weighted average duration greater than ten, say twelve, then the manager would need to sell off high duration bonds (those with small coupons or long maturities) and acquire low duration bonds (those with high coupons and short maturities) until the average falls to the desired duration of ten.

Futures can serve as a useful substitute for this portfolio rebalancing. Rather than having to sell the carefully selected bonds currently in the portfolio, the manager can use a long-term bond futures contract as a substitute for a bond sale. Futures contracts have a duration, as cash bonds do. As a short futures position is added to the bond portfolio, the short position is added with a negative weighting into the portfolio duration calculation; this serves to lower the weighted average portfolio duration to the desired number. By using short futures positions rather than selling physical bonds, the manager can keep any valuable high duration bonds in the portfolio while still immunizing the portfolio against the two competing risks. We discuss the precise number of contracts needed in the last section of this chapter.

A second use for duration arises in the interest rate vulnerability of banks and savings and loans. Most banks and savings and loans hold relatively long maturity assets (commercial loans and long-term mortgages) against liabilities that are generally of a much shorter maturity (demand deposits, savings accounts, and CDs). The assets, with long maturities, have a higher duration than the liabilities, and consequently a higher price volatility when rates change. Because of this mismatch in asset and liability maturity, financial institutions are particularly vulnerable in an environment of rising rates. As rates rise, the value of the assets and liabilities fall, but asset values fall by much more. This serves to diminish quite severely the net equity component—the net capital worth—of the financial institution during a period of rising rates.

Banks have attempted to adjust their asset and liability maturity through various means, decreasing loan life or attempting to increase the maturity of their sources of funds. However, it is a difficult process and involves adjustments that may be unpopular with loan customers and potential investors.

An alternative to these relatively difficult adjustments is to use futures to adjust down the duration of the bank's assets. As with the portfolio just discussed, adding short futures positions to the bank's asset portfolio decreases the duration of the total asset position. This eventually brings asset and liability duration and price volatility more closely in line and eliminates the vulnerability of shareholders' equity to periods of rising interest rates.

HEDGE RATIO DETERMINATION

When hedging financial assets, a futures position should be used so that the change in the cash asset's value, when interest rates change, is exactly offset by the change in value on the futures position. This equivalence of cash value change to futures value change is known as dollar equivalence. Achieving dollar equivalence may mean that the hedger does not necessarily hold futures contracts equal in face value to the cash position. For instance, the issuance of $1 million in corporate bonds hedged short with the $100,000 Treasury bond futures contract may require more or less than ten contracts (10 × $100,000 = $1 million face value) for a perfect hedge. This is because cash and futures instruments generally have different coupon rates and maturities, resulting in different changes in dollar value for the same change in interest rates. It is thus necessary to calculate the number of futures contracts needed to attain dollar equivalence, or what is the same thing, to estimate a hedge ratio, the proportion of the cash portfolio to be hedged with a futures position.

BASIS RISK

The achievement of dollar equivalence in financial futures is related closely to the idea of a perfect hedge in commodity futures. In agricultural futures, the objective of the hedge is an equal change in cash and futures, but this idea is expressed in the basis. The basis is the current spot price less the futures price, $(S_t - F_t)$. If the basis does not change from the initiation of the hedge to the hedge's end, then the hedge is considered a perfect one.

To illustrate, assume the cash price of a T-bond at initiation of a short hedge is 100, while the futures price is 85. The basis at initiation is, therefore, 15 $(S_t - F_t = 100 - 85 = 15)$. If prices decline over the hedge life, then the hedger is losing money on the cash asset but gaining on the futures position. Assume that at the end of the hedge, the cash price has fallen to 90, and the futures price has fallen to 75, so that the basis at the hedge's end is still 15 (90 − 75 = 15). This is indeed a perfect hedge in that the change in the futures price has exactly offset the change in the cash price; the futures position has gained 10 in falling from 85 to 75 while the cash has lost 10 (100 to 90). Thus, the achievement of a perfect hedge involves achieving as closely as possible a zero change in the basis, or dollar equivalence.

If the hedger would achieve dollar equivalence, the hedge would constitute a riskless position. However, it is not possible in most cases to eliminate the hedger's risk totally. The hedger is still subject to basis risk, the possibility that the futures position does not wholly offset the loss on the cash, or that the basis changes over the life of the hedge. Thus, the hedger has exchanged one risk for another, smaller one: the hedger has shifted from bearing the risk of the total spot price change to bearing the risk of a basis change. In most cases, if the hedge has been constructed well, the basis risk is much smaller than the total risk of spot price change.

Of course, there are many reasons why the basis changes through time. We have considered some sources of differential price volatility related to coupon and maturity differences in a cross hedge, as well as differences in yield volatility related to risk. Another source of basis risk involves the elements of futures pricing: changes in the relationship between short-term and long-term yields, or the cost of carry, result in changes between the spot and futures prices. Additionally, as the contract draws closer to maturity, the cost of carry naturally declines and at maturity, the futures price converges to the spot price and the basis becomes zero. Thus, the achievement of a perfect hedge involves eliminating as much as possible the basis risk arising from various sources.

Several approaches have been taken to address this problem, resulting in a number of models of hedging behavior and in a number of different hedge ratios. The most common models and their derivation are discussed next. Although the models and the ratios look quite different, based as they are on different aspects of the hedging problem, they result in quite similar futures positions. This is because they all have, as an underlying objective, the achievement of dollar equivalence in the hedge.

BASIS POINT VALUE MODEL

Perhaps the simplest approach to analyzing the hedging problem is to look at the change in value of the cash position compared to the change in the value of the futures contract when rates change by a small amount. If rates change by one basis point, or by .01 percent, the loss in value of the total cash position held can be calculated and compared to the gain in value on one futures contract. This indicates the number of contracts needed for dollar equivalence. If a one basis point change in rates results in a $5,000 loss on the cash position and a $2,500 gain on one futures contract, then $5,000/$2,500, or two contracts are needed to completely hedge the cash position. The basis point value (bpv) hedge ratio, then, is calculated as the ratio of the bpv change in the cash to the bpv change in the futures:

bpv(cash)/bpv(futures) = Hedge Ratio.

As an illustration, consider the holder of $1 million of one-year commercial paper. A one basis point rise in rates results in a loss of $100:

$.0001 \times \$1{,}000{,}000 \times (360/360) = \$100.$

If the hedger sold the $1 million ninety-day Eurodollar contract as a hedge, the value of one short futures contract would rise by $25 if rates rose by one basis point:

$.0001 \times \$1{,}000{,}000 \times (90/360) = \$25.$

Thus, the hedger would need four contracts for dollar equivalence:

bpv(cash)/bpv(futures) = \$100/\$25 = 4.

One further adjustment needs to be made in the calculation to account for any differences in yield volatility between the cash asset and the asset underlying the futures contract. For instance, if commercial paper rates were twice as volatile as Eurodollar rates, then as rates rose the cash position would experience a two bpv change for every one bpv change in the futures contract. The hedger would thus need twice as many futures contracts as previously calculated, or a total of eight, for dollar equivalence:

bpv(cash)/bpv(futures) × volatility cash/futures = HR

(\$100/\$25) × 2 = 8 contracts

The volatility adjustment can generally be estimated through a regression of past commercial paper rate changes (CP) against Eurodollar rate (ED) changes:

Δ CP rates = $a + b\Delta$ ED rates.

Here the slope coefficient b would be the volatility adjustment factor.

The calculation of the number of futures contracts needed to hedge a long-term coupon bond cash position under the bpv model is similar but slightly more complex. As an illustration of the reasoning involved, let us consider hedging a \$1 million bond portfolio using the \$100,000 T-bond futures contract. (See table 10–2.) For simplicity, let us assume that the bond portfolio consists of ten bonds of \$100,000 face value with a 10 3/4 percent coupon and three years to maturity. If rates change by one basis point from their current 10 percent level, then the price for one bond falls by \$25.29, from 101.865 to 101.839.

We can ask the same question regarding the T-bond futures contract: if rates change from 10 to 10.01, what will happen to the futures price?

The answer depends on which bond is cheapest to deliver (CTD). Because the futures price is based on the price of the CTD and the cost of carry, the volatility of the futures price is the same as that of the CTD. As the CTD price changes, the change is transferred to the futures price. The CTD price and the futures price differ by the conversion factor:

Table 10-2. Hedge Example, Basis Point Value Model

$$N_f = \frac{\text{bpv(cash)}}{\text{bpv(CTD)/CF}}$$

Basis point value change, cash bond:
Cash bond = 10 3/4 % coupon, 3 years to maturity, $100,000 face value
Current rate: 10.00%

Price = Present value at current rate

at 10% $= \sum_{t=1}^{3} \frac{\$10{,}750}{(1.10)^t} + \frac{\$100{,}000}{(1.10)^3}$

= $101,865.14

at 10.01% $= \sum_{t=1}^{3} \frac{\$10{,}750}{(1.101)^t} + \frac{\$100{,}000}{(1.101)^3}$

= $101,839.94

bpv = $101,865.14 – 101,839.94 = $25.20

Basis point value change, futures:
Cheapest to deliver = 7 1/2 % coupon, 29-year bond, $100,000 face value
Conversion factor = 0.9436

Present value of CTD at 10%:

$= \sum_{t=1}^{29} \frac{\$7{,}500}{(1.10)^t} + \frac{\$100{,}000}{(1.10)^{29}}$

= $76,575.98

Present value at 10.01%:

$= \sum_{t=1}^{29} \frac{\$7{,}500}{(1.101)^t} + \frac{\$100{,}000}{(1.101)^{29}}$

= $76,501.36

bpv, CTD = $76,575.98 – $76,501.62 = $74.36

bpv, futures = $74.36/0.9436 = $78.80

HR $= \frac{\$25.20}{\$74.36/0.9436} = 0.3197$

CF × Futures Price = CTD price

or

$$\Delta \text{FP} = \Delta \text{CTD price/CF} \qquad (10\text{–}4)$$

Using equation 10–4, then, the calculation of bpv change on the futures contract is a two-step process: the bpv change of the underlying CTD must be calculated, and then adjusted by its conversion factor to arrive at the futures bpv change.

Assume that the cheapest to deliver bond underlying the futures contract is a 7 1/2 percent coupon, twenty-nine-years to maturity security, with a conversion factor of 0.9436. If rates rise from 10.00 to 10.01, the price of the bond changes by $74.36. This leads to a change in the futures price of Δ CTD/CF, $74.36/0.9436, or $78.80. Thus, the hedge ratio necessary to arrive at dollar equivalence is equal to 0.32:

$25.20/($74.36/0.9436) = 0.3197 or 0.32

Thus, approximately 32 percent of the cash position value should be hedged with the nearby T-bond contract. In general, the number of contracts to use is found by multiplying the hedge ratio by: (value of cash position/value of one futures contract). If, for instance, the portfolio manager has ten of the bonds in a portfolio, the cash position would be worth (at 10 percent yield) 10 × $101,865 = $1,018,650. At a 10 percent yield, each futures contract is currently priced at $81,152 (the value of an 8 percent coupon, 15-year maturity bond standard underlying the futures contract). The hedger should use four contracts:

($1,018,650/$81,152) × 0.32 = 4 contracts

If the hedger used a hedge ratio of 1.00, matching the dollar value of the portfolio with an equivalent dollar value in futures contracts, the number of contracts necessary would be twelve:

($1,018,650/$81,152) × 1.0 = 12.55 contracts

Because the futures contract is three times as volatile as the cash portfolio (changing by $78.80 per basis point versus $25.50 per basis point), fewer futures (one-third as many) are needed. The bpv hedge makes adjustments for differing coupons and maturities between the cash position and the futures contract.

If this were a cross hedge, involving, for example, a corporate 10 3/4 percent, three-year bond, then an adjustment would also be needed for differing rate volatility between Treasury rates and corporate bond rates. We can run a regression of three-year Treasury rates against three-year corporate rates. If the slope coefficient is

1.18 (corporate rates are 1.18 times more volatile than Treasury rates), the hedge ratio would become 0.377:

[$25.20/($74.36/0.9436)] × 1.18 = 0.377

and the number of contracts to hedge the corporate bond would be five:

0.377 × ($1,018,650/$81,152) = 4.732 or 5 contracts.

In sum, the bpv hedge ratio model directly compares the change in value of the cash position and the futures at a small interest rate change of one basis point. The ratio of loss in value on one cash bond to the gain in value on one futures contract is the hedge ratio. If it is a cross hedge, the hedge ratio must be adjusted by the relative volatility of cash yield to futures yield.

PORTFOLIO MODEL

Johnson was the first to apply modern portfolio theory to the hedging problem.[3] The hedged position can be treated as a two-asset portfolio, cash and futures; the risk-averse hedger's objective is to minimize this portfolio's risk. Assuming the hedged portfolio is efficient, then minimizing the portfolio's risk involves minimizing the variance of the portfolio's return. This objective is quite similar to dollar equivalence: a hedge position with zero variance of total return is indeed one in which fluctuations in futures value equal fluctuations in cash value. The hedge ratio obtained from this approach is expressed in terms of covariance and variance of futures and cash price changes.

This minimum risk hedge ratio is derived in equation 5-10:

$$\text{HR} = \frac{\sigma_{s\Delta f\Delta}}{\sigma^2_{f\Delta}}$$

The Johnson, or portfolio model, is a popular one because it is relatively easy to use. The hedge ratio is the coefficient of a regression of spot price changes on futures price changes. Thus, estimating the minimum variance hedge ratio involves regressing past spot price changes on past futures price changes. The model also gives a measure of hedging effectiveness, the R^2 of the regression equation:

$$\text{effectiveness} = \rho_{s\Delta f\Delta} = R^2$$

The R^2, based on past data, gives an indication of the "goodness of fit" between the changes in price of the particular futures and the changes in price of the cash position. Thus, the regression results also supply the probable effectiveness of the hedge. This is useful when attempting to choose which futures contract would give the best hedge results. The higher the R^2, the more that futures price changes track the cash position price changes.

If we look again at hedging the 10 3/4 percent, three-year bonds with the nearby T-bond contract, table 10–3 shows the results obtained from the bond with a nearby T-bond futures contract. Past daily futures price changes are regressed on daily cash price changes:

Δ cash price $= a + b \times \Delta$ futures price.

If we use two months of data, the regression coefficient is 0.23. The hedge ratio indicates the futures price has, on average, been four times more volatile than the cash price. If the futures price changed by $100, the cash price would have changed by $23, on average.

Again, the number of futures contracts to use is obtained by multiplying the hedge ratio by the relative value of cash position to futures:

($1,018,650/$81,152) × 0.23 = 2.88 or 3 contracts

The number of futures contracts is far less than would be required if the hedger matched dollar value in the cash position and futures position. With the futures price four times as volatile as the cash price, one-quarter of the dollar matching number is required. This is also one contract less than that called for in the bpv model. This illustrates the difference in results that can be obtained using different data sources for models with quite similar objectives (dollar equivalence versus minimum price volatility). As we discuss later, results obtained under the portfolio model are quite sensitive to the data used in the estimation.

Also, the R^2 of the regression is 0.92, which indicates that the hedge will be 92 percent effective, or that 92 percent of the variance of the cash price changes will be eliminated through the hedge.

In sum, the portfolio hedge model treats the hedged position as a two-asset portfolio and minimizes the risk, or variance, of return of the hedged position. The resulting hedge ratio is a regression coefficient, and the R^2 of the regression serves as an indicator of the effectiveness of the hedge.

DURATION MODEL

Yet a third approach to the hedging problem models the objective of dollar equivalence directly.[4] The idea behind the duration model hedge is that, at the end

Table 10-3. Hedge Example, Portfolio (Variance Minimization) Model

$HR = \text{Cov}(\Delta FP, \Delta SP)/\text{Var}(\Delta FP)$

Regression results:

10 3/4%, 3-year maturity bond (y) versus nearby (June 1987) futures contract (x)

($y = a + bx$)

b: 0.2341

a: −2.7781

R^2: 0.92

$HR = 0.2341$

Number of contracts = ($1,018,650/$81,152) × 0.23 = 2.88

of the hedge, the change in value of the total cash position (S_i) due to rate volatility based on a standard or base rate as the risk-free rate (R_f) (dS_i/dR_f) will be equal to the change in value of the futures position (dV_i/dR_f) or:

$$dS_i/dR_f + dV_i/dR_f \times N_f = 0$$

(with N_f = number of futures contracts per unit of cash position, V_i = value of futures position, including any cash flow generated through margin).

By substituting further for the two derivatives, a solution for N_f is found which involves readily calculable quantities:

$$N_f = D_c/(1 + R_c) \times (1 + R_{fut})/D_f \times S_i/F_i$$

(with R_c, R_{fut} = the expected yield to maturity of the cash instrument and instrument underlying the futures contract, respectively; D_c, D_f = duration of the cash asset and futures contract, respectively, and F_i = the futures price.) The Appendix to this chapter contains the specific derivation of this hedge ratio.

Recall that the measure of volatility of an asset, ΔS, is equal to the adjusted duration, $-D/(1 + R)$. Thus, this hedge ratio involves the same essential components as the basis point value hedge. The volatility of the cash asset, $D_c/(1 + R_c)$, is compared to the volatility of the futures price, $D_f/(1 + R_{fut})$. The number of contracts is determined by multiplying this relative volatility by: (the value of the cash portfolio/value of the futures contract). If the futures and cash had the same volatility, the number of contracts would be equal to dollar matching, cash value/futures value.

Table 10-4. Hedge Example, Duration Model

$$N_f = \frac{D_c}{(1 + R_c)} \times \frac{(1 + R_{fut})}{D_{fut}} \times \frac{S_i}{F_i}$$

Cash bond = \$100,000 face value, 10 3/4% coupon, 3 years to maturity

Rate in cash market $(1 + R_c) = 1.10$
Price of cash bond (S_i) = \$101,865
Duration of cash bond $(D_c) = 2.721$

Futures contract = Nearby (June) contract

Rate in futures market $(1 + R_{fut}) = 1.104$
Price of futures contract (F) \$79,968
Duration of cheapest to deliver $(D_{fut}) = 10.445$

$$N_f = \frac{(2.721)}{(1.10)} \times \frac{(1.104)}{(10.445)} \times \frac{(\$101{,}865)}{(\$79{,}968)}$$

$$= 0.333$$

Using again the three-year, 10 3/4 percent bonds as the cash position, we can calculate the duration hedge ratio. For this model, we require the price, yield, and duration of the cash bond, taken from table 10-1. We also require the rate and price in the futures market. See table 10-4. With a rate of 10.40 percent in the futures market, the futures price is \$79,968 (the value of the 8 percent, fifteen-year bond at 10.40 percent yield). The duration of the CTD at a yield of 10.4 percent is 10.445. Therefore, the hedge ratio is:

$$[2.721/(1.10)] \times [(1.104)/10.445] \times (\$101{,}865/\$79{,}968) = 0.333 \text{ contracts}$$

This is on a per bond basis. Thus, with ten bonds in the cash position, the hedger should use 10 × 0.333, or 3.3 contracts.

Even though the three hedge ratio models just discussed look quite different, the examples as shown in table 10-2 through 10-4 result in quite similar hedge positions. In all three, the volatility of the cash position is compared to the volatility of the futures. The three methods differ primarily in the measure of volatility. Indeed, it has been shown mathematically by A. Toevs and M. Jacobs that the portfolio model and the duration model are, in fact, equivalent hedge ratios.[5] The chief difference between them concerns the relative costs of data collection and estimation. The regression in the portfolio model requires representative past data: if the cash position is relatively new, or if interest rate volatility and thus price behavior is expected to change in the future hedge period, then previous data may be inadequate to estimate a ratio. In addition, the regressions required on a multiple bond portfolio could be quite onerous. For these reasons, the duration model ratio may be easier to apply.

HEDGE MANAGEMENT

The calculation of an optimal hedge ratio is by no means the only decision required of the hedger during the hedging process. Other choices must also be made of a less theoretical nature but just as critical to the success of the hedge. Indeed, before the calculation of a hedge ratio can be made, both the specific contract and the contract maturity month must be specified.

Beyond using futures to hedge in a strict sense, it is possible to use financial futures to achieve other objectives, here most notably to achieve a particular portfolio duration as part of an immunization strategy. Other uses of financial futures involve various dividend strategies as well as portfolio insurance; we discuss these applications in chapter 11 for stock index futures and in chapter 13 for options.

HEDGE INITIATION: GENERAL CONSIDERATIONS

SHOULD A HEDGE BE INITIATED? The decision to initiate a hedge program involves considerations particular to the institution doing the hedging. Initiating a hedge program for the first time generally entails a comparison of the probable rate exposure (loss in value or income due to probable interest rate volatility) against the cost of organizing a hedge program (personnel and training, position monitoring, and control procedures). Many books and articles are available addressing the problems of specific institutions.[6]

OVERALL HEDGE OR INDIVIDUAL HEDGE? One aspect of the initial decision that requires further discussion involves the general approach taken to the institution's interest rate risk. It is theoretically possible to analyze an institution's total risk exposure and position and hedge against this overall risk; this is considered a macro hedge. It is also possible to focus more narrowly on individual aspects of an institution's risk, for instance the finance function related to short-term financial decisions such as issuance of commercial paper and short-term cash disbursements or the long-term decisions like bond financing and capital expenditures. Treating these individual risks as separate hedge problems is called a micro hedge. Ideally, if there were perfect and continuous flows of information through the organization, a centralized macro position should be the same as the sum of the institution's many individual micro hedges.[7] However, because perfect information flow is difficult to achieve, there is always a danger in a micro hedge that the individual hedge positions will add up to an increased overall risk for the institution. In addition, micro hedges may involve substantially higher transaction costs. Ultimately, most of the issues involved in the choice between a micro and a macro approach concern the relative costs of achieving a perfect or adequate information flow in an institution compared to the cost of a suboptimal set of micro hedges. Many institutions divide the hedging problem along lines of control of firm responsibility, and initiate hedges at a departmental level.

CAN THE INTEREST RATE RISK BE HEDGED WITH FUTURES? The decision of whether to hedge a particular interest rate problem also depends heavily on the effectiveness achievable from the set of futures contracts available. That is, most institutions' risk positions involve a cross hedge, and an important aspect of the hedge decision involves a comparison of the institution's particular unhedged position against the results achievable using the futures positions available to it. At present no rule can help managers decide the optimal correlation level of cash position movement to possible futures movement; a frequently used practitioner's guide is between 80 and 90 percent correlation. A correlation below 80 percent between a futures and cash position will probably result in a reduction in risk through the hedge that is less than the expense required to achieve it. An example of an interest rate risk that is difficult to hedge for this reason is a position tied to the prime rate. Being an administered rather than a market-determined rate, the prime is not highly correlated to other short-term rates such as the T-bill, Eurodollar, or CD rates. As such, it is a difficult interest rate risk to hedge with the contracts currently available.

A number of studies have addressed the problem of an optimal cross hedge for some assets having no close substitute in the futures market. For instance, both convertible and junk bonds differ in rate volatility from Treasury or high-grade corporate bonds in having a strong but variable equity component. Improved results have been achieved in cross hedging these bonds when equity index contracts are added to the hedge position.[8] Similarly, low-grade corporate bonds and municipal bonds, both of which have relative rate volatilities between T-bonds (more volatile) and T-bills (less volatile) can be more effectively hedged using a combined bill/bond futures position. As these examples show, the construction of an effective cross hedge can be as much an art as a science.

WHICH MATURITY MONTH? The simplest approach to selecting a maturity month is to choose the delivery most closely associated with the termination of the particular interest rate exposure. A treasurer hedging the issuance of commercial paper in six months, would use a contract dated as closely as possible to six months from the present. The primary problem with such an approach is the lack of volume in the deferred months of most contracts. If a substantial futures position is required to hedge, then the hedger may have to pay with a considerable price change to execute the needed volume of contracts. The alternative, and also widely used approach, is to execute a roll hedge. A roll hedge involves using the nearby contract (in the amount necessary to assure dollar equivalence) until just before the contract matures; the position is then rolled over into the next, now nearby, contract. The choice between rolling the hedge forward or matching, while a serious one on the practitioner's level, has received little attention in finance literature.

M. Pitts and R.W. Kopprasch address a common and related problem in hedging, the choice of month when the interest rate exposure lies between the available months.[9] For instance, a treasurer could be interested in a May issuance date for the commercial paper, and must choose between the March and June futures contracts currently available in short-term rate futures. Neither contract is optimal. The June contract may not be correlated sufficiently to an early May commercial paper rate. On the other hand, the use of a March contract involves rolling over at some point into June. Because rates on succeeding nonstorable commodity contracts may not be strongly related, there is uncertainty surrounding the gain or loss resulting from closing out the position in one month and reestablishing it at a rate perhaps quite different in another month. The authors find that a higher effectiveness is obtained when the hedger uses both maturities in a proportion related to the gap between the rate exposure date and the nearby contract. In general, the proportion of deferred contracts in the hedge is related to: (number of days between rate exposure and nearby contract maturity)/(number of days between nearby and deferred maturity). If the commercial paper issue date were May 15, sixty days from the March maturity, the hedger should use a proportion of 60/90, or two-third of the hedge in the June contract. The closer to the nearby contract is the rate exposure, the fewer deferred contracts need to be used.

A less passive approach to maturity selection than maturity matching involves choosing based on basis relations of the contracts. If, for instance, the June T-bond contract were known to be overpriced, the short hedger would have a preference for this contract rather than one that might be more closely matched with the rate exposure. The long hedger would wish to avoid the June contract for the same reason. Similarly, a predicted change, such as a flattening, in the shape of the yield curve and, thus, the cost of carrying might lead the long hedger to avoid the nearby and choose the deferred.[10] In these instances, the choice depends on expected changes in the basis on the contracts available.

ROLL, STACK, AND STRIP HEDGES. Yet another approach to maturity selection involves a common problem in bank management. It is usual bank practice to fund relatively long-term fixed rate loans (for instance, one year) with short-term sources of funds such as three-month jumbo CDs. This practice leads to a consistent gap between the maturity of sources and use of funds, or of liabilities and assets, that continually exposes the financial institution to the risk of rising rates. In this instance, the bank's three quarterly gaps require resetting the CD rate at the end of three, six, and nine months from today. The objective here is to eliminate this quarterly interest rate risk compared to the one-year fixed-rate loan, or to extend the quarterly gap as close as possible to one year from today. This approach to the interest rate risk is, of course, a micro one in that it considers this rate exposure in isolation from the bank's total asset and liability position.

As an illustration of the problem, let us consider a bank that has today funded a one-year $1 million fixed-rate loan at 10 percent with $1 million of 8 percent three-month CDs. At initiation of the loan, the spread or profit on the loan is fixed for the first quarter at 200 basis points (10 percent less 8 percent); the bank would like to ensure the same spread over the life of the loan. Thus, the bank must hedge against rising CD rates, and lock in as closely as possible a rate of 8 percent on its CDs over the life of the loan. Table 10–5 shows a possible interest rate scenario for the CD rates: each quarter, CD rates rise by 1 percent, and the average effective rate on the CDs over the year becomes 9.5 percent. The spread, or profit on the loan, is 50 basis points rather than 200. The bank must be able to construct a hedge so that the futures position makes up the $15,000 in additional CD interest expense if rates do indeed rise. Table 10–5 shows the hedge results under various choices of contract maturity. The CD contract is used, so no basis risk arises solely from cross hedging. Also, for simplicity, it is assumed that the yield curve is flat and, while rising, does not change shape during the hedge year. Finally, the value of one basis point change in yield on a $1 million ninety-day CD contract is equal to $25. Thus, a change in yield from 8 percent to 9 percent (or a change in futures price from 92 to 91) results in a change in value on the contract of $25 × 100 basis points = $2,500.

Tabe 10–5 shows the result of a roll hedge. With this strategy, the hedger matches maturity with exposure as it occurs. The hedger sells a March futures contract initially, letting it mature, and then sells a June futures, in this way rolling out of one contract and into another as the CDs are refunded.[11] As table 10–5 shows, a roll hedge extends the quarterly gap, but only by one quarter. Each succeeding rollover results in an additional shortfall of $2,500, so that overall the bank "loses" $7,500 in interest for the year, or locks in an effective rate of 8.75 percent rather than the desired 8 percent.

Table 10–5 shows the results from a stack hedge. Here, the hedger initially "stacks" a position in the nearby contract equivalent to the three quarterly refundings. As these mature, the hedger rolls over the hedge into the next (now nearby) contract, but using fewer contracts. As the quarterly refundings are completed, fewer contracts are needed each time. Two June futures are used when the hedge is rolled over in March, and then one September futures contract when the hedge is rolled over in

June. As the results show, this strategy gives an effective rate of 8 percent, the hedge objective.

The third approach involves the strip hedge. Table 10-5 shows the results. The hedger sells a strip of futures at the initiation of the hedge, selling one contract in each of the three delivery months (March, June, September). With the strip hedge as well, the bank has succeeded in extending the gap for the full year, and locks in an effective interest rate of 8 percent.

Both strip and stack hedges result in an effective rate equal to the hedger's objective. Which of these to use depends heavily on such issues as the timing of interest rate changes and the shape of the yield curve. Because it relies on the earlier months of the hedge, the stack hedge is more vulnerable to the timing of rate changes. If rates change more in the later quarters than in the earlier, then the stack hedge is less effective. The strip hedge is not so dependent on the timing of rate changes because all of the futures positions are initiated at the same time.

Additionally, the stack hedge is also less effective in that it can involve a much larger loss from basis convergence than the strip if the yield curve has a positive and decreasing slope—the most common configuration—and rates are stable. (See table 10-6).

Assume rates are stable throughout the hedge period, and the three-month CD rate is 9.25 percent in March, June, and September. If the hedger maintains the hedge for the full three quarters, a short hedge consistently loses money. To see this, remember that futures rates in equilibrium are equal to the implied forward rate for that time period, as shown in table 10-6. As time passes, the futures rate converges to the actual rate at maturity of the contract, in the example, 9.25 percent. Thus, the March futures rate falls from 10.00 percent to 9.25 percent, and the loss for the hedge period is 75 basis points per March contract. With a total of six contracts (three in the March futures, two in the June, and one in the September), the stack experiences a greater total loss from convergence over one quarter at a time (450 basis points) than the three contracts involved in the strip, involving convergence over nine months (350 basis points). Finally, the rate fixed on any short-term contract for the strip hedge is equal to the IFR of the contract at hedge initiation. The rise in futures price of 75 points on the March contract would result in an effective CD rate in March of 9.25 percent, the current rate, plus 75 basis points, the futures loss, or 10.00 percent, the futures rate at initiation. Similarly, the CD rate in June is equal to 9.25 percent plus 125 basis points, or 10.50 percent, the futures rate on the June contract at initiation. Table 10-6 includes a comparison of stack and strip hedges if the yield curve is upward sloping and the slope is constant. Here there is no difference in performance due to convergence. Again, the usual yield curve configuration is upward sloping with decreasing slope.

Table 10-5. Comparison of Rolling, Strip, and Stack Hedges

Cash Position: $1,000,000 fixed-rate loan at 10% with quarterly refinancing of $1,000,000 CDs.

Interest rate scenario: CD interest rates rise by 1% per quarter from initial 8%.

Quarter	*Rate*	*Quarterly Interest Expense on CDs*	*Incremental Expense over 8 %*
1	8%	$20,000	—
2	9	22,500	$2,500
3	10	25,000	5,000
4	11	27,500	7,500

Average effective rate for 4 quarters: 9.5%

CD Futures: Rates and (prices) at quarterly refunding.

	Rates and (Prices)			
Contract	*Jan. 2*	*March 30*	*June 30*	*Sept 30*
March	8% (92)	9% (91)	—	—
June	8 (92)	9 (91)	10% (90)	—
September	8 (92)	9 (91)	10 (90)	11% (89)

Roll Hedge

Strategy		*Hedge Dollar Gain*	*Interest Expense = Cash Expense-Gain in Futures*	*Effective Rate*
Jan. 2:	Sell 1 March futures at 92			
March 30:	Offset March futures at 91 Sell 1 June futures at 91	(92−91=100 bp) × $25/bp=$2,500	$22,500−$2,500=$20,000	8%

June 30:	Offset June futures at 90 Sell 1 Sept. futures at 90	(91 − 90 = 100bp) × $25/bp = $2,500	25,000 − 2,500 = 22,500	9
Sept. 30:	Offset Sept. futures at 89	(90 − 89 = 100 bp) × $25/bp = $2,500	27,500 − 2,500 = 25,000	10

Average effective rate with hedge = (.08 + .08 + .09 + .10)/4 = 8.75%.

Stack Hedge

Strategy		*Hedge Dollar Gain*	*Interest Expense = Cash Expense-Gain in Futures*	*Effective Rate*
Jan. 2:	Sell 3 March futures at 92			
March 30:	Offset March futures at 91 Sell 2 June futures at 91	(3 × (92 − 91) = 3 × 100bp) × $25/bp = $7500	$22,500 − $7,500 = $15,000	6%
June 30:	Offset June futures at 90 Sell 1 Sept. futures at 90	(2 × (91 − 90) = 2 × 100bp) × $25/bp = $5000	25,500 − 5,000 = 20,000	8
Sept. 30:	Offset Sept. futures at 89	(1 × (90 − 89) = 1 × 100bp) × $25/bp = $2500	27,500 − 2,500 = 25,000	10

Average effective rate = (.08 + .06 + .08 + .10)/4 = 8%

Strip Hedge

Strategy		*Hedge Dollar Gain*	*Interest Expense = Cash Expense-Gain in Futures*	*Effective Rate*
Jan. 2:	Sell 1 March futures at 92 Sell 1 June futures at 92 Sell 1 Sept. futures at 92			
Mar. 30:	Offset March futures at 91	(92 − 91 = 100bp) × $25/bp = $2500	$22,500 − $2,500 = $20,000	8%
June 30:	Offset June futures at 90	(92 − 90 = 200bp) × $25/bp = $5000	25,000 − 5,000 = 20,000	8
Sept. 30:	Offset Sept. futures at 89	(92 − 89 = 300bp) × $25/bp = $7500	27,500 − 7,000 = 20,000	8

Average effective rate = (.08 + .08 + .08 + .08)/4 = 8%

Table 10-6. Comparison of Stack and Strip Hedges
(Stable and Upwardly Sloping Yield Curve)

1. Assume futures prices reflect IFRs of upwardly sloping yield curve.
2. Assume yield curve stable over 9-month period.

Current short-term yield:	9.25%
3-month IFR (Mar.-June):	10.00%
3-month IFR (June-Sept.):	10.50%
3-month IFR (Sept.-Dec.):	10.75%

CD futures: Rates and (prices) at quarterly refunding:

	Futures		
	March	*June*	*September*
On January 2:	10.00% (90.0)	10.50% (89.5)	10.75% (89.25)
March 30:	9.25 (90.75)	10.00 (90.0)	10.50 (89.5)
June 30:	—	9.25 (90.75)	10.00 (90)
Sept. 30:	—	—	9.25 (90.75)

Loss due to convergence:

Stack hedge:	March contract	3 × 75 bp
	June contract	2 × 75 bp
	Sept. contract	1 × 75 bp

Total: 225 + 150 + 75 = 450 basis points

Strip hedge:	March contract	1 × 75 bp
	June contract	1 × 125 bp
	Sept. contract	1 × 150 bp

Total: 75 × 125 × 150 = 350 basis points

1. Assume futures prices reflect IFRs of upwardly sloping yield curve.
2. Assume yield curve stable over 9-month period.
3. Assume slope of yield curve is a constant.

Current short-term rate:	9.25%
3-month IFR (Mar.-June):	10.25%
3-month IFR (June-Sept.):	11.25%
3-month IFR (Sept.-Dec.):	12.25%

CD futures: Rates and (futures prices) at quarterly refunding:

	Futures		
	March	*June*	*September*
On January 2:	10.25% (89.75)	11.25% (88.75)	12.25% (87.75)
March 30:	9.25 (90.75)	10.25 (89.75)	11.25 (88.75)
June 30:	—	9.25 (90.75)	10.25 (89.75)
Sept. 30:	—	—	9.25 (90.75)

Table 10-6 continued

Loss due to convergence:			
Stack hedge:	March contract:	3 × 100 bp	
	June contract:	2 × 100 bp	
	Sept. contract:	1 × 100 bp	
Total: 300 + 200 + 100 = 600 basis points			
Strip hedge:	March contract:	1 × 100 bp	
	June contract:	1 × 200 bp	
	Sept. contract:	1 × 300 bp	
Total: 100 + 200 + 300 = 600 basis points			

The basic effectiveness of a strip hedge versus a stack hedge depends strongly on the path of interest rate changes during the hedge and expected rates at various times. Table 10-7 shows a more realistic interest rate path and the results of the two hedges. In January the yield curve is as before, upward sloping but with a decreasing slope. By March the still rising yield curve has become more shallow. In June the rates fall and the curve steepens; and finally, in September rates rise by 200 basis points. The strip hedge results in an effective quarterly CD rate equal to the futures rate on the contracts as of the initiation of the hedge. The stack hedge is vulnerable to the timing of rate changes. For instance, the 200 basis point fall in rates and rise in futures price in the third quarter results in a large loss on the two short futures contracts, and a quarterly CD rate of 12.50 percent rather than 8 percent unhedged. Overall, the stack hedge leads to a better result, an effective average rate of 9.9375 percent, than the strip's effective rate of 10.75 percent although both are worse than the effective rate if unhedged (9.3125 percent).

In sum, the choice of hedge maturity can depend on probable interest rate and yield curve movements. The strip hedge always results in an effective rate equal to the futures rate at initiation of the hedge. The hedger knows the final result of the hedge at the beginning of the strip hedge. The result of the stack hedge is more dependent on the timing of interest rate moves, and could be considered more risky than the strip hedge if rates are particularly volatile.

HEDGING LONG-TERM MATURITIES

What if the gap had been a longer one initially? That is, what if the fixed-rate loan had had a maturity of one and one-half years? Here, the bank would want to extend the gap for one and one-half years with a strip of futures involving five contracts, the March of this year, June, September, December, and March of next year. It

Table 10-7. Comparison of Stack and Strip Hedges
(Changing Yield Curve)

Yield Curves:

January:	Upward sloping and decreasing yield curve
March:	Rates rise, yield curve shallow
June:	Rates fall, curve steepens
September:	Rates rise by 200 basis points

CD futures: Rates and (futures prices) at quarterly refunding:

	Futures		
	March	*June*	*September*
On January 2:	10.00% (90)	10.50% (89.5)	10.75% (89.25)
March 30	10.00 (90)	10.25 (89.25)	10.35 (89.15)
June 30:	—	8.00 (92)	9.00 (91)
September 30:	—	—	10.00 (90)

Loss due to convergence:

Stack hedge:	March contract	3 × 0 bp
	June contract	2 × (225) bp
	September contract	1 × 200 bp
Effective rate:	9.25% + 10.00% + (8.00% + 4.50% = 12.50%) + (10.00% − 2.00% = 8%) = (9.25 + 10 + 12.50 + 8)/4 = 9.9375%	
Strip hedge:	March contract	1 × 0 bp
	June contract	1 × (250) bp
	September contract	1 × (75) bp
Effective rate:	9.25% + 10.00% + (8.00% + 2.50 = 10.50%) + (10.00% + .75% = 10.75%) = (9.25 + 10.00 + 10.50 + 10.75)/4 = 10.125%	
Unhedged:		
Effective rate:	(9.25% + 10.00% + 8.00% + 10.00%)/4 = 9.3125%	

may not be possible to execute such a hedge, however, if the futures contract does not have maturity months of more than one year. (This is currently the case, for instance, in the CD contract). In this case, the best that is available to the hedger is a rolling strip hedge. This is a combination of a full strip with the contracts currently available at initiation (March, June, September, December), and subsequent rollover into the newly available deferred March contract as the nearby March matures (see table 10-8). Obviously, as the example shows, the rolling strip does not result in 100 percent effectiveness; there is a shortfall of $2,500 due to the necessity to roll over when the deferred March becomes available.

Another partial solution to the lack of deferred months involves the truncated strip hedge (table 10–8). Consider again the original one-year fixed-rate loan. It may be that the most deferred maturities (here, September), while available for trading, do not have sufficient volume to allow the hedger to use them in the full strip hedge without a substantial sacrifice in price. In this case, an alternative to the full strip is the truncated strip: the hedger doubles up positions on the nearby and leaves off the deferred part of the strip. Again, the full strip would be the optimal choice; the truncated strip involves some slippage in the profit on the deferred contracts ($2,500) which raises the effective rate to 8.25 percent from the target 8 percent. The stacking of the earlier months is, in some sense, an "overhedge" on the underlying cash position and is vulnerable, as the stack was, to the timing of the change in rates. If rates had risen by 2 percent in the first quarter and remained flat for the second quarter, the truncated strip would have been even less effective when compared to the full strip results.

As can be seen from the previous example, it is difficult to hedge a long-term commitment in the futures market. Generally, a futures contract has maturities extending for at most two years from today, and volume in the very deferred months is generally low. There are alternatives to using futures to hedge interest rate risk, however, and some of these methods offer a better opportunity to hedge such long-term positions. Because the use of such alternative instruments is outside the scope of this text, these alternative hedge methods are discussed only briefly.[12]

SWAPS. Swaps generally involve the exchange between two parties of their payment obligations.[13] For instance, a company may swap with another its fixed debt payment denominated in British pounds for a fixed debt payment denominated in U.S. dollars. Similarly, the swap may involve the exchange of floating rate payments for fixed-rate payments, a hedge of interest rate volatility.

The earliest swaps involved exchanges of foreign currency obligations; the following example of such a swap illustrates the essentials and objective of the agreement.

Assume a U.S. company has borrowed $170,000 in the British capital market at a favorable rate of 10 percent for five years. The interest payments, denominated in pounds, represent substantial currency risk for the company. Currently, the exchange rate for the pound is $1.70/£, and the company is obligated to pay 10,000 pounds (in current value, $17,000) in interest per year. If, however, the pound rises in value against the dollar, the value of the debt payments to the U.S. firm would be greater than $17,000 per year, and the favorable interest rate of 10 percent would in effect be lost.

The U.S. company can arrange to swap its fixed foreign currency obligation with another firm to obtain a fixed liability denominated in U.S. dollars. Assume a

Table 10-8. Rolling Strip and Truncated Strip Hedges

Cash Position: $1,000,000 fixed rate loan at 10% with quarterly refinancing of $1,000,000 CDs

Interest rate scenario: CD interest rates rise by 1% per quarter from initial 8%.

Quarter	*Rate*	*Quarterly Interest Expense on CDs*	*Incremental Expense over 8%*
1	8%	$20,000	—
2	9	22,500	$ 2,500
3	10	25,000	5,000
4	11	27,500	7,500
5	12	30,000	10,000
6	13	32,500	12,500

Average effective rate for 6 quarters: 10.5%

CD Futures: Prices and rates at quarterly refunding.

	Rates and (Prices)					
Contract	*Jan.2*	*Mar. 30*	*June 30*	*Sep. 30*	*Dec. 30*	*Mar. 30*
March	8% (92)	9% (91)	—	—	—	—
June	8 (92)	9 (91)	10% (90)	—	—	—
Sept.	8 (92)	9 (91)	10 (90)	11% (89)		
Dec.	8 (92)	9 (91)	10 (90)	11 (89)	12% (88)	—
March	—	9 (91)	10 (90)	11 (89)	12 (88)	13% (87)

Rolling Strip Hedge

	Strategy	Hedge Dollar Gain	Interest Expense = Cash Expense-Gain in Futures	Effective Rate
Jan. 2:	Sell 1 March futures at 92			
	Sell 1 June futures at 92			
	Sell 1 Sept. futures at 92			
	Sell 1 Dec. futures at 92			
Mar. 30:	Offset March futures at 91	(92 − 91 = 100bp) × $25/bp = $ 2,500	$22,500 − $ 2,500 = $20,000	8%
	Sell 1 March (deferred) at 91			
June 30:	Offset June futures at 90	(92 − 90 = 200bp) × $25/bp = $ 5,000	$25,000 − 5,000 = 20,000	8
Sept. 30:	Offset Sept. futures at 89	(92 − 89 = 300bp) × $25/bp = $ 7,500	$27,500 − 7,500 = 20,000	8
Dec. 30	Offset Dec. futures at 88	(92 − 88 = 400bp) × $25/bp = $10,000	$30,000 − 10,000 = 20,000	8
Mar. 30:	Offset March futures at 87	(91 − 87 = 400bp) × $25/bp = $10,000	$32,500 − 10,000 = 22,500	9

Average effective rate = (.08 + .08 + .08 + .08 + .08 + .09)/6 = 8.17%

	Strategy	Hedge Dollar Gain	Interest Expense Cash Expense-Gain in Futures	Effective Rate
Jan 2:	Sell 1 March futures at 92			
	Sell 2 June futures at 92			
Mar. 30:	Offset March futures at 91	(92 − 91 = 100bp) × $25/bp = $2500	$25,500 − $ 2,500 = $20,000	8%
June 30:	Offset June futures at 90	(2 × (92 − 90 = 200bp) × $25/bp	$25,000 − 10,000 = 15,500	6
		= $5,000	$27,500 − 10,000 = 27,500	11

Average Effective Rate = (.08 + .08 + .06 + .11)/4 = 8.25%

British company has a similar foreign currency exposure, having borrowed $170,000 in the U.S. at 10 percent for five years. The two companies can agree to swap interest payments to eliminate their foreign currency risk:

U.S. firm:	£10,000/yr. for 5 years	↑
U.K. firm	↓	$17,000/yr for 5 years

After the swap:

U.S. firm	pays $17,000/yr for 5 years
U.K. firm:	pays £10,000/yr for 5 years

For the life of the swap agreement and the loan, the U.S. firm is obligated to pay $17,000 per year no matter what happens to the dollar-British pound exchange rate. In this way, the foreign currency risk has been completely hedged away. (The final value of the principal repayment of £100,000 can be hedged with a five-year forward purchase of pounds or through purchase of an option as described in chapter 13.)

The preceding example has been simplified considerably from reality. There may be no British company involved in the swap, with the other side being taken instead by a bank willing to take on the foreign currency risk exposure. Guarantees against default involving collateral or a third-party guarantee are generally involved.

Swaps have several advantages over futures in hedging away risk. The U.S. firm has effected a five-year hedge, a much longer term than is available with futures contracts. In addition, because the swap is negotiated between private parties, the swap agreement can be customized for the parties involved, reflecting the size and timing of the particular commitment. However, because of this customization and the long-term commitment, swaps are expensive in transactions costs. Further, the hedger loses flexibility. If foreign exchange rates move in the U.S. company's favor, the firm cannot leave the swap to take advantage of this development without paying a substantial penalty.

Finally, the swap is related quite closely to a forward contract: the U.S. company agrees to receive 10,000 pounds every year and to pay $17,000 for it. In essence, the swap is a series of forward contracts for pounds, with the forward price fixed each year at $17,000.

A swap can also involve an exchange of interest payments or interest income between two parties. Generally, the swap involves the exchange of fixed-rate for floating-rate obligations. In addition, it is common for interest swaps to take advantage of differences in relative borrowing costs for differently rated borrowers.

For instance, let us assume two companies are currently interested in borrowing $100,000 for five years. Assume one firm with a relatively low credit rating would like to borrow in the fixed-rate market, while the other high-rated firm would like to borrow in the floating-rate market. The lower-rated corporation (LRC) can borrow at a fixed-rate cost of 10 percent, and a floating rate of 0.5 percent over the London Interbank Offered Rate (LIBOR). The higher-rated corporation (HRC) can borrow at a fixed rate of 8 percent, and a floating rate 0.25 percent over LIBOR:

Corporation	**Fixed**	**Floating**
High rated	8%	LIBOR + 25 basis pts
Low rated	10	LIBOR + 50 basis pts

Although the interest cost for the LRC is higher for both obligations, it has a relative advantage in the floating rate, paying only a 25-basis-point difference for its credit risk (LIBOR + 0.25 percent versus LIBOR + 0.50 percent) as opposed to paying a 200-basis-point difference in the fixed-rate obligation (8.00 percent versus 10 percent). Both corporations can benefit from this relative advantage through a swap. First, the HRC borrows $100,000 at a fixed rate of 8 percent, and the LRC borrows $100,000 at 0.5 percent over LIBOR. Second, the two corporations swap payment streams: HRC takes on the floating-rate obligation at LIBOR, and LRC takes on the 8 percent fixed rate plus an additional 0.5 percent expense. Both parties have borrowed in their preferred market and secured cheaper financing through the swap than would be available otherwise: HRC pays a floating rate of LIBOR rather than LIBOR + 25, and LRC pays a fixed rate of 8.5 percent rather than 10 percent. Both original obligations are met: 8.50 percent is available to pay the 8 percent fixed, with 50 basis points remaining to cover the LIBOR plus 50.

Although the example emphasizes the usual motive for swaps and comparative advantage in rates, the swap mechanism can be used solely to swap out of a floating-rate obligation and into a fixed rate, thus ending interest rate risk, or in effect hedging the floating rate over its entire life. Again, the swap's advantages of longer term and customization must be balanced against the higher cost and loss of flexibility compared to hedging with futures.

The choice of methods to hedge long-term risk—futures or swaps—depends in part on the particular cost structure and experience of the hedger, as well as the probable course of interest rates.

OVER-THE-COUNTER OPTIONS. It is possible to use OTC options, which can have a longer life than futures, to set a floor or ceiling on interest rate expense or income. We discuss these options as well as exchange-traded options in chapter 13.

FUTURES IN IMMUNIZATION AND PORTFOLIO MANAGEMENT

As discussed at the beginning of this chapter, there are times when a portfolio manager wants to achieve a certain portfolio duration, whether as part of an immunization strategy or as part of an active management program. Banks and savings and loans want to adjust the duration of their asset portfolio in relation to the duration of their liabilities. Financial futures can be used to do this in a flexible and relatively cheap way.

As an illustration, let us consider a portfolio manager with a holding period of three years. To immunize the portfolio against the interest rate risks of coupon reinvestment and principal loss, the manager would need to hold a portfolio with a duration of three. Currently, the portfolio consist of $500,000 worth of bonds with a weighted average duration of five. To reduce the duration of the cash portfolio, the manager could sell off the long term or low-coupon bonds and replace them with lower duration bonds having high coupons or short maturities. The manager could also adjust the duration down to the desired three by using futures as a substitute for this cash transaction, adding a short futures position in sufficient size to achieve the duration of three.

The short futures contracts necessary to achieve this number is a function of the portfolio composition and the duration of the bond underlying the futures contract. Ideally, the manager would like a $500,000 value portfolio (P_p) with a duration of three (D_c). Currently, the manager has a $500,000 portfolio with a duration of five to which must be added short futures contracts (N_f) that have a duration (D_f) and a current price of F:

$$\text{Ideal Portfolio} = (D_c \times P_p) = \text{Current Portfolio} + \text{Futures Position}$$
$$= (D_c \times P_p) + (D_f \times F \times N_f)$$

Assume the cheapest to deliver underlying the T-bond contract has a duration of eight and the futures is currently priced at $85,000; then to find N_f, we simply substitute in the known quantities:

$$\text{Ideal Porfolio} = 3 \times \$500{,}000 = \text{Current Portfolio} + \text{Futures}$$
$$= 5 \times \$500{,}000 + 8 \times \$85{,}000 \times N_f$$

or

$$3 \times \$500{,}000 = 5 \times \$500{,}000 + 8 \times \$85{,}000 \times N_f$$
$$N_f = -1.47 \text{ contracts}$$

By selling 1 1/2 futures contracts, the manager can immunize the portfolio. The number of futures necessary to sell is relatively small due to the high duration of the CTD underlying the contract, especially as compared to the ideal and actual portfolio durations. With the portfolio immunized, the yield on the investment over the three-year holding period should be equal to the current yield to maturity of the portfolio.

Since duration changes both through time and in response to rate changes, the manager finds that the duration of the position must be adjusted to maintain the immunization strategy. The advantage of using futures to achieve immunization is that the number of contracts, and thus the portfolio duration, can be adjusted quickly and easily by selling more or buying back some contracts. In addition, the transaction costs for futures can be less than those of a cash transaction.

ACTIVE MANAGEMENT. Not all managers choose a passive immunization strategy. If interest rates are expected to decrease, a manager may want to take advantage of this by increasing the duration, and thus price appreciation of the portfolio. Similarly, if rates were expected to rise, the manager may want to decrease the portfolio duration to a small number to decrease the price volatility (here, loss) of the portfolio. Ultimately, if rates are expected to increase by a large amount, the manager may want to decrease the portfolio duration to zero, or to a full, dollar equivalence, hedged position. The usual duration adjustment without futures would involve a sale of high duration and purchase of low duration bonds, and ultimately, if rates rise high enough, the conversion of the portfolio to cash equivalents (short-term Treasury securities held to their maturity). With futures, the manager could work within the framework of duration adjustment to achieve any duration desired on the basis of expected rate moves and portfolio risk objectives. Again, because they are easy to buy and sell, futures have a flexibility that can enhance the portfolio manager's market timing ability.

The variable purchase and sale of futures in relation to rate movements is the idea behind portfolio insurance programs. Portfolio insurance combines active portfolio management and market timing with a hedge program. As rates move down, the manager would increase duration and have no short futures positions in the portfolio. To increase duration, additional long futures might be included. However, if rates increase, the manager would adjust the duration and the futures position to increase protection and would begin to add short futures contracts to the portfolio. Finally, if rates increase sufficiently, the portfolio would be 100 percent hedged with enough short futures contracts to bring the volatility of the portfolio to zero. The adjustment of the duration and the particular duration needed are closely related to the price behavior of options. Thus, the desired duration of the portfolio, and the specific number of futures needed to adjust the portfolio, are discussed in more detail in chapter 13.

SYNTHETIC SECURITIES. With a perfect hedge (duration = 0), the return to the portfolio should be close to the risk-free rate of return. That is, if the hedged position is risk free, the return on the position should be the risk-free rate of return. To see this more clearly, it is necessary to show the cash flows involved in a perfect, 100 percent hedged position more fully. If the hedger bought a bond, the cash flow from holding it unhedged would be equal to the original purchase price, a negative cash flow ($-S_t$) plus the long-term yield received over time (yS_t). A perfect hedge position would involve selling a futures contract on the cash bond and receiving the futures price ($= S_t + (r - y)S_t$). The total cash flow, then, from the perfect hedge, would be equal to:

$$(-S_t + yS_t) + (S_t + (r - y)S_t) = rS_t \tag{10-5}$$

The total return to a perfect hedge would be equal to the risk-free, short-term rate embedded in the futures contract. This serves to illustrate the true nature of hedging with futures. A full, 100 percent hedge, with duration equal to zero, results in a total investment return of the short-term, risk-free rate. The achievement of dollar equivalence, or zero price volatility, should indeed result in a risk-free position earning the risk-free rate. Using futures with a portfolio can thus result in the creation of synthetic securities. The fully hedged position is in reality a synthetic short-term security paying the risk-free rate of return. The fully hedged position is equivalent to selling off the entire portfolio and investing in cash equivalents.

THE ARBITRAGE TRANSACTION. Finally, the basis of the arbitrage transaction, and its return, is shown in equation 10–5. The arbitrage transactions include buying the bond, selling the futures (as in equation 10–5) and financing the bond purchase at the current short-term borrowing rate (r_{bor}):

$$(-S_t + yS_t) + (S_t - yS_t + r_{fut}S_t) - r_{bor}S_t \tag{10-6}$$

With the price of the bond, S_t, and the long-term yield, y, fixed, the mispricing of the futures would result in an implied short-term rate, r_{fut}, that is too high compared to current market short-term rates. As equation 10–6 shows, the return on the arbitrage depends on the size of the short-term rate implied by the futures, r_{fut}, compared to the short-term borrowing rate of the arbitrageur, r_{bor}.

APPENDIX: DERIVATION OF DURATION HEDGE RATIO

Given bond pricing equation 10–1, we can express the derivative of the cash instrument price with respect to changes in the risk-free rate as:

$$\frac{dS_i}{dR_f} = \frac{dS_i}{d(1 + R_c)} \times \frac{d(1 + R_c)}{dR_f} = \frac{d\sum_{t=1}^{m} C_t/(1 + R_c)^t}{d(1 + R_c)} \times \frac{d(1 + R_c)}{dR_f} \tag{10-7}$$

A similar expression can be used for the derivative of the futures value. Here, we know that the futures price is set so that the value at initiation (V_i) is equal to 0. We also know that the value of the contract is the cash flow expected to be received while holding the contract ($\Sigma_{t=i}^{T} CF_t$) less the purchase price (F_i):

$$V_i = \sum_{t=i}^{T} CF_t/(1 + R_{\text{fut}}) - F_i = 0 \tag{10-8}$$

We can take the derivative of 10-8 with respect to R_f:

$$\frac{dV_i}{dR_f} = \frac{d\left(\Sigma_{t=i}^{T} CF_t/(1 + R_{\text{fut}}) - F_i\right)}{d(1 + R_{\text{fut}})} \times \frac{d(1 + R_{\text{fut}})}{dR_f} \tag{10-9}$$

With the objective of the hedge as dollar equivalence in the cash position versus the futures position:

$$\frac{dS_i}{dR_f} + \frac{dV_i}{dR_f} = 0 \tag{10-10}$$

equation 10-7 and equation 10-9 can be substituted into equation 10-10:

$$\frac{d\left(\Sigma_{t=1}^{m} C_t/(1 + R_c\right)}{d(1 + R_c)} \times \frac{d(1 + R_c)}{dR_f} + \frac{d\left(\Sigma_{t=i}^{T} CF_t/(1 + R_{\text{fut}}) - F_i\right)}{d(1 + R_{\text{fut}})} \times \frac{d(1 + R_{\text{fut}})}{dR_f} = 0 \tag{10-11}$$

This can be simplied to:

$$\frac{1}{(1 + R_c)} \times \frac{-\Sigma_{t-1}^{m} tC_t}{(1 + R_c)} \times \frac{d(1 + R_c)}{dR_f} + \frac{N_f}{(1 + R_{\text{fut}})} \times \frac{\Sigma_{t=i}^{T} - tCF_t}{(1 + R_{\text{fut}})} \times \frac{d(1 + R_{\text{fut}})}{dR_f} = 0 \tag{10-12}$$

and a solution for N_f derived:

$$N_f = \frac{-(1 + R_{\text{fut}})}{(1 + R_c)} \times \frac{\dfrac{\Sigma_{t=1}^{m} tC_t}{(1 + R_c)}}{\dfrac{\Sigma_{t=i}^{T} tCF_t}{(1 + R_{\text{fut}})}} \times \frac{d(1 + R_c)/dR_f}{d(1 + R_{\text{fut}})/dR_f} \tag{10-13}$$

By substituting the expression for duration, N_f can be expressed as a function of rates, prices, and durations:

$$N_f = \frac{D_c}{(1 + R_c)} \times \frac{(1 + R_{\text{fut}})}{D_f} \times \frac{S_i}{F_i} \times \frac{d(1 + R_c)/dR_f}{d(1 + R_{\text{fut}})/dR_f} \qquad (10\text{–}14)$$

It is customary, when using this model, to assume the yield curve is flat. This is a common assumption in calculations, and is implied when a single discount rate, the yield to maturity, is used to discount the cash flows of a bond no matter when those cash flows occur. With this assumption, the yields and prices in equation 10–14, which refer to the end of the hedge period, also refer to current rates, rates at the initiation of the hedge. Obviously, this is a crucial assumption to obtain a solution for N_f in an observable form.

In addition, it is also common to assume $d(1 + R_c)/dR_f = d(1 + R_{\text{fut}})/dR_f$, or that the cash and futures assets show similar rate volatility against the standard, risk-free rate. If this is not the case, an adjustment must be made to equation 10–14, as with the bpv model, for differing volatility of cash and futures rates.

NOTES

1. B. Malkiel, "Expectations, Bond Prices, and the Term Structure of Interest Rates." *Quarterly Journal of Economics* 76 (1962): 197–218.
2. Duration has received substantial treatment in the finance literature. For a general introduction, see F.K. Reilly and R. Sidhu, "The Many Uses of Bond Duration," *Financial Analysts Journal* 36 (1980): 58–72. For a more thorough discussion, see G.O. Bierwag, *Duration Analysis* (Cambridge, Mass.: Ballinger Publishing Co., 1987).
3. L. Johnson, "Theory of Hedging and Speculation in Commodity Futures," *Review of Economic Studies* 27 (1960): 139–51.
4. The duration model is also called the Price Sensitivity Model and was first developed in R. Kolb and R. Chiang, "Improving Hedging Performance Using Interest Rate Futures," *Financial Management* 10 (1981): 72–79.
5. A. Toevs and M. Jacob, "Futures and Alternative Hedge Ratio Methodologies," *Journal of Portfolio Management* 12 (1986): 60–70.
6. There are many practitioner texts available. See, for example, chapter 12 in N.H. Rothstein, *The Handbook of Financial Futures* (New York: McGraw-Hill, 1984); S. Figlewski, *Hedging with Financial Futures for Institutional Investors* (Cambridge: Mass.: Ballinger Publishing Co., 1986); J. Labuszewski and J. Nyhoff, *Trading Financial Futures* (New York: John Wiley and Sons, 1988); E.W. Schwarz, J.M. Hill, and T. Schneeweis, *Financial Futures* (Homewood, Ill.: Richard D. Irwin, 1986); E.W. Schwarz, *How to Use Interest Rate Futures* (Homewood, Ill.: Dow Jones-Irwin, 1979).
7. R. Kolb, S.G. Timme, and G. Gay, "Macro vs. Micro Futures Hedges at Commercial Banks," *Journal of Futures Markets* 4 (1984): 47–51.

8. R. Grieves, "Hedging Corporate Bond Portfolios." *Journal of Portfolio Management* 12 (1986): 23–26.
9. M. Pitts and R.W. Kopprasch, "Reducing Intertemporal Risk in Financial Futures and Hedging," *Journal of Futures Markets* 7 (1987): 11–13.
10. A rise in the short-term rate relative to the long-term yield would reduce the net cost of carrying. With a positively sloping yield curve, deferred contracts would be expected to rise relative to nearby. This is also the justification for a bear spread (short position in nearby futures and long position in deferred futures); see chapter 9.
11. Note that the dollar equivalence hedge ignores interest accrual; that is, the CD is assumed to involve $1 million each quarter rather than $1 million plus accrued interest.
12. For a comprehensive discussion of alternative means to hedge interest rate risk, see R.B. Platt, *Controlling Interest Rate Risk* (New York: John Wiley & Sons, 1986.)
13. For a general introduction to swaps, see C.W. Smith, C.W. Smithson, and L.M. Wakeman, "The Evolving Market for Swaps" in *The Revolution in Corporate Finance*. ed. J. Stern and D.H. Chew. (Oxford: Basil Blackwell, 1986).

STOCK INDEX FUTURES

11

A stock index futures contract is an agreement to buy or sell a well-diversified stock portfolio represented by a stock index. The value of the contract is generally assigned as $500 times the futures price or futures index level. Thus, if Standard & Poor's 500 (S&P500) March futures price is equal to an index level of 300, then a long futures position in the S&P500 index represents the right to "buy" $500 × 300, or $150,000 worth of the S&P500 portfolio. There are two key differences between index futures and other financial futures discussed previously: First, there is no physical delivery of the commodity. Settlement of the contract involves a cash settlement, paying or receiving the difference between the initial futures price and the offsetting futures price or the final, delivery day settlement price. Indeed, because the contracts are marked-to-market daily, the difference in cash received or paid at the offset or maturity of the contract is really the difference between the previous day's settlement price and the offset or delivery day price. Second, and more important, the underlying commodity is an average of the prices of a selected sample of stocks. The futures price or index level refers to an average of the price or performance of a particular, usually well-diversified, stock portfolio. With index futures, then, the concept of a futures contract has been broadened considerably to include a futures on a commodity which is an average of essentially heterogeneous commodities, and the possibility of delivering these commodities need no longer be considered when proposing a futures contract. The extension of index trading in indexes other than stock portfolios is discussed in the last section of this chapter.

Because an index futures contract represents a particular index, its pricing and use in hedging depends on the characteristics of the underlying index and its construction. We discuss the calculation of the indexes and the effect on the use of their futures in the first section.

Similar to the interest rate futures discussed in chapter 9, the value of a stock index futures can be determined through the cost of carry model. As with Treasury bonds or other storable commodities, the portfolio represented by the index can be purchased and carried through time for delivery into a distant maturity contract. In the case of stock index futures, however, the cost of carry relates to the short-term interest rate over the carry period and the dividend yield received on the underlying portfolio. The cost of carry model, as applied to index futures, is discussed in the second section of this chapter.

Stock index futures can transfer the risk of price change in stock prices to another, a speculator, more willing to undertake the risk. As with interest rate futures, a portfolio manager holding an inventory of stocks is subject to a loss if stock prices decline. Provided the spot portfolio held is a well-diversified one, the portfolio manager can hedge the risk of a general stock market decline by selling index futures. If the market does decline, index futures prices decline as well, and the short futures position serves to make up the loss experienced on the cash portfolio.

Similarly, a portfolio manager may expect a cash inflow at some point in the future; this would be used to invest in stocks. In this case, the manager can use index futures to hedge against general price increases during the interim by going long in index futures. If prices do rise, then the long position makes up the loss involved in buying stocks at a now higher price.

Beyond simple hedging of price risk, index futures can be used for a variety of other portfolio management purposes: Index futures can adjust the beta or systematic risk of a portfolio to any level desired, aiding the manager in market timing strategies. Thus, an actively managed portfolio can be hedged selectively against market declines by decreasing the portfolio beta with short index futures, a form of portfolio insurance. Similarly, index futures can increase the beta of a portfolio in anticipation of a general increase in market level. In addition, index futures can also be used in market selection strategies to adjust the beta of a portfolio of currently undervalued stocks. In this way, a manager can purchase the stocks most likely to appreciate in value, yielding more than the risk-adjusted rate of return, while maintaining a given level of risk exposure (beta) to overall market movements. Finally, because index futures offer a way to participate in the capital gains component of portfolio return separated from the dividend yield component, index futures can be used in various dividend separation strategies. All of these applications are discussed in the third section.

INDEX CONSTRUCTION

To determine the value of a particular index futures contract, multiply the futures price or index level by a specific dollar multiplier. For most index futures, the index level is multiplied by $500; for the Major Market Index (MMI) contract, the index is multiplied by $250. For instance, if the March S&P500 contract is trading at a futures price of 285.55, the value of the contract is $500 × 285.55, or $142,775. One futures contract thus represents a position in $142,775 worth of the S&P500 portfolio.

The various stock indexes differ in the sample of stocks used to calculate the index, the method of weighting the various stock prices, and the method of calculating the average. Some of the characteristics of the indexes underlying the current contracts are summarized in table 11-1.

STOCK SAMPLE

As table 11-1 shows, most of the index contracts are based on a large sample of stocks. For instance, the New York Stock Exchange (NYSE) index contract, trading on the New York Futures Exchange (NYFE), contains all of the stocks listed on the NYSE. This index thus contains stocks of companies conforming to NYSE listing requirements, based on such characteristics as the number of shares held publicly and the size of earnings of the company. As another example, the Value Line (VL) index contract, traded on the Kansas City Board of Trade (KCBOT) contains 1,683 stocks chosen by the A. Bernhardt Company, the company responsible for the Value Line index, includes stocks traded on the NYSE, the American Stock Exchange, and the over-the-counter (OTC) market. The choice of stocks to include in the index can affect the valuation or hedging use of the index futures.

Because the value of the index futures is based on a cost of carry model, any arbitrage transaction involves purchase or sale of the underlying portfolio, much in the same way the bond arbitrage involved purchase or sale of a Treasury bond. Thus, the number and types of stocks included in the index portfolio have an effect on the ease of arbitrage and consequently on the maintenance of an accurate futures price. The

Table 11-1. Currently Traded Stock Index Futures

Contract	S&P500	NYSE	Value Line
Exchange	Chicago Mercantile Exchange	New York Futures Exchange	Kansas City Board of Trade
Value	\$500 × futures index level	\$500 × futures index level	\$500 × futures index level
Stocks in index	500	1500+	1,683
Market	All NYSE	All NYSE	10% OTC; 90% NYSE
Sampling method	Top blue chip selected by Standard and Poor's	All stocks listed on New York Stock Exchange	Selected by A. Bernhardt Co. (Value Line) for analysis
Calculation	Value-weighted average	Value-weighted average	Equal-weighted average
Contract	Major Market	Russell 2,000	Russell 3,000
Exchange	Chicago Board of Trade	Chicago Board of Trade	New York Futures Exchange
Value	\$250 × futures index level	\$500 × futures index level	\$500 × futures index level
Stocks in index	20	2,000	3,000
Market	All NYSE	52% OTC; 36% NYSE	86% NYSE; 11% OTC
Sampling method	Industrial blue chips	Ranked 1001–3000 highest capitalization	Highest capitalization stocks
Calculation	Price-weighted average	Equal-weighted average	Value-weighted average

sample of stocks has its greatest effect on the MMI and the VL contract. The MMI consists of just twenty stocks. Consequently, it is the easiest to arbitrage exactly; purchase or sale of these twenty blue chip, large capitalization stocks is relatively easy and generally can be effected with little price movement.

On the other hand, the VL is much more difficult to arbitrage. Because about 10 percent of the index is based on less actively traded OTC stocks, there can often be a significant lag between the time important economic news reaches the market and the time a transaction in one of these OTC stocks takes place. This means that the VL index, based as it is on the last transaction price of the stocks, may not reflect the true, current value of the index portfolio at a given moment. If an arbitrageur were to attempt to buy the index portfolio at the currently quoted index level, the actual cost, or current transaction value of the index, might differ from the index quoted. For this reason, the VL futures have received less attention from arbitrageurs and volume remains relatively low.

The VL futures contract, however, has an advantage in hedging use because of its construction. Most portfolio managers hold OTC stocks as part of their portfolios; this means that the VL futures may more closely represent the particular cash portfolio that a manager would want to hedge. The other indexes (MMI, S&P500, and NYSE) represent large, well-capitalized, frequently traded stocks.

INDEX CALCULATION

The stock prices used in calculating the index can be weighted equally, weighted by market value (number of shares times the price per share), or weighted by the price of stock (e.g., a $10 stock receives twice the weight of a $5 stock). Table 11-2 gives an example of the construction of a three-stock index using different weighting schemes, and the effect that the particular weighting has on the index level.

Table 11-2. Index Calculations Using Various Weighting Schemes

			Price		
Stock	*Shares*	*Value (Day 1)*	*(Day 1)*	*(Day 2)*	*Percentage Increase*
A	75	$1,875	$25	$25	0
B	375	3,750	10	15	50
C	50	250	5	10	100

Calculations:

Value-weighted index:

Day 1 index: (75 × $25) + (375 × $10) + (50 × $5) = 4,125

Day 2 index: (75 × $30) + (375 × $15) + (50 × $10) = 5,750

Percentage increase = 36.2

Price-weighted index:

Day 1 index: ($25 + $10 + $5)/3 = 13.33

Day 2 index: ($25 + $15 + $10)/3 = 16.33

Percentage increase = 25

Equal-weighted index (geometric average):

Change in index value, day 1 to day 2:

(25/25) × (15/10) × (10/5) = 3.0

$$\sqrt[3]{3.0} = 1.44$$

Percentage increase = 44

Table 11-2 shows three indexes and their percentage change in value over one day of trading. The percentage change tends to reflect, as expected, the change in value of the highest-weighted stock. For the value-weighted index, stock B has the greatest weight, twice that of stock A and fifteen times that of C. Thus, the change in the index value of 36 percent reflects primarily the 50 percent increase in value of B although it is diminished by A's 0 percent change. On the other hand, the price-weighted index follows stock A, which has two-and-a-half times the weight of B and five times that of C. The percentage change in the price-weighted index is thus a relatively low 25 percent. With equal weighting, C's 100 percent increase receives more influence, and the equal-weighted index increase is 44 percent. Which index presents a true picture of the market depends on the use to which the index is put and how representative of the market a particular stock is considered.[1] For our purposes, because each index is biased toward its highest-weighted stocks, this bias has an impact on the construction of a portfolio to imitate the index in an arbitrage transaction.

In general, a value-weighted index reflects the price movement of the more highly capitalized stocks in the index such as General Motors, IBM, and oil stocks. This is true of the S&P500 and NYSE indexes. This means that it is relatively easy for an arbitrageur to construct a spot portfolio to imitate the S&P500 using fewer than the full 500 or 2,000 stocks. Currently, approximately 200 of the more highly capitalized stocks are commonly used in an arbitrage portfolio, and result in an almost-perfect substitute for the larger index. Thus, the possibility of a cash loss relative to the futures position due to incomplete convergence at maturity, or the trading risk in an arbitrage, may be relatively low for the S&P500 or the NYSE.

Arithmetic weighting generally emphasizes the price movements of the highest-priced stocks in the index. An arbitrage portfolio for this index should be constructed to include the highest-priced stocks. However, because the only index to be weighted in this manner is the MMI with only 20 stocks, the usual practice is to include all of the stocks in the MMI in an index portfolio.

Finally, the use of equal weighting in an index emphasizes, relative to other indexes, the movement of smaller, less well-capitalized companies. Value Line, by equal weighting, reflects the movements of the smaller OTC stocks selected for the index. This may be an advantage in using the futures for hedging, since OTC stocks may be a large component in the particular cash portfolio being hedged. However, as mentioned previously, this emphasis on OTC stocks makes the VL futures more difficult to arbitrage due to lags in trading.

In addition, equal weighting requires continuous readjustment in the underlying cash portfolio to maintain the equal weighting. To see this, consider an arbitrageur who has bought, in equal dollar amounts, the stocks in the VL portfolio. As trading occurs, the arbitrageur must sell off a certain amount of any stock that rises in price to maintain the equal weighting relative to the other stocks. Similarly, any price decline in a stock requires the purchase of more of that stock to maintain the equal dollar value of the stocks. Consequently, as prices change through time, and as the index changes, the arbitrageur would need to buy and sell stock continuously, in varying quantities, to maintain a portfolio comparable to the index. For this reason, the VL contract is used less in arbitrage and has much less volume than the other index futures.

STOCK INDEX FUTURES PRICING

PRICING MODELS

Stock index futures, like long-term coupon contracts, can be priced according to the cost of carry model. The pricing of stock index futures under this model is complicated, however, by several factors peculiar to index futures: First, the composition of the "cash commodity" in most cases is a large, well-diversified portfolio consisting of at least 500 stocks. Thus, arbitrage arguments based on the ability to acquire the spot commodity and carry it forward are generally not exact when applied to the portfolios represented by the S&P500 or NYSE, and are even less so, as discussed, for the Value Line Index. Second, the stock index used for the futures contract is typically calculated without dividends. Thus, the particular payment pattern of dividends expected through time as well as the uncertainty as to their size and to the marginal tax rate applied to dividends and capital gains relative to the futures transactions can complicate the pricing analysis.

Despite the theoretical difficulties involved in applying the cost of carry model, several pricing models are used in arbitrage; we discuss these later. Most of the cost of carry pricing models for index futures rely on the equivalence of returns between two different investment portfolios, one including a forward contract on the index portfolio, the other containing the index portfolio itself. By constructing the two portfolios so that they have equivalent returns, the futures price can be solved for and expressed as a function of the index portfolio price (spot price or index level), expected interest rates, and dividend payments.

For instance, assume the following two investment strategies are available. In one, the index portfolio is purchased for I_t dollars. The dollar return (R_1) on this portfolio at the end of the period (at T) is equal to the change in price ($I_T - I_t$, with I_T unknown at t) plus dividends paid (D):

$$R_1 = (I_T - I_t) + D \qquad (11\text{-}1)$$

A second strategy involves investing I_t dollars in a risk-free asset paying a rate of interest r and buying a forward contract, at a price equal to F_t, for the delivery of the index portfolio at T. The return (R_2) is the change in the forward price ($F_T - F_t$) and the interest earned on the I_T dollars (rI_t). With convergence of the forward price at T to $I_T (F_T = I_T)$, the return on this strategy equals:

$$R_2 = (I_T - F_t) + rI_t \quad (11\text{–}2)$$

Both strategies are equivalent in risk (involving investment in the index portfolio or its forward); thus, the two returns should be the same. With R_1 equal to R_2:

$$(I_T - I_t) + D = (I_T - F_t) + rI_t \quad (11\text{–}3)$$

The forward price (F_t) can be solved for:

$$F_t = I_t(1 + r) - D$$

or:

$$F_t = I_t + (r - d)I_t \quad (11\text{–}4)$$

(with d = the dividend yield on the index portfolio).

The forward price in this simple model is equivalent to the cost of carry price for bonds in chapter 9 and agricultural commodities in chapter 3; the forward price reflects the value of the spot commodity today (I_t) and the cost of carry. Here, the cost of carry involves the interest expense of carrying the index portfolio through the carry period less the dividend income earned from holding the portfolio.

A much more rigorous model of the pricing of stock index futures has been presented by B. Cornell and K.R. French.[2] In their paper, the price of a stock index futures contract reflects the expected price of the portfolio at the maturity of the contract less a term comprising expected dividend payments and reinvestment income. The more complex expression arises from the allowance for dividend reinvestment and financing at a time dependent rate, $r_{t,T}$, as well as for continuous compounding:

$$F(t) = I_t e^{r(T-t)} - (D/r)(e^{r(T-t)} - 1) \quad (11\text{–}5)$$

This pricing equation is essentially the continuous compounding version of equation 11–4. The price of the forward contract is equal to the terminal compounded value of the portfolio in a continuous time framework (in equation 11–4, $I_t(1 + r)$), less the value of dividends received (here, the dividend yield is D/r) during the period by the holder of the index portfolio. The derivation of this model and its extension to include uncertain interest rates and dividend payments is in the appendix to this chapter.

In sum, the basis in stock index futures reflects the cost of carry, here consisting of both borrowing cost and dividends received. Because both the interest cost over the carry period and the value of the dividends to be received and their reinvestment value are uncertain at the beginning of the period, the cost of carry used to set futures prices must reflect expected interest rates and expected dividends. Also, as with long-term coupon bonds, the basis can be either positive or negative, depending on the expected relative sizes of dividends compared to borrowing costs.

We can go back to the simple cost of carry model in equation 11–4 and calculate the equilibrium futures price of the S&P500 (see table 11–3). We assume the current S&P500 index level is 300. For a full three-month carry period, the interest cost to borrow the purchase price of the S&P500 portfolio is equal to the current short-term rate of 8 percent on the 300 × \$500 = \$150,000 portfolio for three months (= 0.08 × \$150,000 × (90/360)), or \$3,000. In index points, this is equal to six (\$3,000/\$500 per index point = 6). Thus, the futures seller would want at least 300 + 6 = 306 to compensate for the cost of carry. However, some of this cost is offset by the dividend yield paid on the portfolio during the carry period. With an annual dividend yield of 4 percent, the portfolio holder can expect to receive \$1,500 for the three-month carry period (0.04 × \$150,000 × (90/360)) or three index points (\$1,500/\$500 per index point). Thus, the full cost of carry equilibrium price is 300 + 6 − 3 = 303.

We have calculated the equilibrium futures price as of the beginning of the quarter. If the futures contract is priced at some point within the quarter, however, an allowance must be made for the noncontinuous payment of dividends. The dividend cash flow expected to be received over the carry period can vary within the quarter depending on when companies are expected to declare a dividend during the carry period. For instance, if the portfolio is acquired 30 days after the beginning of the quarter, with two-thirds of the three-month carry period left in the contract, only approximately 20 percent of the dividends may have been paid, based on historic averages. Thus, the cost of carry component of the portfolio at this point would involve a dividend cash flow of fully 80 percent of the quarter's dividend yield over only two-thirds of the carrying period. If the portfolio is acquired sixty days after the beginning of the quarter, with only one-third of the carrying period remaining, most dividends have been paid. The holder of the portfolio can expect to receive approximately 5 percent of the quarter's dividends even though one-third of the carry period remains. Thus, the cost of carry does not decline linearly over time as it does for the long-term bond contract; the dividend payment pattern is discontinuous and affects the cost of carry in a discontinuous fashion. As table 11–3 shows, the equilibrium futures price for a contract purchased at 60 days to maturity involves a net cost of carry that is not two-thirds of the net cost for the full quarter. The equilibrium futures price at 60 days from maturity is 301.60 rather than 302.

Table 11-3. Pricing of Stock Index Futures Contract

Three months to maturity

Current S&P500 index level: 300 (300 × $500 = $150,000)
Short-term interest rate: 8%
Dividend yield (annual): 4%
Carry period: 3 months

Equilibrium futures price = Current index + Cost of carrying

Cost of carry:

a. Borrowing cost:

$0.08 \times 300 \times (90/360) = 6.00$ index points
$(= 0.08 \times 300 \times \$500 \times 90/360 = \$3{,}000)$

b. Dividend yield:

$0.04 \times 300 \times (90/360) = 3.00$ index points
$(= 0.04 \times 300 \times \$500 \times 90/360 = \$1{,}500)$

Equilibrium futures price = $300 + 6.00 - 3.00 = 303.00$

60 days to maturity

Current S&P500 index level: 300 ($500 × 300 = $150,000)
Short-term interest rate: 8%
Dividend yield (annual): 4%
Carry period: 60 days

Price assuming continuous dividends	*Price assuming discontinuous dividends*
Cost of carry:	
a. Borrowing cost:	
$0.08 \times 300 \times (60/360) = 4.00$ index points	$0.08 \times 300 \times (60/360) = 4.00$ index points
b. Dividend yield	
$0.04 \times 300 \times (60/360) = 2.00$ index points	$0.04/4 \times 300 \times 0.80^{*} = 2.4$ index points
Equilibrium futures price:	
$300 + 4 - 2 = 302$	$300 + 4 - 2.4 = 301.60$

Assumes 80% of quarter's 1% dividend yield is received in the 60-day period until maturity.

ARBITRAGE

If the futures price does not equal the current index value plus the cost of carry, an arbitrage transaction—buying the commodity for one price and simultaneously selling it at a higher price—is possible. The arbitrage on the MMI futures presented in table 11-4 shows the transactions if the futures price is too high.

At the beginning of the quarter, the cost of carry for the index reflects an inflow of one quarter's dividend yield of 1 percent (4 percent dividend yield per year) and an outflow reflecting the financing of the index portfolio at a 10 percent annualized repo rate. With a current index of 445.50, the net cost of carry, expressed in index points, is 6.6825 ($445.50 + (10\%/4 - 1\%)445.50 = 445.50 + 6.6825$). Therefore, the equilibrium futures price should be equal to the current index level, 445.50, plus the cost of carry, 6.6825, or 452.1825. However, the March futures is selling for 456.10. Thus, it is possible to secure an arbitrage profit by buying the index portfolio and carrying it to March for 452.1825 while simultaneously selling the portfolio into the futures market for March delivery at 456.10. The arbitrage profit should be 3.9175 index points, or $979.375 (= 3.9175 × $250) per contract, minus commissions. The arbitrage example in table 11-4 also illustrates the translations necessary among index levels, actual dollar value, and number of shares.

There are two major differences between the index arbitrage and the other cost of carry arbitrage involving T-bonds discussed in chapter 9. First, in the case of the index portfolio, the arbitrageur must acquire positions in individual stocks which, when added together, equal the index as it is constructed and match the futures contract in value. The MMI index is constructed on a price-weighted basis. The total dollar value of an investment in one share in each of the twenty stocks in the index can be obtained by multiplying the index by the current divisor. To see this, go back to table 11-2. As shown there, if the index level is equal to 16.66, then the value of an investment of one share each is equal to 16.66 × 3, or (25 + 15 + 10). However, unlike the simple average in table 11-2, in which the total is divided by the number of stocks in the index, the MMI uses the divisor to adjust as well for stock dividends and stock splits. The current divisor for the MMI is 2.25, which differs from twenty because of the effect of past splits and other activity in the stock.[3] If the current index level is equal to 445.20, the dollar value of one share in each of the twenty stocks must be 445.20 × 2.25, or $1,002.375. In other words, if one buys one share of each of the twenty stocks in the index, the total portfolio value would be equal to $1,002.375. Each futures contract calls for delivery of a specific dollar value of stock, here $250 × the index value worth of the portfolio per contract, in this case $111,375 (445.20 × $250 = $111,375). The number of shares of each stock required for purchase to match this dollar value thus involves buying: $111,375 worth of stock per contract/$1,002.375 per share = 111.11 shares of stock per contract for each of the twenty stocks. The position can be scaled up so that the arbitrage portfolio involves a whole number of shares in each stock. To avoid odd lots of stock, for instance, 1,000 shares in each of the twenty stocks can be used. One thousand shares of each stock is equal to nine futures contracts (9 contracts × 111.11 shares per contract = 999.99 or 1,000 shares in each stock); this allows the arbitrage to proceed on an equivalent dollar basis, cash to futures.

Table 11-4. Arbitrage

Stock Index Futures

Time: January 2
Current futures price, March delivery: 456.10
Current index level: 445.20

Cost of Carrying:

1. Financing of index portfolio at 10% for 1 quarter (in index points):
   $0.10 \times (90/360) \times 445.50 = 11.1375$
2. Expected dividend payment on index portfolio for 1 quarter (in index points):
   $0.04 \times (90/360) \times 445.50 = 4.455$

Equilibrium futures price:

$I_t + (r - d)I_t$

$445.50 + 11.1375 - 4.455 = 452.1825$

Arbitrage Transactions:

January 2

1. Sell 9 MMI March futures at 456.10
   (Promise to sell 9 contracts × \$250 × 456.10 = \$1,026,225 at maturity on Mar. 18)
2. Buy index portfolio at 445.50
   (1,000 shares of stock in each of 20 stocks at varying prices to replicate MMI = \$1,002.375 per share × 1,000 shares = \$1,002,375.[a]
3. Finance stock purchase at 10% for 90 days
   (Promise to repay \$1,002,375.00 × 0.10/4) = \$25,059.375 interest plus \$1,002,375 principal = \$1,027,434.375)

   Receive 1% dividend yield on \$1,002,375.00 worth of stock portfolio = \$10,023.75 through quarter; assume no reinvestment.

March 18 (maturity of contract):

1. Cash settle on March futures at 456.10
   (Pay or receive difference between sales price and settlement price = (456.10 − 456.10) × \$250 × 9 contracts = \$0)
2. Sell portfolio at 456.10
   (Receive 456.10 × 2.25 × 1,000 shares = \$1,026,225.00)
3. Repay \$1,027,434.375

   Arbitrage profit: \$1,026,225.00 + \$10,023.75 − \$1,027,434.375 = \$8,814.375

Decline in Index:

March 18:

1. Cash settle on March futures at 450
   (Pay or receive difference between sales price and settlement price = (456.10 − 450) × \$250 × 9 contracts = \$13,725)

Table 11-4. (Continued)

2. Sell portfolio at 450
   (Receive 450 × 2.25 × 1,000 shares = $1,012,500)
3. Repay $1,027,434.375
   Arbitrage profit: $1,012,500 + $13,725 + $10,023.75 − $1,027,434,375 =$8,814.375

[a]With an index level of 445.20, and a current divisor for the MMI index at 2.25, the dollar value of 1 share of each of the 20 stocks in the MMI is 2.25 × 445.20 = $1,002.375.

Each futures contract is worth $250 × 445.50 = $111,375; thus, to buy a portfolio constructed like the MMI and equal in value to the futures position, would require buying $111,375 per contract/$1,002.375 per share = 111.11 shares of stock in each of the 20 stocks. To deal with round lots, 9 × 111.11, or 1,000 shares of stock in each of the stocks is purchased, for a total of $1,002,375 invested in the MMI portfolio. This is equivalent to the investment of 9 contracts × $111,375 in the futures contract, or $1,002,375.00 (equilibrium price).

The initial arbitrage transactions involve (1) buying the index portfolio for $1,002,375 (1,000 shares × $1,002.375 per share); (2) selling nine March index contracts; and (3) financing the portfolio purchase at the 10 percent repo rate for three months. In the intervening quarter, as the portfolio holder carries the index portfolio for the three-month carry period, $10,023.75 in dividend payments (1 percent dividend yield on $1,002,375 worth of stocks) would be received.

The unwinding of the arbitrage demonstrates the second major difference in the index arbitrage. At maturity, the index futures is cash settled; that is, the futures holder receives the cash difference between the initial sales price and the final offset price, equal at maturity of the contract to the current cash index level. For simplicity, the index at maturity is assumed to be equal to the initial futures price, 456.10, so that the cash settlement involves no cash flow. The arbitrageur now has to dispose of the cash portfolio to pay back the borrowing and extract the arbitrage profit. Assume that the portfolio can be sold at the settlement index value of 456.10. This would involve a value of 456.10 × 2.25 = $1,026.225 per one share in each of the twenty stocks × 1,000 shares of stock = $1,026,225. After paying back the principal and interest on the borrowing of $1,027,434.375, there remains $8,814.375 in arbitrage profit.

The example illustrates the vital necessity of unwinding the cash position at the same time the futures contract is settled. The arbitrage profit would no longer be a certain $8,814.375 if the arbitrageur waits until after settlement to sell the cash portfolio. Waiting until the next day runs the risk of a stock price change, decreasing the arbitrage profit if stock prices decline from the settlement index level, or increasing the arbitrage profit if stock prices rise the next day.

Further, the arbitrage profit is locked in even if the futures price differs from its initial level of 456.10 at settlement as long as the arbitrageur sells the portfolio at the futures settlement (see table 11–4). If the futures price had declined to 450, the arbitrageur would have realized a profit on the futures of 9 × (456.10 − 450), or 54.9 index points (or \$250 × 54.9 = \$13,725). However, this would be exactly offset by the decline in value of the cash portfolio. The index level of 450 means that the total value of the twenty stocks is now equal to \$1,012,500 (450 index level × 2.25 divisor = \$1,012.50 per share × 1,000 shares in portfolio = \$1,012,500). This represents a loss of \$13,714.00. (This discrepancy between \$13,725 and \$13,714 represents the rounding on 111.11 shares.) The arbitrage profit, if the cash portfolio is sold at the same time the futures contract is settled, remains at \$8,814.375. (The calculation of the arbitrage profit if the index settles at 460 is left to the reader.)

PROGRAM TRADING. Another aspect of the index arbitrage that has received attention is the use of program trading. Buying the individual blocks of stock required to construct an index portfolio for use in the arbitrage generally depends on program trading. Program trading is a term describing the buying or selling of large blocks of stock usually through computer orders to the New York Stock Exchange's Designated Order Turnaround (DOT) system. (A block trade is one for over 100,000 shares of stock.) This system routes the order electronically to the specialist assigned to the stock. In this way, buyers can construct baskets of stock, or index portfolios, quickly and efficiently via almost instantaneous computer executions. The use of computers to route large orders to the specialist has reversed the previous practice of unwinding large positions "upstairs" or off the exchanges. It can also lead to liquidity problems on the floor, as happened on October 19, 1987.

With institutional, rather than individual, trading accounting for a larger percentage of trading on the exchanges, program trading—computerized trading of large blocks of stocks—is used not only for index arbitrage but also for other institutional purposes. Index funds can be constructed through the system almost instantaneously to match the performance of a particular index of stocks. With program trading, it is also possible to sell varying percentages of a well-diversified portfolio and substitute into money market assets. Program trading thus enables a portfolio manager to hedge the value of a portfolio by physically selling the stocks and replacing the portfolio with a short-term, risk-free investment in Treasury bills. Whether a manager uses program trading or futures to hedge depends at times on the relative pricing of the index portfolio compared to the index futures. That is, if the futures price is in disequilibrium, a manager would be more likely to sell the overpriced asset to hedge. In the example in table 11–4, the futures, being priced too high compared to its equilibrium value, would be the choice of a manager who wants to sell. On the other hand, the index stocks themselves would be the choice of a manager who wanted to buy to hedge.

In sum, the development of program trading has had several results. First, there is a close relationship between the futures market and the stock market through index arbitrage. Another linkage between the two markets is the use of both futures and physical stock transactions to construct index funds for portfolio purposes, or to hedge market movement. Second, the controversy continues over whether the ability of institutions to buy or sell large quantities of stock almost instantaneously is fair to individual investors who do not trade this way. Third, there are questions about the effect program trading has on stock values. Do the prices of stocks included in the index reflect economic factors fundamental to the stock itself, or do they now reflect marketwide developments, or even factors relating to developments in the futures-index relationship? Fourth, index trading increases stock price volatility because stock movements may now reflect futures-index pricing rather than economic information. Several proposals have been made to deal with the effects of program trading. The use of the DOT computer system can be suspended if stock prices appear especially volatile in one day of trading. (Arbitrage can still take place, but it must be done with physical orders to the specialist on the floor.) A basket contract for spot delivery may be introduced on the NYSE. This would be a spot equivalent of the index futures contract, and would allow the purchase and sale of the index with a separate specialist.

THE TRIPLE WITCHING HOUR AND ARBITRAGE EFFECTS. The necessity of selling off the cash portfolio in the same instant as the futures settles at maturity can obviously have a major effect on the stock market. As long as the cash portfolio is sold at the settlement index value, the arbitrage profit is locked in no matter what the settlement index happens to be. As a consequence, the natural reluctance of a stock seller to flood the market with large sell orders is eliminated with the arbitrage. Indeed, the cash settlement aspect of the arbitrage requires concentrated transactions in the stock market on the close of the settlement day.

These large transactions have led to a great deal of volatility in both the stock and futures markets at the close of trading on the maturity day of the futures. With related arbitrage trading and unwinding of positions in the options market as well (see chapter 13), the last hour of trading on the maturity day has been called the triple witching hour. It has been difficult to measure the true severity of this arbitrage effect. In the most thorough study of the question to date, H.R. Stoll and R. Whaley found two major effects on the stock market from the arbitrage.[4] First, the volatility of stock prices included in the S&P500 increased significantly on futures expiration dates; these effects have been detected on minute-by-minute stock price data. Second, there have been large price reversals on expiration days, equal to about 0.3 to 0.5 percent of the closing index value. This is equivalent in magnitude to the reversals occurring in the market as the result of very large block trades. The difference in this case is that the reversals are not dispersed through the day as is normal in block trading, but are concentrated in the last 15 minutes of trading on the expiration day.

Is this arbitrage effect a serious problem? Several aspects of the effect should be noted: First, it is usually not possible to anticipate the direction of movement, whether up or down, at the last hour of trading; this means that it is generally not possible to make significant profits from the triple witching hour. The reasons for this are twofold. One, it is just as likely that the reverse arbitrage would be the appropriate one to execute. That is, it is just as likely that the futures contract could be underpriced in relation to the equilibrium price. In this case, the arbitrage would involve (*a*) buying the futures, and (*b*) selling the stocks in the index short, using the stock proceeds for a short-term investment in Treasury bills over the carry period, with the requirement that the arbitrageur pay the dividends on the short stock as they occur. At maturity, the unwinding of this arbitrage would then involve buying in the stock market to cover the short positions. Thus, the price effect of an index arbitrage can be negative (selling stock) or positive (buying back stock) or both, depending on the relative number of trades that have been executed when a mispricing has occurred. Two, the arbitrage can be unwound at an earlier time if the mispricing corrects itself before maturity. For instance, in table 11-4, the arbitrage profit would also be earned if the three initial transactions were executed and then reversed if the futures price moved immediately to its equilibrium value of 452.1825. Thus, the holding of the arbitrage transaction to maturity guarantees the arbitrage profit but is not essential. This means that the number of arbitrage positions remaining to be unwound at maturity is difficult to estimate ahead of time.

Second, the Chicago Mercantile Exchange has changed the settlement procedure for the S&P500 futures contract, and this appears to have decreased the volatility of stock prices on maturity day. The last day of trading in the contract has been moved to Thursday from Friday, and the settlement price for the futures is the index level at the opening of trading on the next day (Friday). This method allows the stock specialist to cope with the balance of arbitrage buy or sell orders in a stock before the market opens. In addition, prices can readjust during the full day of trading after settlement.

OCTOBER 19-20, 1987. Another aspect of index arbitrage has to do with its possible contribution to the severity of the market downturn of October 19-20, 1987. Derivative markets—both futures and options—have grown since 1982, and the markets are strongly interrelated. Stock index futures prices, as discussed earlier, are based on the level of the current index and thus current individual stock prices; any mispricing, if large enough, results in simultaneous trades in futures and the stocks underlying the index. Futures also substitute for various transactions in the stock market. It is now common to construct and hold index portfolios; index futures can replace an index portfolio if the futures are cheap relative to owning the index itself or can serve as a temporary substitute for a cash index purchase or sale when funds flow in or out of the portfolio. Also, stock index futures are used interchangeably with the sale or purchase of the stock portfolio itself to hedge against value changes in a well-diversified portfolio. Further, dynamic hedging strategies for stock portfolios based on variable hedge ratios—increasing (or decreasing) the level of hedging depending on whether stock market prices move down or up—can involve stock or futures transactions that vary in intensity in response to market movements. Thus, the markets for futures and stocks are not only interrelated but respond strongly to changes in relative prices between markets and to changes in market levels.

Although the cause of the market downturn of October 19–20, 1987, and even the events themselves, continue to be hotly debated, one of the main concerns of various studies has been whether the method of trading stocks, index futures, and options contributed to the market decline and its remarkable speed.[5] It is generally felt that the use of the futures market for dynamic hedging sales, coupled with index arbitrage, could have led to a "market meltdown." In this framework, the use of the futures market for selling, both for dynamic hedging purposes and as a substitute for sales transactions impossible to implement at that time in the stock market, drove futures prices below their equilibrium levels.[6] This mispricing in turn led index arbitrageurs to buy the low-priced futures and sell the stocks underlying the index. These arbitrage transactions led to further downward pressure on stock prices and continued selling of index futures, repeating the downward spiral.

The evidence relating to whether this spiral did indeed take place and the place of futures trading within it is inconclusive. Evidence from the SEC study shows that only 20 percent of futures transactions on October 19 was related to portfolio insurance or dynamic hedging.[7] A more telling piece of evidence is the severe market downturn in foreign exchanges at the same time. Most of these foreign stock markets do not have significant index futures markets and, as important, do not have comparable levels of institutional trading or comparable market-making mechanisms, especially program trading. This seems to indicate that the speed of the downturn was not caused by trading mechanics alone. Further, other factors contributing to the market downturn include the disorderly conditions in the stock market, as well as liquidity problems arising from market clearing.[8] Thus, futures trading—index arbitrage and portfolio insurance—in and of itself does not seem to have been the primary cause of the rapid market decline in October of 1987.

OTHER INSTITUTIONAL CONSIDERATIONS. There are several institutional constraints on the efficiency of the arbitrage which may prevent an exact equilibrium in the futures price. For instance, the example in table 11-4 showed the arbitrageur buying the entire portfolio represented by the MMI index. For the futures that trade on the larger indexes, the arbitrageur may buy only a fraction of the portfolio to keep transaction costs down. As noted earlier, 200 stocks are generally sufficient to successfully mimic the S&P500 performance. Because the cash portfolio used in the arbitrage is not the exact portfolio underlying the contract, there is some risk in the arbitrage, and the final portfolio value may not converge to the index price at maturity. In addition, transaction costs involved in assembling a portfolio include not only the outright commission costs for the individual stock purchases but also the spread between the bid and asked price for a large block share trade. Although the ability to execute transactions on a portfolio of stocks is well developed, the price effects of such block transactions must be considered part of the transaction costs of the arbitrage. Further, and more important, there can be a lag between index calculation and actual transaction prices in the market. Thus, the current index level may not truly represent the actual purchase or sale price. This discrepancy between transaction value and the index obviously increases the risk of the arbitrage and changes the arbitrage profit available. Indeed, on October 19, the lack of timely or accurate stock prices and the DOT system's failure to function discouraged index arbitrage from taking place. Also, as with bond futures arbitrage, the arbitrage profit may not be exact due to any cash flow consequences of marking-to-market on the futures contract during the arbitrage. Finally, the arbitrage profit depends on after-tax quantities rather than the before-tax amounts that have been discussed here.

Given the prevalence and success of arbitrage activity in the index futures market, the efficiency of index futures prices has not been the subject of intense academic investigation. Although Cornell and French found early evidence of a mispricing,[9] according to S. Figlewski,[10] E.M. Saunders, and A. Mahajan,[11] the general consensus is that index futures are efficiently priced.

HEDGING

Stock index futures can be used for a wide variety of hedging purposes. Portfolio managers holding well-diversified stock portfolios for a mutual fund, pension fund, or investment trust, all have the same basic "inventory" problem for which futures were developed: they must hold a portfolio of assets over some time period, the value of which can change in a random fashion. To hedge against losses in value on the cash position, the portfolio manager would sell stock index futures. Thus, stock index futures can be used in much the same way as interest rate futures, or even commodity futures.

Index futures are also used for very short-term hedging. Stock market professionals, those whose business requires taking large temporary positions in blocks of stock, often use stock index futures to hedge the risk of price change over relatively short time periods. An investment banking firm underwriting a stock issue is at risk of a price decline between its payment to the issuing firm for the new stock and the eventual resale of the stock in the market. Similarly, a brokerage house may hold large blocks of a stock temporarily as it seeks to unwind a block trade for an institutional investor without disrupting the market price for the shares. Risk arbitrageurs, those who buy or sell blocks of shares in anticipation of a merger offer or other activity in a stock, are subject to considerable short-term risk of price movements on the stock they hold. Each of these market professionals may seek to hedge all or a portion of their exposure to stock price changes.

In addition to those firms whose business it is to invest in stocks short- or long-term, corporations may also use stock index futures to hedge stock price changes. This use derives from the development of shelf registration for new stock issues. Under shelf registration, the firm receives regulatory permission to issue a certain number of shares of its stock over a two-year period, with the timing of the issuance at the discretion of the corporation. Thus, a corporate treasurer could hedge against a general decline in stock prices while waiting for the appropriate moment to issue the new stock.

HEDGE RATIO

Since the basis point value and duration models discussed in chapter 9 cannot be applied to index futures, the usual approach to the hedge ratio centers on the portfolio model. That is, the hedge ratio is one which is designed to minimize the risk or variance of the hedged position, a two-asset portfolio. From chapter 5, the optimal hedge ratio under this model is:

$$\text{HR} = \text{Cov}\,(\text{FP}\Delta,\ SP\Delta)/\text{Var}(FP\Delta) \qquad (11\text{-}6)$$

The hedge ratio can be considered the beta of the stock portfolio with the futures contract. The hedge ratio is generally estimated by regressing changes in value of the cash position against changes in the price of the futures contract chosen for hedging. In addition, the R^2 of this regression gives a measure of the expected effectiveness of the hedge. Examples of short and long hedges with stock index futures are given in tables 11–5 and 11–6, respectively.

SHORT HEDGE

Assume that a pension fund has invested $100 million of long-term funds in a well-diversified stock portfolio (see table 11–5). Due to inflation fears, the stock market has been declining slowly for the last month. To protect the value of the portfolio from further erosion, a pension fund manager sells stock index futures on the S&P500 index. From a regression of past price changes of the portfolio versus the

Table 11-5. Short Hedge in Stock Index Futures

Date: April 1 Current futures price, June delivery: 275 Value of portfolio: $100 million	Regression results: Δ portfolio price = $a + b\Delta$futures price $b = 0.82$ $R^2 = 0.925$
Futures	*Spot Portfolio*
April 1: Sell 596 June contracts at 275	
Value of futures position: 596 × 275 × $500 = $81,950,000	Value of spot position: $100,000,000
June: Buy 596 June contracts at 264.50	
Value of futures position: 596 × 264.50 × $500 = $78,821,000	Value of spot position: $96,375,000*
Gain = $3,129,000	Loss = $3,625,000

*Assume 4% loss in value on spot portfolio.

Table 11-6. Long Hedge in Stock Index Futures

Date: September 1 Current futures price, December delivery: 204.50 Current VL index level: 214.00 Estimated value of dividend payment: $75,000	Regression results: Δ portfolio price = $a + b\Delta$futures price $b = 0.95$ $R^2 = 0.98$
Futures	*Spot Position*
Sept. 1: Buy 1 December futures at 204.50	
Value of futures position: 204.50 × $500 × 1 = $102,250	Index shares which can be purchased with $75,000: $75,000/$214 = 350.5 index shares
Dec. 15: Sell 1 December futures at 214.50	Index level at 225
Value of futures position: 214.50 × $500 × 1 = $112,250 Gain = $10,000	Index shares which can be purchased with $75,000 $75,000/$225 = 333.33 index shares
Net result: Number of index shares which can be purchased at end of hedge: ($75,000 + $10,000 gain in futures) / $225 = 377.77 index shares	

futures contract, the hedge ratio is calculated to be 0.82 (with an R^2 of 0.925). The current futures price is 275. Assuming the regression relationship remains relatively stable, the portfolio manager sells 596 futures contracts, or contracts representing 82 percent of the value of the spot portfolio:

$$N_f = (\text{value of spot portfolio/value of futures}) \times \text{HR}$$
$$= (\$100{,}000{,}000)/(500 \times 275) \times 0.82$$
$$= 596.36 \text{ or } 596 \text{ contracts}$$

With 596 contracts, the value of the futures position at initiation of the hedge is \$81,950,000 (\$500 × 275 × 596 contracts = \$81,950,000).

In two months the portfolio manager decides that the general market decline has ended and lifts the hedge. The value of the stock portfolio has fallen by 4 percent, to \$96,375,000. The futures price has fallen as well, by approximately 4 percent, to 264.50, resulting in a gain of \$3,129,000 (596 contracts × \$500 × (275 − 264.50) = \$3,129,000). The hedge has been 86 percent effective: the futures position has gained \$3,129,000 versus a loss of \$3,625,000 on the spot portfolio. The effectiveness is relatively low because this is a cross hedge of the S&P500 futures with a stock portfolio constructed by the pension fund. Also, the hedge ratio and effectiveness measure (R^2) have been estimated from past price information, and may not reflect changes in new information, dividend payout patterns, or interest levels. Finally, this illustrates a passive or static hedge. The portfolio manager could have hedged more selectively, varying the percentage of the portfolio hedged depending on estimates of potential market movements. For a discussion of dynamic hedging strategies, see chapter 13.

LONG HEDGE

A long hedge is shown in table 11-6. Here, the manager of a \$15 million mutual fund indexed to the Value Line index expects to receive dividend payments of \$75,000 on the fund at the end of the quarter. On receipt, the manager plans to reinvest the money in the portfolio to maintain the present portfolio composition as closely as possible. Thus, the manager would like to hedge against a rise in the general market level until receipt of the dividends. The current Value Line index is 214. To quantify the current value of the \$75,000 investment in the Value Line, the idea of an index share is useful. An index share is the amount of the index portfolio with a value equal to \$1.00 times the index. With a level of 214, an index share in the Value Line is worth \$1.00 × 214, or \$214. At this level, \$75,000 could buy 350.5 index shares (\$75,000/\$214 per index share). If the Value Line index rose before the end of the quarter, \$75,000 would be able to buy fewer index shares. The regression results are:

hedge ratio = 0.95, R^2 = 0.98. The current futures price is 204.50; the number of long futures contracts necessary to hedge is:

$$N_f = \$75{,}000/(\$500 \times 204.5) \times 0.95$$
$$= 0.695, \text{ or } 1 \text{ contract}$$

Because of the indivisibility of futures contracts, the dividend payment is overhedged.

A few days before the maturity of the contract, the Value Line index is at 225, and the futures is at 224.50. At the current index level of 225, the $75,000 dividend payment can purchase only 333.33 index shares ($75,000/$225 per index share = 333.33) compared to the original 350.5. With the $10,000 gain in the futures market (1 contract × $500 × (224.50 − 204.50) = $10,000), the number of index shares to be purchased becomes 377.77 (($75,000 + $10,000)/$215 = 377.77). The hedge has protected the purchase value of the dividend payment and also resulted in a large profit. There are two reasons for this: First, the futures position was an overhedge. Second, the basis was favorable for the long hedger. The basis was 9.5 at initiation (214 − 204.5), and almost 0 (225 − 224.50) at the end of the hedge and maturity of the contract. In this case, the futures rose by much more, almost ten index points, than the index.

STOCK BETAS

Because the beta of stocks with the market index are commonly calculated and readily available, those betas have been suggested as an alternative hedge ratio for stock portfolios.[12] The beta of a stock portfolio is a function of the portfolio's covariance with the general market, or market portfolio, and the variance of the market portfolio. If the market portfolio is assumed to be the index underlying a particular futures contract, for instance, the S&P500, then:

$$\text{beta(portfolio)} = \text{Cov}(\text{FP}\Delta, \text{I}\Delta)/\text{Var}(\text{I}\Delta).$$

Thus, the hedge ratio in equation 11–6 and the stock beta of the portfolio are equivalent only under special conditions, that is, when the futures contract is perfectly correlated with its underlying index. This can occur only if there is no basis risk. From the pricing equation for stock index futures, the basis ($I_t - F_t$) is a function of the cost of carry for the portfolio, depending on short-term interest rates and the dividend yield on the index portfolio. Thus, only if short-term rates and dividend payments are nonrandom are the two quantities, the stock beta and the portfolio hedge ratio, the same.[13]

Most of the empirical evidence related to hedging with index futures has found that the futures are an effective hedging mechanism. For instance, J. Hill and T. Schneeweis found that the portfolio hedge ratio worked well with index futures and the spot index, eliminating up to 70 percent of the variability of the spot index value.[14] J. Junkus and C.F. Lee compared the hedging behavior of three index futures and four hedge strategies; here, too, all of the index futures reduced risk substantially under the various strategies.[15] Finally, D. Graham and R. Jennings tested the hedging performance of the S&P500 futures against portfolios of stock with varying systematic risk (beta) and dividend yield.[16] They found that the hedge effectiveness of the futures with portfolios was 50 percent less than with the index itself. In addition, the effectiveness of the hedge strategy varied with beta and dividend yield on the portfolio.

PORTFOLIO MANAGEMENT WITH INDEX FUTURES

Because the stock index futures contract is closely linked to the underlying index portfolio through the cost of carry, it can be used as a substitute for the index portfolio or a well-diversified portfolio. In particular, the index futures can substitute for an investment in an index fund, a portfolio whose performance is tied explicitly to the performance of a general market index. In addition, the index futures can adjust the beta of a cash portfolio to any desired level. The ability to adjust up or down to a target beta allows a manager to actively manage the portfolio, increasing or decreasing market exposure as the market is forecasted to increase or decrease. This process of market timing has recently been called portfolio insurance or dynamic hedging. Similarly, the beta of a portfolio with undervalued stocks whose rate of return is expected to be greater than a risk-adjusted rate of return can be adjusted to maintain a specified risk level while awaiting the expected increase in the specific stock return. This process is referred to as market selection. Finally, the index futures can separate out the dividend component of stock return from the capital gains component. Such decoupling allows an investment manager to pursue a high-dividend return strategy while hedging against market movement, or to pursue a zero-dividend strategy if that has tax benefits or portfolio income benefits over a portfolio containing both capital gains and ordinary income.

INDEX PORTFOLIO

In deriving the pricing equation for stock index futures, we stated earlier that an investment in the index portfolio was equivalent to an investment in the index futures contract and an investment in pure discount bonds or T-bills. Thus, the index futures contract, in conjunction with a purchase of T-bills, can replicate the performance of the well-diversified portfolio represented by the index.

Constructing a portfolio whose performance tracks the returns of a stock index is a common method of passive portfolio management. The use of such portfolios, or index funds, arose from the implications of modern portfolio theory. If the stock market is efficient, and shares are accurately priced to reflect their known level of risk, then the return on any stock or portfolio reflects its risk level. Numerous studies have concluded that stock prices are, by and large, efficient; prices tend to reflect all available information about them. Thus, it is extremely difficult to find mispriced shares and to construct a portfolio with a rate of return greater than its expected, risk-adjusted rate of return. A portfolio manager who holds a large number of shares in a stock portfolio tends, on average, to achieve a rate of return equivalent to that of a well-diversified portfolio, the overall market rate of return for the period. Indeed, because there are costs associated with active portfolio management—research costs associated with seeking out shares that may be mispriced, transaction costs in buying and selling mispriced shares—the return on such a managed portfolio tends to be less than that achieved by a simple buy-and-hold policy. Thus, index portfolios are constructed to mimic some broad-based stock index, such as the S&P500; such a passive approach minimizes transaction costs and allows the holder to receive the full rate of return on the market index.

A position in stock index futures, together with an investment in T-bills, can replicate the performance of such an index fund and generally can do so at lower cost. To see this, compare the performance of an investment in an index fund tied to the S&P500 with the performance of an equivalent investment in S&P500 futures and T-bills (see table 11–7). With three-month T-bills at a rate of 6 percent, the current S&P500 index at 300, and an expected dividend yield of 4 percent, the equilibrium futures price on January 2 of the S&P500 March futures must be 301.50. The possibility of arbitrage keeps the actual futures price close to this level. An investor with $1.5 million available for investment, would have a choice between two investment strategies: (*a*) buying $1.5 million of the S&P500 index portfolio, or (*b*) going long $1.5 million/($500/contract) × 300 = 10 S&P500 March contracts (with no cash flow involved) and investing $1.5 million in three-month T-bills paying a 6 percent yield.

At the end of the three-month investment period, the dollar return on the two strategies is the same. The key difference between the two strategies is in transaction costs. The round trip commission costs for an S&P500 futures are approximately $25 per contract. Thus, the transaction cost for an index fund of $1.5 million would be $250 using futures. The commission on a stock transaction is approximately $0.075 per share. If the average share price is $50, then the $1.5 million portfolio would contain approximately 30,000 shares, for a total commission cost of $2,250. This transaction cost advantage must, of course, be compared to the unknown cash flow consequences of the use of futures rather than a stock portfolio. If prices rise, then the futures strategy results in a positive cash flow through the intervening period; this

Table 11–7. Comparison of Index Fund and Futures plus T-bill Position

Buy \$1.5 million of S&P500 portfolio	Buy 10 S&P500 futures*
	Buy \$1.5 million of 3-month T-bills
Index level = 300	Futures price = 301.50
Dividend yield = 4%/year	T-bill yield = 6% annually
Market Rises 5% over 3 months	
Index level = 315	*Maturity of contract*
Capital gains:	Futures market receipt:
Portfolio value =	
1.05 × \$1.5 million = \$1.575 million	(315 − 301.50) × 500 × 10 = \$67,500
Dividend Yield:	T-bill receipt:
0.01 × \$1.5 million = \$15,000	\$1.5 million $(1.06)^{0.25}$ = \$1.522 million
Total:	Total:
\$1,575,000 + \$15,000 = \$1,590,000	\$1,522,010.77 + \$67,500 =
	\$1,589,510.77
(Totals unequal due to use of integer number of contracts.)	
Market declines 5% over 3 months	
Index level = 285	*Maturity of contract:*
Capital losses:	Futures loss:
Portfolio value =	
(1 − 0.05) × \$1.5 million =	(295 − 301.50) × \$500 × 10 =
\$1,425,000	(\$82,500)
Dividend yield:	Treasury bill receipt:
0.01 × \$1.5 million = \$15,000	\$1.5 million $(1.06)^{0.25}$ = \$1,522,010.77
Total:	Total:
\$1,425,000 + \$15,000 = \$1,440,000	\$1,522,010.77 − \$82,500 =
	\$1,439,510.77
(Totals unequal due to use of integer number of futures contracts.)	

*Long number of contracts to equal \$1.5 million at futures price of 301.50, value of 1 contract = 301.50 × \$500 = \$150,750

\$1,500,000/\$150,750 per contract = 9.95 or 10 contracts

cash is available for reinvestment, thus increasing the return available through the futures strategy. Similarly, a decrease in the market can result in margin calls on the futures strategy. Thus, the two strategies also differ in the timing of cash flows, with losses and gains on the futures strategy realized by the investor as they occur, while any losses or gains on the cash portfolio are deferred until the end of the investment period.

The equality of return depends on two assumptions: First, that the actual futures price was equal to the equilibrium futures price; and second, that actual dividend payments on the portfolio equal the expected dividend payments. The futures strategy could yield a rate of return higher than the index portfolio if the investor could take advantage of any temporary underpricing of the futures contract. That is, the investor could reap a quasi-arbitrage differential rate of return by buying the futures at something less than the equilibrium futures price. Similarly, if dividend returns were less than expected, the futures strategy would yield a higher rate of return. Thus, the opportunity to construct an index fund using futures can yield a higher return than through the stock market due to transaction costs; this advantage also depends on margin cash flow, actual dividend yield, and futures pricing.

Finally, using index futures to construct an index fund has an additional advantage when the fund is one tied to foreign stocks. Given the availability for trading a variety of foreign stock indexes—the Nikkei, traded on the Singapore Monetary Exchange; the Financial Times Index, traded on the London International Financial Futures Exchange; and the Toronto Stock Exchange Index, traded on the Toronto Futures Exchange—it is possible to use futures to diversify a portfolio globally without the necessity of buying actual foreign shares. Thus, an index futures contract can add considerably to a portfolio manager's flexibility in structuring international investments.

PORTFOLIO BETA ADJUSTMENT

Active portfolio management involves two general strategies: In one, the manager attempts to anticipate changes in the general market level. If prices are expected to drop, the manager would reduce market exposure by investing primarily in low beta stocks, or by leaving the stock market entirely and investing fully in short-term, risk-free assets. If prices are expected to rise, on the other hand, the manager would increase market exposure, investing in high beta stocks whose performance magnifies market trends. This strategy is similar to the adjustment of duration in a bond portfolio in response to expected changes in interest rates. This approach is generally labeled market timing.

A second strategy—market selection—involves the purchase of undervalued stocks or the sale of overvalued stocks in anticipation of a correction in the price. If the stocks are truly mispriced, then the manager obtains a rate of return on a portfolio of these stocks that is greater than the portfolio's risk-adjusted rate of return. The ability to generate a rate of return in excess of that based on risk level has been incorporated in a measure of portfolio performance called alpha. The equilibrium excess rate of return on the portfolio, that is, the rate of return in excess of the risk-free rate of return is a function of its systematic risk:

$$E(R_p) - R_f = \text{beta} \times (E(R_m) - R_f)$$

(R_p is the rate of return on the portfolio; R_f is the risk-free rate of return; R_m is the return on the market portfolio; and beta is a measure of the systematic, or non-diversifiable risk, of the portfolio.)

A positive performance by a manager would result in a rate of return on the portfolio greater than expected, or what is called a positive alpha:

$$\begin{aligned} \text{alpha} &= \text{actual portfolio return} - \text{expected} \\ &= (R_p - R_f) - (E(R_p) - R_f) \\ &= (R_p - R_f) - \text{beta} \times (E(R_m) - R_f). \end{aligned}$$

Thus, the goal of market selection is to construct a portfolio with a high alpha.

Index futures can be used in both of these strategies, market timing and stock selection. In the case of market timing, the portfolio manager faces the necessity of many stock transactions as the portfolio structure is altered in anticipation of market changes. If the market is expected to fall, the manager must sell off high beta stocks and substitute into low beta stocks or into a short-term, risk-free portfolio. If the market is expected to rise, the manager must adjust the portfolio holdings to high beta stocks. The transaction costs necessary to effect these restructurings can be large. Index futures can substitute for these cash transactions; the portfolio manager can adjust the portfolio beta to almost any desired level without buying and selling stocks. Futures also have an advantage in being, at times, more liquid, with faster transaction times.

MARKET TIMING. As an example, assume a manager currently holds a $10 million stock portfolio with a beta of 1.2. The manager expects the market to decline in the next month. If this is so, the portfolio could suffer a loss in value even larger than the market decline because the portfolio is structured to be 120 percent more volatile than the general market portfolio. The manager would like to decrease the portfolio's market exposure to a more manageable level, and chooses a relatively low beta of 0.1. The manager needs to sell enough futures contracts, with a beta equal to one, so that the total position, stock portfolio plus futures, has a beta of 0.1. The calculation of the number of contracts required to do this is relatively straightforward. The manager would like to construct an ideal portfolio, with a beta of 0.1, out of the current portfolio (beta = 1.2) and a short futures position (beta = 1.0) Using the S&P500 futures, with a current futures price of 300 and a current dollar value of $500 × 300, or $150,000:

$$\text{ideal} = \text{current} + \text{futures}$$

$$\text{Value of ideal portfolio} \times \text{beta} = \text{Value of current portfolio} \times \text{beta} + \text{value of futures} \times 1.00$$

$$\$10 \text{ million} \times 0.1 = \$10 \text{ million} \times 1.2 + N_f \times \$500 \times 300 \times 1.00$$

$$N_f = (\$10 \text{ million} \times 0.1 - \$10 \text{ million} \times 1.2)/\$500 \times 300 \times 1.00$$

$$= (\$1 \text{ million} - \$12 \text{ million})/\$150{,}000$$

$$= -73.33 \text{ contracts.}$$

Thus, the manager must sell approximately 73 S&P500 futures contracts to attain an overall beta level of 0.10. Similar calculations can be made for the case in which the manager would seek to increase market exposure to some desired level.

Besides the advantage to index futures from their lower transaction costs, the index futures method also allows a more precise adjustment with much less difficulty. In using stock purchases or sales to adjust the beta, it would be difficult to find just the right set of stocks to achieve a portfolio beta of 0.1, and there would inevitably be some slippage from 0.1 due to stock selection, round lot transactions, and limitations on the proportion invested in any one stock. In addition, low beta stocks are not common, and finding a sufficient number might prove difficult. Finally, as the portfolio becomes less diversified with the addition of primarily low beta stocks, there is a risk that the portfolio will be more exposed to nonsystematic, or stock-specific risk.

The idea of using short futures positions in market timing has led to the widespread practice of portfolio insurance strategies. With this strategy, the portfolio manager sells index futures when stock prices begin to decline. As prices continue to decline, the manager sells more index futures. At the limit, if prices decline sufficiently, the portfolio beta is reduced to 0.00, and the overall return on the portfolio is equal to the risk-free rate of return.[17] The purchase of a stock portfolio involves purchase of the index ($-I$) and receipt of the dividend (dI) and has a dollar return of:

$$-I + dI$$

A short futures position involves receipt of the futures price:

$$I + (r - d)I$$

the total hedged position, stock portfolio plus short futures, has a return of:

$$(-I + dI) + (I + (r - d)I) = rI.$$

On the other hand, if prices begin to rise, the short futures positions are offset; a long futures position may be added to increase market exposure. Thus, the upward potential for portfolio returns is not diminished, while the returns on the portfolio are protected since the short futures position puts a floor on the return (here, the risk-free rate) on the portfolio. This is an example of a very simple insurance strategy. The manager can, of course, substitute other floor levels for the risk exposure and structure a number of risk-return payoff patterns for the portfolio.[18]

STOCK SELECTION. In the case of stock selection, the use of index futures again relates to portfolio beta adjustment. In selecting stocks for a portfolio on the basis of a high alpha, the manager may find that the risk, or beta of the portfolio, becomes too high. For instance, the manager may find after stock selection that the beta of the chosen portfolio is equal to 2.5, an unacceptably high risk level given the portfolio objectives.

Without the use of index futures, the manager would be forced to divest the portfolio of some of the high alpha stocks to adjust the total portfolio beta downward. However, in selling off these particular high alpha, high beta stocks, the managers would also sacrifice portfolio performance.

As an example, consider the portfolio in table 11–8. With a current risk-free rate of 6.5 percent and a market risk premium of 3.5 percent, the equilibrium excess return on the portfolio is 8.75 percent. However, the realized return from the mispriced stocks is greater than this, 10.25 percent. Thus, the portfolio's alpha is 1.5 percent. If the manager adjusts the portfolio beta to 1, a 60 percent reduction, by selling 60 percent of the stock portfolio and investing the proceeds in Treasury bills (beta = 0), the alpha would be reduced by 60 percent as well, falling from 1.5 percent of 0.6 percent. With index futures, the manager can separate the beta adjustment problem from the alpha level of the portfolio. The manager would retain the full portfolio, with an alpha of 1.5 percent, while selling fifteen S&P500 index futures contracts.

DIVIDEND STRATEGIES

The use of index futures in dividend strategies arose out of tax rate differentials for corporate investment in stocks. If stocks are held by a corporation for forty-six days, 80 percent of the dividends on those stocks are excluded from taxable income. Thus, a corporation could earn an after-tax short-term investment rate above current money market rates by buying high-dividend yield stocks prior to dividend payment and holding the stock for the appropriate length of time to qualify for the 80 percent exclusion. Adverse price moves on the portfolio of stocks during the holding period could be hedged with a short position in stock index futures. (An alternative hedging vehicle would be to write calls on the individual stocks in the portfolio, or to buy puts; see chapter 13.) This dividend strategy is available only to corporations.

Table 11-8. Portfolio Alpha with and without Futures

Current portfolio:

Portfolio beta = 2.5
Risk-free rate = 6.5%
Market return = 10%

Equilibrium expected return: 6.5% + 2.5(10% − 6.5%) = 15.25%
Equilibrium excess return: 15.25% − 6.5% = 8.75%
Expected excess return: 10.25%

Portfolio alpha: 10.25 − 8.75 = 1.5

Without futures:

Invested: 60% T-bills and 40% in portfolio with beta = 2.5

Portfolio beta = 1.00

Equilibrium expected return: 6.5% + 1.00(10% − 6.5%) = 10%
Equilibrium excess return: 10% − 6.5% = 3.5%
Expected excess return: 0.40 × 10.25 = 4.1%

Portfolio alpha: 4.1% − 3.5% = 0.6%

With futures:

Futures required to reduce portfolio beta to 1.00:

at a futures index level of 301.50:

Ideal portfolio = Current portfolio + futures position

$\$1.5 \text{ million} \times 1.0 = \$1.5 \text{ million} \times 2.5 + N_f \times 500 \times 300 \times 1.00$

$N_f = 14.9$ or 15 futures contracts

Portfolio beta = 1.00

Equilibrium expected return on stock portfolio: 6.5% + 2.5(10% − 6.5%) = 15.25%
Equilibrium excess return: 15.25% − 6.5% = 8.75%
Expected excess return: 10.25%

Portfolio alpha: 10.25 − 8.75 = 1.5

Another dividend strategy involving index futures relates to the behavior of stock prices around the exdividend date. The fall in the price when the stock goes exdividend is less than the dividend payment.[19] Thus, an investor could earn excess returns by buying high dividend stocks before the exdividend day, receiving the dividend payment, and selling the stock on the exdividend date. Again, while the stocks are held, the investor is subject to a risk of price decline on the portfolio (the market-wide risk component), and this could be hedged away through a short index futures hedge.

Finally, A.F. Herbst and N.O. Ordway argue that stock index futures contracts can be a superior investment vehicle if the investor desires to avoid dividend payments on stocks and their (then higher) tax on dividend income over capital gains.[20] That is, a stock index futures contract with an investment in T-bills can be used to construct a portfolio whose return is free of dividend payments but matches the capital gains component of an investment in the underlying index portfolio. Such a futures strategy had a tax advantage over investment in an ordinary stock portfolio.

Although the tax advantage is no longer as strong as in 1984, avoiding dividend payments is still a consideration to portfolio managers who wish to construct an index portfolio. The periodic payment of dividends to an index portfolio requires a rebalancing of stock positions. This is because the funds received as dividends must be invested in the index as quickly as possible to maintain indexing; if the dividends are retained as cash or cash equivalents (T-bills), the performance of the total position no longer matches the index. With stock index futures, there is no need to consider the problem of periodic dividend payment and portfolio rebalancing.

OTHER INDEX FUTURES

The development of a futures contract traded on an index with cash delivery has offered opportunities previously unavailable to the speculator and hedger. The discussion that follows is a brief summary of some of the new index contracts. Index contracts cover a wide array of financial products, with very individual characteristics peculiar to their construction. Thus, the discussion highlights a particularly innovative aspect of the contract, or a use of the contract that had been previously unavailable.

MUNICIPAL BOND FUTURES

One of the primary characteristics of a commodity suitable for futures trading is homogeneity or fungibility: each unit of the commodity is nearly identical to any other. However, much of the risk of a financial asset is related to its particular characteristics. That is, a portfolio of bonds has a different risk-return profile, and interest rate volatility, depending on the bond issuer, tax treatment, coupon and maturity, and other defining features. This is particularly true of junk bonds. These high-yield, low-grade debt instruments are very sensitive to issuer characteristics such as cash flow, and take on the characteristics of equity as a default grows more likely. The problem of interest rate volatility and risk characteristics has also been increased in recent years with the securitization of mortgages, accounts receivable, and car loans. With these debt instruments, the bond risk depends very strongly on the particular character of the assets underlying the bonds: the creditworthiness of the underlying creditor, payback schedule, and assumed maturity—even geographic location. Thus, the management of financial assets, and the use of interest rate futures to manage interest rate risk, has become complicated by the wide variety of debt instruments available. The only long-term debt contract available for hedging bond risk has been the long-term Treasury bond contract. This is expecially true with the decline in popularity of the Government National Mortgage Association (GNMA) contract.

A potential solution to the problem of bond fungibility is the development of an index on a type of bond. The first traded futures of this kind is the Muni Bond Index offered by the Chicago Board of Trade.

The index represents the prices of 40 municipal and general revenue bonds. The bonds are selected by a group of brokerage firms (market makers for the muni bonds) comprising the Bond Buyer. The bonds must meet such requirements as maturity (nineteen or more years), size (greater than $50 million), callability (must be callable between seven and sixteen years after index inclusion), fixed coupon, rating (A or higher by Moody's), and lack of any unusual features. The index is computed twice daily by the five brokers. The forty bonds are priced by the brokers, the highest and lowest prices are dropped, and the remaining three prices are averaged and converted to a price based on a yield of 8 percent. This makes the Bond Index price comparable to the 8 percent coupon T-bond and T-note contracts also traded at the Chicago Board of Trade. Issues are replaced by new bonds twice monthly depending on trading volume.[21]

The computation of the index involves some difficulties. Prices on bonds depend strongly on the frequency of trading; unlike stocks, most bonds trade relatively infrequently. Thus, the index cannot be computed frequently, or the prices included in the index may not be current. The choices of bonds and the number to include are also problematic. Even though a "good" representation of the commonly held muni bonds is desirable, the number of bonds to include is limited by the necessity to find trade prices for them. Finally, the composition of the index changes frequently. This has the virtue of allowing the index's composition to reflect current portfolios (a criticism leveled at stock indexes). However, this also means that the index does not have a long-term history with which to compare current level or volatility. This can diminish its use as a forecasting mechanism and also lead to difficulties in the calculation of a hedge ratio.

Despite the difficulty of calculating an index of bond prices, there has been great interest in having a futures contract on other bond indexes. For instance, there are currently several planned proposals for a corporate bond index futures.

DOLLAR INDEXES

A second category in which indexes are particularly needed is in the foreign currency market. While there are individual dollar/foreign currency futures contracts, there has been demand for some measure of overall dollar strength. In addition, many bond portfolio managers and multinational corporations are subject to multiple-currency risk against the dollar. For such speculative and hedging uses, there are currently two dollar index futures.

One futures is based on the Federal Reserve trade-weighted dollar index. This is the U.S. Dollar Index^{sm} traded on the Financial Instrument Exchange (FINEX) of the New York Cotton Exchange. Currently ten countries are represented in the index. The weights are determined by relative share of world trade; the index uses as a base year 1973, when foreign currency values were first allowed to float. The index is officially calculated daily by the Federal Reserve; it is also calculated by the exchange every 30 seconds for use with the futures contract.[22]

The second futures is based on the European Monetary System (EMS), and represents the value of a fixed amount of each of the ten EMS countries' currencies. This is the European Currency Unit (ECU) futures traded at the Chicago Mercantile Exchange.[23] The value of the European Currency Unit in dollars reflects a market-weighted average of the dollar with respect to ten European Common Market currencies. Unlike the dollar index, the ECU is an actual currency, and bonds and bank accounts are available in ECU-denominated units.

Both the indexes present the opportunity to speculate on relative dollar movement against a basket of currencies. In this respect, the dollar indexes resemble the speculative opportunities presented by the stock market indexes. In addition, the futures also allow a trader to speculate on a specific foreign currency movement against the currency basket. For instance, the Japanese yen futures contract can be used in conjunction with the ECU to speculate on the relative value of the yen against European currencies.

Because the ECU is correlated with other, nonincluded currencies, it is also possible to use the ECU to hedge or speculate on the movements of such currencies as the Austrian schilling, a currency for which there is no futures contract available.

The two contracts can also hedge against overall dollar movement. Many multinational corporations with U.S. headquarters have exposure to foreign currency risk in a variety of countries, and the risk changes through time as customer accounts are paid or initiated and as suppliers deliver or receive payment. Rather than hedge each currency exposure separately, thus holding positions in a multiplicity of contracts, the multinational can hedge against overall dollar risk with one contract. Similarly, the holder of a global portfolio can hedge against the general decline in currency value of repatriated dividends and capital gains with the contracts.

OTHER INDEXES

A further development in index futures was the introduction of contracts on general price levels. For instance, the Commodity Research Bureau (CRB) index futures contract traded on the New York Futures Exchange offers a vehicle to hedge or speculate on the general level of futures prices for selected commodities. This index is an average of 27 futures prices, with representative futures from the major commodity groupings such as livestock, energy, grains, and metals.[24] A contract on the Consumer Price Index was offered by the Coffee, Sugar, and Cocoa Exchange as a means to hedge or speculate on the rate of U.S. inflation. Currently, this futures contract is not trading.

One problem with such indexes is the specificity of the index. That is, there may not be sufficient interest or volume in a contract correlated to particular prices. A case in point is the trading of an index on over-the-counter stocks. Both a NASDAQ and an S&P500 OTC index failed to develop sufficient volume to continue trading, and proposals to trade other high tech or energy stock indexes have been postponed. Thus, the very quality that makes the index a desirable innovation, its particular characteristics, can be its greatest liability.

APPENDIX: DERIVATION OF THE CORNELL AND FRENCH MODEL

Even though more complex, the Cornell and French (CF) model involves the same reasoning as the simpler model discussed in the chapter.

Under perfect market assumptions, an investor can acquire one of two portfolios with equivalent terminal value.[25]

Portfolio 1. Today (at time t), acquire a portfolio of stocks worth I_t and invest all of the dividends paid during the holding period in risk-free bonds paying r. The initial investment required is I_t:

$$\text{Inv}_1 = I_t \tag{11-7}$$

Assuming continuous compounding of the dividends, the value of this portfolio at time T is equal to the terminal value of the stock portfolio (I_T) and the sum of the invested dividends:

$$\text{Value}_1 = I_T + D\int_t^T e^{r(T-w)}\,dw \tag{11-8}$$

The second expression on the right side is the summation over the time interval $(T - t)$ of the dividends and income reinvested at r_t. Solving the integral:

$$\text{Value}_1 = I_T + (D/r)(e^{r(T-t)} - 1) \tag{11-9}$$

Portfolio 2. Acquire a forward contract at a price of F_t (maturity at T) and also invest the sum of:

$$\text{Inv}_2 = (F_t + D/r(e^{r(T-t)} - 1) \times e^{-r(T-t)} \tag{11-10}$$

dollars in pure discount bonds.[26] The initial investment in this alternative is the price of the bonds; the forward contract involves no cash flow at the outset.

The terminal value of this alternative is equal to the face value of the discount bond, $F_t + D/r(e^{r(T-t)} - 1)$, and the change in the forward price $(F_T - F_t)$. With convergence of the futures price to the spot price at maturity, the terminal value of portfolio 2 is equal to:

$$\text{Value}_2 = I_T + (D/r)(e^{r(T-t)} - 1) \tag{11-11}$$

If the terminal value of portfolios 1 and 2 are the same, then the two portfolios should be priced the same initially.

Therefore:

$$\text{Inv}_1 = \text{Inv}_2 \tag{11-12}$$

Substituting equations 11–7 and 11 10 into 11–12:

$$I_t = (F_t + D/r(e^{r(T-t)} - 1))e^{-r(T-t)} \tag{11-13}$$

The forward price is then equal to:

$$F_t = I_t e^{r(T-t)} - (D/r)(e^{r(T-t)} - 1) \tag{11-14}$$

As noted earlier, this is the continuous-time version of equations 11–4: the value of the futures contract is equal to the compounded value of the index less the compounded value of the dividend payments received (with the dividend yield equal to D/r).

This model can be broadened to include more realistic departures from perfect market assumptions. For instance, it was assumed that the reinvestment rate for dividends was known at the start of the period, and that the rate paid on the discount bond was constant throughout the carry period. We can allow dividends to be reinvested at a changing and uncertain rate, $R_{t,T}$, the rate in force from the payment of the dividend at any time t to the maturity of the futures contract at T. We can also allow interest earned on the discount bond to vary throughout the period, or to be time-dependent as well: $r_{t,T}$. It was also assumed that dividends were paid in fixed dollar amounts, D. We can allow dividends paid to fluctuate through time; the dividend payment received at any time t is set at D_t. Finally, the model can be made more realistic by including taxes. Assume capital gains are taxed at a rate g, ordinary income is taxed at rate i, and futures trading is taxed at rate f.[27] The capital gains portion of the portfolio, I_T, is reduced by gI_T, and interest earned and dividends paid are reduced by i. When all of these adjustments are made, the portfolio argument results in a modified equation.

$$F_t = (I_t(e^{(1-i)r_{t,T}(T-t)} - g) - \int_t^T (1 - i)D(w)e^{(1-i)R_{t,w,T}(T-w)}dw)/(1 - g)$$

Here, the ordinary income tax rate reduces both the effective dividend yield and the interest rate; these effects are partially offsetting. The effect of the capital gains tax is complex, and depends in part on the size of the forward price relative to the spot portfolio value. Finally, the forward tax rate does not enter into the equation. This is because the tax on a forward transaction merely reduces the size of the return $(I_T - F_T)$. This reduction in return can be offset by entering into a larger initial forward position. Therefore, the forward tax rate does not change the price, only the size of the contract. Although more complex than equation 11–14, the forward price is still a function of the terminal index value (now reduced by the various tax rates) less the intervening reinvested dividend payments.

NOTES

1. For a discussion of the significance of the sample of stocks and weighting method for index movements, see J.H. Lorie and M.T. Hamilton, "Stock Market Indexes," in *Modern Developments in Investment Management*, ed. J.H. Lorie and R. Brealey (Hinsdale, Ill: Dryden Press, 1978), pp. 78–93.
2. B. Cornell and K.R. French, "Taxes and the Pricing of Stock Index Futures," *Journal of Finance* 38 (1983): 675–94.
3. As an illustration of the effect of a stock split, assume that stock A in table 11–2 split 2 for 1 on day 2, so that the number of shares is now equal to 2 × 75, or 150 shares, and the price is halved to $12.50. The price decline is solely related to the split. To maintain the index level of 18.33 with the new split, the price of A, the divisor, can be adjusted so that the new price-weighted average, using a share price of $12.50, is equal to the old price-weighted average. To do this, the three stock prices ($12.50 + 15 + 10) must be divided by 2.045 to equal 16.66.
4. H.R. Stoll and R. Whaley, "Expiration Day Effects of Index Options and Futures," Monograph Series in Finance and Economics. Monograph 1986-3. (New York: NYU-Salomon Brothers Center for the Study of Financial Institutions, 1986.
5. The studies include the Brady Commission report, and those by the SEC, the General Accounting Office, the New York Stock Exchange, the Chicago Mercantile Exchange, and the Commodity Futures Trading Commission. For a discussion of the studies' findings, see

F.R. Edwards, "Studies of the 1987 Stock Market Crash: Review and Appraisal," Working Paper CSFM168, Center for the Study of Futures Markets, Columbia University, 1988.

6. There were many severe dislocations in the stock trading system on October 19, 1987. The huge trading volume resulted in a breakdown in the NYSE's computer systems as well as the communication linkage between the major stock exchanges and the electronic over-the-counter stock system. In addition, large order imbalances resulted in very late openings of major stocks as well as disorderly price changes in individual stocks throughout the day.
7. Security and Exchange Commission study.
8. The severity of variation margin calls and the lack of coordination of margin between positions in the stock market and derivative markets created severe liquidity problems at many clearing firms.
9. Cornell and French, "Taxes and Pricing."
10. S. Figlewski, "Hedging Performance and Basis Risk in Stock Index Futures," *Journal of Finance* 39 (1984): 657–69.
11. E.M. Saunders and A. Mahajan, "An Empirical Examination of Composite Stock Index Futures Pricing," *Journal of Futures Markets* 8 (1988): 211–28.
12. Because of modern portfolio theory, which relates the return on an asset to its systematic risk or beta, the betas of most stocks have been estimated and are generally available.
13. Several studies have examined the relative effectiveness of the beta ratio and the portfolio hedge ratio; they found the hedge ratio is more effective in hedging price variability in all instances (Figlewski, "Hedging Performance"; and J. Junkus, "Hedge Ratios in Up and Down Markets," in *Advances in Futures and Options Research,* ed. F. Fabozzi, (Greenwich, Conn.: JAI Press, 1987), pp. 279–290.
14. J. Hill and T. Schneeweis, "Reducing Volatility with Financial Futures," *Financial Analysts Journal* 41 (1984): 35–40.
15. J. Junkus and C.F. Lee, "Use of Three Stock Index Futures in Hedging Decisions," *Journal of Futures Markets* 5 (1985): 201–22.
16. D. Graham and R. Jennings, "Systematic Risk, Dividend Yield, and the Hedging Performance of Stock Index Futures," *Journal of Futures Markets* 7 (1987): 1–13.
17. The specific beta desired on the portfolio in relation to the market level depends strongly on index option pricing. For a discussion of how to effect portfolio insurance or dynamic hedging strategies, see chapter 13.
18. For a discussion of portfolio insurance using index futures, see M. Rubenstein, "Alternative Paths to Portfolio Insurance," *Financial Analysts Journal* 41 (1983): 42–52; and T.J. O'Brien, "The Mechanics of Portfolio Insurance," *Journal of Portfolio Management,* Spring 1987, 40–47.
19. J. Lakonishok and T. Vermaelen, "Tax Induced Trading around Ex-dividend Days," *Journal of Financial Economics* 16 (1986): 287–319.
20. A.F. Herbst and N.O. Ordway, "Stock Index Futures Contracts and the Separability of Returns," *Journal of Futures Markets* 4 (1984): 87–102.
21. For a complete summary of the Muni Index futures contract characteristics, see *The CBOT's Municipal Bond Futures Contract.* (Chicago Board of Trade, 1985).
22. For a further discussion of the U.S. Dollar Index contract, see *U.S. Dollar Index Futures and Options on U.S. Dollar Index Futures.* (New York: Financial Instrument Exchange, 1987).

23. Finex also offers an ECU contract. For a fuller discussion of the ECU contract, see *ECU Futures: Composition and Application.* (Chicago Mercantile Exchange, 1986).
24. For a fuller discussion of the CRB contract, see *The CRB Futures Price Index,* (New York Futures Exchange, 1986).
25. In particular, it is assumed that: (*a*) there are no taxes, transaction costs, or restrictions on short sales; (*b*) assets are perfectly divisible; (*c*) investors can borrow or lend at a constant, risk-free rate; and (*d*) D dollars per period of dividends are paid continuously.
26. Pure discount bonds are similar to Treasury bills. There are no intervening interest payments and the difference between the purchase price and the maturity face value equals the interest earned on the bond. In terms of continuous compounding, a bond with a maturity face value of X dollars is priced at $Xe^{-r(T-t)}$ to earn r interest during the period $(T - t)$. The price $Xe^{-r(T-t)}$ is the continuous compounding equivalent of $X/(1 + r)^t$.
27. Under the 1987 tax revisions, the tax rates on capital gains and dividends are the same, or $g = i$.

FOREIGN CURRENCY

12

Perhaps more than most markets, the foreign exchange (forex) market seems mysterious and complex. A major reason for this may be the nature of most forex transactions. Fully 95 percent of these transactions are between major banks (the interbank market) and all transactions are done in a telecommunications network rather than on a centralized, visible exchange. Fewer individuals speculate in the spot foreign exchange as they do in stocks and, to a lesser degree, in bonds. Indeed, one of the innovative aspects of foreign currency futures trading has been its accessibility to the individual speculator.

The first section of this chapter describes the major forex markets: spot, forward, futures, and options; their basic organization; and the transactions common to them. The second section discusses the theoretical determinants of exchange rates, both spot and forward, with special attention paid to the Interest Rate Parity Theorem. Finally, the last section illustrates the uses of futures contracts for forex hedging.

ORGANIZATION OF THE MARKET

The major centers of forex activity are New York, London, and Tokyo; there is also considerable activity in Zurich, Frankfurt, Paris, Brussels, and Hong Kong. The market operates essentially twenty-four hours a day as major bank operators in the forex market pass the forex book—outstanding positions of the bank in various currencies—from Tokyo to London to New York and back to Tokyo during a twenty-four-hour period. In the United States, the twelve largest U.S. banks, all money center banks in New York, are the major forex dealers. Also, two or three broker firms bring banks together for larger forex transactions, preserve anonymity, and also function as a central network. Besides the international banks, other participants include multinational industrial and oil firms and commodities dealers, mostly in metals.

The vast majority of forex transactions involve the U.S. dollar. In fact, there are very few direct cross-currency—say deutsch mark (DM) to French francs (Fr)—transactions to obtain needed currency. The centrality of the U.S. dollar results from a variety of causes. Historically, the U.S. dollar served as the common denominator of the international payments system under the 1944 Bretton Woods system. Additionally, the sheer size and strength of the U.S. economy is a factor. Generally, the volume of trading in a particular currency depends on the degree of development of its capital markets, lack of government control over the market mechanism and over international capital flows, and also at times its historical relation to former colonial possessions. Table 12-1 lists the most frequently traded currencies. Economic size or position in international trade may matter little; see, for instance, Japan's standing compared to Switzerland's.

Table 12-1. Estimated Currency Composition of Foreign Exchange Trading

Currency	Percentage of total transactions	Currency	Percentage of total transactions
U.S. dollar	99%	French franc	6
German mark	40	Dutch guilder	5
British pound	15	Belgian franc	2
Swiss franc	18	Italian lira	1
Canadian dollar	5	Swedish krona	1
Japanese yen	5	Other	3
		Total	200%

Source: Ian H. Giddy, "Measuring the World Foreign Exchange Market." *Columbia Journal of World Business,* Winter 1979, p. 41. Reprinted with permission.

Note: Total adds to 200% because two currencies are involved in every foreign exchange transaction.

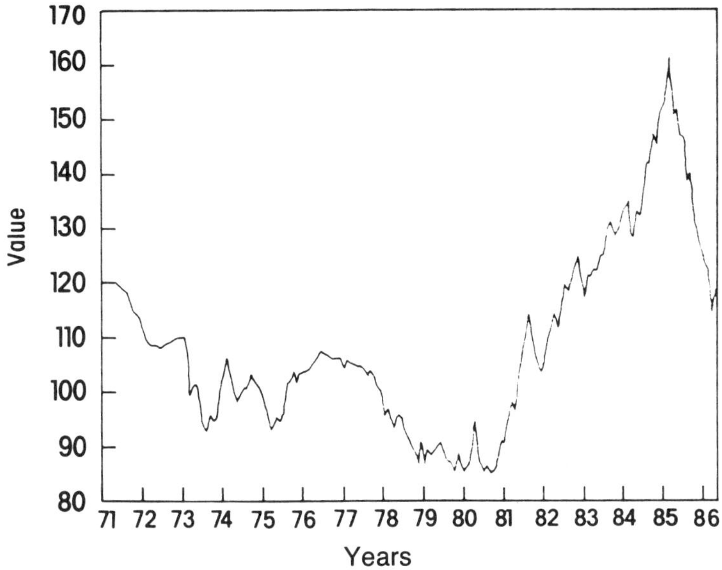

Source: U.S. Dollar Index Futures, Financial Instrument Exchange, division of the New York Cotton Exchange, 1987, p. 7

*The dollar index indicates the value of the dollar against a value-weighted basket of the currencies of U.S. major trading partners. 1973 value = 100.

Figure 12–1. U.S. Dollar Index[sm] 1971–1986 *(monthly spot values)*

The volatility of exchange rates has increased considerably in the past fifteen years. Since the abandonment of fixed exchange rates by the United States and its trading partners in 1972, the U.S. dollar has appreciated and depreciated against such currencies as the Japanese yen (¥) and the British pound (£) within a relatively wide range. (See figure 12–1). This has increased the element of risk in foreign trade and has led to the development of many risk-shifting devices, including but not limited to futures. Because of this increased volatility, speculation has also increased and many major banks run currency desks designed in part to speculate on short-term forex movements. Despite the attempts to establish a "dirty float" system—a system in which central banks allow floating exchange rates but set consensus upper and lower bounds on the rates—or to refix currency values to a specific commodity price or an index of commodity prices, volatility in forex will likely continue.

There are then a relatively large number of different markets organized for forex dealings and risk-shifting. Besides the spot market, for delivery in one to two days, there is also a large market in forward contracts. In addition, there are futures on foreign currency, options on physical currency, both exchange-traded and over-the-counter, options on futures, and forex swap agreements.[1]

FORWARD MARKET

Similar to forward contracts developed for agricultural commodities, the forward market in forex transfers risk from one party to another. The underlying reasons for foreign currency transactions are the requirements of international trade and payments; transactions in either goods or services are generally paid for in the currency of the seller. Thus, the buyer in any international transaction must generally arrange to purchase the required foreign currency before delivery of the goods. There are also times when the seller will, as part of the negotiations of a transaction, accept foreign currency in payment. Because the two trading partners presumably earn a profit margin from buying and selling, and not from speculation in changes in the exchange rate, there is a corresponding need for some mechanism to fix the price of the required foreign currency before the transaction occurs. The usual mechanism is a forward contract between the trader and a bank; the trader buys the required foreign currency, or sells the currency to be received, for a later delivery at a price (an exchange rate) fixed today. The bank in turn either leaves its forward commitment uncovered, or executes a matching forward contract with another customer or bank.

A typical forward contract is illustrated in table 12–2. A U.S. importer of pâté from Strasbourg expects a shipment in one month's time for a total of 2,500,000 French francs (Fr). The current dollar value of the payment is $500,000 (the spot exchange rate is 5Fr/$ making each franc worth $0.20). There is a risk, however, that in one month the dollar will have depreciated against the franc, requiring more dollars to cover the 2,500,000 Fr purchase. For instance, if the exchange rate is 4 Fr/$ making each franc worth $0.25, the pâté importer would have to pay $625,000 for the shipment (2,500,000Fr × $0.25/Fr = $625,000). To fix the price today, the importer would enter into a forward contract with a bank for 2,500,000 Fr to be delivered in one month at the one-month forward rate. Assume the one-month forward rate quoted is 4.85 Fr/$ ($0.21/Fr). With acceptance of this rate, the importer would fix the payment for the shipment at $525,000 (2,500,000Fr × $0.21/Fr = $525,000) and would know the profit margin on the pâté with certainty.

The bank in this instance now has an outstanding position in one-month forward French francs, and is subject to the risk of a dollar depreciation. The bank has promised to sell francs and buy dollars at a fixed rate of 4.85Fr/$ ($0.21/Fr). If the dollar depreciates in the interim, then the bank would receive dollars from the importer that are worth less. Or, what is the same thing, with the franc appreciated against the dollar, the bank would have to give the importer francs at a fixed price when they are, indeed, worth more. If the bank had to buy francs in one month to make delivery to the trader, then the bank would have to pay the higher exchange

Table 12–2. Foreign Currency Forward Transaction

Current spot rate: $0.20/French francs (Fr) (= 5Fr/$)
Forward rate, 1-month delivery = $0.21/Fr (= 4.85Fr/$)
Importer expects shipment of pâté in one month; will be billed Fr2,500,000
  Current value of pâté in dollars = $500,000
  (Fr2,500,000 × $0.20/Fr = $500,000)
To fix the value of the shipment, the importer buys Fr2,500,000 for delivery in 1 month
  Value of pâté fixed in dollars = $525,000
  (Fr2,500,000 × $0.21/Fr = $525,000)

rate for the francs. Thus, as the bank has promised to sell francs in one month at a fixed price of 4.85Fr/$ ($0.21/Fr), the bank would now like to arrange to buy francs for one month delivery at 4.85Fr/$ ($0.21/Fr) or better (4.85Fr/$ or more; $0.21/Fr or less).

Quotes on forex rates are available daily for both spot transactions and for various fixed forward dates (generally 30, 90, and 180 days forward). Table 12–3 shows the forex page from the *Wall Street Journal.* Only the major currencies, six in all, are quoted for forward delivery. Quotes are expressed both in $/foreign currency units called European terms and in foreign currency units/$ called American terms. Each is the inverse of the other. For instance, if spot Swiss francs are worth $0.6254/SFr, then it must be that there are 1/0.6254, or 1.5990 Swiss francs per dollar. Similarly, for Swiss francs to be delivered in 30 days, $.6274 buys one Swiss franc ($.6274/SFr) or $1.00 buys (1/.6274 =) 1.5940 Swiss francs. The prices represented here are for relatively large, $1 million or more, transactions; the quotes represent a middle range between the bid and ask rates. Most foreign currency rates are expressed to four decimal places, and the fourth digit to the right of the decimal point is called a point. Thus, from Wednesday to Thursday, the Swiss franc exchange rate moved 135 points, from $.6389/SFr to $.6254/SFr. In this instance, the dollar appreciated against the Swiss franc; in European terms, it took $0.6389 to buy a Swiss franc on Wednesday, but only $0.6254 to buy a Swiss franc on Thursday. In American terms, $1.00 would buy 1.5652 Swiss francs on Wednesday, but more, 1.5990, on Thursday.

When trading foreign currency during the day, traders generally quote foreign currency rates in a slightly different way than that presented in table 12–3. For instance, in trading British pounds, a bank in New York may quote the following on a telex for the spot, 30, 90, and 180 day forward pound rates:

Britain	1.6365/1.6367	2 to 3	12 to 15	20 to 25

The first pair of quotes is the bid-ask spot rates: the trader is willing to buy pounds for $1.6365, or sell them for two points higher, $1.6367. The next pair is quoted in

Table 12-3. Foreign Exchange Rates

FOREIGN EXCHANGE

Wednesday, August 5, 1987

The New York foreign exchange selling rates below apply to trading among banks in amounts of $1 million and more, as quoted at 3 p.m. Eastern time by Bankers Trust Co. Retail transactions provide fewer units of foreign currency per dollar.

Country	U.S. $ equiv. Wed.	U.S. $ equiv. Tues.	Currency per U.S. $ Wed.	Currency per U.S. $ Tues.
Argentina (Austral)	.5114	.5114	1.9555	1.9555
Australia (Dollar)	.7025	.6993	1.4235	1.4300
Austria (Schilling)	.07576	.07547	13.20	13.25
Belgium (Franc)				
Commercial rate	.02572	.02557	38.88	39.11
Financial rate	.02563	.02537	39.01	39.42
Brazil (Cruzado)	.02165	.02165	46.19	46.20
Britain (Pound)	1.5800	1.5748	.6329	.6350
30-Day Forward	1.5774	1.5722	.6340	.6361
90-Day Forward	1.5716	1.5663	.6363	.6384
180-Day Forward	1.5636	1.5578	.6395	.6419
Canada (Dollar)	.7559	.7551	1.3229	1.3244
30-Day Forward	.7544	.7536	1.3255	1.3270
90-Day Forward	.7519	.7511	1.3299	1.3313
180-Day Forward	.7474	.7468	1.3379	1.3390
Chile (Official rate)	.004534	.004534	220.55	220.55
China (Yuan)	.2687	.2687	3.721	3.721
Colombia (Peso)	.004035	.004035	247.81	247.81
Denmark (Krone)	.1403	.1395	7.1300	7.1700
Ecuador (Sucre)				
Official rate	.005089	.005089	196.50	196.50
Floating rate	.006079	.006079	164.50	164.50
Finland (Markka)	.2203	.2191	4.5400	4.5650
France (Franc)	.1597	.1592	6.2615	6.2825
30-Day Forward	.1596	.1591	6.2662	6.2871
90-Day Forward	.1593	.1588	6.2765	6.2965
180-Day Forward	.1589	.1583	6.2950	6.3164
Greece (Drachma)	.007077	.007037	141.30	142.10
Hong Kong (Dollar)	.1281	.1281	7.8080	7.8080
India (Rupee)	.07622	.07616	13.12	13.13
Indonesia (Rupiah)	.0006090	.0006090	1642.00	1642.00
Ireland (Punt)	1.4260	1.4255	.7013	.7015
Israel (Shekel)	.6180	.6180	1.618	1.618
Italy (Lira)	.0007346	.0007321	1361.00	1366.00
Japan (Yen)	.006631	.006594	150.80	151.65
30-Day Forward	.006651	.006615	150.35	151.18
90-Day Forward	.006685	.006648	149.58	150.43
180-Day Forward	.006739	.006703	148.38	149.19
Jordan (Dinar)	2.8818	2.8818	.347	.347
Kuwait (Dinar)	3.5223	3.5223	.2839	.2839
Lebanon (Pound)	.006920	.006920	144.50	144.50
Malaysia (Ringgit)	.3932	.3932	2.5435	2.5435
Malta (Lira)	2.8369	2.8369	.3525	.3525
Mexico (Peso)				
Floating rate	.0007047	.0007047	1419.00	1419.00
Netherland (Guilder)	.4731	.4707	2.1135	2.1244
New Zealand (Dollar)	.5755	.5705	1.7376	1.7528
Norway (Krone)	.1460	.1450	6.8475	6.8950
Pakistan (Rupee)	.0571	.05698	17.50	17.55
Peru (Inti)	.06293	.06293	15.89	15.89
Philippines (Peso)	.04895	.04895	20.43	20.43
Portugal (Escudo)	.006821	.006803	146.60	147.00
Saudi Arabia (Riyal)	.2666	.2666	3.751	3.751
Singapore (Dollar)	.4738	.4735	2.1105	2.1120
South Africa (Rand)				
Commercial rate	.4840	.4850	2.0661	2.0619
Financial rate	.3050	.3075	3.2787	3.2520
South Korea (Won)	.001238	.001238	808.00	808.00
Spain (Peseta)	.007844	.007822	127.48	127.85
Sweden (Krona)	.1528	.1521	6.5450	6.5750
Switzerland (Franc)	.6254	.6389	1.5990	1.5652
30-Day Forward	.6274	.6410	1.5940	1.5601
90-Day Forward	.6308	.6443	1.5854	1.5520
180-Day Forward	.6363	.6503	1.5717	1.5377
Taiwan (Dollar)	.03275	.03268	30.53	30.60
Thailand (Baht)	.03854	.03854	25.[illegible]5	25.95
Turkey (Lira)	.001139	.001139	878.04	878.04
United Arab (Dirham)	.2723	.2723	3.673	3.673
Uruguay (New Peso)				
Financial	.004348	.004348	230.00	230.00
Venezuela (Bolivar)				
Official rate	.1333	.1333	7.50	7.50
Floating rate	.03503	.03503	28.55	28.55
W. Germany (Mark)	.5319	.5297	1.8800	1.8880
30-Day Forward	.5333	.5311	1.8752	1.8828
90-Day Forward	.5361	.5338	1.8654	1.8732
180-Day Forward	.5402	.5381	1.8513	1.8585
SDR	1.25807	1.25738	0.794870	0.795303
ECU	1.10345	1.10597	....	....

Special Drawing Rights are based on exchange rates for the U.S., West German, British, French and Japanese currencies. Source: International Monetary Fund.

points and refers to the one-month forward rate. The forward rates are quoted in terms of the spot rate. If the first number is smaller than the second, as it is here, the first is added to the bid and the second is added to the ask to get the forward rates. The trader is indicating a willingness to buy pounds for one month forward for \$1.6365 + 2 points, or \$1.6367, and sell pounds for \$1.6370 (\$1.6367 + 3 points). Similarly, the ninety-day forward rates are \$1.6365 + 12 = \$1.6377 bid and \$1.6367 + 15 = \$1.6382 ask. When the first number is smaller, as it is here, the forward rate is said to be at a premium to the spot rate; the forward rate is higher than the spot. A premium means that the dollar's value against the pound is dropping as it goes from spot rate (\$1.6365/£) to thirty days (\$1.6367/£) to ninety days (\$1.6377/£).

On the other hand, a trader in New York might quote the Canadian dollar (C\$) as follows:

Canada	0.7071/0.7075	5 to 3	9 to 7	15 to 13

Here, the forward rates are at a discount to the spot quote because the first number is larger, and the forward quote is found by subtracting the numbers, respectively, from the bid and ask spot quotes. In this case, the trader is willing to buy Canadian dollars for \$.7071/C\$ and sell for \$.7075/C\$ today and to buy Canadian dollars for \$.7066/C\$ (\$.7071 − 5 points = .7066) and sell them for \$.7072/C\$ (.7075 − 3 points = .7072) for delivery in thirty days.

SWAPS

As the forward trade example shows, banks in the forex market have numerous commitments to buy and sell currency at various points in the future. At times, these commitments cancel out, leaving the bank with no net forex exposure. However, this is not generally the case, and the bank may wish to reduce this outstanding, unmatched risk. One way to do this is to execute a swap, the simultaneous purchase and sale of a foreign currency for different delivery dates, the dates chosen to correspond to two of the bank's unmatched exposures. Table 12–4 illustrates a swap.

A bank has a British pound to dollar gap of twenty-nine days caused by a mismatch between sale and purchase, having arranged to sell £1 million at \$1.75/£ in twenty-one days from today and to buy them back twenty-nine days later (fifty days from today) at \$1.65/£. However, the bank must arrange to purchase the £1 million to deliver in twenty-one days, and arrange as well to sell the £1 million when it receives them in fifty days. A broker arranges a swap for the bank for twenty-one and fifty days. In twenty-one days, the bank meets its forward commitment to sell £1 million at \$1.75/£ by buying £1 million through the swap at \$1.725/£. The total profit on this transaction is \$25,000. In fifty days, the bank buys £1 million at the agreed-on

Table 12-4. Foreign Currency Swap

Position in the forward market:
1. A sale of £1 million at $1.75/£ in 21 days (a value of $1.75 million or £1 million)
2. A purchase of £1 million at $1.65/£ in 50 days (a value of $1.65 million or £1 million)

Swap transactions:
1. A purchase of £1 million at $1.725/£ in 21 days
2. A sale of £1 million at $1.64/£ in 50 days

Profit/(Loss) on swap transactions:

1. in 21 days:	
Buy £1 million at $1.725/£, pay:	$1,725,000
Sell £1 million at $1.75/£, receive:	$1,750,000
Profit/(loss):	$25,000
2. in 50 days:	
Buy £1 million at $1.65/£, pay:	$1,650,000
Sell £1 million at $1.64/£, receive:	$1,640,000
Profit/(loss)	($10,000)
Total net profit	$15,000

forward rate of $1.65/£; through the swap agreement, the banks sells the £1 million and receives $1.64/£, losing $10,000 on this part of the transaction. In the example, it is possible for the bank to profit on the swap on a net basis due to the differences between its current position and fixed prices in the forward market and the prices involved in the swap. In this instance, the bank has arranged to cover its risk exposure and make a small profit of $15,000. Of course, the bank could choose to leave the gap uncovered if it anticipates that the exchange rate will move in its favor between now and twenty-one days or between now and fifty days.[2]

FUTURES CONTRACTS

In 1972 in response to the increased volatility of exchange rates, the IMM at the Chicago Mercantile Exchange initiated trading in futures contracts on selected foreign currencies. As might be expected, the choice of currencies to trade was influenced in large part by the already developed forward market in foreign currencies. Sample futures prices from the *Wall Street Journal* are listed in table 12-5. As the table shows, the size of the contracts in dollar terms is roughly similar to the investment required for other futures contracts. For example, the value of the West German deutsch mark contract is approximately $74,162 (closing price, nearby contract; $0.5933/DM × 125,000 DM/contract = $74,162.50/contract), while the British

Table 12-5. Foreign Currency Futures Prices

–FINANCIAL–

BRITISH POUND (IMM)–25,000 pounds; $ per pound								
Mar	1.7560	1.7615	1.7535	1.7560	+ .0115	1.8845	1.5870	36,923
June	1.7450	1.7500	1.7430	1.7440	+ .0115	1.8780	1.5280	2,828
Est vol 6,890; vol Tues 20,284; open Int 37,784, –89.								
CANADIAN DOLLAR (IMM)–100,000 dlrs.; $ per Can $								
Mar	.7871	.7875	.7848	.7864	–.0015	.7898	.7052	20,922
June	.7841	.7847	.7820	.7834	–.0017	.7870	.7325	4,002
Sept	.7800	.7807	.7787	.7804	–.0019	.7847	.7307	736
Dec	.7776	.7784	.7765	.7774	–.0021	.7825	.7390	234
Est vol 3,964; vol Tues 2,672; open Int 25,950, –226.								
JAPANESE YEN (IMM) 12.5 million yen; $ per yen (.00)								
Mar	.7775	.7791	.7761	.7769	–.0005	.8320	.6672	49,463
June	.7824	.7841	.7812	.7819	–.0005	.8390	.6735	3,167
Sept	.7874	.7885	.7874	.7875	–.0005	.8485	.7075	212
Est vol 20,130; vol Tues 17,517; open Int 52,946, –602.								
SWISS FRANC (IMM)–125,000 francs-$ per franc								
Mar	.7254	.7275	.7243	.7252	+.0021	.7955	.6450	32,183
June	.7337	.7359	.7325	.7334	+.0021	.8040	.6580	2,183
Sept	.7420	.7435	.7408	.7415	+.0019	.8120	.6950	97
Est vol 21,844; vol Tues 29,630; open Int 34,500, –90.								
W. GERMAN MARK (IMM)–125,000 marks; $ per mark								
Mar	.5928	.5946	.5923	.5933	+.0027	.6426	.5359	43,811
June	.5975	.5995	.5972	.5981	+.0027	.6494	.5410	6,431
Sept	.6028	.6040	.6028	.6033	+.0027	.6555	.5609	218
Est vol 16,077; vol Tues 20,787; open Int 50,564, –256.								

Reproduced from table 2-1.

pound is $43,900 ($1.7560/£ × £25,000/contract). Thus, it is possible for an individual investor to use the futures market to speculate or hedge in foreign currencies, an opportunity previously unavailable in the much larger denominated spot and forward interbank market.

The foreign currency futures market is unusual in that a large, well-developed forward market coexists with it, serving different market needs and market participants. The existence of a well-established forward market facilitated the development of the more standardized futures market. The foreign currency futures were the first of the financial futures, and as such were considered relatively experimental at the time. The design of the contract borrowed heavily from the established practice of the forward market, and the proposal for the contracts relied in part on the obvious success of the forward market for its economic justification.

As with other futures markets, the foreign currency futures differ from the forward market in important respects. Futures are standardized contracts, with set size and delivery specifications, in marked contrast to the bank-to-customer negotiated terms of the forward market. The futures contracts come with the entire security guarantee (margin, marking-to-market, clearinghouse guarantees) of the futures market, and so rely less on the need to establish customer-to-bank credit lines as the forward market does. Most important, the futures rarely result in delivery, while the forward market has evolved in large measure to facilitate the acquisition of needed foreign currency for various future time periods. Surprisingly, despite the economies of scale presumably following from contract standardization, there seems to be little difference in transaction costs (bid-ask spread) between the two markets.[3]

OPTIONS

There are also options on foreign currency, the right but not the obligation to buy or sell foreign currency at a fixed exchange rate for a specified time period. The valuation and uses of options contracts are discussed in chapter 13. The substantial size of worldwide foreign currency dealings, both spot and forward, has caused the development of a number of hedging and speculative alternatives, a selection much wider than that available for any other underlying market, either commodity or interest rate. The foreign currency market supports not only separate and large forward and futures markets, but also a large market in both exchange-traded and over-the-counter options instruments, and options on both futures and on the physical commodity itself.

THE DETERMINANTS OF EXCHANGE RATES IN SPOT AND FORWARD MARKETS

The exchange rate, or the price of foreign currency, responds to a large number of factors affecting its supply and demand. Certain fundamental price relationships hold, however inexactly, in the spot or forward market, and we discuss these next. In addition, some of the individual primary factors influencing exchange rates are discussed briefly.

THE EXCHANGE RATE IN SPOT MARKETS

TRIANGULAR ARBITRAGE. In the spot market, triangular arbitrage ensures that exchange rates between countries are mutually consistent; that is, the rates across two pairs of currencies (for instance, the \$/DM rate and the DM/£ rate) determines the equilibrium cross-exchange rate for the third pair (here, the \$/£ rate). If the rates between the three currencies are not consistent, an arbitrage profit is possible.

For instance, assume the dollar to DM exchange rate is \$.53/DM and the DM to pound rate is 2.96DM/£. This implies a dollar to pound cross-rate of \$1.57/£ (or 0.64£/\$):

$$\$0.53/\text{DM} \times 2.96\text{DM}/£ = \$1.57/£ \qquad (12\text{–}1)$$

If one of the pairs were out of line, there would be an arbitrage possibility, an ability to buy one of the currencies at a cheap price and simultaneously sell it at a higher price. For instance, if the \$/£ rate were \$1.70/£ rather than the equilibrium \$1.57/£, this would imply a disequilibrium. In equation 12–1, the implied \$/£ cross-rate is \$1.57/£. A rate of \$1.70/£ undervalues the dollar or overvalues the pound. It would be profitable to convert dollars to pounds via the cheaper DM rate of equation 12–1, \$1.57/£, and then use these pounds to buy back dollars at a much better rate (\$1.70/£). An arbitrageur could, for example, take \$530 and convert it to DM (\$530/\$0.53/DM = 1,000DM) and use the 1,000DM to acquire pounds (1,000DM/ 2.96 DM/£ = 337.84£). An arbitrageur who converted the pounds to dollars using the favorable \$1.70/£ rate, would receive \$574.33 (337.84£ × £1.70/\$ = \$574.33). Thus, the arbitrageur could use the discrepancy in rates to pay \$530 and acquire, after currency translations, \$574.33 with no risk. Obviously, the arbitrage would continue until the dollar/pound cross rate is driven back to equilibrium cross-rate of \$1.57/£. In reality, of course, the equilibrium relation does not hold exactly due to transaction costs and bid-ask spreads between the currencies, but the relationship is close.

DETERMINATION OF SPOT RATES. The determination of spot exchange rates depends on a multitude of factors whose relative influence changes through time. At its simplest, the exchange rate between two countries depends on the supply and demand of the one currency relative to the other. This supply and demand depends on the trade between the two countries, the relative demand and supply for goods and services. For instance, if the United States buys Japanese semiconductors and cars, this requires selling dollars for Japanese yen. All things being equal, selling dollars for yen could decrease the value of the dollar against the yen: The \$/¥ rate would increase; a lower value for the dollar requires more dollars to buy one Japanese yen; therefore, the \$/¥ rate would rise to reflect this. Similarly, when the United States sells Coca-Cola and Cray computers to West Germany, this involves buying dollars and selling deutsch marks to pay for them, and the \$/DM rate can be expected to decline. Buying dollars with marks increases the dollar's value; fewer dollars would be needed to buy one mark, and the \$/DM rate would decline. Not only goods and services, but also capital flows, affect the exchange rate: If Japanese investors buy U.S. Treasury bonds— like selling Coca-Cola and Cray computers— this causes the dollar's value to rise against the foreign currency, and the \$/¥ rate to decline. This flow of goods, services, and capital is summarized in the balance of payments between two countries. A balance of payments deficit with Japan means that, on net, the United States is importing more goods from Japan (or investing dollars there, or even sending out dollars for aid or grants to Japan) than the Japanese are importing from the United States. This would mean a decline of the dollar compared to the yen as dollars are sold and yen are bought to pay for the goods, or to pay for the investment, or to use the aid.

The balance of payments between any two countries is influenced in turn by many factors. High national income may increase a balance of payments deficit as the citizens of the country can afford to import more goods. Relative prices between countries also influence the balance of payments: If prices of British agricultural products are high relative to U.S. products, the United States may export such goods to Britain, increasing the balance of payments of the United States relative to the United Kingdom. Of course, interest rates influence the balance of payments and the exchange rate. Higher interest rates in the United States compared to other countries result in a net inflow of foreign capital, at least initially. Eventually, the return on those investments in dividends or interest payments must flow out of the United States. Of course, the level of interest rates in the United States is in turn affected by many other domestic and international factors.

Other influences on the dollar exchange rate are at work as well. Political instability tends to strengthen the U.S. dollar, as investors preferentially invest their capital in a safe haven. Import quotas and tariffs can influence the amount of foreign trade, and through this the exchange rate. Capital restrictions, such as fixed official exchange rates and restrictions on the amount of currency leaving or entering a country, can influence the exchange rate directly. Even changes in the price of oil (denominated in dollars internationally) can change the demand or supply of dollars versus other currencies. Thus, there is no simple set of factors to use in judging the direction of a currency's value against the dollar. It is this great uncertainty, of course, that is responsible for the speculative interest in foreign currency and the demand for a way to hedge against foreign currency fluctuations.

THE EXCHANGE RATE IN FORWARD MARKETS

INTEREST RATE PARITY THEOREM. As with the spot market, certain price relations must hold in the forward market, or else arbitrage will occur. The best known of these is the Interest Rate Parity Theorem (IRPT). Under this theorem, there is a relationship between the interest rates of two countries, their spot exchange rate, and their forward exchange rate.

The idea behind the IRPT is that the rate of interest on similar investments should be the same in any two countries, provided that the forward exchange rate between the two countries can be hedged. The two key conditions are: First, the investor has a choice between investing in two countries of equivalent risk, however defined. Second, if the dollars are invested in a foreign country, the investor has the opportunity to fix the exchange rate at which they are converted back to U.S. dollars at the end of the investment period. Because these two conditions may not hold exactly, the IRPT is a useful approximation rather than an exact relationship.

As an example, assume a U.S. investor can invest $1,000 in a risk-free U.S. Treasury bill for three months at a rate of 6.25 percent. The investor can also invest in Britain in a three-month government obligation (also considered risk-free) at a rate of 7.5 percent. Which is a better investment, or are they equivalent? This depends on the

Table 12-6. Comparison of Investment Returns
(Interest Rate Parity Theorem)

Situation: US 3-month rate = 6.25%
UK 3-month rate = 7.50%
Spot British pound/$ rate = 0.67£/$ ($1.50/£)
3-month forward $/£ rate = $1.50/£ (0.67£/$)
Interest Rate Parity Theorem does not hold:
(1.0625) ≠ (0.67£/$) × (1.0750) × ($1.50/£)

Dollar proceeds from U.S. investment:
$1,000 + ($1,000 × 0.0625 × 90/360) = $1,015.63

Dollar proceeds from British investment:

1. Conversion to British pounds today:
   $1,000 × 0.67£/$ = £670
2. Investment at 7.50% for 3 months:
   £670 + (£670 × 0.0750 × 90/360) = £682.56
3. Reconversion to dollars at end of investment:
   £682.56 × $1.50/£ = $1,018.75

exchange rate between dollars and pounds, and, more important, on the forward exchange rate of pounds into dollars three months from now. If the investor converts dollars to pounds, buys the three-month British bill, and at the same time fixes the rate at which the pounds can be reconverted into dollars in three months, the two rates can be compared. If both investments are risk-free, the returns on the two alternative investments should be the same.

Table 12-6 shows the calculation of the realized rate of return on the two investments. The U.S. investment yields a return of 6.25% over the three months, or an end-of-investment amount of $1,000 + ($1,000 × 0.0625 × 90/360) = $1,015.63. The British investment involves converting the $1,000 to pounds (equal to $1,000 × 0.67£/$ = £670), and investing this at 7.5 percent; at the end of the three-month period, the investor would have £670 + (670 × 0.0750 × 90/360) = £682.56. Converting this to dollars at the fixed forward rate of $1.50/£ gives the investor $1,018.75 (682.56 × $1.50/£ = $1,018.75). Thus, with the fixed forward rate of 0.67£/$, the two investment returns are not equivalent. As the two investments are assumed equal in risk, all investors prefer to convert dollars to pounds, invest in Britain, and hedge the value of the investment at the fixed forward rate. The differential buying and selling pressure on the exchange rates and the British short-term investment force the rates to adjust until there is no preference for the British investment over the U.S. one, or until the investment rates are the same:

$$(1 + r_{US}) = (£/\$)_{spot} \times (1 + r_{UK}) \times (\$/£)_{forward} \quad (12\text{-}2)$$

This is the Interest Rate Parity Theorem: there is a necessary relationship between the U.S. interest rate, the British interest rate, and the two exchange rates, spot and forward. If the relationship does not hold, there is a preference for one investment alternative over the other, and the rates equilibrate through these preferential transactions. In the preceding example, the adjustment would be as follows: the British interest rate would be expected to fall as more investors preferentially demanded to buy the British investment. Similarly, the U.S. interest rate would rise as investors sell U.S. investments in favor of the British, or preferentially choose to invest in the British asset. In addition, the £/$ rate would fall as the preference for spot pounds over dollars dominated. The pound would become more valuable against the dollar, or the dollar would become cheaper against the pound; in this case, it would take fewer pounds to buy one dollar, and the £/$ would fall. Similarly, the forward $/£ rate would fall as investors sold pounds forward for dollars in three months.

If the discrepancy is large enough, an arbitrage can also take place. If the British investment yields more, as it does here, then it would be profitable to borrow the dollars in the United States at the current rate of 6.25 percent (owing $1,015.63 in three months) (the left side of equation 12–2) and arrange the British investment (the right side of equation 12–2). The dollar value of the British investment at the end of the three months would be $1,018.75, enough to repay the U.S. loan and have a risk-free $3.12 profit remaining, with no initial investment. Again, this arbitrage would continue until the rates adjust and equation 12–2 holds exactly. This is called a covered interest arbitrage.

The success of the arbitrage and the equilibrium relation itself depend on the free flow of capital across borders, completely flexible exchange rates, and an equality in tax treatment of the two investments across countries. In addition, the arbitrage assumes that one can borrow at the U.S. rate and lend at the British rate, or in reverse if the relationship is in disequilibrium in the other direction. Finally, transaction costs are ignored as is any risk of default on the forward contract. For all of these reasons, equation 12–2 may not hold exactly but is useful as an approximation.

Another form of the IRPT expresses the equilibrium relation in the percentage change of the forward rate over the current spot rate. Multiplying equation 12–2 out, simplifying, and dropping a cross-term gives the IRPT in its more usual form:

$$r_{US} - r_{UK} = ((£/\$_{forw} - (£/\$)_{spot}) / (£/\$)_{spot} \qquad (12\text{–}3)$$

Here, equation 12–3 states that the percentage change between the spot and forward exchange rate (right side) is related to the difference between the two countries' spot interest rates. For instance, with the British rate at 7.50 percent, the United States at 6.25 percent, and the spot pound to dollar rate at 0.67£/$, the equilibrium forward $/£ rate is $1.475/£.

PURCHASING POWER PARITY THEOREM. There is a second relationship between exchange rates that concerns the relative price level between two countries for common goods. This is the Purchasing Power Parity Theorem (PPPT), and it is simply that the price of a common good should be the same in two countries. As an illustration, assume that a Dresden porcelain costs 100DM in Dresden, and the current DM/$ exchange rate is 2DM/$. The equilibrium price of a Dresden porcelain in Chicago is $50 (100DM/2DM/$ = $50). If the Chicago price were $75, then there would be an arbitrage opportunity. An astute trader could buy Dresden porcelains in Dresden for 100 DM (or $50) per figurine and then sell them in Chicago for $75 (or 150DM), making a $25 (or 50DM) arbitrage profit. This assumes, of course, that there are no tariffs or quotas on these figurines; the arbitrage also ignores transportation and transaction costs. However, net of these charges, the relationship should hold.

PPPT's relevance for forward rates arises from the fact that the exchange rate-relative price level relationship must be consistent over time as well. That is, forward exchange rates must be consistent with the expected change in relative price level between the two countries. If the inflation rate in Germany is expected to be 10 percent, then the Dresden porcelain can be expected to sell for 110DM in one year. If there were no inflation in the United States, then the equilibrium expected price for the Dresden porcelain in the United States would be $50. This implies a DM/$ exchange rate a year from now of 2.20DM/$. If the relative purchasing power of the dollar and the DM is expected to change with the German price level rising 10 percent and the U.S. price level constant, the forward exchange rate must reflect this expected 10 percent change. This is merely a restatement of the IRPT (equation 12-2) in slightly different form: The forward exchange rate depends on the relative difference in interest rates, including expectations on inflation over the future time period, between the two countries.

MODERN THEORY. So far the discussion of forward exchange rates and their relation to spot exchange rates and price levels or interest rate levels has emphasized the role of an arbitrageur in determining the forward rate. The Modern Theory argues that the forward rate depends on both the arbitrageur's transactions and the speculator, and that one or the other (or both) may dominate the market and set the equilibrium forward rate.

The arbitrageur enters into forward contracts, buying or selling, in response to interest rate differentials. In the previous IRPT example with pounds and dollars (table 12-6), the arbitrageur found it profitable to enter into a long forward contract, buying dollars/selling pounds for three-month delivery. The arbitrage possibility arose because the forward dollar/pound rate was out of equilibrium with the current spot exchange rate and interest rate differential between the two countries. Arbitrageurs are expected to buy dollars and sell pounds forward if the $/£ forward rate is too high, as in the example. Additionally, the arbitrageur can be expected to sell

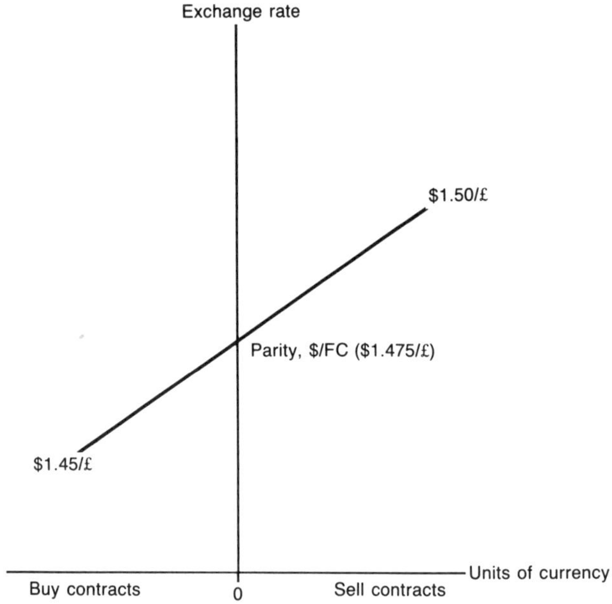

Figure 12–2. Supply Schedule, Arbitrageur

dollars and buy pounds in the forward market (reverse the arbitrage) if the rate is too low. Thus, the arbitrageur has a supply schedule for the forward contract that is a function of the market forward rate compared to the equilibrium rate (see figure 12–2).

Speculators, however, another group of participants in the forward market, buy and sell forward contracts in response to expectations regarding the spot price in some future time period. A speculator who sees a discrepancy between the forward rate in the market and the subjective expected spot rate, can buy or sell a forward contract in the hope of a speculative return for superior forecasting ability. If the expected spot rate is higher than the market forward rate prevailing, then the speculator would buy the forward contract at what is, to the speculator, an attractive price. For instance, despite a forward rate of $1.80/£, the speculator who expected the $/£ rate to be $1.70/£ would buy dollars forward. In this case, the speculator expects that the dollar will be worth more against the British pound (it will take $1.70 to buy a pound) than the forward market indicates (at $1.80/£ in the forward market). With the $/£ forward rate undervaluing the dollar, the speculator would buy dollars forward at this cheap rate. Thus, the demand schedule for the $/£ forward contract for the speculator depends on the discrepancy between the speculator's

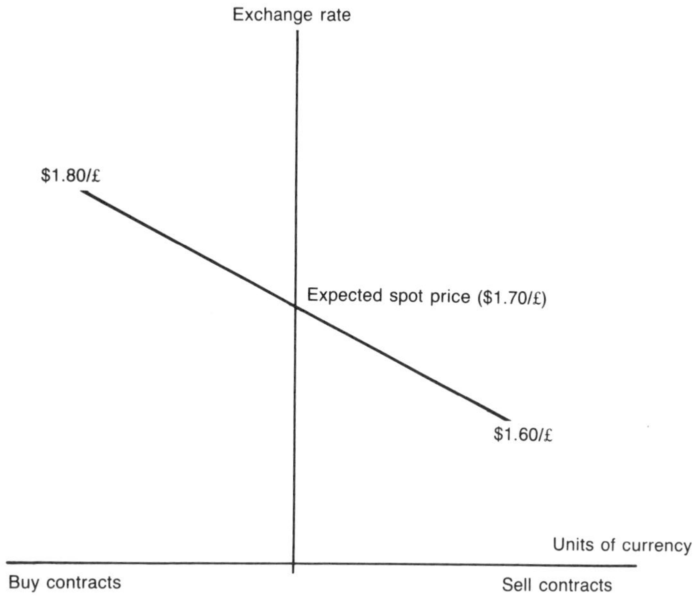

Figure 12–3. Demand Schedule, Speculator

expected spot rate ($1.70/£) and the forward rate in the market ($1.80/£). When the forward rate in the market is high compared to the speculator's expectations as it is here, forward contracts are purchased. Similarly, if the forward market rate were too low (for instance, $1.60/£), compared to the expected rate, the speculator would sell dollars and buy British pounds in the forward market. The speculator's demand schedule for the forward contract is shown in figure 12–3.

The forward exchange rate depends on both arbitrageurs and speculators, and is determined by the supply and demand schedules for forward contracts of the two competing market groups. The equilibrium forward rate is determined at the intersection of the two schedules (see figure 12–4). Thus, the equilibrium* rate is where supply equals demand, in this case, approximately $1.60/£. Because this is a classic supply-demand analysis, the equilibrium* exchange rate depends on such characteristics of supply and demand as the exchange rate elasticity of the arbitrageur versus the speculator, and most important, the expected exchange rate of the speculator group. Figure 12–4 attempts to explain a common problem in foreign exchange markets, that the IRPT and its related PPPT may not hold for long periods of time. This lack of correspondence between a reasonable theory and market conditions is explained by the presence of a speculator group that acts on expectations. In this case (figure 12–4), the speculator group causes the equilibrium* forward exchange rate to

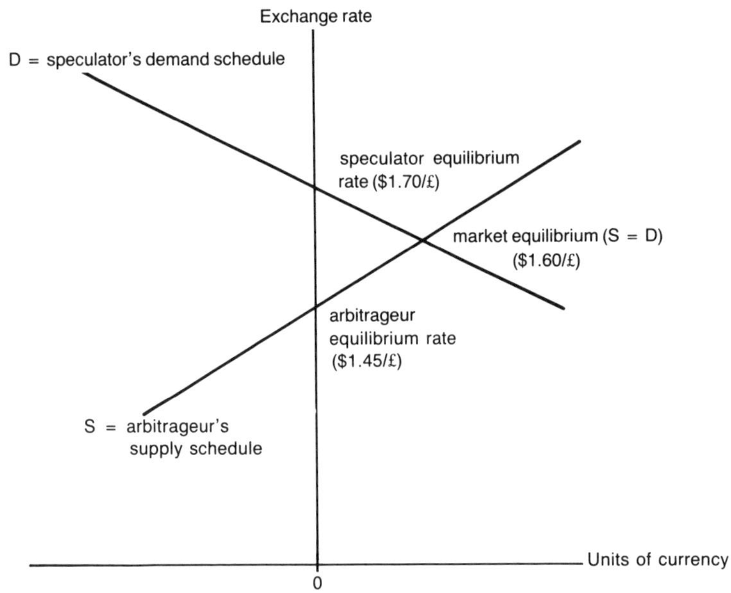

Figure 12-4. Intersection of Supply and Demand for Forward Contracts *(Equilibrium Forward Rate)*

remain at $1.60/£ when the IRPT would result in an equilibrium forward rate of $1.45/£. Unfortunately, the speculator curve, the equilibrium* rate, and the general Modern Theory, depend strongly on the expectations of the speculator group. It is not easy to empirically test whether the Modern Theory is a valid explanation of the failure of the IRPT to hold.[4]

HEDGING FOREIGN CURRENCY EXPOSURE

The purpose of the forward market in forex is the acquisition or disposal of foreign currency to finance international trade. The use of foreign currency futures, on the other hand, can include risk-shifting activities that necessitate neither delivery nor receipt of actual currency. This section discusses different hedging activities and illustrates some of the uses of foreign currency futures.

SHORT HEDGE

Assume an international portfolio manager based in the United States has taken a substantial position in the Japanese equity market. Even though the rate of return on the Japanese stock market is expected to be quite favorable, the manager is concerned about the eventual repatriation of the funds to the United States. The manager decides to use the Japanese yen futures contract at the CME to hedge against a dollar appreciation/yen depreciation during the investment period. The contracts are all priced in European terms (\$/unit of foreign currency). The manager would use a short hedge; if the price of the futures contract declines, this would indicate a dollar appreciation/yen depreciation. It would take more yen to buy one dollar. Table 12-7 illustrates the short hedge. The ¥ contract, unlike the others traded on the Chicago Mercantile Exchange, is quoted in four significant digits but with an implied "0.00" in front of the price. For instance, if the ¥ futures price is quoted at \$0.3821, the actual price is \$0.003821/¥.

With a spot rate of \$.006750/¥ (or 148.15¥/\$), the manager calculates the value of the equity investment in the Japanese market as \$525,000 × 148.15¥/\$ =

Table 12-7. Short Hedge

Situation today:

Spot rate: \$0.006750/¥ (= 148.15¥/\$)
6-month futures contract price: \$0.006687/¥ (= 149.54¥/\$)

Cash:	Futures:
Cash value of equity investment = ¥77,777,777 (\$525,000)	Sell 7 contracts at \$0,006687/¥ (= 149.54¥/\$) Value of futures position = 7 contracts × 12.5 million ¥/contract × \$0.006687/¥ = \$585,112.50

In 5 months:

Spot rate: \$0.005975/¥ (= 167.36¥/\$)

Cash:	Futures:
Cash value of equity investment = ¥97,223,440 (\$580,922.00) (25% capital gain in ¥; 11% capital gain in dollars)	Buy back 7 contracts at \$0.005960/¥ (= 167.82¥/\$) Value of futures position = 7 contracts × 12.5 million ¥/contract × \$0.005960/¥ = \$521,500.00 Futures profit: (\$0.006687/¥ − \$0.005960/¥ × 7 contracts × 12.5 million¥/contract = \$63,612.50

Ending dollar value of equity investment:
\$580,922.00 + \$63,612.50 = \$644,534.50
(23% capital gain in dollars)

¥77,777,777. The current futures price for a six-month delivery contract is \$0.006687/¥. With delivery terms of 12.5 million ¥ per contract, the manager sells seven contracts (¥77,777,777/12.5 million yen per contract = 6.22 contracts). This represents a slight overhedge on the current value of the spot equity portfolio, but the value of the portfolio is expected to increase through capital gains.

In five months, the manager is ready to sell the shares in the Japanese market and convert the proceeds to dollars. As the manager expected, the position has grown; it is now ¥97,223,440, a 25 percent capital gain on the Japanese equity investment. However, the spot rate is now \$0.005975/¥, so that the equity position in dollars is worth only \$580,922, an 11 percent capital gain in dollars due to the yen's depreciation against the dollar. In the futures market, the short futures position has gained in value due to the dollar appreciation, and the futures price on the seven contracts is now \$0,005960/¥. The profit on the seven contracts in dollars is thus: 7 contracts × (\$0.006035/¥ − \$0.005960/¥) × 12.5 million ¥/contract = \$63,612.50. Thus, the total dollar value, cash and futures, of the equity investment is now \$644,534.50 (\$580,922.00 in equity value at current exchange rate + \$63,612.50 profit on the futures contract), a 23 percent increase over the beginning dollar value of \$525,000.

LONG HEDGE

As an illustration of a long hedge in currency futures, assume that in three months the U.S. division of a Canadian firm will pay a dividend to the parent firm. The division manager estimates that the quarter's profit will be \$2.5 million; of this, 50 percent is expected to be paid to the Canadian parent firm. At the current spot rate, this would be worth C\$1,658,875 (\$1,250,000 × C\$1.3271/\$). The manager would like to hedge against a dollar depreciation against the Canadian dollar for the three months so that the payment to the parent company is close to C\$1,658,875. The manager buys Canadian dollar futures: if the dollar does depreciate against the Canadian dollar, the futures price will rise. The current spot and futures prices are listed in table 12-8. With each contract denominated as C\$100,000, the manager buys seventeen contracts (C\$1,658,875/C\$100,000 per contract = 16.58 contracts).

As table 12-8 shows, in three months the dollar has, indeed, depreciated against the Canadian dollar. The manager has the \$1,250,000 to repatriate to Canada, and the value in Canadian dollars is now C\$1,515,125 (\$1,250,000 × C\$1.2121/\$), a loss of C\$143,750 over the original planned dividend. However, the futures has increased in value, and the profit on the futures of \$133,450 can be added to the remittance. In Canadian dollars, this is equal to C\$110,096.25. The full amount paid as a dividend to the parent firm is thus C\$1,515,125 + C\$110,096.25 = C\$1,625,221.25, which is close to the original value of C\$1,658,875.

Table 12-8. Long Hedge

Situation today:	
Spot rate: C$1.3271/$ (= $0.7535/C$)	
3-month futures contract price: $0.7465 (= C$1.3396/$)	
Cash:	Futures:
Cash value of expected dividend = $1,250,000 (C$1,658,875)	Buy 17 contracts at $0.7465/C$ (= C$1.3396/$) Value of futures position = 17 contracts × C$100,000 per contract × $0.7465/C$ = $1,269,000
In 3 months:	
Spot rate: C$1.2121/$ (= $0.8250/C$)	
Futures contract price: $0.8250/C$ (= 1.2121C$/$)	
Cash:	Futures:
Cash value of dividend = $1,250,000 (C$1,515,125) Cash loss = (C$1,658,875 − C$1,515,125) = C$143,750	Sell 17 contracts at $0.8250/C$ (= $1.2121/C$) Value of futures position = 17 contracts × C$100,000 per contract × $0.8250/C$ = $1,402,500 Futures profit: ($0.8250/C$ − $0.7465/C$) × 17 contracts × C$100,000/contract = $133,450 (=C$110,096.25)
Ending Canadian dollar value of dividend: C$1,515,125 + C$110,096.25 = C$1,625,221.25	

HEDGING FOREIGN CURRENCY EXPOSURE IN FOREIGN CURRENCIES WITHOUT FUTURES

An exposure in a currency without a futures contract (for instance, the Italian lira) may be hedged if the foreign currency in question is correlated with some other currency on which contracts trade. That is, it may be possible to hedge against a decline in the value of the Dutch gilder versus the dollar by using a Swiss franc contract. The European Monetary System stipulates that the cross-exchange rates between member currencies can fluctuate away from a fixed par value by only 2¼ percent (some countries have large margins; in addition, intervention is voluntary). Thus, the nine countries in the EMS can be expected to have a relatively high correlation of exchange rates against the dollar; EMS currencies moving together against the dollar through the system (Danish krone, Belgian franc, Greek drachma) may be correlated highly enough with the futures currencies to be hedgeable. Indeed, many European currencies, even outside the EMS, tend to move together against the dollar. For instance, the deutsch mark has a correlation coefficient against the dollar of greater than 95 percent with the Austrian schilling (0.971), the Belgian franc (0.952), and the Italian lira (0.953).

HEDGING INTEREST RATE RISK IN A FOREIGN COUNTRY

R. Kolb, G. Gay, and J. Jordan have shown that it is possible to hedge against the risk of foreign interest rate fluctuations using currency forward contracts and a U.S. interest rate futures contract.[5] The forward contracts translate the foreign currency into U.S. dollars at the beginning of the hedge and translate it back after the hedge; the interest rate futures contract serves to hedge the expected short-term rate in the United States. As an example, assume an international portfolio manager will have a certain amount of foreign currency to invest three months from now. The manager knows the current three- and six-month rates on investments in the foreign currency, and can estimate an expected ninety-day investment rate three months from now. The problem is to hedge against a drop in rates in the foreign country between now and when the manager receives the foreign currency in three months.

Table 12–9 illustrates the problem for an investment in France. At current three- and six-month French rates, the portfolio manager can expect to invest the planned receipt of 25 million French francs at an implied forward rate of 8.50 percent. At this rate, the investment would be worth Fr25,515,100 at the end of the three-month investment period six months from today. The manager would like to hedge against a decline in the French rate and can do this through the use of forward contracts and a T-bill futures contract. (See table 12–9.)

Today, the manager must:

1. Arrange to convert the foreign currency into dollars at its receipt by selling the Fr25 million forward at a three-month forward rate of \$0.1594/Fr. This locks in receipt of \$3,985,000 (Fr25,000,000 × \$0.1594/Fr = \$3,985,000).

2. Hedge the investment rate on the three-month investment by buying (hedge against rate decline) four T-bill futures contracts. The futures price for three-month delivery reflects the implied forward rate in the U.S. of 7.75% (\$1,000,000 − (0.0775 × 90/360 × \$1,000,000) = \$980,625). Anticipating approximately \$4 million in receipt, buy four futures contracts for delivery in three months.

Table 12–9. Hedging Foreign Interest Rate Risk

	Interest Rates			*Exchange Rates*		
Country	*3-month*	*6-month*	*3-month forward*	*Spot*	*3-month forward*	*6-month forward*
France	7.50%	8.00%	8.50%	6.3492Fr/$	6.2735Fr/$	6.2893Fr/$
United States	6.25	7.00	7.75	$0.1575/Fr	$0.1594/Fr	$0.1590/Fr

Expect receipt of Fr25 million in 3 months.

Expected investment income on 3-month investment 3 months from today:

Fr25,000,000 × $(1.085)^{0.25}$ = Fr25,515,110

Today:

1. Sell Fr25 million 3 months forward at $0.1594; will receive (Fr25,000,000 × $0.1594/Fr = $3,985,000) in 3 months.
2. Buy 4 Treasury bill futures for delivery in 3 months; will pay (FP = $980,625) × 4 = $3,922,500 in 3 months.
3. Sell $4 million 6 months forward at $0,1590; will receive ($4,000,000/$0.1590/Fr = Fr25,161,600) in 3 months.

In 3 months:

4. Receive Fr25 million.
5. Convert to U.S. dollars at $0.1594/Fr; receive $3,985,000.
6. Take delivery of 4 U.S. Treasury bills in futures market; pay 4 × ($980,625) = $3,922,500[a]

In 6 months:

7. Have $62,500 in excess funds from steps 5 and 6.
8. Receive $4 million for maturity of T-bills.
9. Convert to French francs at $0.1590; receive Fr25,550,281 ($4,000,000 + $62,500) × (6.2893FR/$)

[a]The portfolio manager will have $62,500 remaining after paying for the Treasury bills; the excess can be invested at the current 3-month U.S. rate and, in 3 months, include the proceeds in a reconversion back to French francs. The excess is ignored here.

3. Finally, hedge the repatriated value of the investment at the end of the investment's life (six months from today) by selling $4 million for francs forward six months at the six-month rate (6.2904Fr/$). The transactions and the results are listed in table 12–9. There is slippage in the example because of the unitary nature of the futures position. There is $62,500 remaining when the manager takes delivery of the Treasury bills in the futures market (steps 5 and 6) ($3,985,000 − $3,922,500 = $62,500). Ignoring any reinvestment, the $62,500 can be repatriated into French francs as well three months later. The total sum obtained is thus ($4,000,000 + $62,500) × 6.2893Fr/$ = Fr25,550,281.

As table 12–9 shows, the portfolio manager has hedged the French franc investment rate through using the forward market for currencies and the futures market for interest rate instruments. All of the rates are consistent with the implied forward rate for French investments of 8.50 percent: The forward U.S.-French franc exchange rates reflect the three- and six-month spot rates; the U.S. T-bill futures contract reflects the U.S. implied forward rate; and the French implied forward rate is locked in through the combination of the forward currency rates and the U.S. implied forward rate. The actual rate on the investment is 9.09 percent (Fr25,000,000 $\times$ $(1.0909)^{0.25}$ = Fr25,550,281). Thus, with three transactions the portfolio manager can convert the francs to be received into dollars at a known rate, hedge a U.S. investment at a known rate, and also reconvert the dollars back into French francs at a known rate, fixing a foreign interest rate using currency forward contracts and a U.S. interest rate futures contract.

NOTES

1. For a fuller introduction to hedging practices, see A. Loosigian, *Foreign Exchange Futures* (Homewood, Ill.: Dow Jones-Irwin, 1981).
2. Swaps on foreign currency are also discussed in chapter 11.
3. For a discussion of transaction costs, see J. Peterson, "A Study of Transaction Costs in the Forward and Futures Exchange Markets during the Years of Floating Exchange Rates" (Ph.D. diss., University of Notre Dame, 1980).
4. For a more complete explanation of the Modern Theory, see J. Hilley, C. Beidleman, and J. Greenleaf, "Does Covered Interest Arbitrage Dominate in Foreign Exchange Markets?" *Columbia Journal of World Business* 14 (Winter, 1979): 99–107; and H. Stokes and H. Neuburger, "Interest Arbitrage, Forward Speculation, and the Determination of the Forward Exchange Rate." *Columbia Journal of World Business* 14 (Winter 1979): 86–98.
5. R. Kolb, G. Gay, and J. Jordan, "Hedging International Interest Rate Risk," Working Paper. The discussion follows that in R. Kolb, *Interest Rate Futures* (Reston, Va: Reston Publishing, 1984).

OPTIONS ON FUTURES

13

Prior to 1973 options were either banned completely for domestic commodities regulated under the Commodities Exchange Act of 1936 or traded only in an informal, off-exchange market for unregulated commodities such as metals and for individual stocks. In 1973, the Chicago Board Options Exchange (CBOE), an exchange for trading call options on stocks opened; since then both trading volume and the number of contracts offered have increased enormously. Put options on stocks were introduced in June 1977.

Despite the great success of options on stocks, options on physical commodities and futures have been subject to considerable regulatory discussion. Because of this, trading of these options has been introduced very slowly, or in some cases, not at all. Options on stock index futures and on stock indexes themselves were the first options of this kind to trade in the United States. Options on the S&P500 index futures and the New York Stock Exchange (NYSE) index futures were introduced in January 1983 on the Chicago Mercantile Exchange (CME) and the New York

Futures Exchange (NYSE), respectively. The first option on an index of stocks, the S&P100, has been trading since March 1983. The S&P100 has been particularly successful, and is now the single most active option in all markets. Other options on actuals include currencies at the Philadelphia Exchange, as well as on other stock indexes such as the Major Market Index at the American Stock Exchange (AMEX) and the S&P500 (CBOE).

Options on interest rate futures and physical interest rate assets have also been introduced. The Treasury bond futures option contract at the CBOT has been the most successful option on futures, with two-thirds of the volume of options on futures trading concentrated in this option alone in 1987.

Options on agricultural futures have been introduced more slowly because of the past history of abuse associated with agricultural options. In the 1930s abuses in the trading of agricultural options affected the futures markets for these commodities. Options were sometimes used to accumulate huge hidden positions in the futures markets, and often prices in the futures markets were subject to large swings arising from dealings in the options markets. Consequently, options on regulated commodities were, as noted, forbidden under the 1936 Commodities Exchange Act.

In 1981 the Commodity Futures Trading Commission (CFTC) initiated a three-year pilot program in options on commodity futures. Under the program, each exchange was allowed to trade two options on futures. Generally, the most popular commodity futures on each exchange were chosen for options trading. The CBOT began trading in soybean and corn futures options, the CME initiated trading in live cattle and hog futures options, and the COMEX, gold options. The program has been so successful that, after a review in late 1985, the pilot program was amended to allow up to eight futures options to be traded at each exchange. Currently, there are a wide variety of options on futures offered for trading. Although there are options on physical currencies and financial instruments, there are no options traded on physical agricultural commodities.

The first section of this chapter introduces the terminology of options trading, which borrows heavily from stock options practices. The second section discusses some of the possible uses of options on futures, and contrasts options use with futures use. In the third section, we review the Black-Scholes stock options pricing model and apply it to the pricing of options on futures. Finally, the last section discusses new developments in hedging involving options.

TERMINOLOGY OF OPTIONS MARKETS AND THEIR MECHANICS

An option contract gives its owner the right to buy (a *call* option) or sell (a *put* option) an underlying asset for a certain price, the *exercise* price or *strike* price, for a limited period of time.

On exercise of the option, the holder of a call option on a futures contract has the right to assume a long position in the underlying futures contract at a futures price equal to the strike price of the option. Similarly, the put option holder has the right to assume a short futures position at the strike price. For instance, a U.S. Treasury bond call option with a strike price of 66 and June maturity gives its holder the right to a long T-bond futures contract for June delivery at a futures price of 66. If the current price of the June futures contract is greater than 66, for instance 80, the option to buy is valuable and probably will be exercised. If the current futures price is less than 66, say 50, the option holder can obtain a long futures position at a lower price by using the futures market directly, and the option probably will not be exercised. If the futures price remains below 66 until expiration, the call option will not be exercised and will expire worthless.

Similarly, a U.S. T-bond put option with a strike price of 70 gives the option holder the right to a short U.S. T-bond futures position at a futures price of 70. In this case, the option is valuable if the futures price is below 70, say 55. On exercise, the option holder receives a short futures contract at a futures price of 70 when the futures is trading at 55. With a put option, the option will expire worthless if the futures price remains above the option strike price.

One of the major differences between options and futures relates to the limited risk of options contracts. In contrast to a futures contract, an option gives the holder the right, but *not* the obligation, to buy or sell at the exercise price. Taking the underlying futures position is at the option holder's discretion. If the current futures price moves against the option holder by, for instance, declining below the exercise price of the call option, the option will not be exercised and simply expire. Another difference between options and futures is that the buyer of an option makes only one payment, the price of the option or the *premium*, when the option is bought. Losses on the option are thus limited to this premium paid; if the option expires without exercise, the buyer loses the premium. This is in contrast to a futures position, in which the holder is obligated to make delivery, and thus has unlimited price risk unless the position is offset before contract delivery. The option buyer posts no margin. There is no cash flow to or from an option holder over the life of the option as there is to the margin account over the life of the futures.

Although an option buyer has no obligation to undertake the underlying futures position, the option seller does. By selling, or writing, the option, the seller assumes the obligation to take the appropriate futures position opposite the option buyer if the option is exercised by the buyer. Thus, the seller of the T-bond call option must, on exercise, take a short position in the June T-bond futures contract at a futures price of 66. Similarly, the writer of a put option must assume a long position in the futures contract if the option is exercised by the buyer. If the option is not exercised before it expires, the writer keeps the premium of the option. Because of the underlying obligations involved in selling an option, the writer is required to post both the margin on the underlying futures contract and the premium received for the option when it is sold.

DESCRIPTION OF AN OPTION, BUYING, EXERCISE

To fully describe an option requires six characteristics:

1. The option is a put or call; that is, the option represents the right to a short or a long position in the underlying futures contract, respectively. The seller/writer of a call is obligated to assume a short position in the underlying futures contract; the put writer is obligated to take a long position.

2. The underlying futures contract.

3. The exercise price or strike price, the price at which the futures position can be entered into on exercise of the option. At the initiation of trading, exercise prices are fixed by the exchange at certain price intervals from the current futures price. For example, if the deutsch mark (DM) March futures is currently quoted at a price of 0.4241, options trade on the DM futures with exercise prices of 0.40, 0.41, 0.42, 0.43, and 0.44. New exercise prices are added as the futures price moves up or down. The price of the option is determined by the consensus of the market; the exercise price of the option is fixed for the option contract by the exchange.

4. The number of futures represented by the option. Generally, the futures options currently traded entitle the option holder to a position in one futures contract. This differs slightly from a stock option involving 100 shares of the underlying stock.

5. The maturity or expiration date of the option. Most currently traded futures options expire in the same month as the underlying futures. Generally, the option expires just before the first delivery day of the futures. Many of the current options are on financial futures, and expire on a quarterly cycle. For instance, the S&P500 futures options are traded on a March-June-September-December cycle.

6. An option can be an American or European option. An American option can be exercised at any time; there is no fixed delivery or exercise period as there is in futures trading. European options can be exercised only at expiration; few are currently traded in the United States.

Table 13–1 shows a sample page of price quotations for futures options from the *Wall Street Journal.* The options prices are quoted in terms of the underlying futures contract. Thus, the corn futures call option for September expiration with a strike price of 180 (180 cents/bushel) has a price expressed in cents per bushel, here 22 1/2

Table 13-1. Options on Futures

FUTURES OPTIONS

Wednesday, February 10, 1988.

–AGRICULTURAL–

CORN (CBT) 5,000 bu.; cents per bu.

Strike Price	Calls–Settle Mar-c	May-c	Jly-c	Puts–Settle Mar-p	May-p	Jly-p
180	22½	28½	32½	⅛	⅜	⅞
190	12¾	19	23	¼	1¼	2½
200	3¾	11¾	17	1¼	3¾	5
210	⅝	7	12	8	8½	9¼
220	⅛	3¾	7¾	16¾	14¾	15
230	⅛	1⅞	5	....	....	....

Est. vol. 2,000, Tues vol. 1,043 calls, 370 puts
Open interest Tues 23,466 calls, 23,892 puts

SOYBEANS (CBT) 5,000 bu.; cents per bu.

Strike Price	Calls–Settle Mar-c	May-c	Jly-c	Puts–Settle Mar-p	May-p	Jly-p
575	37½	48½	61½	½	3¾	8
600	13½	30½	43	2⅛	9¾	15
625	2⅛	18	30	15	23	27
650	⅝	10½	21	37½	39½	42½
675	⅛	5½	15½	62½	60	60½
700	⅛	3¼	11	97½	....	....

Est. vol. 3,500, Tues vol. 1,890 calls, 1,287 puts
Open interest Tues 46,078 calls, 25,402 puts

SOYBEAN MEAL (CBT) 100 tons; $ per ton

Strike Price	Calls–Settle Mar-c	May-c	Jly-c	Puts–Settle Mar-p	May-p	Jly-p
165	13.10	....	....	0.10	2.00	3.30
170	8.40	11.00	....	0.45	3.00	4.75
175	4.00	7.50	10.75	1.00	4.50	6.85
180	1.40	5.00	8.50	3.25	7.50	9.00
185	0.70	3.50	6.85	7.50	10.50	12.00
190	0.35	2.50	5.25	12.30	14.75	15.50

Est. vol. 200, Tues vol. 298 calls, 251 puts
Open interest Tues 6,919 calls, 4,232 puts

SOYBEAN OIL (CBT) 60,000 lbs.; cents per lb.

Strike Price	Calls–Settle Mar-c	May-c	Jly-c	Puts–Settle Mar-p	May-p	Jly-p
19	2.230	2.620	....	.005	.120	.210
20	1.240	1.750	2.050	.020	.250	.430
21	.400	1.200	1.440	.190	.600	.720
22	.090	.630	1.080	.860	1.130	1.350
23	.040	.420	.750	1.810	1.920	2.030
24	.005	.270	.550	....	....	....

Est. vol. 150, Tues vol. 121 calls, 142 puts
Open interest Tues 7,886 calls, 5,123 puts

WHEAT (CBT) 5,000 bu.; cents per bu.

Strike Price	Calls–Settle Mar-c	May-c	Jly-c	Puts–Settle Mar-p	May-p	Jly-p
310	20¾	28	28	½	4⅞	10
320	13¾	21	23	2	[illegible]	13
330	[illegible]	[illegible]	[illegible]	[illegible]	[illegible]	[illegible]

–METALS–

COPPER (CMX) 25,000 lbs.; cents per lb.

Strike Price	Calls–Last Mar-C	May-C	Jly-C	Puts–Last Mar-P	May-P	Jly-P
96	6.05	9.50	7.60	0.35	11.95	17.65
98	4.20	8.80	7.25	0.60	13.25	19.20
100	2.80	8.35	6.90	1.10	14.75	20.85
105	0.85	6.90	5.90	4.15	18.25	24.70
110	0.20	5.60	5.05	8.50	21.90	28.70
115	0.10	4.65	4.30	13.35	25.90	32.90

Est. vol. 3,000, Tues vol. 1,308 calls, 675 puts
Open interest Tues 38,255 calls, 16,549 puts

GOLD (CMX) 100 troy ounces; dollars per troy ounce

Strike Price	Calls–Last Apr-C	Jun-C	Aug-C	Puts–Last Apr-P	Jun-P	Aug-P
400	45.40	52.30	57.50	1.60	4.60	6.20
420	27.10	35.80	41.50	3.20	7.60	9.60
440	11.40	20.80	28.00	7.50	12.50	15.20
460	3.30	10.50	17.50	19.40	22.00	24.50
480	1.30	5.50	10.90	37.10	37.00	37.00
500	0.60	2.90	6.60	56.70	54.40	52.00

Est. vol. 7,300, Tues vol. 4,756 calls, 8,590 puts
Open interest Tues 59,847 calls, 47,353 puts

SILVER (CMX) 5,000 troy ounces; cents per troy ounce

Strike Price	Calls–Last Mar-C	May-C	Jly-C	Puts–Last Mar-P	May-P	Jly-P
575	55.5	71.5	86.0	0.30	8.5	15.5
600	31.5	53.5	67.0	1.0	15.5	22.0
625	10.5	38.0	54.0	5.0	24.0	33.5
650	2.5	26.0	42.5	22.0	35.0	43.5
675	0.70	18.0	33.0	45.0	54.5	61.5
700	0.30	12.5	25.5	69.5	73.0	77.5

Est. vol. 2,000, Tues vol. 1,789 calls, 898 puts
Open interest Tues 39,461 calls, 12,170 puts

–FINANCIAL–

BRITISH POUND (IMM) 25,000 pounds; cents per pound

Strike Price	Calls–Settle Mar-c	Apr-c	May-c	Puts–Settle Mar-p	Apr-p	May-p
1700	6.15	....	....	0.70	2.00	....
1725	4.20	....	5.50	1.25	2.95	3.70
1750	2.65	....	....	2.10	4.10	....
1775	1.55	2.50	....	3.40	5.60	....
1800	0.85	1.75	....	5.20	7.30	....
1825	0.50	1.25	....	7.30	19.15	....

Est. vol. 1,855, Tues vol. 1,333 calls, 1,733 puts
Open interest Tues; 21,946 calls, 20,347 puts

W. GERMAN MARK (IMM) 125,000 marks, cents per mark

Strike Price	Calls–Settle Mar-c	Apr-c	May-c	Puts–Settle Mar-p	Apr-p	May-p
57	2.51	....	....	0.19	0.38	....
[illegible]	[illegible]	[illegible]	....	0.37	0.63	....

T-BONDS (CBT) $100,000; points and 64ths of 100%

Strike Price	Calls–Last Mar-c	Jun-c	Sep-c	Puts–Last Mar-p	Jun-p	Sep-p
101	....	....	....	....	....	....

Est. vol. 3,000, Tues vol. 5,119 calls, 1,138 puts
Open interest Tues;45,045 calls, 29,493 puts

–INDEXES–

MUNICIPAL BOND INDEX (CBT) $100,000; pts. & 64ths of 100%

Strike Price	Calls–Settle Mar-c	Jun-c	Sep-c	Puts–Settle Mar-p	Jun-p	Sep-p
88	4-00	3-34	....	0-40	2-51	....
90	2-40	2-30	....	1-21	3-44	....
92	1-33	....	....	....	....	....
94	0-51	....	....	....	....	....
96	....	....	....	....	....	....
98	....	....	....	....	....	....

Est. vol. 190, Tues vol. 963 calls, 820 puts
Open interest Tues;8,551 calls, 9,449 puts

NYSE COMPOSITE INDEX (NYFE) $500 times premium

Strike Price	Calls–Settle Mar-c	Jun-c		Puts–Settle Mar-p	Jun-p	
142	6.90	11.70	....	4.25	8.50	....
144	5.70	10.55	....	4.95	9.15	....
146	4.55	9.45	....	5.95	10.15	....
148	3.50	8.45	....	6.80	11.05	....
150	2.60	7.50	....	7.90	12.10	....
152	2.00	6.70	....	9.10	13.20	....

Est. vol. 60, Tues vol. 46 calls, 62 puts
Open interest Tuesday; 897 calls, 526 puts

S&P 500 STOCK INDEX (CME) $500 times premium

Strike Price	Calls–Settle Feb-c	Mar-c	Jn-c	Puts–Settle Feb-p	Mar-p	Jun-p
250	10.30	14.35	22.90	2.35	6.45	13.95
255	6.55	11.05	20.05	3.50	8.15	15.90
260	3.60	8.15	17.40	5.60	10.25	18.15
265	1.95	5.75	14.95	8.95	12.75	....
270	0.85	3.80	12.70	....	15.80	....
275	0.40	2.45	10.80	....	....	....

Est. vol. 1,951; Tues vol. 810 calls; 2,087 puts
Open interest Tues; 18,805 calls; 19,216 puts

Other Futures Options

Cocoa (CSCE) 10 metric tons; $ per ton

Strike	May-c	Jly-c	Sep-c	May-p	Jly-p	Sep-p
1700	65	167	169	35	102	77

Est. vol. 42. Tues vol. 14. Op. Int. 847.

Pork Bellies (CME) 40,000 lbs.; cents per lb.

Strike	Mar-c	May-c	Jly-c	Mar-p	May-p	Jly-p
58	1.40	[illegible]	[illegible]	[illegible]	[illegible]	[illegible]

Est. vol. 26. Tue[illegible]

Lumber [illegible]

cents/bushel. For the 5,000 bushel contract, the value of the option is, therefore, 5,000 bushels × 22 1/2 cents per bushel, or $1,125.

Buying or selling futures options is quite similar in operation to futures trading. An order to buy or sell is relayed from a broker to a trader on the options exchange floor who attempts in open outcry to fill the order. As with futures, options trading also involves a central clearinghouse jointly owned by exchange members. The clearinghouse is a buyer to every seller and a seller to every buyer.

To exercise an option, the option buyer tenders notice to a clearing member who notifies the clearinghouse. The clearinghouse assigns the notice on a random basis to one or more clearing members with an open short or written position in the same kind of option. The clearing member can assign the notice to one or more of its customers in any manner it chooses as long as a description of this process has been approved by the exchange. Exercise of an option is an overnight transaction; notice received by the clearinghouse by the end of the day is effective on the next business day. At the beginning of trading on this next business day, the two parties in the exercise and assignment have an appropriate short or long position in the underlying futures. Margin on the futures must then be posted, and the positions are marked-to-market at the settlement price at the end of the day.

GENERAL DETERMINANTS OF AN OPTION'S PRICE

As with any speculative contract, the price of an option is determined by the supply and demand for the contract. However, particular determinants of an option's price are derived from the nature of the contract. We discuss an option pricing equation in more detail in a subsequent section and give a general description of the five variables determining the price here.

Obviously, the price of an option depends strongly on the underlying futures price. When the futures price is above a call option strike price, or the futures price is below the put strike price, the option is said to be "in the money." The premium then reflects in part the amount that would be realized if this option were exercised now. This portion of the option premium is its *intrinsic value.* For instance, the T-bond call option discussed previously had an exercise price of 66 and the futures price was 80. In this case, the intrinsic value of the option is 80 less 66, or 14 ($14,000). In addition to this intrinsic value, the premium also reflects a component related to the possibility of future favorable price movement before expiration, the *time value* of the option. Thus, the premium for an "in the money" option consists of both intrinsic and time value. For instance, the T-bond put option discussed earlier has an exercise price of 70 and the futures price is trading at 55. This option may have a premium of 18; 15 represents the intrinsic value (70 − 55), the value realized on exercise, and 3 represents the time value of the option.

An "out of the money" option is a call option with a strike price greater than the current futures price or a put option with a strike price less than the current futures price. For this option the premium consists solely of the time value. For instance, a T-bond put option may have an exercise price of 80 when the T-bond futures price is 90. In this case, there is no intrinsic value in the premium. The premium would still be positive, though small, representing the chance that the futures price may decline to 80 or less before expiration. The premium is never negative.

Time is the second pricing factor. The more time to expiration of the option, the greater is the probability of successful exercise for both puts and calls, and thus the larger is the time value component of the premium.

Besides the underlying futures price and the time to maturity, the option premium is also influenced by the strike price of the option, the third factor. The lower the strike price of a call option, or the higher the strike price of a put option, the greater is the probability of successful exercise and the greater the intrinsic value component of the option price. This can be seen in the comparison of two T-bond put options, one with an exercise price of 80, the other with an exercise price of 90. Obviously, the right to sell at 90 would be more valuable and thus the higher priced option.

A fourth determinant of the option price relates to the volatility of the underlying futures price; the more variable is the futures price, the greater is the probability of successful exercise for both a put or a call. Thus a higher futures price variance contributes to a larger option premium.

The fifth pricing factor is less obvious. Although a call option increases in value as the current futures price rises, actual payment of the strike price is deferred until exercise or expiration of the option. During a call option's life, the intrinsic value of an option depends on the difference between the current futures price and the *present value* of the deferred strike price. The higher the market interest rate, the lower the present value of this deferred payment and the higher the value of the option to the holder. Thus, the value of a call option rises as interest rates rise.

By contrast, during the life of a put option, the intrinsic value depends on the current futures price and the present value of the strike price to be received on exercise or expiration. Thus, in the case of a put option, the present value of the strike price represents a positive cash flow to the put holder. Higher interest rates lower the value of this deferred receipt and thus the value of the put option. In either case, because of the deferred nature of the payment or receipt of the strike price, an option's value depends on the level of market interest rates.

DELTA FACTOR

A commonly used concept in options trading is the delta factor. The delta of an option measures the relationship between a change in the option's price and the change in the underlying futures price. For example, if a call option has a delta of 0.50, this means that a rise of, say, $1,000 in the futures price results in a rise of $500 in the price of the option. Deltas for long call options are positive because a rise in the futures price results in a rise in the call option price. A written call option position, on the other hand, has a negative delta; the written call (the obligation to take a short position in the underlying futures at the fixed exercise price) decreases in value as the futures price rises. Similarly, a put option position has a negative delta because a rise in the futures price is accompanied by a decline in the put option price. A written put obligation to buy the futures at the fixed exercise price has a positive delta; the written put increases in value as the futures price rises.

Because of the complex interaction of time to maturity, interest rates, and other factors in determining the price of an option, the delta of an option is not a stable number. In general, an option at or near the money has a delta around 0.50. As an option becomes increasingly in the money, however, its delta approaches positive or negative one. For a call option, a very high futures price means almost certain exercise. Thus, the call option value reponds very closely to changes in the futures price, approaching a perfect 100 percent correlation as exercise becomes more certain. Similarly, as an option becomes increasingly out of the money, its delta approaches zero. Changes in the futures price affect it less and less as it becomes almost certain that the option will expire without exercise. Time to maturity affects the delta also. As time to maturity decreases, deltas become more unstable and gravitate to one (for an in-the-money option) at an accelerating rate. Option deltas are discussed later when we explain using options in dynamic hedges and in speculative combination strategies.

WHY OPTIONS ON FUTURES?

It may seem that trading options on futures is a rather indirect method of tracking commodity price movements, and that options traded on the physical commodity itself would be a more efficient financial instrument. Two reasons can be given for the emergence of markets in options on futures rather than on actuals: First, options traded on futures are subject to less of a liquidity constraint on exercise. While the cash market supply of any commodity is limited, the available supply deliverable against the option on a futures contract can be expanded to an unlimited extent by futures traders. Thus, potential liquidity problems are much less severe with options on futures. Second, the capital requirements for taking a position on exercise of the option on a futures contract (e.g., posting margin) are typically much smaller than that required for exercise of an option on the commodity itself, which involves posting the entire cash value of the strike price. Options on futures thus allow a greater access to the hedging/speculative opportunities represented in the options market than options on the physical commodity itself.

Nevertheless, there are currently a few commodities in which there is an option on a futures contract and also an option on the actual commodity. For instance, gold has been a very popular commodity for options trading. Options on gold futures currently trade on the Commodities Exchange (COMEX) in New York and at the Chicago Mercantile Exchange (CME) and on several foreign exchanges (Argentina); options on actual gold are traded on the AMEX in New York, as well as in Montreal, Vancouver, and Amsterdam. Similarly, there are options traded on T-bond futures (at the CBOT) and on cash T-bonds (at the CBOE). In addition, there are options on cash commodities, particularly indexes, that have no futures option counterpart.

The development of the options market on futures contracts has broadened considerably the risk-return possibilities available to traders in futures contracts. As we discuss next, the difference in potential profit and loss characteristics between futures and options permits a much wider range of potential outcomes for an individual investor than are available with futures alone.

THE USES OF BUYING PUTS AND CALLS

In analyzing positions in options and combinations of options and futures it is helpful to use a profit diagram. This graphic presentation shows the possible profit from buying or selling an option as a function of changes in the value of the underlying commodity (here, the futures contract). To simplify the profit diagram, the option's value is considered at expiration when there is no time value remaining in the price.

Figure 13–1 portrays the profits and losses possible from a call option as the futures price varies. If the futures price is less than the option exercise price (X) at expiration, the option expires worthless and there is a loss on the call option equal to the premium paid (here, intrinsic value equals 0). As the futures price rises above the exercise price, the intrinsic value of the option becomes positive, and the value of the option rises $1.00 for every dollar increase in the futures price. Break even occurs when the futures price has risen enough to overcome the premium paid for the option, or when the futures price is equal to the exercise price of the option plus the premium paid.

Figure 13–1 shows the profit and loss resulting from a long futures position bought at the exercise price. The profit diagram makes apparent the considerable difference

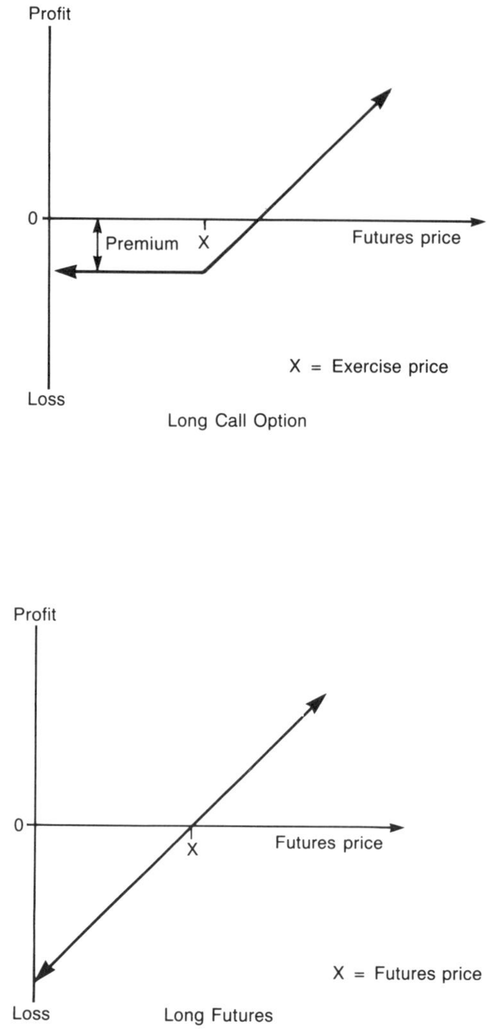

Figure 13-1. Long Call Option and Long Futures

in outcomes possible with a futures contract as opposed to an options contract as the futures price declines.

A similar diagram can be constructed for the put option (see figure 13-2). The put option represents the right to sell at the exercise price. The put expires worthless if the current futures price is greater than the exercise price, because the option holder can sell in the futures market directly at a higher price than the option exercise price. Again, the loss on the option position is equal to the premium paid. Similarly, the

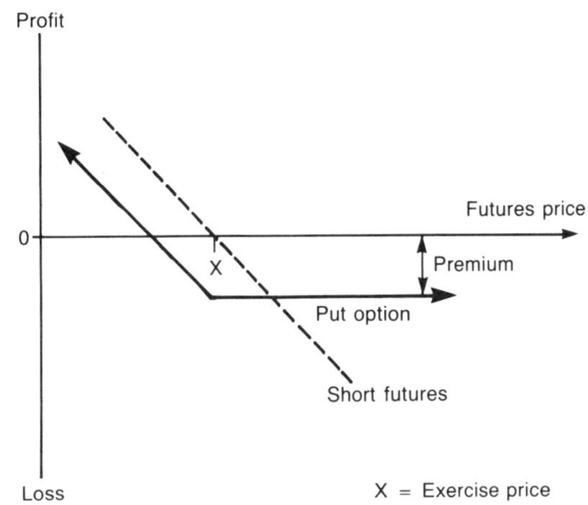

Figure 13-2. Put Option

option gains in intrinsic value, dollar for dollar, as the futures price declines. Break even occurs when the futures price has declined to the exercise price less the premium paid. The put option has positive value if prices decline, yet simply expires if prices increase. This payoff pattern is attractive to an individual who wants to hedge against price declines and still capture upside potential if prices increase.

CALLS

As can be seen from the profit diagram for a call in figure 13-1, this option represents a profit opportunity if the futures price rises. It can be used, then, much like a long futures position, for speculative and hedging purposes. If, for technical or fundamental reasons, speculators feel that a price increase is expected, they can buy a long futures position or buy a call option. The key difference between the strategies is the insurance nature of the call option—once having paid the premium for the option, the speculator's losses are fixed at that amount no matter where the futures price (and the underlying commodity price) settles. The call option holder fixes exactly the maximum loss on the position when it is initiated. In contrast, the long futures position can in theory result in unlimited losses, and the size of the loss, and margin calls if any, are unknown. However, because the call option involves this premium payment, the underlying futures price must rise by at least that amount to break even on the option. For the long futures, no initial payment must be overcome, and any increase in the futures price accrues to the long futures position immediately.

The buyer of a call option has some flexibility in the amount of premium paid and thus the break-even point. Purchase of an out-of-the-money call where the futures price is less than the exercise price involves a smaller premium because the option price involves only the time value. However, the futures price must rise from its current level to the exercise price and beyond before the call's speculative position results in a positive profit. On the other hand, buying an in-the-money call option involves a bigger premium, but the futures price is already above the exercise price. Which of these options to buy depends on the probability of a futures price increase of some size and the relative premiums, which in turn depend strongly on the expected volatility of the underlying futures price.

Similarly, the call option can be used in place of a long futures for hedging purposes. If, for instance, a money manager expects to receive a sum for investment some time in the future, a call option on an interest rate futures contract can be bought now to hedge against a decrease in investment rates (increase in price) between now and the receipt of the funds. If rates do fall, figure 13–1 shows that the call option increases in value and serves to offset the opportunity cost of investment at the now lower rate. Again, there are two major differences between hedging with options and hedging with futures: First, the buyer of a call must pay for this protection at initiation of the hedge with the premium. Second, the loss on the option is limited to the premium paid. Thus, the call option hedge does not fix a rate for the money manager. Instead, the call option establishes a *floor* on the investment rate if rates fall. Table 13–2 illustrates the outcome of a call option hedge.

Assume a money manager expects to receive $1 million in four months, and expects to invest the money in short-term, three-month securities. The expected three-month money market rate is 10 percent, and the money manager would like to hedge against a rate decline over the next four months. The manager can buy an at-the-money Eurodollar futures call option with a premium of 0.30 basis points, or $750 (30 bp × $25/basis point = $750). The manager pays $750, thereby establishing a floor on the investment of 9.7 percent (10% − 0.30 = 9.7%). If rates do fall to 9 percent, the manager will receive only $22,500 in investment income on the $1 million. With the profit on the call option position of $1,750, however, the effective interest rate earned is 9.7 percent. As can be seen from the table, this is the effective interest rate on the investment with the call option no matter how far interest rates fall. Thus, the manager has effectively hedged the fall in rates, and secured a 9.7 percent interest income. If rates remain the same, the money manager can invest at 10 percent but the option premium of $750 lowers the effective rate to 9.7 percent. The real difference in hedging with options rather than futures is illustrated in the case of a *rise* in interest rates. With a rise in rates (decrease in futures prices), the call option expires without exercise. The manager is thus free to invest at the current 11 percent market rate, and the effective rate is reduced only by the cost of the premium (30 basis points). Thus, any rise in rates accrues to the money manager, less the premium paid.

Table 13–2. Hedging Short-Term Rates with a Futures Option

Expected short-term rate: 10%

Eurodollar futures call option:

Exercise price:	90 (10%)
Premium:	0.30 basis points ($750)
Maturity:	4 months from today

Outcomes:

Rates fall to 9% (Price at expiration = 91):

Interest receipt for 3-month investment:
$1,000,000 × 0.09 × (90/360) = $22,500

Proceeds from option:

intrinsic value: (91 − 91) =	100 basis points
less premium:	30 basis points
total:	70 basis points or $1,750

Total interest income: $22,500 + $1,750 = $24,250
Effective interest rate: 9.7%

Rates remain at 10% (Price at expiration = 90):

Interest receipt for 3-month investment:
$1,000,000 × 0.10 × (90/360) = $25,000

Proceeds from option:

intrinsic value: (90 −90) =	0 basis points
less premium:	30 basis points
total:	−30 basis points or $750 loss

Total interest income: $25,000 − $750 = $24,250
Effective interest rate: 9.7%

Rates rise to 11%

Interest receipt for 3-month investment:

$1,000,000 × 0.11 × (90/360) = $27,500

Proceeds from option:

intrinsic value: (90 × 90) =	0 basis points
less premium:	30 basis points
total:	−30 basis point or $750 loss

Total interest income: $27,500 − $750 = $26,700
Effective interest rate: 10.7%

Call options can thus be used to fix a *minimum rate,* or a *maximum price* to be paid, on a financial instrument. This ability is particularly useful to a potential investor or to anyone with an anticipated long position in an underlying financial instrument. This ability can be extended as well to physical commodities: use of a call option effects a *cap* on commodity prices. As we have seen, the call option fixes a maximum price to be paid for the underlying commodity. Thus, any potential buyer of raw materials such as a food processor or miller, can fix a cap or ceiling on input price while retaining the ability to profit from a decline in commodity price.

Figure 13–3 illustrates the expected return and risk (standard deviation of return) of a hedge with a call option. The unhedged position (the $1 million investment in four months) has an expected return of 10 percent, the current expected rate, but there is a possibility of the rate being higher or lower by the time the investment is made. With a call option, the lowest rate possible is 9.7 percent, and the distribution of possible returns is truncated at this point. There is still, however, a possibility of higher returns with the call option, because it will expire worthless, and the cash position will be unhedged, if rates rise. Thus, the distribution of returns with a call option is truncated at the left and skewed to the right. This is in contrast to the hedge with a long futures position; the expected return for a perfect hedge (dollar equivalence) results in a fixed rate of 10 percent.

Which instrument, futures or option, is better for hedging? Table 13–3 contrasts the results of a physical commodity hedge using options and futures.

Table 13–3 illustrates a long hedge in corn futures from chapter 8, example 7, and the results of the same hedge using a call option in place of futures. The cash price of corn as of April, the initiation of the hedge, is $2.74 per bushel, and the processor hedges a planned July purchase by buying a July corn futures contract at $2.95 per bushel. At the end of the hedge, with a cash corn price in July of $2.99, the hedger's effective cash price with the futures hedge is $2.84 ($2.99 less the gain in the futures market of 0.15 equal to $2.84, or in another expression, $2.74 plus a change in basis of 0.10 = $2.84).

As with the futures contract, the call option gains in value if cash corn prices rise and serves to offset the higher grain price the processor must now pay. Using a July 2.90 call option with a price of $0.07 5/8, the effective cash price is higher than with futures, $2.86 5/8 ($2.99 less the net 12 3/8 gain on the call option).

It will always be true that the ceiling price fixed by the option will be greater than that fixed by the futures; the difference is the time value of the option premium, here $0.02 5/8. We can see this by comparing the price fixed with the two instruments.

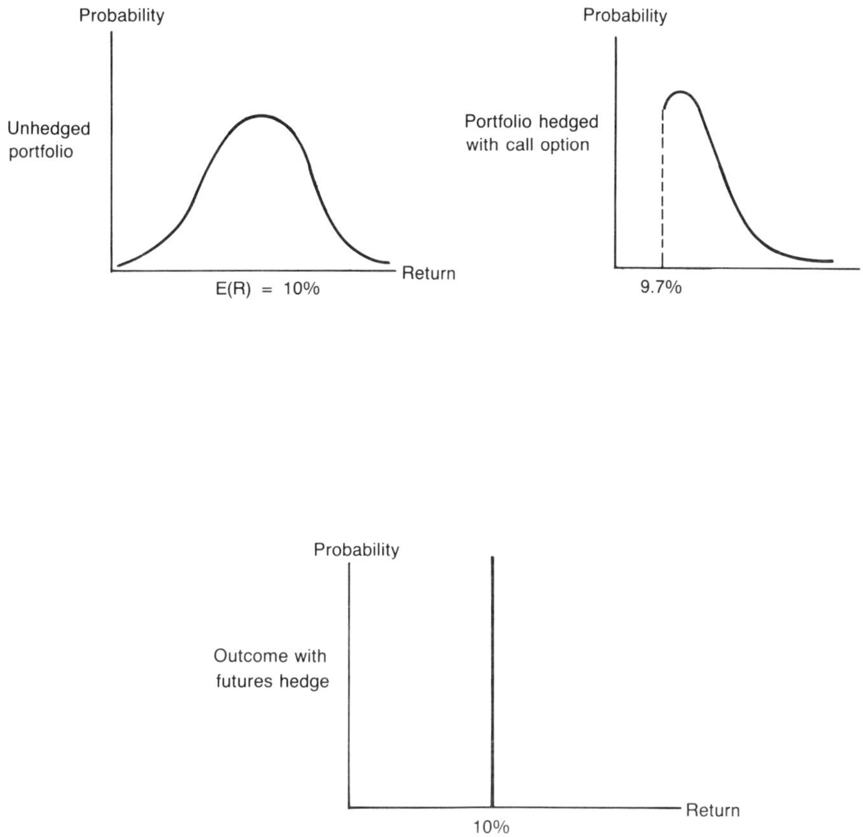

Figure 13-3. Expected Return and Risk

As we have seen, the price fixed in the futures market, P_f, is equal to the cash price at the initiation of the hedge (S_1) plus the change in the spot price ($S_2 - S_1$) less the change in the futures price ($F_2 - F_1$):

$$P_f = S_1 + (S_2 - S_1) - (F_2 - F_1) \tag{13-1}$$

For the call option, the price fixed is the final spot price, S_2, (here, \$2.99) plus the premium paid, *Prem*, (7 5/8) less the worth of the option at expiration ($F_2 - X$), the final futures price F_2 less the exercise price X, (here 3.10 − 2.90):

$$P_{opt} = S_2 + Prem - (F_2 - X) \tag{13-2}$$

Table 13-3. Hedging with Futures and Options

Situation: Date: April 1		
Current cash price = \$2.74/bushel		
July futures price = \$2.95/bushel		
July 2.90 call option price = 7 5/8 cents/bushel		
Outcomes:	*Price increase*	*Price decrease*
Prices at July maturity:		
Cash	\$2.99	\$2.50
Futures	3.10	2.61
Strategy		
Long futures hedge		
Cash gain/(loss)	(\$0.25)	\$0.24
Futures gain/(loss)	0.15	(0.34)
Final price to buyer	\$2.84	\$2.84
Put option hedge		
Cash gain/(loss)	(\$0.25)	\$0.24
Option final value	0.20	0.00
Option premium paid	(0.07625)	(0.07625)
Option gain/(loss)	0.12375	(0.07625)
Final price to buyer	\$2.86625	\$2.57625

We can rewrite equation 13-2 to show its similarity to equation 13-1. Note that the premium is equal to the time value (TV) plus the intrinsic value when it is purchased $(F_1 - X)$. In addition, the spot price at the end of the hedge is equal to the initial spot price plus the change in the spot price over the hedge period $(S_2 = S_1 + (S_2 - S_1))$. Substituting these into equation 13-2:

$$P_{opt} = S_1 + (S_2 - S_1) + TV + (F_1 - X) - (F_2 - X) \tag{13-3}$$

and simplifying:

$$P_{opt} = S_1 + (S_2 - S_1) - (F_2 - F_1) + TV \tag{13-4}$$

Note that the difference between the ceiling price of the option in equation 13-4 and the ceiling price of the futures in equation 13-1 is the time value. Although the ceiling price fixed is higher for the option, the real advantage of the option over the futures is evident if the cash price falls. (See table 13-3). If the spot price falls to \$2.50 between April and July, the effective cash price is still \$2.84 (\$2.50 plus the futures market loss of 0.34) with the long futures position. With the call option, however, the processor is able to participate in any favorable cash price declines. The call option merely expires without exercise and the processor loses the premium paid. In this case, the effective cash price is \$2.50 plus the premium paid, 7 5/8, or \$2.57 5/8. Again, when the processor uses options to hedge, a ceiling price is established for the cash transaction. This is in contrast to the futures hedge in which, depending on the basis, the hedger "locks in" a price for the cash transaction regardless of what cash price eventually occurs.

There are other, institutional differences between using futures and options. The cash flow can differ considerably over the life of the hedge between the two instruments. The option hedger is not liable for margin calls as would have been the case for the futures hedger in our example when prices fell. The option buyer is required to pay only the initial option premium no matter what movements occur in the cash price. However, the option buyer is required to pay the purchase price at initiation; the futures user is required to post margin, which can take the form of interest-bearing assets. Thus, the initial cash flow is less with futures. Finally, the option hedger has a choice of strike prices and option premiums to use to structure the hedge. The hedger could have used a call option that was out of the money (with a strike price greater than \$2.95) for which a smaller premium would have been paid. However, using this option affects the ceiling price achieved. Such an option lowers the price at which its favorable effect comes into play. The processor would fix a higher price of purchase.

Hedging with options may require an adjustment to the hedge ratio similar to those discussed in chapter 10 for interest rate futures. In the case of options, the adjustment depends on the delta factor of the option. The delta factor relates to the expected percentage change in the premium of the option to the percentage change in the futures price. If a call option delta is 0.50, for example, this means that the call option increases in value by \$0.50 when the futures price increases by \$1. Deltas are especially important in hedging if the option is going to be sold before expiration. This is because the difference between purchase and sale premium on the option is directly related to changes in the futures price through the delta. If the option is held to maturity, the delta will be close to 1 or 0.

In hedging, the expected change in the value of the options position should be matched to the change in the underlying futures price. For instance, if the delta of the option used for hedging is 0.50, two options should be used so that the change in value of the total options position (2×0.50, or 1.00) is equal to the change in the futures (1.00). In the corn hedge example discussed earlier, the delta of the option at initiation was 0.71, so only one options contract should be used, although the hedge was held to maturity of the option. This calculation also assumes that the futures price underlying the option and the spot commodity being hedged are highly correlated, and do not require adjustment in their relative price volatility. The numerical calculation of deltas for options is discussed in greater detail in the pricing section of this chapter. Of course, the greater the number of options contracts bought or sold to hedge, the greater the commission charges and the larger the total premium paid.

PUTS

Just as a call option can substitute for a long futures position or a long hedge, a put option can substitute for a short futures or short hedge. If prices are expected to fall, the speculator can purchase a put option. As figure 13–2 shows, the purchase of an at-the-money put option has the same profit potential as a short futures position if the price does decline (adjusted by the premium paid for the option). Again, the put holder has an advantage if prices move up. If prices rise, the put holder suffers only the loss of the premium, while the futures position has, in theory, unlimited loses.

Thus, the use of a put option rather than a short futures to speculate depends on several factors. A put holder does not begin to profit from the position until the premium is overcome, so the choice of option or futures depends in part on the size of the premium paid compared to the expected decline in value of the futures. The choice also depends on the expected likelihood of an adverse price move. Finally, as discussed in the case of a call, the cash flows differ; an option position requires a large initial cash flow (premium) but there is no possibility of any other cash flow (margin call) over the life of the speculative position.

A put option can also substitute for a short futures hedge. Table 13–4 illustrates the use of a put option on T-bonds. In the example, the effect of differences in exercise price is also discussed. Assume that a portfolio manager holds $10 million face value of a Treasury bond, the 8 3/4 percent with a thirty-year maturity. The current price of the bonds is 99.7, while the futures price is 89 22/32. The manager would like the hedged position to retain a value for the bonds as close to $99,700, the current price, as possible. The manager believes rates will rise in the next six weeks (bond prices will fall) and wants to hedge short or buy put options to protect the value of the portfolio. Assume that the manager buys 10 put options; the choices regarding premium and exercise price are listed in the table. At the end of six weeks, the options expire and the futures enter the delivery month. The results are given for two final cash bond prices, 95 (yields have risen to 9.40 percent), and 99 (yields have risen slightly to 8.95 percent).

Because the underlying asset on the option was the futures rather than the spot, the fall in value of the spot was not hedged completely. While the cash bond fell from $99,700 to $95,000, the futures price fell by only approximately half that, from $89,687.50 to $87,600. This highlights one of the problems with hedging cash with an option on the futures: unless the cash and futures move by the same amount (the basis is stable), the hedge is not exact. In this case, the best hedge was the option that was the most in the money at initiation; the intrinsic value at expiration more

Table 13-4. Treasury Bond Hedge, Differing Exercise Prices

Current Treasury bond price (8 3/4%, 30-year):	99.7 (8.82%)
Current futures price:	89 22/32 (89.6875) (9.131%)

Options available (all prices expressed in percent of par):

		Final price at expiration	
		Bond = 95	*Bond* = 99
Exercise price	*Premium*	*FP* = 87.6	*FP* = 91.25
86	16/64 ($250)	0	0
88	38/64 ($593.75)	400	0
90	1 18/64 ($1,812.50)	$2,400	0
92	2 35/64 ($2,546.875)	$4,400	$750

Effective cash bond value (Cash price at 95.00):

Exercise price	
86	$95,000 + $0 − $250 = $94,750
88	$95,000 + $400 − $593.75 = $94,806.25
90	$95,000 + $2,400 − $1,812.50 = $95,587.50
92	$95,000 + $4,400 − $2,546.875 = $96,853.125

Effective cash bond value (Cash price at 99.00):

Exercise price	
86	$99,000 + $0 − $250 = $98,750
88	$99,000 + $0 − $593.75 = $98,406.25
90	$99,000 + $0 − $1,812.50 = $97,187.50
92	$99,000 + $750 − $2,546.875 − $97,203.125

than made up for the higher premium paid for it; the final hedged value of the bond was $96,853, compared to the initial value of $99,700. With a final cash price of $99,000, on the other hand, most of the options were not hedges at all, and the premium represents almost a dead loss.

As the example shows, the success of the options hedge depends on the relative changes in the price of the cash item being hedged compared to the futures underlying the option. As to the exercise price, the choice depends on the relative premiums to be paid for the higher protection against the probable move in the futures price over the hedge period. As the example shows, heding with options can be expensive if the cash price remains relatively close to its initial value.

Figure 13-4 illustrates the expected risk and return of a hedge with a put option. Although the unhedged position has an expected return of 8.8 percent, there is a possibility that interest rates will change. If rates rise, the value of the bond falls, and the overall return on the bond could be less than 8.80 percent. Similarly, if interest rates fall, the value of the bond rises, and the overall return could be greater than 8.80 percent. With a long put option in combination with the bond portfolio, the possible returns are truncated: because the put has value (after the premium) if prices fall, the option position makes up the cash loss. Thus, the put option fixes a floor price for the bond—$96,853 in the example—or a lower limit on the possible rate of return on the portfolio. On the other hand, the upside potential of the portfolio if prices rise and rates fall is left intact after the premium.

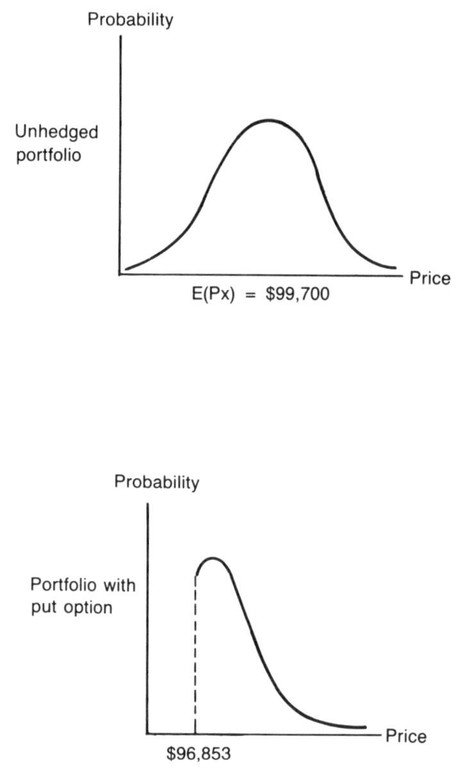

Figure 13-4. Expected Price and Risk (Short Hedge)

WRITING PUTS AND CALLS

On exercise, the seller or writer of an option is obligated to take a futures position opposite that of the option holder. Thus, writing a call obligates the seller to establish a short position as the other side of the call option holder's long futures position. The writer can either sell a covered option by possessing the underlying futures position when the option is written, or a naked option by acquiring the futures position only if the options is exercised by the buyer. The potential profit and risk on a covered option differs considerably from that of a naked option.

The profit diagram for writing a naked call option is given in figure 13-5. If the futures price is less than the exercise price at the expiration of a call option, the call option is not exercised and the writer is allowed to keep the full premium received. This is the maximum profit possible from writing a call option. However, writing an uncovered call exposes the writer to the risk of loss if the price of the futures contract rises. With a futures price greater than the exercise price at expiration, the call will be exercised. The option writer must then go to the futures market and buy a futures contract at the current futures price and resell it to the call option holder at the (lower) exercise price, thus incurring a loss. The loss due to the acquisition and resale of the futures contract may be covered by the premium received, but once the premium is exhausted, the potential loss is unlimited. Because of this large loss potential, the writer of a naked option must post both the margin on the potential underlying futures position and the full option premium received.

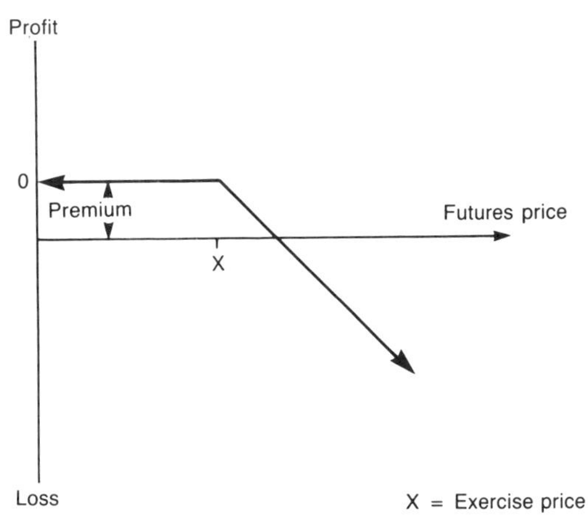

Figure 13-5. Written Call Option (Uncovered)

Maximum profit for writing an uncovered call option occurs if prices remain constant or decline. Because of the limited profit resulting from a price decline with this option position, the motivation for this strategy arises primarily from the possibility of an enhanced return to capital from collecting premiums rather than outright price speculation. An option writer tends to be better capitalized than an option holder because of the margin involved. Table 13–5 gives a numerical example of the profit and loss from writing a naked call.

For example, a speculator who follows the live cattle market decides to enhance investment income by writing a call option on the nearby live cattle futures contract. Currently, the speculator has no position in cattle futures. The current futures price is 60.50 dollars/hundredweight (cwt), and the premium on selling one call option with exercise price equal to 58 is $3.25/cwt (equal to $1,300 on the contract). If the futures price at expiration of the option is 58 or lower, the option expires without exercise and the speculator keeps the 3.25 premium. However, if the futures price at expiration is 60, the option is exercised. The speculator must go to the futures market and go long a live cattle futures at the current futures price of 60 and immediately sell or offset at the exercise price of 58. The speculator loses $2/cwt on the option exercise; the net premium income is reduced by 2 to 1.25 (equal to $500). If the futures price is even higher at expiration, at 62, the option exercise costs the speculator 62 − 58, or $4/cwt. This results in a net loss on the written call of 4 − 3.25, or 0.75 ($300). Each dollar increase in the futures price results in a further loss of $400 on the written call.

The profit diagram on a naked put option is given in figure 13–6. A similar line of reasoning applies to the put writer. The writer retains the premium if the futures

Table 13–5. Writing an Uncovered Call
(dollars/hundredweight)

Current nearby futures price: 60.50
Live cattle futures option price (X = 58) = 3.25

Profit/(loss) on position at option expiration:

	Final futures price			
	56	*58*	*60**	*62**
Premium received	3.25	3.25	3.25	3.25
Loss on exercise	0.00	0.00	(2.00)	(4.00)
Net profit/(loss)	3.25	3.25	1.25	(0.75)

*In the money at expiration and exercised.

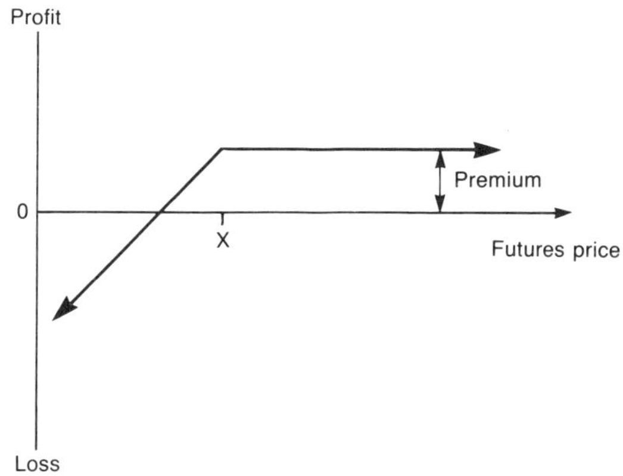

Figure 13-6. Written Put Option (Uncovered)

price is greater than the exercise price at expiration; but if the futures price is less than the exercise price at expiration, and the option is exercised, losses occur. The writer is then obliged to go to the futures market, sell a futures contract at the current futures price, and then offset by buying at the higher exercise price in fulfillment of the options contract, incurring a loss. With a put, the writer generates income if futures prices rise or remain constant.

Writing a *covered* option differs from the naked strategy because the profit or loss arising from the underlying futures position is combined with the profit or loss from the option. For instance, assume the holder of a long futures position sells a call option on the futures with an exercise price equal to the initial futures price (see figure 13-7). For this covered call option, a futures price greater than the exercise price at expiration results in a net gain on the total position. The option writer simply offsets, or sells, the long futures contract at the acquisition price, the exercise price, and retains only the premium. The futures gain is offset by the option loss, except for the premium. However, if the futures price declines to less than the exercise price, losses on the total position can result. In this case, the option is not exercised but the option writer/long futures holder suffers losses on the long futures position. The premium income from the option can cover part of the loss on the futures contract, but beyond this the losses on the long futures contract are unlimited. This is in contrast to the naked call writer for whom maximum losses occur if the futures price rises and the writer is obliged on exercise to buy and then resell the futures contract for a loss. However, in either case the maximum profit involved in writing the option is the premium received. A similar line of reasoning holds for writing covered put

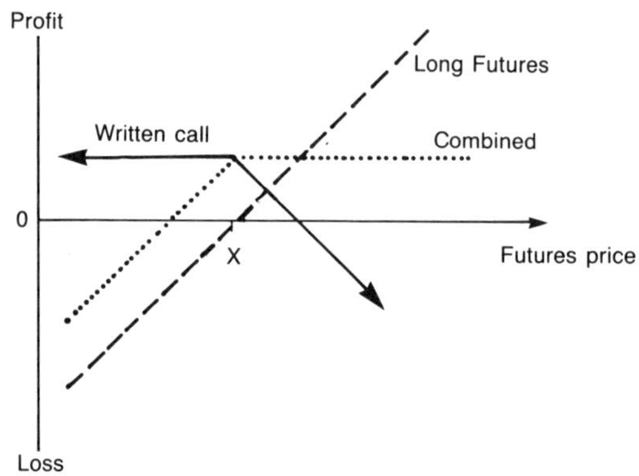

Figure 13-7. Long Futures, Written Call Combined

options. A numerical example of the profit from writing a covered call is given in table 13-6.

Assume that an investment firm is holding both physical gold and long gold futures in anticipation of a long-run increase in gold prices. However, for the next six weeks, the firm expects little movement in gold prices as traders wait for another price-setting meeting of OPEC. Gold futures options are traded at the COMEX; a portfolio manager decides to write a covered call with an exercise price equal to the current price of the nearby gold futures, $460/oz. The premium received is $9.80 per ounce for the contract, equal to $9,800 on the 100 ounce contract. Gold futures would have to increase in price to $460 plus $9.80, or $469.80 at expiration before the combined position would generate a net profit less than that of the gold futures held alone. Obviously, the portfolio manager would write the call only if it were felt that futures prices would remain within the range of $460 to $469.80. If futures prices fall, the written option serves as a partial hedge on the value of the futures due to the $9,800 premium received. However, if the futures price falls below $460 less $9.80, or $450.2, the combined position will begin to suffer a loss as well.

Finally, the profit diagram for the combined position (long futures, written call) is identical to that of a written put (figure 13-6). As we discuss later, this ability to generate an equivalent put option position through a combination of a long futures and a written call allows us to derive a relationship between the price of a put option and the price of a call option plus the underlying futures, called the put-call parity.

Writing covered calls has become a popular way to enhance bond portfolio return. Indeed, it is so prevalent that regular "buy-write" programs are instituted to time the writing of calls for maximum premium income. If the price of the underlying futures

Table 13-6. Writing a Covered Call
(dollars/oz.)

Current nearby futures price = 460.0
Gold futures option (X = 460) 9.8

Profit/(loss) on position at option expiration:

	Final futures price			
	455	*460*	*465**	*470**
Premium received	9.8	9.8	9.8	9.8
Futures profit/(loss)	(5.0)	(0.0)	5.0	10.0
Option profit/(loss)	0.0	0.0	(5.0)	(10.0)
Net profit/(loss)	4.8	9.8	9.8	9.8
Profit/(loss) on gold futures held alone	(5.0)	0.0	5.0	10.0

*Option is in the money at expiration and is exercised.

is expected to remain relatively stable—that is, interest rates are expected to remain at the same level or fall slightly—the portfolio holder can increase the return to the portfolio by writing calls. The same strategy for stock index futures options can enhance the return if stock prices are expected to remain the same or increase slightly. The probability of exercise if there is an adverse price move can be reduced by writing an out-of-the-money option, one whose exercise price is away from the current futures price. Of course, the premium income on such an option is less.

Besides using simple options positions to speculate, hedge, or increase investment income, it is also possible to use combinations of futures options to achieve a variety of risk-return profiles. The following section describes a purely speculative strategy, straddles, and the next section discusses spreads in options and their uses.

STRADDLES

A straddle in the options market involves the purchase or sale of two options contracts, a put and call, with the same exercise price and the same maturity. A buy straddle involves buying a put and call option. Either half of the straddle, called a leg, can be entered into separately.

BUY STRADDLE. With a buy straddle in options, it is possible for the straddle holder to have the right to both a long and a short position in the underlying futures contract for the same delivery and the same contract price. This position and the corresponding profit/loss potential is obviously not available to the speculator using the futures market alone.

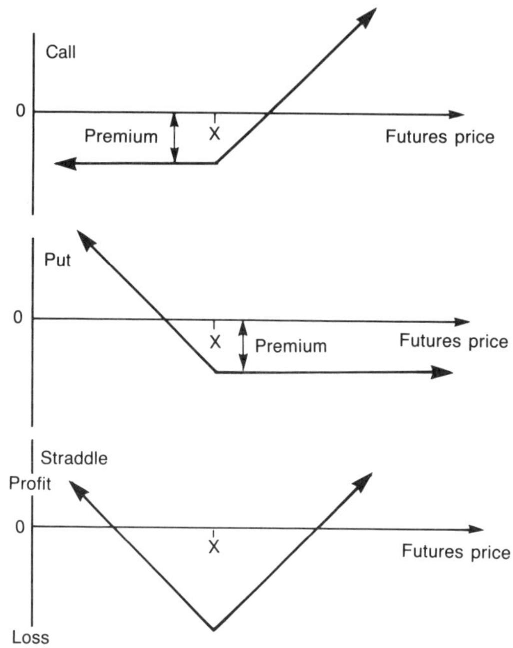

Figure 13-8. Buy Straddle

A buy straddle allows the options holder to profit from major price moves in the underlying futures contract in either direction. The profit potential of this strategy is portrayed in figure 13-8 and consists of the put and call diagrams combined. At a futures price less than the exercise price, the call option portion of the straddle expires without exercise and the straddle position reflects the profit potential of the put option alone (less the two premiums). Similarly, at a futures price greater than the exercise price, the put option portion of the straddle expires worthless and the total profit on the straddle reflects the profit on the call option less the two premiums. Thus, on a net profit basis, the straddle results in a V-shaped profit pattern, with unlimited profit potential at futures prices away from the exercise price in either direction. Because the straddle involves buying two options, the put and the call, the largest possible loss on the straddle is equal to the combined premium of the two options. This maximum loss occurs at the point where the futures price at expiration equals the strike price. Break even occurs at the point where the futures price has risen or fallen by more than the two premiums paid. A buy straddle is used, then, when major price movement is expected. A numerical example of a buy straddle is presented in table 13-7.

Table 13-7. Buying a Straddle
(dollars/barrel)

Current nearby futures price = 20.19
Gasoline futures option price (X = 20): Put = 0.54
Call = 1.72

Buy straddle: buy put and call with same exercise price

Profit / (loss) on position at option expiration:

	Final futures price				
	16	*18*	*20*	*22*	*24*
Premium paid	(2.26)	(2.26)	(2.26)	(2.26)	(2.26)
Profit on call	0.00	0.00	0.00	2.00	4.00
Profit on put	4.00	2.00	0.00	0.00	0.00
Net profit / (loss)	1.74	(0.26)	(2.26)	(0.26)	1.74

Assume a speculator has been following the oil market for the past year. Recently, OPEC has had difficulty in formulating a pricing strategy that its members can agree to. If the current framework falls apart, Saudi Arabia may increase production substantially, driving oil prices to record lows. However, a Bahrainese terrorist group has threatened to block the Straits of Hormuz; this would cause oil prices to skyrocket. The speculator decides that a buy straddle is the best strategy in this situation. With the current nearby futures contract at $20.19 per barrel, the speculator can buy a slightly out-of-the-money put (with exercise price equal to $20) for $0.54, and buy an in-the-money call (with exercise price equal to $20) for $1.72, for a combined premium of $2.26. The futures price must rise to $22.26 before the straddle is profitable on the upside. The price must decline to $20 less $2.26, or $17.74, before the straddle is profitable on the downside. As shown in table 13-7, at a futures price of $22 the call option enables the speculator to take a long futures position at an exercise price of $20 and offset at $22, making $2 on the exercise. This does not quite overcome the premium paid, and the straddle results in a net loss of $0.26. If the futures price declines to $16, on the other hand, the put enables the speculator to sell the futures at $20, and offset at $16, for a profit of $4 on the put exercise. The overall profit on the straddle is $4 less $2.26, or $1.74.

SELL STRADDLE. A sell straddle, on the other hand, involves the simultaneous sale of a put and call with the same exercise price and expiration (see figure 13-9). It arises from the income-generating possibilities of writing options, in this case both puts and calls. Again, the combined position is a simple addition of the individual written put and call shown in figures 13-5 and 13-6. Here, if the futures price at expiration is equal to the exercise price of the two options, neither the put nor the call can be exercised and the seller retains both the premiums paid. This represents the maximum profit possible on the sell straddle. However, it is most unusual for a futures price to

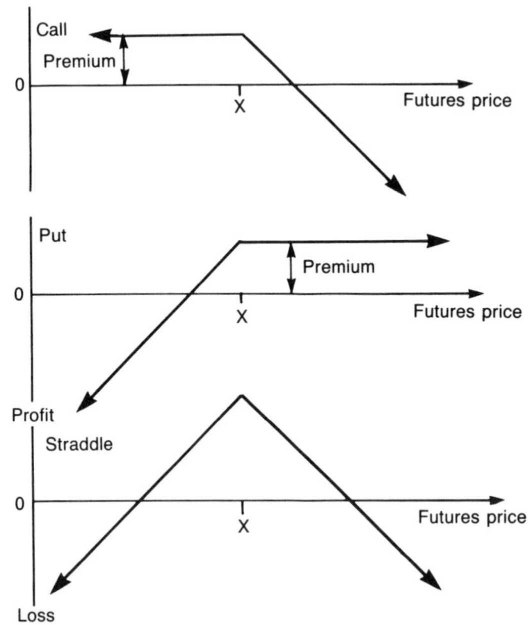

Figure 13–9. Sell Straddle

remain at a certain level over time. Thus, if the futures price rises, and at expiration is greater than the exercise price, the call option is in the money and can be exercised against the option seller while the put option expires worthless. The profit on the combined position reflects the premiums received for the options less the loss on the call option. Thus, the straddle seller gains a positive profit if the futures price changes by less than the two premiums received. Similar reasoning applies to the outcome if the futures price declines. In this case, the put option portion generates losses and the combined position reflects the two premiums received less the loss on the put. A sell straddle, then, is a strategy used to profit during those times when futures prices are expected to remain nearly unchanged. A numerical example of a sell straddle is given in table 13–8.

In table 13–8, an investor with interests in the soybean market decides that prices will remain fairly stable over the next month. The current nearby futures price is at 527 cents per bushel. The investor writes two options for their premium, a put with exercise price equal to 525 cents per bushel for 12¾ cents per bushel (equal to $637.50 on the 5,000 bushel contract) and a call with an exercise price of 525 for 15¾ (equal to $787.50). The investor receives a total of 28½ ($1,425) in income premium. This is the maximum profit. If futures prices rise to 525 plus 28½, or 553½, the straddle produces a net loss. There is a loss as well if the futures price is less than 525 minus 28½, or 496½.

Table 13-8. Selling a Straddle
(cents/bushel)

Current nearby futures price = 527
Soybean futures option price (X = 525): Put = 12¾
Call = 15¾
Sell straddle: sell put and call with same exercise price
Profit / (loss) on position at option expiration:

	Final futures price				
	495	*500*	*525*	*550*	*575*
Premium received	28.50	28.50	28.50	28.50	28.50
Profit / (loss) on call	0.00	0.00	0.00	(25.00)	(50.00)
Profit / (loss) on put	(50.00)	(25.00)	0.00	0.00	0.00
Net profit / (loss)	(21.50)	3.50	28.50	3.50	(21.50)

It is evident that the expected profit from the sell straddle is vulnerable to movements in the underlying futures price. It is possible to use the delta factor discussed earlier to partially insulate a straddle profit from these movements, and to allow the writer of the sell straddle to profit from the declining time value of the written options as they near expiration.

Under a "delta neutral" strategy, the writer of the sell straddle should seek to sell puts and calls in a ratio to maintain an aggregate delta of zero. If the individual deltas of the options contracts in the straddle sum to zero, as the futures price moves away from the options exercise price the positive or negative change in the option value should then cancel out. What is left for the straddle writer in this case is to wait for the options to expire. If the straddle writer succeeds in keeping the position's delta at zero until expiration, then the trader retains the full amount of the time value of the options' premiums even if the futures price has moved away from the exercise price.

This "delta neutral" strategy must be a dynamic one. Because deltas of individual options change as the futures price and time to maturity change, the position usually has to be adjusted by selling or buying puts and calls to maintain the overall zero delta through time. Similar to a pure sell straddle, this strategy works best in markets in which there are no sudden large movements in the underlying futures price.

Because neither written option is covered in a simple straddle, the margin requirements for a naked sell straddle are quite high: initial margin for one futures contract and the two premiums received for the options. Margin requirements change as futures prices move away from the exercise price, resulting in the necessity to post additional margins.

SPREADS

A spread involves the purchase and sale of two options, either two calls or two puts. Two spread trades are possible with options: One, the horizontal or calendar spread, involves the simultaneous purchase and sale of two calls or two puts differing only by maturity. The second spread is the vertical spread involving the simultaneous purchase and sale of two calls or two puts differing only in exercise price. (The term *vertical* probably arose from the placement of the options prices on the newspaper page; see table 13–1).

As with spreads in futures, the speculator or spreader in options expects to make a profit through changes in the price difference, or spread, between the two instruments through time. For a vertical spread, the change in the spread comes about through differences in the responsiveness of options prices to changes in the underlying futures price. That is, the price of the bought option is expected to increase more than the price of the sold option as futures prices change. In other words, the bought option has a higher delta in absolute value than the sold option. For a horizontal spread, on the other hand, the change in the spread comes about through time decay, the speed at which the time value component decreases.

Because a spread involves both a purchase and a sale of an option, the spreader has either a positive or negative cash flow at the initiation of the spread. If the option purchased costs more than that written, then the spreader has "bought the spread" or paid to set up the initial transaction. If the option purchased costs less, then the spreader has "sold the spread" and receives a cash flow at the initiation of the spread.

HORIZONTAL SPREADS. The economic rationale for the horizontal or time spread involves the speed at which the time value component of an option's price decreases. The time value component of a nearby maturity option always decreases at a rate faster than that of the more deferred maturity option, assuming that nothing else changes, including the underlying futures price. This is because the time value of an option is proportionate to the square root of the time to maturity. Thus, if a one-month maturity S&P100 option has a time value of $100, a four-month maturity option has a time value of $200. The time value increases as a function of the square root of time to maturity, in this case $\sqrt{4}$, or 2 times. Similarly, the time value of a nine-month maturity option would be $\sqrt{9}$ times that of a one-month maturity option, or $300.

For any holding period, the price of the nearby option should decline more quickly than the price of the deferred. Thus, over time, it is expected that the spread between the two options will widen. The classic time spread involves writing a short-term option while purchasing a long-term option. For instance, the speculator could write an at-the-money one-month S&P100 option for $150 and simultaneously buy an

Table 13-9. Horizontal Spread
(1 index point = $100)

Current index level = 305
Index option price: Nearby = (X = 305) = 1.50
Deferred = (X = 305) = 2.50

Horizontal spread: Buy deferred option and sell nearby with same exercise price
Profit / (loss) on position at first option expiration:

	Final Index Value	
	305	*350*
Net premium	(1.00)	(1.00)
Value at first option expiration		
Nearby	0.00	45.00
Deferred	1.73	45.50
Net / (loss)	0.73	(0.50)

at-the-money four-month option for $250. (See table 13-9.) The speculator has bought the spread, and the initial spread between option premiums is $100. If the S&P100 futures price remains unchanged at 305, the one-month option expires without being exercised and the premium is retained. The four-month option also declines in value as it becomes a three-month option, but the loss on the long option is not as large as the premium retained on the one-month: the time value component has decreased from $200 to $173 ($\sqrt{3}$, or 1.73 times $100) for a loss of $27. Here, then, the spread has widened from $100 at initiation to $173 ($173 less $0). The profit on the spread was $73 (change in the spread, or the premium kept, $100, less the loss on the option remaining ($27)). In percentage terms, the spreader received $73 on a one-month net investment of $100.

The major risk involved in the time spread involves the possibility of a large increase in the underlying futures price. Because the short-term option has little time value to its premium, a futures price increase, involving an increase in intrinsic value, causes the nearer term option to increase more rapidly than the deferred. In other words, the delta of the in-the-money option closer to maturity is nearer to 1.0. In this case, it is possible for the loss on the nearby written option to be greater than the gain on the long deferred. If the S&P100 had risen to 350, both options might be trading near their intrinsic value of $45, narrowing the spread to near 0. The result of the spread in this case in shown in table 13-9. Note the larger relative increase in the price of the short-term option in response to the rise in the index value. Despite the decay in the time premium over the month, it rose in value from 1.5, or $150, to 4.5, or $450, while the longer term rose from 2.5 to 4.55. The spread narrowed rather than widened as expected, going from $100 to $50.

Table 13-10. Call Bull Spread
(cents/ounce)

Current nearby futures price = 773
Silver futures option prices: Calls (X = 800) = 15
(X = 750) = 38.5
Puts (X = 800) = 37.5
(X = 750) = 11

Bull spread: Buy 750 call for 38.5
Sell 800 call for 15

Profit / (loss) on position at option expiration:

	Final futures price				
	725	*750*	*775*	*800*	*825*
Premium received	(23.5)	(23.5)	(23.5)	(23.5)	(23.5)
Profit / (loss) on 750	0.0	0.0	25.0	50.0	75.0
Profit / (loss) on 800	0.0	0.0	0.0	0.0	(25.0)
Net profit / (loss)	(23.5)	(23.5)	1.5	26.5	26.5

It is also possible to implement a reverse calendar spread by buying the nearby and writing the deferred. This strategy would be successful if the futures price rallied in the short term. In this case, the spread would generate profits based on market judgment rather than on the mathematics of time value movement. However, with the reverse time spread, the margin requirements change dramatically after the expiration of the short-term leg of the spread. After expiration, the speculator is exposed to the risks of a naked written option position (the deferred).

VERTICAL SPREAD. Unlike the time spread, the construction of a vertical spread can be shown on a profit diagram. There are two vertical spreads, bull or bear, depending on the relative size of the exercise prices of the puts or calls. The bullish spread results in positive profits as the futures price rises; the bearish when the futures price falls.

BULL SPREAD. Both the bull and the bear spread can be constructed from two put or call options. Figure 13-10 shows the construction of the bull spread using two calls and the bull spread using two puts. A call bull spread involves buying the call with the lower exercise price (X_l) and selling the call with the higher exercise price (X_h). Being bullish, one would want to buy the option with the most upward potential. In this case, this involves buying the call with the lower exercise price. Because the purchased call has a higher profit potential (a lower exercise price), the premium paid for it is greater than that received from the written call; the bullish speculator buys the spread. If both options expire without being exercised, that is, the futures price

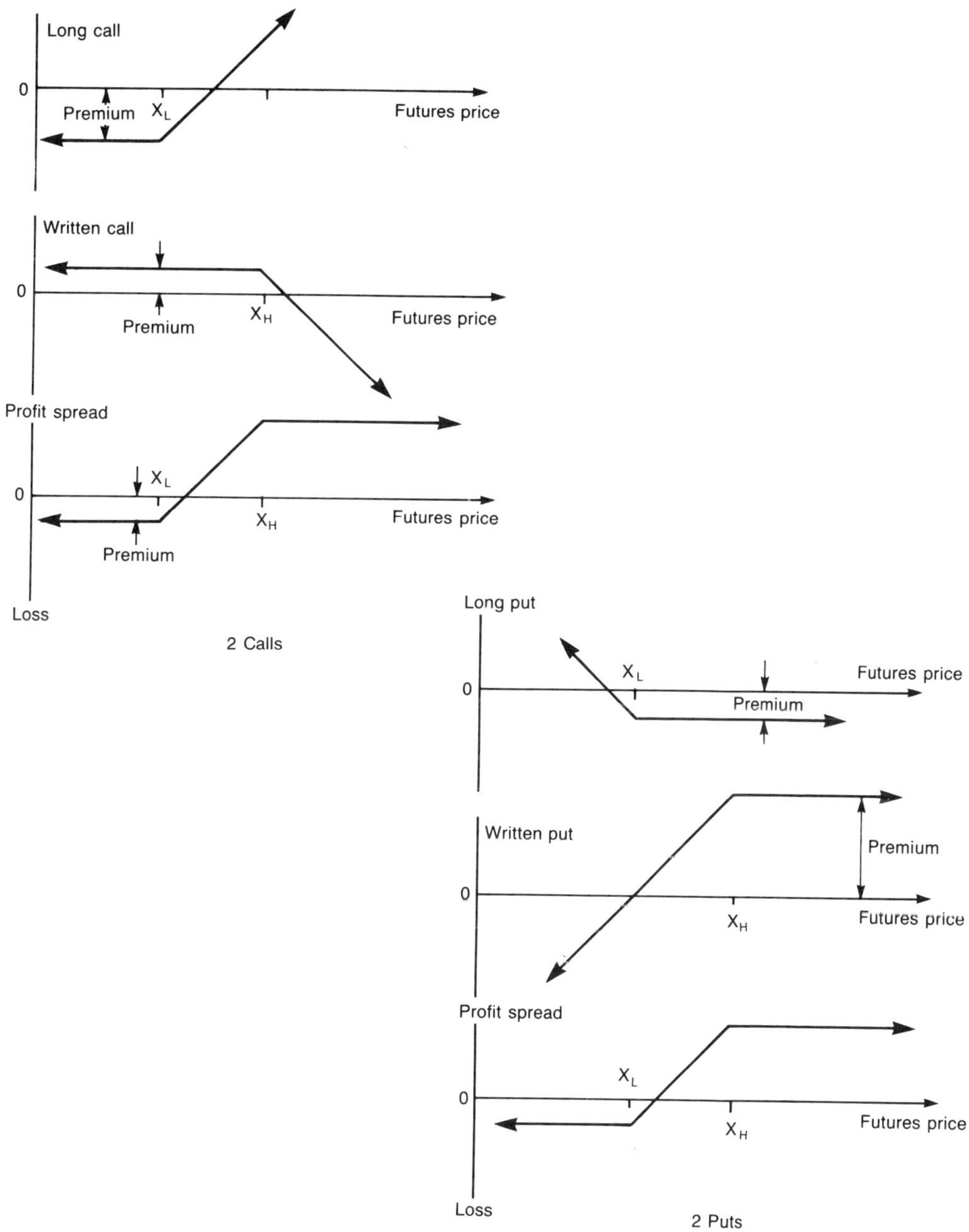

Figure 13-10. Bull Spread: Two Puts and Two Calls

is less than or equal to the lower exercise price, the spreader loses the premium on the purchased call while retaining the premium from the written call. The spreader thus has a net loss, the difference between the two premiums. This is the maximum loss on the bull spread. Between X_l and X_h, the purchased call increases in value and eventually breaks even and generates a positive profit. This, added to the premium received on the written call, results in a net rising profit pattern for the spread, with a maximum profit attained at X_h. Beyond X_h, the additional profit resulting from exercise of the purchased call by the spreader is exactly offset by the loss resulting from the exercise of the written call against the spreader. The total gain on the spread is always equal to the difference in strike price between X_h and X_l, less the premium paid. The total spread pattern thus shows a limited profit with high or rising futures prices and a limited loss with low futures prices. Note that the spread has a well-defined risk-reward profile. Maximum loss is always the net premium paid, while maximum profit is always equal to the difference between the exercise prices of the two options less the premium paid. Thus, it is possible for the potential spreader to know beforehand the risk and return for the strategy. The spread, while making a profit under rising prices, is not as profitable here as an outright call option position would be. This emphasizes the primary purpose of a spread trade, a relatively lower risk position with a correspondingly lower possible reward. A numerical example of a bull spread is given in table 13–10.

Assume a speculator believes that silver futures prices will rise and is considering the use of a bull call spread. The current nearby futures price is 773 cents per ounce. The 750 call is thus in the money, and its price is equal to 38.5. The 800 is out of the money and selling for 15. The spreader can purchase the spread (buy the 750 call for 38.5 and sell the 800 call for 15), for a net premium of 23.5 (equal to $1,175 on the 5,000 ounce contract). The maximum loss on the strategy would then be 23.5. As the futures price rises above 775, the bought call increases in value while the sold call remains unexercised. The bought call has a positive value equal in general terms to (FP − 750). At a futures price beyond 800, the written call (800) is liable to exercise, and can result in a loss of (FP − 800). Thus, the total position has a value in general of (FP − 750) − (FP − 800), or (800 − 750 = 100), less the premium paid of 23.5, or 100 − 23.5 = 26.5.

Should the speculator take on the spread? There are several factors to consider. The risk/reward ratio here is relatively low, 26.5/23.5. At the same time, the break-even point on the spread is 750 plus 23.6, or 773.6; the futures price would not have to rise by much for the spread to be profitable. As a third consideration, a rule of thumb used by many market practitioners is that the spread must be bought for a net premium of 40 percent or less of the difference in exercise prices (e.g., the net premium paid should be no more than 40 percent of the 800-750 difference, or 20). Thus, the speculator must decide if the risk and reward of this particular spread is suitable for the investment objectives.

Table 13–11. Put Bull Spread
(cents/ounce)

Current nearby futures price = 773
Silver futures option prices: Calls (X = 750) = 38.5
(X = 800) = 15
Puts (X = 750) = 11
(X = 800) = 37.5

Bull spread: Buy 750 put for 11.00
Sell 800 put for 37.5

Profit / (loss) on position at option expiration:

	Final futures price				
	725	*750*	*775*	*800*	*825*
Premium received	26.5	26.5	26.5	26.5	26.5
Profit / (loss) on 750	25.0	0.0	0.0	0.0	0.0
Profit / (loss) on 800	(75.0)	(50.0)	(25.0)	0.0	0.0
Net profit / (loss)	(23.5)	(23.5)	1.5	26.5	26.5

A bull spread can also be constructed using two puts, and the reasoning behind the net profit pattern is similar to the call bull spread. The put bull spread is constructed by buying a put with an exercise price (X_l) lower than the exercise price of the put option that is sold (X_h). (See figure 13–10). If both options expire without being exercised at futures prices greater than the higher exercise price, the spreader retains the written put premium while losing the purchase put premium. Because the written put has a higher exercise price, it has a greater intrinsic value than the purchased put and the spread results in a net positive profit at higher futures prices. This is also the maximum profit on the put bull spread. As futures prices decline, the written put is exercised against the spreader, and the losses eventually overcome the premium received. Finally, at futures prices less than X_l, the purchased put begins to generate profits, matching losses on the written put. Again, the net profit pattern results in limited losses with lower futures prices and limited profits at higher futures prices. A numerical example of a put bull spread is given in table 13–11.

Assume a put bull spread is constructed with the silver options discussed previously. In the case of a bullish sentiment, the speculator sells the option with the greatest profit potential on the upside, the put with the higher exercise price. The put with the lower exercise price is bought. Here, the net premium is 26.5 per ounce (receive 37.5 for the written 800 and pay 11 for the bought 750 for a net receipt of 37.5 less 11, or 26.5). The speculator is selling the spread. This difference in premiums is the maximum profit on the spread. If the futures price indeed rises, then both puts expire without exercise, and the net premium received is retained. If the futures price falls, then the written put has a value of (800 − FP), and it will be exercised. The bought put has a value of (750 − FP). The total loss of the spread is thus (750 − FP) − (800 − FP) plus the premium of 26.5, or − 50 + 26.5 = 23.5. The maximum loss on the spread is the difference in strike prices plus the premium.

Even though the two bull spreads, call and put, can result in equivalent profit and loss, there are differences in implementation between them. A put bull spread involves selling the put with the higher exercise price and thus results in a net positive cash flow at the beginning of the spread. Similarly, the call bull spread involves selling the call with the higher exercise price and results in a net negative cash flow at initiation. However, the call spread has an advantage—the possibility of a premature exercise against the spreader is lower initially. With the call spread, the written option is, at the beginning of the spread, out of the money. This is in contrast to the put spread, in which the written put is, at initiation, in the money and liable to exercise at any time. This potential disruption in the spreader's plans may lead the potential spreader to use the call spread despite the disadvantage of an initial negative cash flow.

BEAR SPREAD. A similar option position can be constructed for a mildly bearish market using either two calls (the call bear spread) or two puts (the put bear spread). (See figure 13–11).) For a call bear spread, the call option with the lower exercise price (X_l) is sold while the call option with the higher exercise price (X_h) is purchased. The option sold has a lower exercise price than the option purchased; therefore, the premium received for it by the spreader will be greater than the premium paid. The net premium received is the maximum profit on the call bear spread. The written call is in the money and liable to premature exercise. If the futures price at expiration is less than X_l, both options expire unexercised, and the net premium is retained. As the futures price rises, the written call is exercised against the spreader, and eventually the loss on this call is greater than the net premium paid. Finally, at futures prices greater than X_h, the purchased call is exercised by the spreader and the resulting profit from the purchased call matches dollar for dollar the additional loss on the written call. The maximum loss is equal to the difference in exercise price less the premium received. Again, the spread results in a limited profit with low or declining futures prices and a limited loss at higher futures prices. An example of a call bear spread is given in table 13–12.

Consider a trader who is bearish on the S&P500. The nearby futures price is currently 311.55. To institute a bear spread, the trader sells the option with the higher premium; if the futures price does fall, the premium will be retained. The trader sells the call option with the lower exercise price (here, 305) for a price of 10.90 and buys the option with the higher exercise price (here, 315) for 5.40, for a net receipt of 5.5 (equal to $2,750 on the index contract). This is the maximum profit on the bear

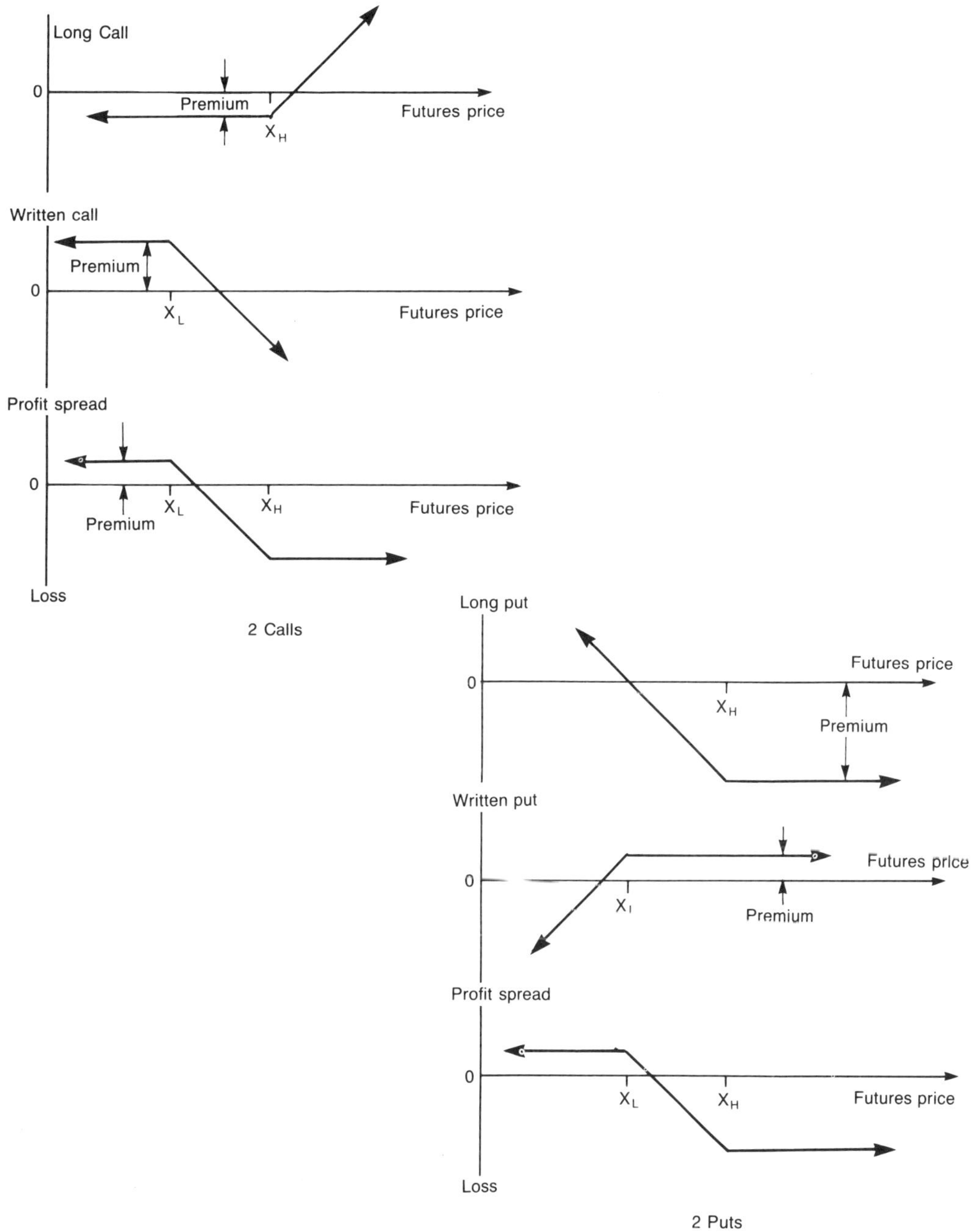

Figure 13-11. Bear Spread: Two Puts and Two Calls

Table 13-12. Call Bear Spread
(index units 1. = $500)

Current nearby futures price = 311.55
S&P500 futures option prices: Calls (X = 305) = 10.90
(X = 315) = 5.40
Puts (X = 305) = 4.40
(X = 315) = 8.80

Bull spread: Buy 315 call for 5.40
Sell 305 call for 10.90

Profit / (loss) on position at option expiration:

	Final futures price				
	300	*305*	*310*	*315*	*320*
Premium received	5.5	5.5	5.5	5.5	5.5
Profit / (loss) on 305	0.0	0.0	(5.0)	(10.0)	(15.0)
Profit / (loss) on 315	0.0	0.0	0.0	0.0	5.0
Net profit / (loss)	5.5	5.5	0.5	(4.5)	(4.5)

spread. If the futures price does fall, both options expire without exercise and the spreader keeps the net premium receipt. If the futures price rises, however, the written call (lower exercise price) will be in the money first, and begin to generate losses equal to (FP − 305). As the futures price rises past 315, the bought call will become in the money as well and generate a profit of (FP − 315). Thus, the total value of the spread is equal to (FP − 315) − (FP − 305) plus the net premium, or − 10 plus 5.5 premium, or −4.5. This is the maximum loss on the spread.

Again, there are several considerations before the spread is undertaken. The reward/risk ratio is a relatively low 5.5/4.5. The break even on the spread is the lower exercise price, 305, plus the premium of 5.5, or 310.5, very close to the current futures price. A rule of thumb for sold spreads is that the net premium received should not be less than 60 percent of the difference in exercise prices. Here, the premium received should be at least 60 percent of 10, or 6.

The profits and losses possible with a bear spread constructed from S&P500 puts is left for the reader who can use the data in table 13-12.

PRICING OF OPTIONS

Options contracts have been successfully valued according to a concise mathematical model first developed by F. Black and M. Scholes.[1] Before we discuss this model in more detail, it will be useful to examine a few conditions that bound the value of an option within a certain range, and to establish a relationship between call prices and put prices on the same underlying futures. Also, because the option pricing model (OPM) has been developed under a simplifying assumption that the option is a European option that can be exercised only at maturity, much of the discussion must focus on European options as we consider their relation to American options.

As we have seen, the value of a call option at maturity is always greater than or equal to zero. The option either expires without exercise, if its exercise price is greater than the current futures price, or is worth its intrinsic value, the difference between the futures price and the exercise price, a positive value. In mathematical notation, the value of a call option, c, is the maximum of either 0 (it expires worthless) or its intrinsic value (the futures price less the exercise price, $F - X$, if F is greater than X).

$$c = \text{Max}\ (0, F - X) \tag{13–5}$$

Thus, the option can never be worth less than $F - X$ if it is in the money meaning the current futures price is greater than the exercise price, since prior to expiration there is also a positive component of the price related to the time value. Further, equation 13–5 states that the option can never be worth more than the underlying futures, even if the option exercise price is zero. Thus, equation 13–5 gives both an upper and lower bound to the option value in relation to the futures price. Later, we present a hedging argument to quantitatively fix the value of the option within these established bounds.

With regard to an American call option that can be exercised prior to maturity, it can be argued that this option will not, in fact, be exercised before the option maturity date. If the American call is exercised prior to maturity, the value on exercise is equal to $F - X$, the amount by which the current futures price is greater than the exercise price. Thus, on exercise, the option holder loses any value associated with the remaining time to maturity of the option. The time value of an option is always positive; thus, the option holder can always make more on the option by sellling it in the options market rather than exercising it. This result simplifies the analysis of American options by avoiding the possibility of premature exercise.[2]

Finally, the price of a put option can be expressed in terms of the call option price, a relationship known as put-call parity. The proof of this relationship involves the construction of a portfolio with one futures contract, one put option, and the sale of one call option. The put and call options have the same maturity and exercise price and refer to the same futures contract. The possible value of the portfolio at expiration of the options is listed in table 13–13. At expiration, the futures price is either greater than the exercise price or the futures price is less than or equal to the exercise price. In the first case, the total value of the portfolio consists of the futures

Table 13-13. Value of Portfolio at Option Expiration

	$F > X$	$F < X$
Value of call	$-(F - X)$	0
Put	0	$X - F$
Futures	F	F
Net value of portfolio	X	X

(worth F), the put option (here, with F greater than X, worth 0) and the call option. Because it has been sold, the value of the call to the writer is negative and reflects the intrinsic value: $-(F - X)$. The net position is thus equal to $F + 0 - (F - X)$, or X. In the second case, the payoff on the net position is the same. With F less than X, the portfolio consists of the futures (value $= F$), the call (which now expires worthless, with a value of 0), and the put (worth its intrinsic value, $X - F$), for a total position of $F + 0 + (X - F)$, or X. Thus, the return on the portfolio is always X, and its current price should equal the value of this net certain payoff discounted back to the present at the risk-free rate of return (r_f).

Thus, with p equal to the price of the put option:

$$F + p - c = X/(1 + r_f) \qquad (13\text{-}6)$$

Rearranging 13-6 gives the put-call parity relationship:

$$(c - p) = F - (X/(1 + r_f)) \qquad (13\text{-}7)$$

Using continuous compounding notation, the put-call relationship can also be expressed as:

$$(c - p) = F - (Xe^{-r_f T}) \qquad (13\text{-}8)$$

(T = the time to maturity of the option and the time when the exercise price will be paid.) This relationship is a useful one; given the price of a call, the value of the equivalent put is immediately known.

There is a necessary relationship between the prices of a put, a call, and the underlying futures. If any of these prices are distorted away from the price relationship in equation 13-8, then an arbitrage opportunity is present. For instance, writing a covered call is equivalent to a written put position. Thus, if the put is overvalued in relation to the call and the futures, the arbitrageur can write the put and at the same time "write" a covered call by buying the call and selling the underlying futures.

Similarly, as table 13–13 indicates, if the call is overvalued, the arbitrageur can write a call and simultaneously buy a futures and a put option.

Because the arbitrage activity in the options market also involves the futures contract, and because with index futures the two markets expire at the same time with no need to avoid physical delivery, the above arbitrage activity serves at times to accentuate the price volatility due to cash-futures index arbitrage (chapter 11). The options market is the third leg of the triple witching hour activity discussed previously with stock index futures expiration. As with the cash-futures arbitrage, the options-futures arbitrage serves to ensure properly priced instruments. H. Stoll and R. Whaley have also tested for increased volatility due to options activity, and found that options do not affect the volatility of the underlying futures in a statistically significant manner.[3]

VALUATION

The valuation of a call option is derived next using an arbitrage argument. If a hedge portfolio can be constructed using the call option and the underlying futures for which the return is certain under all possible conditions, then the return on this portfolio must be equal to the risk-free rate of return. This relation and the boundary conditions discussed previously are used to derive an exact pricing equation for the call option. Because the OPM was derived for stock options, we discuss the model first in terms of stock options and then modify the results for futures options. Finally, the derivation requires some mathematical concepts and assumptions which are discussed later in more detail.

First, the derivation of the Black-Scholes OPM involves a consideration of the returns on a portfolio in continuous rather than discrete time. Thus, the rates of return on the portfolio reflect continuous compounding of the sort in equation 13–8, in which the time interval of compounding is assumed to be infinitely small.

Second, the development of the model relies on mathematical relationships developed under stochastic calculus, a mode of mathematical analysis applied to variables whose values are both uncertain and changing through time. The value of a stochastic variable as it changes through continuous time can be expressed mathematically as a function of the time elapsed and as a function of the increasing uncertainty in its value as time passes. For instance, the instantaneous rate of return on a stock ($d\tilde{r}$) can be expressed as a function of its instantaneous rate of change through time, or drift (k), and its variability or uncertainty through time, or its standard deviation (sd), in a differential equation called an Ito process:

$$d\tilde{r} = (k \times dt) + (sd \times d\tilde{z}) \tag{13–9}$$

The first component of the change in the rate of return ($k \times dt$) reflects movement along a trend line. At any particular moment, the expected value of the return is equal to some initial observed value, r_0, and the movement along a trend as time passes:

$$E(\tilde{r}) = r_0 + (k \times dt) \tag{13–10}$$

So the change in r reflects in part the movement along the trend and the amount of time elapsed, $k \times dt$.

The second component reflects the uncertainty involved in the value of the variable as time passes. Sd is the standard deviation of the rate of return and $d\tilde{z}$ is a variable, or process, that summarizes random changes through time:

$$d\tilde{z} = \tilde{e} \times \sqrt{dt} \tag{13–11}$$

in which $\tilde{e}$ represents white noise, a variable much like the random error in a regression equation.

The OPM assumes that the rate of return of the asset underlying the option can be described in this way. If this is so, then an expression for the changes in the value of the asset price can be obtained:

$$d\tilde{r} = d\tilde{S}/S(t) = (k \times dt) + (sd \times d\tilde{z}) \tag{13–12}$$

or

$$d\tilde{S} = (k \times S(t) \times dt) + (sd \times S(t) \times d\tilde{z}) \tag{13–13}$$

Although complex, equation 13–13 is simply the continuous time description of a well-known process, Brownian motion, or in financial terms, a random walk. Again, it describes the movement in an asset's price through time as a function of a trend, of the time elapsed since initial observation, and the increasing uncertainty in its movement as time elapses.

Besides the preceding assumption on stock price movement, other ideal market conditions are assumed:

1. The underlying stock pays no dividends.
2. The risk-free rate of return, r_f, is known and constant; and it is possible to borrow and lend at this rate.
3. The option is European.

4. There are no transaction costs.
5. There are no restrictions on short sales of stock or on the option.

Under these assumptions, the value of the option is a function of two variables, the underlying asset price and the time to maturity) and three constant terms (the risk-free rate of return, r_f; the exercise price of the option, X; and the variance of the stock's rate of return, *var*).

To derive the pricing equation, it is necessary to construct a risk-free portfolio. If the change in the value of the option given a change in the stock price (the derivative dc/dS, or c_1) is known, then a hedge portfolio can be formed to yield a certain or risk-free rate of return. For instance, if dc/dS is equal to two, the option value increases \$2.00 for every \$1.00 increase in the stock price. If a portfolio is constructed by buying two shares of stock and selling one call option (a hedge ratio of 1/2, or $1/c_1$), then the change in value of the long stock position is exactly offset by the change in value of the short option position. The change in equity on the total position is equal to the change in the stock equity, ΔS, less the change in the short option position, $\Delta c \times (1/c_1)$, or

$$\text{Change in equity} = \Delta S - \Delta c/c_1 \qquad (13\text{–}14)$$

A result from stochastic calculus can be used to expand the expression Δc to reflect the change in the option's value as the stock price changes and as the time to maturity changes:

$$\Delta c = (c_1 \times S) + (c_2 \times t) + (1/2 \times c_{11} \times var \times S^2 \times \Delta t) \qquad (13\text{–}15)$$

(with $c_2 = dc/dt$, and $c_{l})$ – d^2c/dS^2, the second derivative of the option price with respect to the underlying asset price.)

Equation 13–15 is a continuous time version of a total derivative and includes the continuous time expression for the two partial derivatives with respect to time and with respect to stock price change and a third term involving higher order derivatives. In ordinary calculus the third term vanishes; in stochastic calculus, the products of differentials and squared differentials do not disappear at the limit.

Equation 13–15 can be substituted into equation 13–14 and the result simplified to:

$$\text{Change in equity} = -(1/2 \times c_{11} \times var \times S^2 + c_2) \times (\Delta t/c_1) \qquad (13\text{–}16)$$

Because the hedged portfolio results in a perfectly certain return (changes in value of the stock are offset by the call option), equation 13–16 represents a riskless return on equity and should be equal to the risk-free rate of return on the original equity invested in the portfolio:

$$\begin{aligned} \text{Change in equity} &= -(1/2 \times c_{11} \times var \times S^2 + c_2) \times (\Delta t / c_1) \\ &= \text{equity} \times r_f \times \Delta t \\ &= (S - (c/c_1)) \times r_f \times \Delta t \end{aligned} \tag{13-17}$$

Upon simplifying, this gives a differential equation for the value of the option:

$$c_2 = r_f \times c - (r_f \times S \times c_1) - (1/2 \times var \times S^2 \times c_{11}) \tag{13-18}$$

With the boundary condition, equation 13–5, the differential equation, equation 13–18, can be solved to yield an expression for the price of an option:

$$c = SN(d1) - (Xe^{-r_f(T-t)}N(d2)) \tag{13-19}$$

For a more complete discussion of the derivation, see Black and Scholes.[4]

Though appearing complex, the equation basically values an option as a function of the underlying asset, S, less the discounted value of the exercise price, X, to be paid at exercise. $N(d1)$ and $N(d2)$ can be considered "weights" on the stock price and the exercise price components that depend on stock price volatility, time to maturity, and other factors in a complex interaction.

$N(d1)$ refers to the cumulative normal density function of a standard normal random variable, and takes on values between 0 and 1. For instance, $N(d1)$ becomes very close to 1 for long maturity, in-the-money options. For the price of an option like this, then, most of the weighting would be placed on the current value of the stock, with much less weight ($N(d2)$) placed on the exercise price to be paid in the very far future. $d1$ is equal to

$$d1 = \frac{\ln(S/X) + (r_f + 1/2 \times var) \times (T - t)}{(var)(\sqrt{T - t})} \tag{13-20}$$

and

$$d2 = d1 - (var \times \sqrt{T - t}) \tag{13-21}$$

The option price depends on the five factors discussed previously: the underlying asset's price, the time to maturity, the exercise price, the variance of the underlying asset's rate of return, and the risk-free rate of interest. The price of an option does, indeed, increase as the square root of time to maturity, as discussed in the section on spread trades. Except for the variance, the factors are known at any point in time.

If one can assume that a historical variance estimate is accurate enough, then a relatively accurate price can be established for a call option using the OPM. Further, once the call option is priced, the put option price can also be determined.

This pricing equation was developed for an option on stock. Using the same portfolio arguments and boundary conditions, Black derived a pricing equation for futures that is very similar:[5]

$$c = e^{-r_f T}(FN(d1) - XN(d2)) \qquad (13\text{–}22)$$

The pricing formula for futures options can be obtained from the equation for stock options by substituting $Fe^{-r_f T}$ everywhere for S in the original formula. This change results because exercise of the futures option does not involve physical carrying charges (insurance, storage, or interest) that result from the exercise of an option on physicals, either stocks or commodities. Hence, the price for the underlying commodity, F, is a future payment similar to the exercise price, and is discounted back by the risk-free rate of interest, r_f.

A theoretical price for a futures option can be calculated from the formula using market data for the futures price and the risk-free rate, and an estimate of the volatility of the futures return expected during the life of the option. The calculation of a T-bond December option theoretical price is given in table 13–14.

Assume the instantaneous variance of the futures return is equal to 15 percent, and the option is valued as of September 13, when 100 days are left until maturity. If we assume a price of 70 for the futures, so that the option is out of the money, the theoretical price is 3.27, which is completely composed of time premium. On the other hand, if the current T-bond futures price is assumed to be 80, making the option in the money, then the option price would be 7.63.

Obviously, the theoretical price is sensitive to the value used for the variance. Even though historical variance estimates are generally used to derive the theoretical price, the volatility can change rapidly if underlying bond price changes. Thus, the theoretical price should be viewed with caution in deciding whether a market option price is overvalued or undervalued. In addition, the expected volatility determines the price; this means that, if bond prices become more volatile, options become more expensive. This is a common complaint of options users in that the price of an option rises at just the moment that a buyer would most like to use it.

The theoretical price is derived under the assumption that the option is European and will not be exercised before expiration. Futures options are subject to less risk in this regard because there are no cash dividends on the underlying commodity; still there is some danger of premature exercise if the option is very deep in the money. This

Table 13-14. Theoretical Price of a Call Option on Futures
(December 76 option as of September 13)

Assume: $rf = 10\%$ $\quad v^2 = 15\%$ $\quad T = 100/356 = .274$

$X = 76$ $\quad v = .387$

$F = 70$

$$d1 = \frac{\ln(70/76) + (0.10 + 1/2(.15))(.274)}{(.15)(\sqrt{.274})}$$

$$= -.4367$$

$$N(d1) = .3315^*$$

$$d2 = -.4367 - ((.387)(\sqrt{.274}))$$

$$= -.639$$

$$N(d2) = .2611$$

$$c = e^{-.10(.274)}((70)(.3315) - ((76)(.2611)))$$

$$= .973 \times (23.205 - 19.843)$$

$$= 3.271$$

$F = 80$

$$d1 = \frac{\ln(80/76) + (0.10 + 1/2(.15))(.274)}{(.15)(\sqrt{.274})}$$

$$= 1.264$$

$$N(d1) = .9107$$

$$d2 = 1.264 - .203$$

$$= 1.06142$$

$$N(d2) = .8554$$

$$c = e^{-.10(.274)}((80)(.9107) - ((76)(.8554)))$$

$$= 7.628$$

*Cumulative normal probabilities can be obtained from any normal distribution table.

can be seen from the options pricing formula (equation 13–21) if S/X (or F/X for the futures option) is allowed to approach infinity. If F/X approaches infinity, then the theoretical price of the option becomes $(F/X)e^{-r_fT}$, which is less than the value the option would have if exercised, (F/X). If the futures price does rise sufficiently, then the option may be exercised before expiration. Again, the use of a price derived from the model depends on how well the assumptions underlying the model are met.

Finally, the delta of the option, or dc/dS, can be derived from the OPM pricing equation. Taking the derivative of equation 13–19 with respect to S, dc/dS is equal to $N(d1)$. As can be seen from equation 13–20, the option delta depends heavily on the time to maturity $(T - t)$ and whether the option is in or out of the money. As an example, for the option in table 13–14, the delta $N(d1)$ is equal to 0.3315 for an out-of-the-money option and 0.9107 for an in-the-money option. With the call in the money, the sensitivity of the call option price to the underlying futures rises to 0.91, or 91 percent. This is so because the sensitivity of the call option value to changes in the underlying asset is stronger if exercise is more likely. With a futures price of 90, the option delta becomes 0.9971. In general, the delta of an option varies from 0.0 (for deep out of the money) to 0.50 (at the money) to 1.0 (deep in the money) as the underlying asset value changes.

Similarly, the time to maturity affects the option's delta, with the call option price being more sensitive to the asset's value changes as exercise becomes more likely, or as time to maturity approaches zero for an in-the-money option. If the option is out of the money, then the sensitivity of the call option price to the asset becomes less as time to maturity approaches zero. When it is out of the money, it is very likely that the option cannot be exercised, and thus the option does not reflect a meaningful ownership claim on the underlying asset. For instance, from table 13–14, the option's delta with 100 days to maturity is 0.3315 and increases to 0.5478 for an option with 200 days.

OPTIONS IN PORTFOLIO MANAGEMENT

Two recent developments in portfolio management involve the use of options. One, the range forward or cylinder, uses options to construct a hedge for a portfolio that has many of the characteristics of a hedge using futures. Another, portfolio insurance, attempts to replicate an options hedge using futures contracts.

CYLINDERS

A cylinder uses options to fix both a floor and a ceiling on the value of a portfolio, in effect creating a cylinder around the possible value of a portfolio. The usual cylinder involves an over-the-counter (OTC) option rather than an exchange-traded option, with the portfolio manager purchasing a put option in private negotiation with a bank or investment banker. Because it is not traded on an exchange, the OTC option's characteristics can be negotiated. There is a great flexibility in an OTC option concerning the nature of the underlying asset that can be constructed to be equal to the particular bond portfolio being hedged; and the maturity that can be longer than the usual three-month exchange-traded option. However, because of this flexibility and usually longer maturity, OTC options can be expensive. The idea behind the cylinder is to hedge downside price risk with an OTC option and to pay for it with the writing of another OTC option.

To construct a cylinder, the hedger buys a put option on the portfolio. The put option, with an exercise price of X_l, fixes a floor on the portfolio value: no matter how far prices decline, the put option provides a floor on the value equal to X_l less the premium paid. To finance the put option, the portfolio manager writes a call option on the portfolio with a higher exercise price (X_h), in effect giving up to the other party the upside potential of the portfolio beyond X_h. An example of a cylinder on a bond portfolio and the same hedge using futures is given in table 13–15 and figure 13–12.

Assume that the portfolio to be hedged with the cylinder contains one 8 percent, 20-year to maturity Treasury Bond. At the current market rate of 10 percent, the price of the bond is equal to $82,843. A futures hedge, if it were 100 percent effective, would protect this value; if interst rates rise or fall, the value of the portfolio remains at $81,843.

With a cylinder, the portfolio manager buys a put option on the portfolio and finances this option by writing a call option on the portfolio. Assume that the option purchased has an exercise price (X_l) of $79,250, indicating a market yield on the underlying bond portfolio of 10.50 percent, and costs $5,000. Assume that the manager writes a call option whose value is equal to $5,000 also, with an exercise price (X_h) of $86,687 (yield of 9.5 percent). If rates rise, the bond falls in value, but the put option increases; the net effect is to set a floor on the portfolio value of $79,250 (yield of 10.5 percent) equal to the exercise price of the put. If market rates fall, on the other hand, the bond portfolio gains value but the call option results in losses to the manager; the portfolio value is fixed at $86,687.50 ($X_h$). If rates remain between 10.5 percent and 9.5 percent, however, neither of the options has value, and the total position's value is equal to the price of the bond alone. Thus, the manager has fixed a floor on the portfolio value that is less than that achievable with futures, but is also allowed upside appreciation in value greater than that possible using futures. If the manager had used the put option alone, the floor fixed would have been $79,250 less the premium of $5,000, or $74,250, and the upside potential would have been retained.

The cylinder allows some flexibility in the upper and lower bounds of the portfolio value. The manager can choose the degree of protection by varying the exercise prices of the options depending on potential market movements. A variant of the cylinder is the range forward developed by Salomon Brothers. Similar to the cylinder, the range forward involves the purchase of a put and the sale of a call. In this case, the hedger chooses one of the levels, the ceiling or the floor, and the maturity, and Salomon fixes the other end of the range. The choice for Salomon depends

Table 13-15. Hedging Interest Rate Risk, Futures and Options

Assume: Portfolio with $100,000 face value, 8% coupon, 20 years to maturity;
price = $82,843.75 (market yield = 10%)

With futures:

Sell one Treasury bond futures contract at futures price = $82,843.
Assume dollar equivalence achieved

Outcomes:

Interest rate	*Gain or (Loss) on Portfolio*	*Gain or (Loss) on Futures*	*Effective Price*
12%	($12,937.50)	$12,937.50	$82,843
8%	17,156.25	(17,156.25)	82,843

With options:

Buy put option with exercise price = $79,250 (10.5%)
Price = $5,000

Sell call option with exercise price = $86,687.50 (9.5%)
Price = $5,000

Outcomes:

Rate	*Portfolio Value*	*Portfolio Gain or (Loss)*	*Option Value**	*Total Gain or (Loss)*	*Effective Price*
Rates increase:					
11%	$ 75,906.25	($ 6,437.50)	$ 3,343.75	($3,593.70)	$79,250
12%	69,906.25	(12,937.50)	9,343.75	(3,593.70)	79,250
Rates decrease:					
9%	$ 90,781.25	$ 7,937.50	($ 4,039.75)	$3,843.75	$86,687.50
8%	100,000.00	17,156.25	(13,312.50)	3,843.75	86,687.50

*Put option value = X − spot price
Call option value = spot price − X

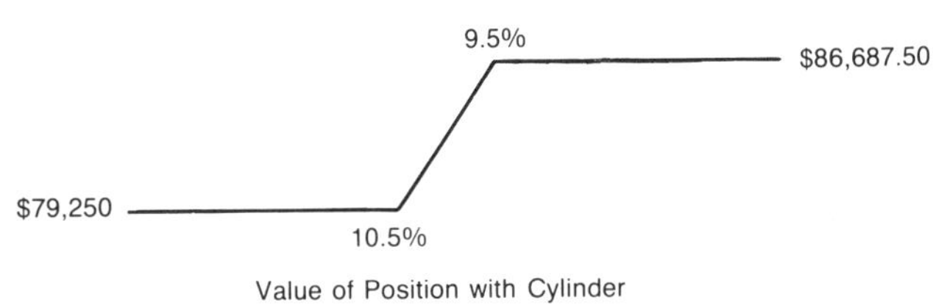

Figure 13-12

in part on its view of the market but also is adjusted so that there is no premium paid. With the range forward, if the price of the asset remains between the floor and ceiling, the hedger pays the spot price in effect for the asset at maturity. If the price settles outside the range, the hedger has fixed the price either at the top or bottom of the established range.

PORTFOLIO INSURANCE

A second development in portfolio management using options concerns portfolio insurance. As discussed in chapter 10, the portfolio manager would like a flexible hedge, one that varies in degree of hedge protection in response to price changes. For a cash portfolio, put options are an excellent hedge becasue the protection afforded by the option varies in response to price changes and, most important, diminishes to zero if asset prices rise sufficiently. As discussed earlier (figure 13–3), a put option can hedge downside losses on the portfolio but expires without exercise if prices rise, thus allowing also for upside potential on the hedged portfolio's value. Further, the degree of protection of the put, its change in value in response to a change in the value of the underlying asset, varies through time depending on the asset's value. This is the option's delta, which can vary from a value of 0.0 to 1.0, depending on the underlying asset's value in relation to the exercise price. Portfolio insurance with futures mimics the responsiveness of put options to spot price changes by utilizing the put option delta to calculate the degree of hedge protection.

As discussed in the previous section on option pricing, the delta of an option changes depending on whether the option is in or out of the money, that is, the underlying asset price is less than or greater than the exercise price. If the asset price falls sufficiently, the put option's delta approaches 1.0; at this asset price level, a $1.00 decrease in the asset value is offset by a $1,00 increase in the value of the put option, resulting in a 100 percent hedged position. At the other extreme, if the asset price rises sufficiently, the put option delta approaches 0.0; at a high asset value, the put option affords no protection, and indeed, none is needed. Thus, the percentage of hedging protection afforded by a put varies as its delta.

In portfolio insurance strategies using futures, the amount of futures hedging is varied to mimic the price responsiveness, or hedging behavior, of a put option on the portfolio. By choosing the implied exercise price, the portfolio manager chooses a level of protection on the portfolio value. As the portfolio value changes from this level, the percentage of the position hedged is adjusted to conform to the put option's delta. If the portfolio value rises sufficiently, no hedge (delta equals 0) is in place. If the value falls sufficiently, a 100 percent hedge is effected (delta equals 1). For intermediate values, the hedge rate is calculated based on the implied exercise price versus the portfolio's current value.

NOTES

1. F. Black and M. Scholes, "The Pricing of Options and Corporate Liabilities," *Journal of Political Economy* 81 (1973): 637–54.
2. Premature exercise may become necessary in stock options when the underlying stock pays a cash dividend and the value of the option is not protected against dividend payments. When dividends are paid, the stock price generally declines by the value of the dividend payment. Because call value declines as the stock price declines, the holder of an option may find it an advantage to exercise the option before dividend payments cause the call value to decrease. Futures do not pay dividends; therefore, the problem of premature exercises is much less severe and is ignored here.
3. H.R. Stoll and R. Whaley, "Expiration Day Effects of Index Options and Futures," Monograph Series in Finance and Economics. Monograph 1986–3. (New York: NYU-Salomon Brothers Center for the Study of Financial Institutions, 1986.)
4. Black and Scholes, "The Pricing of Options."
5. F. Black. "The Pricing of Commodity Contracts." *Journal of Financial Economics* 3 (1976): 161–79.

REGULATION OF FUTURES MARKETS

14

In the United States and in other countries regulatory controversy has surrounded futures markets since their inception. Speculation conjures images of wheeler-dealers and price manipulation that presumably injures the public. Governments then step forward to regulate or forbid trading, often creating troubled industry and government relationships. Regulatory laws in the 1600s did not slow down the feverish tulip bulb speculation the swept Holland where futures markets located in taverns eventually collapsed in 1637 causing thousands of bankruptcies. The Japanese government banned the rice ticket market in 1869, and in 1958 the United States government banned futures trading in onions.

Bad news always captures the headlines before the good news, but futures markets have now existed continuously in the United States for over 120 years without major scandals or market disruptions, and their growth has ballooned in the last decade. There are always controversies and problems requiring regulatory action, but the balance between private and government regulation in the United States seems fairly effective. This chapter reviews the historical development of the regulatory process in the United States and discusses topics of current regulatory concern, mainly from an economic standpoint rather than a legal viewpoint. The chapter concludes with a discussion of performance.

DEVELOPMENT OF THE REGULATORY PROCESS

EXCHANGE SELF-REGULATION

For about the first seventy years, futures trading in the United States was self-regulated by exchanges. The exchanges, primarily owned and controlled by their members, established binding trading rules as problems arose. Exchanges established their own guidelines for trading and business conduct, specified their own contracts for trading, and developed procedures for disciplining members. Over time they have developed their own rule books covering contract terms, trading units, trading months, hours of trading, daily price range, position limits, and delivery procedures and payments. Exchanges were interested in fostering competition and preventing price manipulation that might result in corners, squeezes, or distorted prices.[1] They wanted to assure that prices were representative of commercial value and that traders had full information and equal access to the markets. Existence of exchanges depended on a reputation of integrity, safety, competitiveness, and fairness. Exchanges developed elaborate mechanisms for self-regulation by hearing complaints, arbitrating internal disputes, and penalizing members. In essence, they developed their own legislative, judicial, and administrative procedures, becoming quasi-public regulatory bodies.[2] These elaborate rules and regulations help distinguish futures contracts from forward contracting.

Futures markets would probably not exist without self-regulation. Franklin Edwards argues that these markets are joint ventures among individuals and institutions designed to impose rules and regulations on markets and participants.[3] The distinguishing feature of futures markets is their liquidity in the trading of financial obligations. This results in reduced transaction and information costs in forward contracting. Regulation is not needed to make contracts about future events, but it is needed for organized futures markets to maintain active trading.

Edwards points out there are two institutions central to self-regulation. One is the futures exchanges that establish trading rules; write contracts; and ensure fair, orderly, and efficient markets. The other is the clearing associations that act as guarantors of contracts. Misconduct by a member of either institution affects all the others and undermines public confidence of futures trading. Public participation cannot exist if self-regulation does not ensure markets of high integrity.

Nevertheless, some argue that self-regulation is not likely to be in the public interest. The exchanges are monopolistic institutions restricting membership and denying floor access to nonmembers. Some argue that exchanges exist to restrain competition and create large profits. The competitive structure of trading is not self-sustaining and is inherently vulnerable to colluding by traders if not prohibited by regulations. Before instituting public regulation, one must examine the resulting social benefits and costs vis-a-vis self regulation. Public regulation has been sporadic and not overbearing, often coming on the heels of some well-publicized disruptive event or problem.

LEGISLATIVE HISTORY

The first attempt in Congress to control futures trading was the Hatch Act in 1893 which never passed.[4] The opposing forces were the commodity traders who supported free markets and the right to speculate, and farmers who felt victimized and equated futures trading with gambling.

A staunch opponent to futures trading, Senator Clapper pushed through Congress the Futures Trading Act of 1921 that levied a tax of 20 cents per bushel for transactions off certain exchanges. The courts declared this act unconstitutional, so Congress rewrote the legislation without the taxing provision and enacted it as the Grain Futures Act of 1922. Regulating grain trading only, this legislation required exchanges to be licensed, to prevent manipulation, and to supply the public with trading information.

COMMODITY EXCHANGE ACT. The above legislation with thin, and the first major regulatory legislation came after almost 70 years of futures trading in the form of the Commodity Exchange Act of 1936. The overriding concern was still the effects of speculation, the threat of manipulation and the public's vulnerability to unscrupulous brokers. Farmers blamed the feature of short selling of futures contracts for their low prices. Antispeculation feelings still prevailed.

The 1936 act gave new powers to the Secretary of Agriculture to regulate exchanges. It also established the Commodity Exchange Authority (CEA) that oversaw futures trading for the next thirty-eight years. This act broadened the regulation from grains to all domestic agricultural commodities, but not to important international commodities or metals that remained free of regulation. The act required futures commission merchants to register, declared it unlawful to cheat or defraud customers, banned certain trades like wash sales and options, and gave the CEA powers to deal with market abuses and to prosecute price manipulators. Also, it broadened the licensing of exchanges, declared bucketing orders and misrepresentation of facts illegal, and established authority for auditing accounts and segregating customer funds. Except when amended, the CEA had no authority over the development or introduction of new contracts.

The 1936 act established the case for speculative position and trading limits, a subject of considerable controversy. Trading limits have since been abandoned, but position limits still exist. The legislation on these limits was based on questionable research which argued that large speculators moved prices in their favor. Designed to prevent manipulation and price distortion, the limits apply only to speculators and not to hedgers.

A principal impact of this legislation was statistical. It required traders who held positions exceeding established reporting limits to file reports of cash and futures positions daily with the CEA. This led to semimonthly commitment of traders' reports that indicate aggregate long and short positions of hedgers, speculators, spreaders, and by deduction, nonreporting traders. These detailed reports on open interest and volume along with price changes have been of great interest to traders and academic researchers.

The CEA did not regulate with a heavy hand, and in fact had limited powers to prosecute violators. Several commodities were exempt. It was a complement to strong exchange self regulation. Nevertheless, the CEA played a major role in protecting the public from fraud, deceit, and misuse of funds, and it established extensive surveillance systems to prevent manipulation, corners, squeezes, and unwarranted price distortion. The CEA was to ensure that competition existed.

The 1936 act was amended in 1968 to bring some new contracts like livestock and frozen concentrated orange juice under regulation, to establish minimal financial standards for futures commission merchants, to increase penalties, and to place more responsibility on the exchanges to make and enforce rules. This and other amendments gradually began to recognize the legitimacy of anticipatory hedges by firms like soybean processors and cattle feeders, and cross hedges of hybrid seed corn dealers, bakers, dry corn millers, and other processors into appropriate underlying agricultural contracts. These changes allowed the classification of such firms as hedgers instead of speculators, removing them from the speculative limit constraints.

In the late 1960s and early 1970s activities and events began to change. Volume of trading grew rapidly, new contracts were added at a fast pace, and world events created greater volatility in commodity prices. Some attempts to trade options on unregulated commodities were revealed as fraudulent. Exchanges were paring their rules and the CEA became too small to handle the ballooning industry. Congress was hit with a long list of complaints from producers, firms, and traders. These events led to the passing of the Commodity Futures Trading Act of 1974 establishing the

Commodity Futures Trading Commission (CFTC) with jurisdiction beginning in 1975.

COMMODITY FUTURES TRADING ACT. The Commodity Futures Trading Act left in tact many provisions of the 1936 act, but substantially amended it and brought the presence of strong federal regulation. The 1974 act provided major revisions in government and industry relationships. Of most significance, this act created an independent five-person commission appointed by the president and given broad authority to regulate all futures trading and many exchange activities.

Specifically, the CFTC now regulates all futures contracts in the United States, and achieved the right to approve the introduction of all new contracts.[5] The exchanges must now justify the economic need of a proposed contract to gain CFTC approval before offering it for trading. Also, exchanges must seek CFTC approval for any substantial changes or amendments to contract specifications, exchange bylaws, and trading rules and regulations, except for margins discussed later. The CFTC assumed responsibility for resolving conflicts concerning the number and location of delivery points and the issue of dual trading.[6] The CFTC has emergency powers as well as the power to enjoin and seek injunctions, impose cease and desist orders, and assess civil monetary fines up to $500,000 for each violation of CEA and CFTC regulations. That is, the CFTC is empowered with much more authority than the CEA ever possessed. A main focus of this act is enforcement.

Of much concern to Congress was the protection of public customers from unscrupulous dealers and brokers. Consequently, all persons dealing with customers—commodity pool operators, commodity trading advisors, and associated persons—must register with the CFTC. Their backgrounds and financial standing are subject to scrutiny. This registration is in addition to the existing registration of futures commission merchants.

Despite the stronger roles of the federal government, the same basic regulatory philosophy is maintained through the 1936 act until present. One of these themes is protection of the public, accomplished through licensing exchanges; registering brokers, advisors and dealers; auditing books; disallowing misuse of funds; ensuring proper trades; outlawing fraudulent trades and cheating; publicizing information; and preventing dissemination of false information. The other theme is to prevent price manipulation, distortion, and corners or squeezes through market surveillance; establishing speculative trading limits; requiring extensive reporting; establishing price limit moves; and taking court action when necessary.

Even with several amendments to the 1974 act, there remains concern over the balance between government and self-regulation. The questions are: Which type of regulation is most cost effective? What is the influence of regulation on efficiency?

Does the regulation enhance social welfare? Presumably, regulation is needed because the market has failed somewhere in serving its two basic functions, price discovery and the allocation of risk through the facilitation of hedging. Despite the 1974 act, exchanges still have the authority to determine margin requirements, establish some position limits, specify substitute delivery instruments, provide for cash settlement, and invoke emergency powers such as imposing liquidation trading only. There is always concern over the balance between public and self-regulation, and authorities need a conceptual framework in analyzing the case for regulation and who should do it.[7]

NATIONAL FUTURES ASSOCIATION. There will always be support for government regulation to prevent unfair market practices and excessive speculation that might distort prices. The government must ensure that self-regulation rules do not restrict competition. Now there is a swing back toward self-regulation, with government approval. A private group, the National Futures Association (NFA), has been granted the privilege of supervising firms and futures commission merchants dealing with the public. Independent of exchanges, the NFA is a regulatory organization operated by market participants and funded through a market transaction fee. The intention is to police the activities of dealers and firms who are not members of any exchange. There have been several instances of fraud, cheating, and unscrupulous activities by these individuals and associations, and the industry realizes the importance of public protection.

Specifically, the NFA is responsible for auditing and monitoring the sales practices and financial status of commodity professionals such as futures commission merchants, commodity pool operators, and commodity trading advisors and their agents. Membership is compulsory for these people but not for exchange members. The NFA conducts registration and fitness screening of these professionals and establishes training standards and proficiency tests. These activities assist the NFA in fulfilling its responsibility to enforce ethical standards and customer protection rules. The NFA also has an arbitration system designed for expedient and efficient settlements of commodity claims and disputes between customers and a NFA member or between NFA members. The NFA manages several regulatory activities for the CFTC, freeing the CFTC to concentrate on other oversight activities.

FUTURES TRADING ACT OF 1982. The Futures Trading Act of 1982 further amended the 1974 act, and wrote into law an agreement between the CFTC and the Securities and Exchange Commission (SEC) delineating their respective jurisdictions. This act also put into writing support for expanded industry self-regulation by requiring the NFA to implement a concrete plan for its regulatory activities. This specifically included registration of brokers and dealers.

Another key feature of the act was to authorize $3 million for a study to assess the impact of futures and options trading on the economy including the impact of trading on capital investment, and to determine whether any new laws are needed to protect the national interest. Specifically, congressional concern arose over the rapid expansion of financial futures trading, particularly the emergence of trading in stock index futures and options on futures contracts. Congress wondered whether these new instruments served an economic purpose, were competitive with existing securities markets, and created conflicts among alternative federal regulatory agencies. Congress directed the Federal Reserve Board, SEC, and CFTC to conduct a joint study addressing these issues. In addition, several leading scholars outside the government contributed independent research to these topics.[8] These studies indicate that the institutional arrangements, commercial and financial practices, private rules, and federal regulations are very complex and highly integrated in the attempt to foster efficient and financially secure trading. The studies recommend that public policy toward futures markets be based on thorough understanding of how the markets function, and not on superficially similar features of related markets.

The 1982 act specifically permitted the CFTC to inaugurate a three-year pilot program to trade options on domestic agricultural commodities banned since 1936. The act also authorized the right of commodity investors who suffer financial damages in a commodity futures or related transaction to sue brokers and exchanges if the damages were a result of a violation of the Commodities Exchange Act.[9]

CURRENT ISSUES

There remain several issues of continuing regulatory concern, and of course, new ones always arise as the industry and events change. In this section we highlight a few of them.

MARGINS

The question of whether the federal government or exchanges should control the size or level of margins continues to be debated and battled. The stock market crash of October 19, 1987, brought the issue to the forefront again. The exchanges originally had authority to determine margins, and they have maintained that authority despite many government attempts to assume control of margins.

The hypothesis is that low margins encourage excessive speculation leading to excessive price fluctuations and undermining the integrity of the market. Many regulators believe that timely changes in margins could in some way control price variation and prevent a financial panic resulting from the collapse of a speculative bubble. These same people argue that only the government, and not the exchanges, would have an interest in adjusting margins.

On the other hand, increased margins would increase hedging costs that would lead to decreased use of the futures market and decreased liquidity, a feature that could bring excessive price variability and even further increased hedging costs. High margins reduce available equity capital and increase the financial strain on hedging firms by reducing their ability to hedge away unwanted risks. At 100 percent margins, hedgers would probably carry their own risks, or find other alternatives. Thus, these people argue that for economic efficiency margins should be low; they presume that exchanges are more interested than the government in low margins because of the additional trading.

Thus, there are really two issues: one is the economics of low versus high margins, and the other is the likely attitude or posture of the controlling authority toward margin setting. One reason for the controversy is that margins in the stock market play a very different role than do margins in the futures market; many do not understand the distinction. Controlled by the federal government, margins in securities reflect the downpayment for buying stocks; where the balance must be borrowed. For most investors the margin requirement on stocks is 50 percent of the stock's market value, and this federally regulated minimum has not changed since 1974. It is designed to limit the role of credit in destabilizing stock prices and to prevent the diversification of credit from other productive uses. For the futures market, margins are earnest money put up by both the long and short sides to guarantee the performance of the contract. They are not downpayments, but a means to preserve the financial integrity of the markets by ensuring that both parties are able to fulfill obligations toward the contract. Futures margins are a function of price volatility, and traders are subject to the marking-to-market provision that reduces default risks to a one-day price move.

On the economic side of the issue, it is almost impossible to determine or define if there is excessive speculation in the market, and if there is, whether it is destabilizing or not. Regulators need to address the argument as a benefit-cost issue. Increasing margins increase costs for futures trading and decrease liquidity. This leads to poorer price discovery and a poorer allocation of resources. On the other hand, if low margins do lead to a speculative bubble, what are the costs of such a financial panic? The probability of such a bubble occurring seems low. In addressing the theory of margins, Telser discussed the optimal margin where presumably costs and benefits would be in equilibrium.[10] Unfortunately, there is no convenient formula for determining the optimal margin. Telser argues that increasing margin requirements can decrease open interest and volume which likely leads to increased volatility of futures prices. Hence, proponents of both low and high margin requirements see the end result being excessive or highly variable prices. This demonstrates the lack of existing empirical evidence.

Betsey Kuhn reviews four empirical studies on margins and concludes there is no empirical evidence to show that higher margins control price fluctuations.[11] Large price fluctuations are more likely associated with low rather than high levels of speculation. In fact, one study showed large price variability occurred with high margin levels. William Tomek could not find strong empirical relationships between margin and either volume or open interest because all three variables change as price volatility changes.[12] Michael Hartzmark found that changing margin levels brought a significantly negative response in open interest and volume, but not a statistically significant response in price volatility.[13] Because margin requirements impose costs on traders, he further found that changing margin levels significantly affect the composition of traders in the market, but it is impossible to predict which group of traders will enter or leave.

The other issue in the argument is whether the government would act more quickly and more in the public interest than would the exchanges in margin settings. Edwards reviewed the silver bubble when prices of silver skyrocketed from less than $10 to over $50 an ounce from late 1979 to early 1980.[14] The argument is that governing boards for exchanges are slow to make decisions to prevent panics and bubbles because of the conflict of interest resulting from these board members having market positions. The inference is that the government would act faster, yet in the silver bubble the CFTC was split two for and two against taking emergency action. As a result, the CFTC never acted. The Chicago Board of Trade intervened before both the CFTC and the COMEX exchange in New York where most silver trading was occurring. Hence, it is not necessarily clear that the government has better information, foresight, or judgment in adjusting margins than do the exchanges, nor would the government always act more quickly during an emergency.

A key issue in the debate is that daily price limits are and must be related to the margin requirement. Daily price limits act as protection for the futures commission merchant from a customer losing more money in one day than the margin posted. The limits provide financial protection to brokerage houses and dealers. Typically, commodities requiring small margins often have narrow daily price limits, other factors like contract size and price volatility held constant. Very wide daily price limits would require very large margins. Because exchanges set price limits, they should also have the authority to coordinate margins with those limits.

Thus, it is inappropriate for the government to have the authority to set margins on futures contracts. The CFTC is subject to too much political pressure. More importantly, federal regulators have neither presented a convincing economic justification for governmental authority, nor shown that government officials would act more swiftly or appropriately than exchanges in curbing or preventing so-called excessive speculation. The government already has emergency powers that it can invoke. From a benefit-cost standpoint, self-regulation probably is most appropriate. Tomek concludes that federal regulation is justified only if the exchanges do a poor job of enforcing their own rules.[15] He claims that exchanges have done well in setting margins relative to price variability, and that the benefits are small in moving from self-regulation to public regulation, while the costs are potentially large. Such a move could be counterproductive. Margins should be used only to maintain market integrity and guarantee performance, and not for other uses such as regulating volume, open interest, price behavior, or controlling excessive speculation.[16]

SPECULATIVE POSITION LIMITS

Speculative position limits establish the maximum number of contracts that a speculator can hold at any one time of a specific commodity. These limits apply only to speculators, not to hedgers. Rules for speculative limits were originally established in 1938, but applied to only major commodities. As recently as 1981, only one-quarter of futures commodities had federal positon limits, although some commodities were subject to exchange limits. Over half of the commodities had no speculative limits. However, in 1981 the CFTC adopted rules requiring speculative position limits on all commodity futures contracts. This ruling was an outgrowth of the silver bubble in 1979–80 when a small group of traders was able to acquire a very large number of silver futures contracts, a contract with no position limits. Currently, exchanges set some position limits and the CFTC sets others. There are variations in whether the limits apply to each delivery month or to the contract market.[17]

The notion behind the setting of speculative limits was to curb excessive speculation. Advocates alleged that large speculators were able to move prices in their favor with large trades. Hieronymus reviews the legislative history and assesses the quality of the research base used to establish the legislation.[18] He questions the validity of the research and feels the legislation is based on shaky results. Specifically, although strong correlation existed between the direction of the price change and change in net positions, none of the analysis investigated the relationship between the size of change in price and the size of change in net positions. This research was conducted in the 1920s; a new investigation is needed.

Peck investigated speculation levels in the corn, wheat, and soybean markets and found that declines in speculation were associated with increased price variability.[19] She states that these three markets "do not suffer from excess speculation and may be suffering the effects of inadequate speculation."[20]

There can be a need for large speculators. Large hedgers can force prices out of line and the best defense for that may be large speculators as countervailing power. Large speculators contribute to the price discovery process and can prevent unnecessary price concessions during peak hedging periods. Another argument is that one speculator with a large portion of the open interest may reduce liquidity so much that the position works against the trader.

One focal point of the speculative limit controversy was to define who in the market is a hedger and who is a speculator because the limits apply only to the latter. The 1974 act mandated that the CFTC provide a definition of hedging. The result in 1977 was a long, conceptual definition based on economic context. This definition is in chapter 4; it allows any firm to justify itself as a hedger. The definition also recognizes certain cases of anticipatory and cross hedging as legitimate hedges, thereby exempting these firms from speculative limits. Thus, the legal definition of hedging has important monetary and regulatory implications.

Speculative limits must fit within contract terms and other trading rules. The overall concern is orderly liquidation of a contract at maturity without price manipulation or distortion. Proposals for change are continually made, and in October 1987 the CFTC increased the speculative position limits for many agricultural contracts. Limits must be flexible and appropriate to the circumstances. If problems occur, then maybe limits should apply to all traders during the delivery period.

JURISDICTION

The CFTC has broad jurisdiction over the regulation of *commodities*, a term broadly defined. Technically, the CFTC could have jurisdiction over other markets such as cash markets, but it has made no attempt to regulate beyond futures market transactions. The CFTC would certainly be in court if it attempted any market regulation outside of futures, although it regularly obtains information from reporting futures traders about their cash market positions. Regulation of cash forward contracts and transactions on foreign exchanges are outside the scope of CFTC jurisdiction.

However, the introduction of futures contracts on financial instruments, stock indexes, and options on these contracts brought a jurisdictional dispute between the CFTC and the SEC. The SEC argues it has exclusive jurisdiction over securities and that some of these new contracts relate more to securities than to commodities. The two authorities agreed that the CFTC regulates all futures contracts and options on futures contracts traded on futures exchanges, while the SEC regulates all other securities, options, indexes, and foreign exchange traded on national securities exchanges. This latter group includes options on actual stock indexes and financial instruments. Thus, the regulation of an option on a financial instrument comes from a different authority than an option on a futures contract for the same financial instrument. Certainly, the authority of an agreement between the CFTC and SEC will be tested many times.

The stock market crash of October 19, 1987, again brought national attention to jurisdictional issues and to the regulation of securities and futures markets in general. Several study reports of the events surrounding that day are available, and the conclusions vary in accordance to who commissioned the study. Thus, the debate continues about the role of the futures market in contributing to the crash, or whether the stock market created an unwarranted speculative bubble by itself. Important to note is that all financial markets survived this crash, as opposed to the previous major stock market crash of 1929. So far, no major federal regulatory changes have occurred, and there is little cooperation among the major regulatory bodies toward a coordinated effort. Exchanges have imposed price limits on stock index futures and trading position limits on stock index options. Some major brokerage houses have halted index arbitrage trading for their own accounts, a computerized program method of trading stocks against stock index futures. Debate continues on the setting of margins. Only time will tell if major regulatory and jurisdictional changes are to occur.

DUAL TRADING

Dual trading refers to floor brokers being allowed to trade both customer orders and for their own accounts. Some people contend that dual trading is an inherent conflict of interest, but others argue that floor brokers need their own accounts to trade out mistakes and to supplement their income when trading is slow. Once a borker receives a customer's order, it must be traded before the broker executes a personal order. The floor broker can take the other side of the customer order only if there is specific consent given by the customer. Unfortunately, due to surveillance problems and greed by some, abuses continually occur.

To provide surveillance of the flow of orders, rules instituted several years ago required floor brokers to time stamp customer orders when received and again when executed. The trading day was divided into thiry-minute segments for time-stamping purposes. Although still in effect, this large time span could not detect abusive trade practices occurring within a thirty-minute time bracket. Recently, the CFTC established rules to reduce the thirty-minute bracket to one-minute brackets to reduce dual trading abuses. However, some question the ability of this new rule to curb offenses.[21]

Exchanges are now required to implement trade reconstruction systems to provide a recorded time of trade execution to the nearest minute. Called audit trails, exchanges are free to choose their own method for compliance. Obviously, computers are needed to reconstruct trade sequences for active contracts. In fact, the two largest exchanges in Chicago are considering installing electronic order-routing and execution systems to aid in surveillance as well as alleviate trading problems created by hand signals and hand-carried order slips.[22]

Central to the issue of dual trading is the effect on the quality of the order fills and, subsequently, market liquidity. Without dual trading, low volume markets may cease due to the lack of activity and large price concessions to complete a trade. Nevertheless, abuses remain prevalent in some markets, the situation became so bad that 400 members petitioned the Chicago Mercantile Exchange in 1987 to eliminate the practice of dual trading.

TRIPLE WITCHING HOUR

Once a calendar quarter all index options, stock options, and stock index futures contracts expire simultaneously; this is known as the triple witching hour. Through massive program trading activities associated with these simultaneous expirations, very sudden and volatile price changes occurred in the stock market during the last hour of trading, creating potentially hazardous trading circumstances for small investors. Arbitrageurs establish an index arbitrage to profit from price differentials, simultaneously purchaing or selling stocks against an opposite position in options or stock index futures contracts. The sudden price changes come from unpredictable, large orders placed by these traders unwinding their market positions at the close. Many large entries are computer controlled at large financial institutions.

To reduce these price behavior problems, exchanges are shifting the quarterly expiration of certain stock index futures and options contracts to the opening of trading from the close on those expiration days. They are researching alternative actions, and certainly other changes will come forth depending on their effectiveness and the nature of the remaining problems.

CASH SETTLEMENT

Since 1982 several futures contracts, especially index contracts, but also other financial instruments and a few physical commodities, are settled by cash payments between sellers and buyers rather than delivery of the cash commodity. For some contracts like index contracts, physical delivery is impossible. The key to successful cash settlement is whether reliable cash quotes or indexes are available on a regular basis to determine the final contract value. Such indexes are more feasible and available for financial instruments than for agricultural commodities.

Mechanically, cash settlement contracts differ from actual delivery contracts in that the settlement price on notice day for the former contracts is determined by a cash market index external to the futures market. Convergence between cash and futures prices is assured by setting the futures settlement price equal to a cash market index on the notice day. Arbitrage between cash and futures markets to bring convergence is not necessary in this case.[23] Also, there is no physical delivery in cash settlement markets. Cash settlement contracts can reduce basis risks when futures contracts are priced off average deliverable grades rather than the cheapest deliverable grade as in actual delivery contracts. Average prices change less than those for the cheapest deliverable grade.

Allan Paul reviews several of the policy issues associated with the cash settlement procedure.[24] Foremost is the concern of the effect on prices, including risk shifting effectiveness, market liquidity, and the temporal structure of prices. Related to this is the potential change in basis risks. Some argue that markets with cash settlement are much more difficult to manipulate at delivery time than when delivery is by physical commodity. Only experience will tell. Finally, some people question the economic purpose of cash settlement and the role of the government in regulating it. Expansion of cash settlement seems inevitable, especially to financial instruments, and to physical commodities because of the gains in efficiency; it also encourages the introduction of new contracts where only cash settlement is possible.

TAXES

The 1981 Economic Recovery Tax Act (ERTA) made significant changes in taxing gains and losses resulting from the trading of commodity futures contracts. Before that market positions called tax straddles could be taken in the futures market to defer income into future years. Tax straddles also reduced tax liabilities substantially by converting ordinary income and short-term capital gains into long-term capital gains. None of these features is available any more.

Tax codes treat hedgers differently from speculators. For those who buy and sell futures contracts as part of their business to reduce risks, gains or losses on the contracts are treated as ordinary income or loss. Firms realize these gains and losses whenever they finalize their cash market transactions and simultaneously terminate their futures contracts. Futures transactions then become a part of the ordinary business income.

Taxing for speculators is quite different, however, because futures contracts are treated as capital assets. The most significant change in the ERTA was to require speculators to mark-to-market all contracts held at year end and to include the unrealized gains or losses as income. The mark-to-market concept requires that the contract be treated as if sold for its fair market value on the last business day of the taxable year. This provision, of course, prevents the taxpayer from carrying gains or losses into a subsequent tax year. Contracts terminated during the year accumulate realized gains and losses. All realized and unrealized gains and losses are netted at the end of the year for tax purposes.

ERTA deemed these gains and losses as 40 percent short-term and 60 percent long-term for tax purposes, regardless of the length of time held. In 1986 Congress repealed the capital gains provision from taxes; since 1988 futures trading income has been treated for tax purposes like all other income with a maximum tax rate of 28 percent. However, the mark-to-market concept for taxing at year end still applies to speculators, but not to hedgers. The interesting question remaining for research is how these tax law changes affect traders' behavior, price level, and variability.

MARKET MANIPULATION

The concern over price manipulation is a central focus of federal legislation dating back to 1922. It is also of concern to exchanges as their rules prohibit market manipulation. Congressional preoccupation with manipulation is documented by the existence of at least fourteen sections in the Commodity Exchange Act dealing with the subject.[25] Federal rules and regulations sometimes specifically address manipulation and the need to provide for its prevention. Often accompanying these rules is a set of fines and jail sentences for the guilty. However, most federal legislation addresses manipulation indirectly through establishing rules on other aspects of commodity trading. For example, the CFTC licenses exchanges that must provide their own guidelines for the prevention of manipulation. Federal regulations deal with issues such as speculative position limits, delivery points, dual trading, dissemination of false information, abusive trading practices, market surveillance, reporting market positions, market congestion, and restraint of trade, all dealing in some way with the prevention of manipulation. Also, the CFTC has the power to intervene in markets during an emergency; manipulation is one such instance. Most futures market regulation is concerned with manipulation and the protection of customers.

Despite this concern, Congress has never seen fit to define manipulation, and rightly so. A specific definition is virtually impossible as the circumstances and events surrounding each case are unique and diverse with individual elements of causation. The definition of manipulation has been left to the judicial system, although no case concerning commodity futures contracts has ever reached the U.S. Supreme Court. Hence, various lower courts assume different positions or interpretations.

Actually, the number of known manipulation cases is not large, and they have been reviewed and discussed adequately elsewhere. Hieronymus describes a few classical cases of manipulation around the turn of the century,[26] while others discuss more recent cases.[27] A.C. Johnson reported that from 1945 to 1974 twenty-nine complaints were filed, twenty-eight having to do with commodity futures contracts.[28] Of these twenty-eight, nineteen were settled with some agreement or stipulation, or there was no contest, while only nine were brought to trial. Some argue that the market itself may be the best preventor as several manipulation attempts have been defeated by market action of other traders.[29]

Manipulation involves both an economic and a legal question; exactly what is manipulation remains vague. Thus, manipulation has been decomposed into elements, each with a specific criteria. These criteria assume different levels of importance for each case.

Manipulation has taken on different definitions in various legal cases. In brief, manipulation implies intent to cause a price to be something other than it would have been under normal demand and supply conditions. Defining normal demand and supply conditions becomes a point of academic debate. The elements on which cases focus are: (1) a distorted or artificial price; (2) a dominant or controlling futures position; (3) a dominant or controlling position in deliverable supplies; (4) actions taken to cause an artificial price; and (5) manipulative intent.[30]

Manipulation can occur from either the long side or short side. On the long side, the trader buys nearby futures contracts exceeding the deliverable supply immediately available, accepts delivery on these contracts, and forces a high price on shorts supplying the contracts or physical commodity. This same long trader may also have control over much of the deliverable supply. The cash and futures prices in the delivery market are forced abnormally high in relation to other markets and futures contracts. Interestingly, most manipulation attempts are from the long side.

For short-side manipulation, the trader puts a very large quantity of the commodity into a deliverable position, sells an even larger number of futures contracts and attempts to force down the price with deliveries. To be successful, the deliveries must fall into the hands of those traders who need to establish new short positions to redeliver the commodity, adding to the same price pressure.

Both of the events just described are known as a *corner* where the manipulator's actions during contract expiration contribute either to a cash market shortage or excess deliverable supply. The trader has dominant positions in two markets. In contrast, a *squeeze* occurs because of a scarcity in deliverable supply, due maybe to quality or transportation problems or lack of uncommitted commodity, and the shorts are unable to fulfill their delivery commitments. Thus, they must offset their positions at prices set by the longs, or they must default. Recognize that for a squeeze the scarcity in deliverable supply does not occur because of deliberate action taken by the longs, although they often take advantage of the situation.

The first issue the CFTC must address in a manipulation case is whether an artificial price occurred and whether the traders acted in a manner to cause the distortation. It is never easy to define a normal price, let alone an aberration in that price. For example, if the price of a spot commodity and delivery contract moved $0.10 a bushel on the last day of trading relative to all other contracts and markets, at what point did manipulation occur? If a $0.10 move is manipulation, what about $0.08?

Or $0.06? And so on. The courts carefully scrutinize the action of the traders at the time of the price distortion. They examine whether the accused traders were adding to their positions, liquidating them, or attempting to force an abnormal price on the other side.

An artificial or distorted price must always be defined in relation to some other prices. Four possibilities exist: (1) the price of the futures contract immediately before delivery is high or low relative to the price of the delivered commodity immediately after delivery; (2) the price of the delivery contract is high or low relative to prices of deferred contracts; (3) the cash price of deliverable goods under contract is high or low relative to cash prices of nondeliverable goods; (4) the price of the cheapest to deliver good is bid up relative to the price of more expensive goods, providing multiple grades are deliverable.[31]

The second area that the courts and CFTC must address in alleged manipulation cases is the relative position of the manipulator in the cash and futures markets and the existence of deliverable supply. The prosecution must establish that the manipulator had a dominant or controlling position in the cash and/or futures market. As with artificial price, what constitutes a dominant position is subject to debate and depends on relationships to other markets. There are few specific guidelines or norms available. The courts may find that 60 percent of the market is dominant in one case while in another it may take 90 percent to be dominant. It depends on whether the market position caused congestion in market activity, and the number of trading hours remaining. A trader's domination of the market can increase naturally without taking market positions because open interest declines as termination of trading approaches. So, dominant or controlling positions in cash and futures markets become unique to the case and trading activity of the alleged manipulator.

One of the thornier issues concerns what constitutes deliverable supplies. The courts need to know not only the trader's position relative to open interest, but also the position relative to deliverable supply.[32,33]

Deliverable supply is less than available supply because some commodity does not qualify for delivery, some is committed for processing or shipment, and some is not in a convenient location for delivery. The exact amount is never precise because at certain price levels traders can shift shipping commitments to alternative locations and delay processing commitments. Deliverable supply usually includes all the commodity of reasonable quality in delivery position and certifyable for delivery. This can include that supply outside the delivery location which could be put into delivery position without undue expense. Because this latter action takes time, when to determine deliverable supply during the delivery month can become important. Courts usually define it according to what seems appropriate for the case, but concentrate on the day manipulation occurs. Trader action in accumulating or dispersing supplies during the delivery month usually is important information.

The emphasis on deliverable supplies punctuates the critical nature of delivery terms for the successful trading of futures contracts. Terms defined too broadly make the market difficult to use and discourage deliveries because it may not be clear what the price represents, while too narrow terms can lead to distortion and lack of arbitrage opportunities. Because a manipulator needs to control supply, inappropriate delivery terms and restricted deliverable supply can encourage manipulation. Some argue that cash settlement of futures contracts will eliminate many of these problems, but we need more experience.

Finally, manipulation cases ultimately must show that the trader intended to cause an artificial price, and this is more of a legal than economic issue. The debate centers on whether the trader wanted an artificial price and took actions intentionally and knowingly to create an artificial price. Some argue that traders large enough to manipulate should be knowledgeable about their actions and profits are proof of intent. However, not all manipulation attempts result in profits for the manipulator. Some lose money; others attempt to minimize large losses. Also, profits alone may not be sufficient to prove manipulation.

Intent to manipulate a market is very difficult to prove. One must look at circumstantial evidence and the course of action that the trader took. The evidence is never very direct, and its sufficiency rests with the court and the case at hand.

Sometimes when there is concentration on one side of the market with circumstances appearing like manipulation, there is also concentration on the other side. Only one side can win, and that is the side most likely charged with manipulation. However, in the potato default case of 1976 when the shorts failed to deliver about 1,000 contracts of potatoes, the government charged both the long and short traders with attempted manipulation.

Manipulation cases are decided in the courts, and economists have no theoretical model concerning futures market manipulation. Such a theory would need to address issues such as the delivery process, agents with market power, imperfect information, and financial requirements.[34] Several rules are already in place for prohibiting manipulation, but the appropriateness of government regulation depends on the social costs and benefits of attempting to reduce manipulation, and what incentives exist in the private economy for less manipulable markets. The question remains as to which policies are effective in preventing manipulation.

Albert Kyle offers an initial, but restricted, attempt at such a model.[35] His model addresses the relative price outcomes between two goods of different quality under game-theoretic conditions when the squeezer has privileged information about aggregate hedging. Although the model does not immediately help resolve court cases on manipulation, it does demonstrate how the anonymity of futures trading can allow a large trader with information about hedging orders to profit from taking market positions that create a squeeze.[36]

Nevertheless, despite the preoccupation and concern with manipulation and that it underlies much of the established regulation, there have not been many cases brought to court. Maybe this small number is due to effective regulatory rules, or alternatively, due to the difficulty in proving manipulation once in court. Actually, exchanges have a very strong incentive to prevent manipulation because their success and survival depends on market integrity. If manipulation occurred frequently, traders would quickly find other market alternatives. Manipulation can increase the cost of hedging, or reduce its effectiveness, diminishing the attractiveness of futures markets to hedgers. The lack of high integrity can lead to the demise of futures markets.

PERFORMANCE ISSUES

CONTRACT FAILURE AND SUCCESS

We outlined the common characteristics of futures contracts in chapter 2. However, contracts come and go. Some are successful, then fade out of existence even though they appear to have the necessary characteristics. Other contracts just never get off the floor. Citing failures is not to overlook that some contracts are over one hundred years old and have continued in existence since the inception of futures trading. This section outlines the success and failure of futures contracts.

Following is a partial list of why futures contracts fail, associating principally with agricultural contracts:

1. The contract may be poorly written, favoring either the longs or the shorts. If one side has an advantage through contract terms, the disadvantaged eventually refuse to participate. Turkey futures were active in 1962–63, but dwindled as short hedgers took advantage of the contract specifications. Early contracts for hogs and pork bellies were rewritten to prevent their demise.

2. A boycott by commercial interests with market power may stifle interest in a contract. Allegedly, this was the case for cottonseed oil and wine contracts.

3. The government may ban the contract, such as onions. The potato contract survived many legislative attempts, but eventually failed to survive the marketplace.

4. The contract may lose its economic basis for existence. A fresh egg contract replaced the storage egg contract as egg production became a year-around event. Lard no longer has wide commercial interest. Governmental price fixing and production programs brought a near halt to the cotton contract for several years.

5. Some contracts just fail to attract speculators and, therefore, lack liquidity. Bid-ask spreads become too large, discouraging hedgers. Cause and effect is difficult to determine because if the contract initially had the confidence of hedgers, speculators should follow. However, sometimes speculators show no interest, maybe due to a lack of sufficient price movements.

Before introducing new contracts, exchanges must determine the benefits and costs of the contract and measure the likelihood of success. The costs of introducing a contract can be quite high. Exchanges usually work closely with the industry and commercial firms to obtain the correct specification and generate hedging interests.

Failure occurs among commodity and instrument contracts alike. A glance at table 2-2 shows some recently introduced contracts that quickly failed, especially among financial index contracts. Of recent fame were the highly advertised, competing over-the-counter stock index futures contracts introduced by the Chicago Board of Trade and Chicago Mercantile Exchange in 1985. Despite the several million dollars spent promoting them, both contracts failed. Success is difficult to predict apriori.

Deborah Black claims to have developed a model that can predict the success of financial instrument contracts.[37] Defining success by volume, she found volume related to relative residual risk, cross-hedge liquidity, price volatility, and size of the cash market. If a theoretically perfect hedge is one with no risk, then residual risk is the uncovered portion of a hedged position. Cross-hedge liquidity refers to the liquidity in a related market that could serve as a hedging instrument. Price volatility and size of the cash market are more obvious necessary variables to predict success. The model has been fairly accurate in predicting success and failure of financial instrument contracts.

PERFORMANCE

We presented in chapter 6 a detailed discussion of forward-pricing performance, and hence, efficiency of futures markets. We cited several studies revealing mixed results with respect to forward-pricing abilities of futures markets. Similar evidence was noted for financial instruments in chapter 9.

To our knowledge, however, no one has done a full evaluation of futures markets and their impact on society and social welfare. Models exist which demonstrate that when uncertainty and risk premiums are reduced, production increases. Speculators in accepting price risks may well promote increases in real output. Also, allowing hedgers to manage risks though centralized futures markets lowers overall marketing costs for the industry; this can benefit both producers and consumers.

Futures markets play other roles also, such as in helping secure financial collateral, processing and interpreting information, and allocating scarce resources. To study all these aspects simultaneously in a comprehensive fashion would be difficult without oversimplifying assumptions, so what remains are many partial analyses of market performance, costs, and benefits. Nevertheless, when considering all the roles together, we feel that these markets provide a large net benefit to society and social welfare. Their benefits through the roles just mentioned far exceed their costs. Through trader interpretation of information, the markets provide accurate signals about future demand and supply conditions, thus directing and allocating resources optimally. The continued use of them by commercial firms for over one hundred years speaks to their importance and contribution. Although individuals may think of improvements in the market here and there, no one has developed an alternative market format that can provide more market services at a cheaper cost than the futures markets. Due to their wide acceptance, use, and benefits, futures markets are most likely here to stay. This positive pronouncement, however, is not to deny there can be large costs to individuals and society from misuse of these markets, and the evidence toward that concern is the substantial level of regulation imposed on futures markets.

NOTES

1. Corner and squeeze are defined and illustrated later in this chapter.
2. F.R. Edwards, "The Regulation of Futures Markets: A Conceptual Framework," *Journal of Futures Markets* 1 (1981): 417–39.
3. F.R. Edwards, "Futures Markets in Transition: An Uneasy Balance between Government and Self-Regulation," *Journal of Futures Markets* 3 (1983): 191–205.
4. One of the best short reviews of the legislative history on which we base some of this discussion is J.V. Rainbolt II, "Regulating the Grain Gambler and His Successors," *Hofstra Law Review* 6 (1977): 1–25.
5. For an overview of CFTC regulatory philosophy and practice, see S.M. Phillips, "Regulation of Futures Markets: Theory and Practice," *Review of Research in Futures Markets* 3 (1984): 150–58.
6. Dual trading, discussed later, refers to a floor broker being able to trade for both a personal account and outside customers.
7. Edwards, "The Regulation of Futures Markets."
8. A.E. Peck, ed. *Futures Markets: Regulatory Issues;* and *Futures Markets: Their Economic Role* (Washington, D.C.: American Enterprise Institute, 1985).
9. Futures markets in England are much less closely regulated than in the United States, with the Bank of England providing primarily surveillance and advice to the markets. For a

comparison of market regulation in the two countries, see: G.T. Gemmill, "Regulating Futures Markets: A Review in the Context of British and American Practice," in *Futures Markets: Modeling, Managing, and Monitoring Futures Trading,* ed. M.E. Streit (London: Basil Blackwell, 1983), 295–318.

10. L.G. Telser, "Margins and Futures Contracts," *Journal of Futures Markets* 1 (1981): 225–53.
11. B.A. Kuhn, "Margins: A Review of Literature," *Research on Speculation* (Chicago Board of Trade, 1981), 84–93.
12. W.G. Tomek, "Margins of Futures Contracts: Their Economic Roles and Regulation," in *Futures Markets: Regulatory Issues.* ed. A.E. Peck (Washington, D.C.: American Enterprise Institute, 1985), 143–209.
13. M.L. Hartzmark, "The Effects of Changing Margin Levels on Futures Market Activity, the Composition of Traders in the Market, and Price Performance," *Journal of Business* 59 (1986): S147–S180.
14. Edwards, "Futures Markets in Transition."
15. Tomek, "Margins of Futures Contracts."
16. Hartzmark, "The Effects of Changing Margin Levels."
17. A historical review and analysis of speculative limits is provided by A.B. Paul, "Speculative Position Limits," *Research on Speculation* (Chicago Board of Trade, 1981), 122–36.
18. Hieronymus, *Economics of Futures Trading,* 333–39.
19. A.E. Peck, "Increase Speculative Limits?" *Commodities* 10 (February, 1981): 20–8.
20. For other studies on market performance and speculative adequacy in futures markets, see A.E. Peck. "The Role of Economic Analysis in Futures Market Regulation," *American Journal of Agricultural Economics* 62 (1980): 1037–43; and R.M. Leuthold, "Commercial Use and Speculative Measures of the Livestock Commodity Futures Markets," *Journal of Futures Markets* 3 (1983): 113–35.
21. S.J. Grossman and M.H. Miller, "Economic Costs and Benefits of the Proposed One-Minute Time Bracketing Regulation," *Journal of Futures Markets* 6 (1986): 141–66.
22. This topic relates to the interesting issue of computerizing futures trading. Many activities associated with futures markets are already computerized, except trading itself. Certain aspects of programmed stock trading and hedging stock indexes are already computerized. The benefits of computerized trading focus primarily on gains in efficiency and performance, increased availability of information, and reduced costs. Detractors are concerned about market control and surveillance. Electronic trading in futures markets will likely be predominant some day, but in off-shore markets before in the United States.
23. F.J. Jones, "The Economics of Futures and Options Contracts Based on Cash Settlements," *Journal of Futures Markets* 2 (1982): 63–82.
24. A.B. Paul, "The Role of Cash Settlement in Futures Contract Specification," in *Futures Markets: Regulatory Issues.* ed., A.E. Peck (Washington, D.C.: American Enterprise Institute, 1985), 271–328.
25. P. Johnson, "Key Cases in Manipulation," *Research on Speculation* (Chicago Board of Trade, 1981), 96–107.
26. Hieronymus, *Economics of Futures Trading,* 321–24.
27. P. Johnson, "Key Cases,"; R.W. Gray, "Economic Evidence in Manipulation Cases," *Research on Speculation* (Chicago Board of Trade, 1981), 108–14; and E.T. McDermott,

"Defining Manipulation in Commodity Futures Trading: The Futures 'Squeeze'," *Northwestern University Law Review* 74 (1979): 202–25.

28. A.C. Johnson, *Economic Analysis of Price Manipulation under the Commodity Exchange Act: 1945–1974.* Report prepared for the Commodity Futures Trading Commission under Grant 801-CFTC-76, October, 1976.
29. Gray, "Economic Evidence."
30. T.A. Hieronymus, "Manipulation in Commodity Futures Trading: Toward a Definition," *Hofstra Law Review* 6 (1977): 41–56.
31. R.W. Anderson, "The Industrial Organization of Futures Markets: A Survey," in *The Industrial Organization of Futures Markets,* ed. R.W. Anderson (Lexington, Mass.: Lexington Books, 1984), 1–33.
32. For examples of the data gathered in two alleged manipulation cases, see: T.A. Hieronymus, "How the Practical Aspects of Testimony Directed Some Research," *Research of Speculation* (Chicago Board of Trade, 1981), pp. 52–66.
33. For a thorough discussion of aspects of deliverable supply, see Hieronymus, "Manipulation in Commodity Futures Trading"; and P. Johnson, "Key Cases."
34. Anderson, "Industrial Organization."
35. A.S. Kyle, "A Theory of Futures Market Manipulation," in *The Industrial Organization of Futures Markets.* ed. R.W. Anderson (Lexington, Mass.: Lexington Books, 1984), pp. 141–73.
36. For other models, cases, and discussions of the economics and welfare impacts of hedging, see L.N. Edwards and F.R. Edwards, "A Legal and Economic Analysis of Manipulation in Futures Markets," *Journal of Futures Markets* 4 (1984): 333–66; and R.W. Anderson, "The Regulation of Futures Contract Innovations in the United States," *Journal of Futures Markets* 4 (1984): 297–332.
37. D.G. Black, "Success and Failure of Futures Contracts: Theory and Empirical Evidence." Monograph Series in Finance and Economics. Monograph 1986-1. (New York: NYU-Salomon Brothers Center for the Study of Financial Institutions, 1986).

GLOSSARY

Accrued interest option—One of the seller's options under the CBOT T-bond and note contracts. The choice of whether to deliver the bond into the futures contract or to continue to accrue interest on the bond for another day.

Adjusted duration—Bond or portfolio duration divided by (1 + yield); approximates the percentage change in the bond price for a percentage change in the yield.

Alpha—A measure of excess return on a stock portfolio; the difference between the stock's actual return and the rate of return based on the stock's systematic risk

American option—An option that can be exercised at any time prior to maturity.

Arbitrage—Simultaneous purchase and sale of securities, cash commodities, or futures at different prices to profit from a price discrepancy. In financial, the arbitrage generally involves no net investment by the arbitrageur, and once positions are established, the return is riskless and certain. Includes some aspects of hedging. See Spread.

At the money—An option whose exercise price is equal to the current price of the underlying futures.

Backwardation—Market situation in which futures prices are progressively lower in the distant delivery months.

Basis—The difference between a cash price at a specific location and the price of a particular futures contract.

Basis point—Measurement of a change in the yield of a security; one basis point equals 1/100 of 1 percent.

Basis risk—The risk associated with unexpected changes in the basis between the time a hedge is placed and when it is lifted.

Bear—One who believes prices are too high and will decline.

Bear spread (options)—The purchase of a put (call) with an exercise price greater than the exercise price of the put (call) sold. The two options have the same maturity. The bear spread will have limited profit (loss) if the underlying futures price falls (rises).

Beta—A measure of a stock's risk; the volatility of the stock's return in relation to the market portfolio return. The high the beta, the riskier the stock and the larger the return, on average, expected from holding the stock. A measure of systematic risk.

Bid—An offer to buy a specific quantity of a commodity at a stated price.

Broker—(1) A person paid a fee or commission for acting as an agent in making contracts, sales, or purchases. (2) A floor broker who actually executes someone else's trading orders on the trading floor of an exchange. (3) An account executive who deals with customers and their orders in commission-house offices.

Bucket—Illegal practice of accepting customer orders to buy or sell without executing such orders on an exchange.

Bull—One who believes prices are too low and will advance.

Bull spread (options)—The purchase of a put (call) with an exercise price less than the exercise price of the put (call) sold. The two options have the same maturity. The bull spread will have limited profit (loss) if the underlying futures price rises (falls).

Call option—The right, but not the obligation, to buy the underlying futures contract at a specific price for a length of time.

Carrying charges—(1) Those costs incurred in warehousing the physical commodity, generally including interest, insurance, and storage. (2) Full carrying charge market—A situation in the futures market when the price difference between delivery months reflects the full costs of interest, insurance, and storage.

Cash forward—See Forward Contract.

Certificate of deposit—A short-term obligation of a bank with a fixed maturity, generally less than 270 days. Interest is paid at maturity.

Cheapest to deliver—The bond deliverable into a futures contract that has the largest difference in the seller's favor between the price received in the futures market and the cash market price for it. Because this bond is expected to be delivered, the futures price is based on this bond's cash price.

Clearinghouse—The separate agency associated with a futures exchange through which futures contracts are offset or fulfilled and through which financial settlement is made. (Also called a clearing association.)

Conversion factor—Calculated by the CBOT, the factor adjusts the delivery futures price to reflect the 8 percent coupon, 15-year maturity T-bond underlying the contract and the bond actually delivered. Calculated by pricing the delivered bond at an 8 percent yield as of the futures delivery date and dividing the price by 100. Each deliverable bond would have a different factor for a different maturity contract.

Corner—(1) To corner is to secure such relative control of a commodity or security that its price can be manipulated. (2) In the extreme situation, obtaining contracts requiring the delivery of commodities or securities exceeding the existing quantity of such commodities or securities.

Covered option—An option for which the writer owns the underlying obligated position. A written call is one for which the writer has the long futures position.

Cylinder—A hedge of an interest rate sensitive asset or liability constructed with options. For a long asset position, a put on the asset is sold to protect its value; to pay for this protection, a call option with a higher exercise price is simultaneously written.

Deliverable stocks—Commodities located in exchange-approved storage certified for delivery on futures contracts.

Delivery month—The calendar month during which a futures contract matures.

Delivery notice—The notification of delivery of the actual commodity on the contract, issued by the seller of the futures to the clearinghouse.

Delivery points—Those locations designated by commodity exchanges at which a commodity covered by a futures contract may be delivered in fulfillment of the contract.

Delta—The change in price of an option with respect to a change in the underlying futures price. The delta changes with maturity and the price of the futures contract in relation to the exercise price.

Delta neutral—The purchase (sale) of a varying number of put and call options in a straddle such that the value of the total straddle position is unaffected by changes in the underlying futures price.

Discount—Indicating one price is below another price.

Distant or deferred delivery—Usually means one of the more distant months in which futures trading is taking place.

Dual trading—Allowing floor brokers to execute trades for customers as well as their own accounts.

Duration—The elasticity of bond price with respect to bond yield; a measure of the price volatility of a bond. Also, the weighted average time to maturity of a bond, in which the times when a cash flow is received are weighted by the proportion of the price the cash flow represents.

European option—An option exercisable only at maturity.

Exercise price—The price at which the option holder can buy (call) or sell (put) the underlying futures.

Expiration—The maturity of the option.

Ex-pit transaction—Trades executed, for certain technical reasons, in a location other than the regular exchange trading pit. The futures trade is offset by an accompanying and equal cash transaction. (Also called Exchange for Physicals and Cash-Futures Swaps.)

Forward contract—An agreement to deliver a cash commodity from seller to buyer of specified quality and quantity at a specified future date. Price may or may not be determined. Forward cash contracts are personalized between buyer and seller.

Fungible—The characteristic of being interchangeable.

Futures contract—A transferable, legally binding, agreement to make or take delivery of a standardized amount of a commodity, or standardized minimum quality grades, during a specific month, under terms and conditions established by the federally designated contract market on which trading is conducted.

Hedge ratio—The ratio of the value (number) of futures contracts purchased or sold to the value of the cash commodity or instrument being hedged which minimizes risk.

Hedging—Taking a position in a futures market opposite to a position held in the cash market to minimize the risk of financial loss from an adverse price change; a purchase or sale of futures as a temporary substitute for a cash transaction that will occur later.

Horizontal spread (options)—The purchase and simultaneous sale of two call or two put options differing only in maturity.

Immunization—A portfolio management strategy in which the duration of the portfolio held is set equal to the holding period. If this is done, the total yield on the portfolio is equal to the initial yield to maturity irrespective of any intervening interest rate changes.

Implied forward rate—The expected interest rate for a future time period implied by the level of current yields. Under the Pure Expectations Hypothesis, any expected rate can be estimated by the ratio of the observable long-term rate for a maturity at the end of the period in question to the observable short-term rate for a maturity at the beginning of the period in question.

Implied repo (repurchase) rate—The break-even short-term borrowing rate for the purchase and holding of a cash security in an arbitrage. Given the futures price, the IRR represents the highest rate at which the arbitrageur could borrow in the cash market, or the lowest rate at which the arbitrageur could lend or purchase, and achieve a net zero arbitrage profit.

In the money—An option whose exercise price is greater than the underlying futures price for a call, or less than the futures price for a put.

Intrinsic value—The value of the option if exercised immediately, equal to the price of the underlying futures less the exercise price (call) or the exercise price less the price of the underlying futures (put).

Inverted markets—A futures market in which the nearer months are selling at premiums to the more distant months; hence, a market displaying "inverse carrying charges," characteristic of situations in which supplies are currently in shortage.

Invoice amount—The dollar amount received for delivery of a security into the futures market, equal to the futures price times the conversion factor.

Last trading day—Day on which trading ceases for the maturing (current) delivery month.

LIBOR (London Interbank Offered Rate)—The rate paid on Eurodollar deposits loaned between banks; the rate varies with the maturity of the Eurodollar deposit.

Limit (up or down)—The maximum price advance or decline from the previous day's settlement price permitted in one trading session by the rules of the exchange.

Liquidation—The closing out of a position—often refers to the closing of a long position. "Covering" is sometimes used for the closing of a short position.

Liquid market—A market of sufficient volume where one can buy or sell contracts at little or no price concession.

Long—One who has bought futures contracts or cash commodity and has not yet offset that position.

Long the basis—The purchase of cash commodity and the sale of futures against unsold inventory.

Macrohedge—A hedge of the total risk exposure of an institution; hedges the total interest rate volatility of an institution as a single portfolio of assets.

Margin—The amount deposited by buyers and sellers of futures, to insure performance on contract commitments; serves as a performance bond rather than a downpayment. Initial margin is the amount required when a futures position is opened. Maintenance margin is the minimum amount that must be maintained on deposit at all times.

Margin call—A request to deposit either the original margin at the time of the transaction, or to restore the guarantee to a required minimum level.

Market timing—A portfolio investment strategy designed to shift into or out of stocks depending on the expectation of rising or falling stock prices. If market turning points can be forecasted accurately, the yield on the portfolio should be greater than the yield on the market for the same time period.

Mark-to-market—A daily cash flow system of calculating the gain or loss in each contract position resulting from changes in the contract price at the end of each trading day and adjusting the customer account accordingly.

Maturity—Period within which a futures contract can be settled by delivery of the actual commodity; the period between the first notice day and the last trading day of a commodity futures contract.

Microhedge—A hedge of single asset or liability interest rate risk in an institutional portfolio. See macrohedge.

Nearby delivery—Means the nearest traded contract month.

Net position—The difference between the open contracts long and the open contracts short held in any one commodity.

Notice day—Any day on which notices of intent to deliver on futures contracts may be issued.

Offer—An indication of willingness to sell at a given price; the opposite of bid.

Offset—Usually the liquidation of a long or short futures position by an equal and opposite futures transaction.

Open interest—The total number of futures contracts of a given commodity that have been entered into and not yet offset by opposite futures transactions nor fulfilled by delivery of the commodity; the total number of open transactions.

Out of the money—An option whose exercise price is less than the underlying futures price for a call, or greater than the futures price for a put.

Par—(1) The standard delivery point or points or quality of the commodity represented in the contract that is deliverable at contract price. (2) In bond markets, an index (usually 100) representing the face value of a bond.

Point—Minimum change in price up or down.

Portfolio insurance—The adjustment of a futures position in conjunction with a bond portfolio. The futures are adjusted to imitate the hedging qualities of an option on the portfolio.

Position limit—The maximum number of speculative futures contracts one can hold open under the rules of the CFTC or the exchange on which the contract is traded.

Position trading—An approach to trading in which the trader either buys or sells contracts and holds them for an extended time, as distinguished from a day trader who initiates and offsets positions within a single trading session.

Premium—A price relationship where one price is higher than another price.

Premium (options)—Price of an option, equal to the intrinsic value, if any, plus the time value.

Price limit move—See Limit.

Principal risk—The risk that a change in yield over the holding period of a bond will change the resale value of the bond at the end of the investment.

Profit diagram—A graphic representation of the dollar value of an option in relation to the price of the futures at expiration.

Program trading—The use of computer linkages to the floor of the NYSE to execute trades in a large number of stocks almost simultaneously.

Put option—The right, but not the obligation, to sell the underlying futures at a specified price for a length of time.

Quality option—A seller's option embedded in the CBOT futures delivery specifications. The ability of the seller to choose which of the bonds eligible for delivery to deliver during the maturity month.

Quasi-arbitrage—Preferential purchase or sale of one of two equivalent securities, generally futures versus the cash equivalent. Involves an investment by the quasiarbitrageur; the return on the quasi-arbitrage is higher than the risk-adjusted rate of return by the amount of mispricing on the futures.

Range forward—See Cylinder.

Reinvestment risk—The risk that a change in yield over the holding period of a bond will change the rate at which coupons received can be reinvested.

Reporting level—The number of futures contracts, as determined by the CFTC, above which one must report daily to the exchange and the CFTC with regard to the size of one's position by commodity, by delivery month, and by purpose of trading.

Repurchase agreement (repo)—An agreement to sell securities with a corresponding agreement to buy them back, usually the next day, at a higher price. The agreement is a short-term loan, and the difference in price represents interest on the loan; the securities serve as collateral.

Retender—The right of holders of futures contracts who have been tendered a delivery notice through the clearinghouse to offer the notice for sale on the open market, liquidating their obligation to take delivery under the contract.

Roll hedge—Hedging a long-term asset or liability position with a series of individual maturity futures contracts. When one futures matures, the hedge is rolled over into the next delivery month.

Scalper—A speculator operating on the trading floor who provides market liquidity by buying and selling rapidly, holding positions for a short time, with small profits or losses.

Settlement price—The daily price at which the clearinghouse clears all the day's trades; also a price established by the exchange to settle contracts unliquidated because of acts of God, such as floods, or market congestion and other causes.

Short—The selling side of an open futures contract; also refers to a trader whose net position shows an excess of open sales over open purchases.

Short the basis—The purchase of futures as a hedge against a commitment to sell in the cash or spot market.

Speculator—One who attempts to anticipate commodity price changes and to profit through the sale and purchase or purchase and sale of commodity futures contracts or of the physical commodity; one who does not hedge.

Spot price—The price at which a physical commodity is selling at a given time and place. Same as cash price.

Spread (or) Straddle—The purchase of one futures contract and sale of another, in the expectation that the price relationships between the two will change so that a subsequent offsetting sale and purchase yields a net profit.

Squeeze—Situation in which those short cannot repurchase their contracts, except at a price substantially higher than the value of related contracts in the market.

Stack hedge—An alternative to the strip hedge in which the hedger buys or sells a strip of futures with proportionately more nearby contracts than deferred.

Stock selection—A portfolio investment strategy designed to purchase or sell stocks price lower or higher than their true value based on discounted value of expected cash flow.

Straddle (options)—An option strategy in which a put and call with the same exercise price and maturity are bought (buy straddle) or sold (sell straddle).

Strike price—Exercise price of an option.

Strip hedge—A position using several sequential maturity futures to hedge an interest rate asset or liability maturing at the last contract's delivery.

Strip of futures—The purchase or sale of futures with successive maturities.

Systematic risk—The risk of a stock relative to marketwide movements. It cannot be offset or diversified away by combining the stock with other stocks in a portfolio.

Swap (Currency)—A matched purchase and sale of a foreign currency forward for different delivery dates. The two legs of the swap correspond to an unhedged forward transaction and are designed to match a previously contracted forward sale and purchase.

Tick—See Point.

Time value—That part of an option's price over the intrinsic value tied to the time to maturity.

Triangular arbitrage—Arbitrage effected if there is a disequilibrium between two pairs of foreign currency rates ($\$/FC_1$, $\$/FC_2$) and the cross-rate of those currencies (FC_1/FC_2).

Waiting option—A seller's option embedded in the CBOT bond and note contracts. The ability of the seller to choose when to deliver within the delivery month.

Warehouse receipt—A document evidencing possession by a licensed warehouse of the commodity. To be tenderable of future contracts, they must cover commodities recognized for delivery purposes by the exchange on which futures contracts are traded.

Vertical spread (options)—The simultaneous purchase and sale of two call or two put options differing only by exercise price.

Volume—The number of purchases or sales of a commodity futures contract made during a specific time period.

Write—Sell an option. The sale gives the seller the obligation to buy (put) or sell (call) the futures at the exercise price.

SUBJECT INDEX

AUTHOR INDEX

ABOUT THE AUTHORS

Raymond M. Leuthold has been a professor of agricultural economics at the University of Illinois at Urbana-Champaign since 1967. He teaches courses in futures markets, price analysis, and forecasting. Professor Leuthold has concentrated his research in commodity futures markets on such topics as forward pricing efficiency and performance, basis risks, cash-futures price relationships, risk management (hedging) strategies, influence of futures markets on cash price variability, and optimal hedging strategies for multiple-risk situations. He has published numerous articles on these topics in economics, agricultural economics, and finance journals, and has edited two books on futures markets. He is on the editorial board of *The Journal of Futures Markets.* Professor Leuthold has been the recipient of a Fulbright Research Fellowship to France. He holds a Master's degree in Economics and a Ph.D. in Agricultural Economics, both from the University of Wisconsin at Madison.

Dr. Joan C. Junkus attended the University of Illinois at Urbana-Champaign, receiving a B.S. in Biology in 1974. After three years at Salomon Brothers, Chicago, she returned to the University of Illinois where she received an MBA in 1980 and a Ph.D. in Finance in 1983. She has taught in the Graduate School of Business at the University of California-Irvine and is presently an associate professor of finance at DePaul University in Chicago. She teaches courses in finance, management, futures, and options. Dr. Junkus's major research interests are in the investments field, particularly stock index futures, and in corporate finance, particularly bankruptcy. She has published in several finance journals.

Dr. Jean E. Cordier is a professor of marketing at the Institut de Gestion Internationale Agro-Alimentaire, the agribusiness department of the ESSEC group in France. He holds Master's degrees in Economics and Food Sciences from France and a Ph.D. in Agricultural Economics from the University of Illinois, Urbana-Champaign. Dr. Cordier has had commodity trading experience with a feedmill company in France. He is active as a commodity marketing research consultant for many French firms. Dr. Cordier teaches courses in marketing, futures markets, and price analysis, and has written several professional papers on futures markets, international marketing, information systems, and price forecasting.